Advance Praise

Myers has produced a gem—a commentary worth reading in its entirety. Her narratives and dialogue with previous scholarship never leave the reader wondering about the significance of a particular topic or discussion or the logic of her choices. Her explanations of Johannine language and patterns bring clarity for new scholars and restore a luster for advanced scholars that may have dulled by repeated scouring. Myers's careful delineation of possible relationships between the Gospel and the Letters highlights rather than obscures distinctive facets of each work.

—*Jo-Ann A. Brant*
Professor Emeritus
Goshen College, Indiana

This is a marvelous commentary that bristles with fresh perspectives on and new insights into the interpretation of the Gospel and Letters of John. Alicia Myers opens her study with a clear and measured examination of how the Gospel and Letters can be read together as well as separately, before embarking on a substantial and yet highly accessible literary-rhetorical and sociocultural reading of each of the four texts. A significant and very welcome addition to Johannine studies.

—*Catrin H. Williams*
University of Wales Trinity Saint David

READING JOHN AND 1, 2, 3 JOHN

SMYTH&
HELWYS

Smyth & Helwys Publishing, Inc.
6316 Peake Road
Macon, Georgia 31210-3960
1-800-747-3016
© 2019 by Alicia D. Myers
All rights reserved.

Library of Congress Cataloging-in-Publication Data

Names: Myers, Alicia D., author.
Title: Reading John and 1, 2, 3 John / Alicia D. Myers.
Description: Macon : Smyth & Helwys Publishing, Inc., 2019. | Series:
  Reading the New Testament | Includes bibliographical references.
Identifiers: LCCN 2019023392 (print) | LCCN 2019023393 (ebook) | ISBN
  9781641731560 (paperback) | ISBN 9781641731577 (ebook)
Subjects: LCSH: Bible. John--Commentaries. | Bible. Epistles of
  John--Commentaries.
Classification: LCC BS2601 .M94 2019 (print) | LCC BS2601 (ebook) | DDC
  226.5/07--dc23
LC record available at https://lccn.loc.gov/2019023392
LC ebook record available at https://lccn.loc.gov/2019023393

Reading John and 1, 2, 3 John

A Literary and Theological Commentary

Alicia D. Myers

SMYTH&HELWYS
PUBLISHING, INCORPORATED • MACON, GEORGIA

Reading the New Testament
2nd Series

Also by Alicia D. Myers

Come and Read: Interpretive Approaches to the Gospel of John
(co-edited with Lindsey M. Trozzo)

Blessed among Women? Mothers and Motherhood in the New Testament

Abiding Words: Perspectives on the Use of Scripture in the Gospel of John
(co-edited with Bruce G. Schuchard)

*Characterizing Jesus: A Rhetorical Analysis on the Fourth Gospel's
Use of Scripture in Its Presentation of Jesus*

For Charles H. Talbert

An outstanding scholar and mentor,
As well as a brother committed to a life lived
recognizing Jesus as the Christ, the Son of God

Contents

Editor's Foreword

Like its predecessor (Reading the New Testament) and its companion series (Reading the Old Testament), Reading the New Testament: Second Series seeks to help readers—whether students or scholars, ministers or laypeople—gain a greater understanding of and appreciation for biblical texts in their original contexts. To this good end, commentaries in this series attend not only to lexical, historical, and critical concerns but are also attuned to and interested in, as the subtitle of each volume signals, literary matters and theological meaning.

Whereas some commentaries are committed to the necessary and salutary task of commenting on every jot and tittle (see Matthew 5:18), works in this series seek to trace the thought and observe the craft of biblical authors in a less atomistic manner. While attending to various trees, they are also intent on not missing the forest. Relatedly, while technically undergirded and academically informed, the commentaries within this series are intended for and are meant to be accessible and valuable to a broad readership. The seventeen volumes that will make up Reading the New Testament: Second Series, then, are written *by* scholars but are not exclusively, or even primarily, *for* scholars.

Contributors to this commentary series are accomplished academics, experienced teachers, capable communicators, and professing Christians who are committed to explicating Scripture thoughtfully, clearly, and sympathetically. To the extent that this series results in people reading the twenty-seven New Testament documents with greater skill, care, insight, devotion, and joy, the contributors and editor of Reading the New Testament: Second Series will be grateful and gratified.

Todd D. Still
Baylor University
George W. Truett Theological Seminary
Waco, Texas

Acknowledgments

Three years ago, when Todd Still contacted me about the possibility of writing a commentary on the Gospel and Letters of John, I was excited about the prospect. When I learned it would follow Charles Talbert's 2005 volume in the Reading the New Testament series, I knew that it was a chance I could not let pass by. Although it is daunting to write a single commentary volume on four New Testament books, this was an opportunity to explore a Gospel I have spent most of my career studying while also expanding my understanding of the Letters of John. I am honored that it will follow the work of Charles, my doctoral mentor, to whom I happily dedicate this book.

I am grateful to Todd for his confidence in my ability to contribute a volume on the Gospel and Letters of John, and to Marion Moore at Smyth & Helwys for her quick responses to my questions and concerns. Thanks also to Mikeal Parsons, whose support and advice were invaluable throughout my doctoral years at Baylor and well beyond. I am also fortunate to work at Campbell University, whose faculty development and research programs funded a summer research grant to facilitate my work on this book. The Divinity School, Dean Andy Wakefield, and Assistant Dean Derek Hogan have supported this project with travel funds and flexible class scheduling so that I could make time for writing as well as sharing ideas as I crafted this work. I am surrounded by wonderful colleagues at Campbell University Divinity School and in an environment where I am encouraged to write in a variety of settings without losing sight of the theological value and ministerial impacts of scriptural interpretation. Thanks are also due to the fantastic library staff at Wiggins Library, and especially to Marie Berry, for securing innumerable items through interlibrary loan.

Outside of Campbell, I have the privilege of working with Johannine specialists from around the world and hearing them present their ideas at conferences and through their writings. I have benefited in countless ways from their insights, questions, challenges, and encouragement through the

years. In particular, I would like to thank Jo-Ann Brant, with whom I chaired
the Johannine Literature Section of the SBL for three years. In addition to
her thought-provoking readings of John, Jo-Ann is an outstanding friend
and colleague, always looking for ways to include new voices in the conversation on John and inspiring those who are often silenced to speak out.

My family and friends continue to walk with me as I take on writing
projects, cheering me on to continue moving forward while also providing
me places to slow down and live life together. Jennifer Bashaw and Lindsey
Trozzo have endured me prattling on about odd Johannine theories with
good humor and helpful advice. My husband, Scott, understands my calling
to keep writing and is also the voice of wisdom that calls for me to pause
when I need to. I hope that Keaton and Gavin, my two boys who are my joy,
will know the love of God in their own lives, in part from my own life and
maybe someday from the books I write.

Abbreviations

The abbreviations used conform to the SBL Handbook of Style (2nd edition). Only abbreviations of ancient works are included here and are organized alphabetically by abbreviation rather than by author.

1 Apol.	Justin Martyr, *First Apology*
1 En.	*1 Enoch*
1 Macc.	1 Maccabees
Ad. Apol.	Plutarch, *To Apollonius*
Ad. Marc.	Cicero, *To Marcia*
Adul. amic.	Plutarch, *How to Tell a Flatterer from a Friend*
Ag.	Aeschylus, *Agamemnon*
Agr.	Tacitus, *Agricola*
Alc.	Plutarch, *Life of Alcibiades*
Alleg. Interp.	Philo of Alexandria, *Allegorical Interpretation*
An seni	Plutarch, *On Whether an Old Man Should Engage in Public Affairs*
Apoc. Ab.	*Apocalypse of Abraham*
Apol.	Plato, *Apology*
Aug.	Suetonius, *Life of Augustus*
Caus. plant.	Theophrastus, *De causis plantarum*
Chaer.	Achilles Tatius, *Chaereas and Callirhoe*
Cher.	Philo, *On the Cherubim*
Cho.	Aeschylus, *Libation Bearers*
Claud.	Suetonius, *Life of Claudius*
Comm. Jo.	Origen of Alexandria, *Commentary on John*
De or.	Cicero, *De oratore*
Dial.	Justin Martyr, *Dialogue with Trypo*
Dom.	Suetonius, *Life of Domitian*
Ep.	Seneca, *Letters*

Ep. Tra.	Pliny the Younger, *Letters to Trajan*
Eth. nic.	Aristotle, *Nichomachean Ethics*
Eum.	Aeschylus, *Eumenides*
Gen. an.	Aristotle, *Generation of Animals*
GLAE	*Greek Life of Adam and Eve*
Gos. Pet.	*Gospel of Peter*
Haer.	Irenaeus, *Against Heresies*
Hdt.	Herodotus, *Histories*
Helv.	Seneca, *To Helvetica*
Hist.	Cassius-Dio, *Histories*
Hist. eccl.	Eusebius, *Church History*
Hist.	Tacitus, *Histories*
Hom. Jo.	John Chrysostom, *Homilies on John*
Il.	Homer, *Iliad*
Inst.	Quintilian, *Institutes on Oratory*
J. W.	Josephus, *Jewish War*
Jos. Asen.	*Joseph and Aseneth*
Jub.	*Jubilees*
LXX	Septuagint
Mart. Ascen. Isa.	*Martyrdom and Ascension of Isaiah*
Metam.	Ovid, *Metamorphoses*
Mil.	Cicero, *Pro Milone*
Mor.	Plutarch, *Moralia*
Mos.	Philo, *Life of Moses*
Nat. puer.	Hippocrates, *Nature of a Child*
Nat. Q.	Plutarch, *Natural Questions*
Nic.	Plutarch, *Life of Nicias*
Noct. att.	Aulus Gellius, *Attic Nights*
Od.	Homer, *Odyssey*
Or. Brut.	Cicero, *Orator ad M. Brutum*
p. Pe'ah	Palestinian (Jerusalem) Talmud, *Pe'ah*
Part. an.	Aristotle, *Parts of Animals*
Phaedr.	Plato, *Phaedrus*
Phil.	Sophocles, *Philoctetes*
Post.	Philo, *On the Posterity of Cain*
Prax.	Tertullian, *Against Praxeas*
Prog.	*Progymnasmata*
Pss. Sol.	*Psalms of Solomon*
Resp.	Plato, *Republic*
Rhet.	Aristotle, *Rhetoric*

Rhet. Her.	Pseudo-Cicero, *Rhetorica ad Herennium*
Sir.	Ben Sirach
Sol.	Plutarch, *Life of Solon*
Symp.	Plato, *Symposium*
T. Ab.	*Testament of Abraham*
T. Levi	*Testament of Levi*
T. Mos.	*Testament of Moses*
Tg. Neof.	*Targum Neofiti*
Tg. Ps.-J.	*Targum Pseudo-Jonathan*
Thuc.	Thucydides, *Histories*
Tim.	Plato, *Timaeus*
Tob.	Book of Tobit
Top.	Cicero, *Topica*
Tract. Ev. Jo.	Augustine, *Tractates on John*
Tranq. an.	Plutarch, *On Tranquility of Mind*
Tro.	Euripides, *Trojan Women*
Xen. *Apol.*	Xenophon, *Apology*

I. General Introduction to the Gospel and Letters of John

The Johannine Writings

Reading the Gospel of John along with the three letters that (at least traditionally) bear the same name seems a natural enough enterprise. At the very least, it helps to rescue the letters from near oblivion toward the end of the Christian canon, tucked almost invisibly between two other obscure, and most likely related, letters: 2 Peter and Jude. In the present-day form of the Christian canon, the three segments of what church tradition regards as the "Johannine Writings" are separated by their distinct genres: the Gospel of John; 1–3 John as letters; and the book of Revelation, an apocalypse with its own distinctive features (Hill, 1–3). As the surviving evidence demonstrates, when early Christian communities were collecting writings, the arrangement of material was far from set. Judith Lieu notes the convoluted history of reception for 3 John, in particular, although she says that its "survival" in spite of its brevity might suggest that it "preserves most succinctly a pivotal moment for the tradition as a whole" (2008, 28).

As early as the second century in the writings of Irenaeus (ca. 180 CE), we find an association between the Gospel and 1–2 John, all attributed to the Apostle John, the son of Zebedee and brother of James (*Adv. haer.* 1.16.3 [quoting 2 John 11]; 3.16.8 [quoting 1 John 4:2-3; John 1:14; 1 John 5:1]). Even earlier, however, Irenaeus's teacher, Polycarp of Smyrna (ca. 110–40 CE), shows awareness of 1 John in his *Letter to the Philippians* (7.1 [1 John 4:2-3; 3:8]), and Justin Martyr (ca. 150–60 CE) may also reference at least the Gospel of John in his works (cf. *1 Apol.* 46.2; 61.4; *Dial.* 105.1). Although such attribution is early, it is nevertheless later than the widespread use of the Synoptic Gospels. References to the Johannine writings also hint at persistent debates on their authority (especially 2–3 John and Revelation) because they were used by various Christian groups that were later deemed heretical.

Many scholars suggest the use of the Gospel of John by gnostic teachers, such as Valentinus (ca. 100–160 CE), resulted in a neglect of John's Gospel by church fathers. Charles Hill (11–71) has recently argued against this position, suggesting that later scholars have imposed a "Johannophobia" on the early orthodox teachers of the church. Nevertheless, the paucity of references to 3 John, as well as the diversity of comments on the status of 2–3 John when they are mentioned, indicates continued debate over their status even as the Gospel and 1 John enjoyed a growing acceptance in the latter decades of the second century. The Montanist controversy, for example, when Montanus claimed a special inspiration by the Holy Spirit for himself and his closest disciples predicting the imminent return of Christ, put the book of Revelation in a particularly precarious place among church leaders. Associating this book, the only one of the five that explicitly claims to be written by a "John," with the Gospel served to bolster its otherwise questionable status (Lieu 2008, 25–28).

The Johannine writings, therefore, have a complicated past that is hidden by our contemporary canons and bound Bibles. In the third century, Origen reflected the doubt of apostolic authorship for 2–3 John, and Eusebius also says "not all consider them [2–3 John] genuine" (*Hist. eccl.* 6.25.6–10). According to Eusebius, there were "two persons in Asia" named John, one "the Apostle," who is responsible for the Gospel and 1 John, and the other "the Elder," the author of 2 and 3 John. This tradition traces back to the writings of Papias, as early as 100 CE (*Hist. eccl.* 3.39.5–7). Unlike the Gospel and 1 John, therefore, 2–3 John are not always accorded unmitigated canonical status in early canon lists perhaps because the Johannine writings most likely did not exist in their final form until between 90–110 CE.

The late second-century Muratorian Canon, for example, credits apostolic authorship to the Gospel and 1 John. It also contains a brief reference to "the two" letters bearing John's name after describing some pseudonymous Pauline letters and Jude (lines 10–22, 41). The deteriorated state of the surviving Latin text, however, means that this line could be interpreted as a reference only to 1 and 2 John, leaving the personal 3 John out altogether (Lieu 2008, 26–27). For Origen, the questionable authorship of these writings led to his acknowledgment that they were disputed letters in his time, a status noted in Eusebius's writing above (*Hist. eccl.* 3.24.17–25.3). Georg Strecker suggests that the complicated history of these Johannine writings belies their widespread use and acceptance in their region of origin (xxxv; see also Hill). Yet, as we will see below, determining precisely the provenance of the Johannine writings is still another debate.

Even with this complicated past, there remain good reasons to read the Johannine writings, that is, the Gospel and Letters of John, *together*. I remove the book of Revelation from this discussion due in large part to its distinct genre as well as the fact that it merits a much fuller exploration. This is not to suggest that there is no possible relationship between Revelation and the remainder of the Johannine corpus, but only that such a connection will not be examined here (Keener 2003, 1:126–39). A connection is much easier to ascertain regarding the Gospel and Letters of John, regardless of what one ultimately concludes about their composition histories. As will be shown more fully below, whole phrases, specific descriptions, and theological dispositions are quickly discerned in both the Gospel and 1 John, while 2 John seems to bring together 1 and 3 John (Parsenios 2014, 26–28). Although Revelation has connections to various aspects of these themes, its distinct genre pushes the conversation in different directions and leads the majority of current scholars to ascribe it to a "John" different from the one traditionally credited as the authority behind the Gospel and Letters (Koester 2014b, 65–68; cf. Eusebius, *Hist. eccl.* 3.25.2–4). Reading the Gospel alongside 1–3 John, therefore, not only draws these three, lesser-known letters out from obscurity but also acknowledges a shared relationship between these writings that can elucidate our interpretations of them.

Even with such good reasons to read theses writings together, there are also reasons to remember to read the Gospel and Letters of John *separately*. Lieu is the most stringent advocate of this position. While she acknowledges that these writings all demonstrate a Johannine tradition, she concludes that there is nothing in the letters that "appeals to or assumes knowledge of the Gospel, and indeed that the latter seems unlikely; rather each writing is, largely independently, reworking common or shared traditions" (2008, 8). Lieu ventures to respect the different genres represented (Gospel, exhortation, letters) and author identifications (anonymity in the Gospel and 1 John vs. "the Elder" of 2–3 John) in order to "explore and unfold a text as far as possible first of all within its own terms" (2008, 8). Lieu's warnings are well stated and helpful. She cautions readers against glossing over the real distinctives of the Johannine writings and using the Gospel as the automatic hermeneutical key to all four writings without careful consideration of context and additional possibilities.

In the present commentary, I will offer a middle way in this debate, hearing the warnings of Lieu while also maintaining a closer relationship between the Gospel and Letters than she is willing to argue. My reasons for this decision will be made clearer as the commentary progresses. I will, however, also aim to allow the unique elements of each writing to stand rather than using the Gospel to eclipse the other canonical books. In this way, I will seek to model fruitful ways to read these works both together and separately in order to encounter the theological insights of this ancient, Johannine community as they worked to articulate and to vivify what it means to "believe that the Christ, the Son of God, is Jesus" (John 20:31; 1 John 5:1).

Reading the Gospel and Letters of John Together

The majority position in Johannine scholarship is that one ought to read the Gospel and Letters of John together. As George Parsenios notes (2014, 5), for preeminent John scholar Raymond Brown, the Letters of John were never meant to be read apart from the Gospel. This was not because Brown thought the Gospel explained the Letters but rather that the Letters clarified potentially problematic aspects of Johannine theology from the Gospel that had caused division in the Johannine community (1979, 97; 1982, 69–71). Others have often concluded the opposite, suggesting that literary allusions and theological language from the Gospel, as the more fully developed writing, helps to clarify statements from the Letters (Schnelle; Strecker; Culpepper 2014, 98–99). Especially pronounced, for example, is the overlap between John 13:31–17:26 and 1 John (Reis, Loader). Indeed, the fact that we have at least four writings from the same community of believers—the "Johannine community"—means that we can potentially reconstruct more about the history and theological development of this group of early Christians than we can about any other "church" (*ekklēsia*) described in the New Testament.

Community Theories: One Schism or Two?

The dominant theory of how the Gospel relates to the Letters is that of Brown, put forward shortly after J. Louis Martyn's own influential theory for the history of the Fourth Gospel (Martyn 1968/1979; see also Brown and Moloney 2003). Martyn, influenced by the source, redaction, and compositional theories of his day, argued for three discernable layers within the Fourth Gospel, pointing to a two-level drama of division of the Johannine believers from their synagogue roots. Martyn's layers begin with what he identifies as "low" christological confessions in the Gospel (Jesus is "prophet" or "king") that would have been acceptable to Jewish believers still operating in local synagogues. As the confessions about Jesus grew more elevated (Jesus is "Christ" and "Son of Man"), these believers were expelled from their synagogues and forced to create a new community, the "Johannine community," on their own. After this separation, the confessions of Jesus' identity continued to develop, ultimately reaching the heights of claiming Jesus' divinity and oneness with the Father (John 10:30; 20:28). It was during this time that the Gospel reached its final form (ca. 90s CE).

The significance of Martyn's reading is hard to overestimate, particularly in North American and British spheres of New Testament scholarship. His approach not only provided a historical context for the passages mentioning synagogue expulsion (John 9:22; 12:42; 16:2) but also ostensibly explained John's often troubling characterization of the Jews (*hoi Ioudaioi*, see Myers 2017b). The negative aspects of the Jews were explained by the intra-Jewish conflict of this emerging Christian group as it separated from a first-century Jewish synagogue. Martyn's scholarship has dominated Johannine studies for the last fifty years and can often be found lurking behind readings of the Gospel even when it is not explicitly articulated (cf. Culpepper 1983; Brant 2011; Thompson 2015; Anderson 2011, 2014, 63–81).

Urban von Wahlde's commentary offers the most robust recent developments of Martyn's and Brown's theories. He combines Martyn's work with significant input from Brown to form his own conclusions in his three-volume work (2010, see also von Wahlde 2014). Von Wahlde uses Brown's work because Brown developed Martyn's theory further, continuing the conversation past the layers of tradition in the Gospel to include the Letters as well. Brown describes *four* stages of history for the Johannine community, arguing that the canonical order of the Johannine writings—Gospel, 1, 2, 3 John—is also the chronological order of composition (ca. 90s–100 CE). For Brown, the Letters address not the intra-Jewish schism described in the Gospel but a later schism within the Johannine community itself as false teachers interpreted the Gospel tradition differently, developing theological positions the Elder considered untenable. Brown labels these false teachers "secessionists" who, using the language of 2 John 9, "go beyond" the teaching of Christ, leaving the importance of his incarnation, future eschatology, and ethical behavior behind and claiming authority through inspiration by the Holy Spirit (1979, 109–44).

Although influential, Martyn's and Brown's approaches are not without detractors, two of whom I will mention here. First, regarding the historical reconstruction of the Gospel, is Adele Reinhartz (1992, 2001). Reinhartz agrees with Martyn that the Fourth Gospel demonstrates a splitting between Jews who call Jesus "the Christ" and those who did not, but, she argues, there is no historical evidence for an *expulsion* of the Jesus-believing Jews from local synagogues. Instead, it is just as likely that these believers left of their own accord and that they interpreted their own departure in terms of expulsion. This separation is what prompted them to craft a negative characterization of the non-messianic Jews who remained in the synagogues in their Gospel. Reinhartz's main argument for this reading is that Martyn cannot prove the historicity of Jewish expulsion from synagogues. Moreover, as Reinhartz suggests, Martyn's theory can unwittingly sanction further anti-Jewish readings of the Gospel by justifying the negative presentation of the Jews: that is, they deserve such negativity because they persecuted Christians in the past.

The second group of dissenters is represented by Udo Schnelle who, along with Strecker and a few others, contends for an alternative compositional order and a single schism within the Johannine community as the context for all four writings (Schnelle; Strecker; Talbert 2005; Kinlaw, 70–74). Schnelle suggests that the shortest letters, 2 and 3 John, were written first as quick responses to a developing controversy in the community. This, Schnelle argues, explains the vehemence of 2 and 3 John as the Elder attempted to shortcut an impending crisis: the rejection of the continued importance of Jesus' incarnation. Pamela Kinlaw argues that rather than incarnation, the opponents deny the permanence of Jesus' identity as the Christ; they believe he was "possessed" or "inspired" by the divine Christ for a time but that he is no longer, and, therefore, Jesus is no longer relevant for salvation (107–108). The key verses for these scholars are those that emphasize the need to "confess that Jesus Christ has come in the flesh," found in 1 John 4:2 and his "coming in the flesh" in 2 John 7. Schnelle maintains that while one cannot prove a synagogue expulsion in these writings, one can see a consistent concern to bolster belief in Jesus' incarnation with stories of his emotions (John 2:15-16; 11:33-38), his exhaustion (4:6), and his corporeality even after his resurrection (20:17, 27–28). For these scholars, 2 and 3 John were stop-gap measures that were expounded upon in 1 John and the Gospel, which develop the theological positions of the community to a fuller extent in order to combat the anti-Jesus teachers.

Although all these scholars vary in their historical reconstructions, what is consistent among them is the thought that one *can* read through a text to reconstruct the historical locations of those responsible for writing the Gospel and Letters of John. Furthermore, all these theories assert some sort of literary relationship between the Johannine writings, even if the order of composition fluctuates; these writings should, and indeed were designed, to be read together. Nevertheless, the variety of reconstructions offered above illustrate the more recent shift away from such two-level reading strategies: if we all look at the same data and come to differing conclusions, then perhaps ancient texts are not as transparent as we thought (Kysar 2006; see also Perkins). Richard Bauckham and his students suggest that we have focused too much on "communities" behind the Gospels. He argues instead that these Gospels were always meant for "all Christians" rather than for isolated communities alone (cf. Klink; Bernier; Lamb). Noting the impact of literary and postmodern approaches on Johannine studies, Reinhartz admits her now "conflicted" relationship with historical-critical methods. Rather than stating reconstructed histories with certitude, she encourages all readers to offer "humility, imagination, and good humor," knowing we can only arrive at probabilities and possibilities rather than entirely provable results (2008, 69–70).

Literary and Rhetorical Connections
The search for a history behind the Johannine writings is, in large part, fueled by the literary and rhetorical connections between these works. There are significant words and whole phrases that appear in these writings, linking them together and supporting the conclusion that they come from the same community, or at least a "Johannine" stream of tradition. In this section I will review some of these connections, highlighting aspects of the Johannine works that join them to one another and distinguish them from other sections of the New Testament, starting with the Gospel of John and the Synoptic traditions.

A. John's Gospel and the Synoptic Gospels
John's distinctive voice can first be detected by comparing this Gospel to its Synoptic counterparts: Matthew, Mark, and Luke. That John is still telling the life story of Jesus of Nazareth is clear, not only from the fact that he has the same name and comes from the same town (at least physically) but also due to the familiar characters who resurface in John's account, such as John (the Baptist), Simon Peter, Barabbas, Pilate, and Mary Magdalene. (When referring to John the Baptist in the Gospel of John, I use parentheses around "the Baptist" because he is not identified with this title in this Gospel.) Jesus also acts out several familiar scenes and miracles: he causes a disturbance in the Jerusalem temple, walks on water, feeds a multitude, heals the sick, outwits opponents in debates, and is compared to Moses. There are also references to Scripture, or the Old Testament, that appear in John and in the Synoptics: Isa 40:3 (John 1:23; Matt 3:3; Mark 1:3; Luke 3:4); Ps 118:25 (John 12:13; Matt 21:9; Mark 11:9; cf. Luke 19:38); Isa 6:10 (John 12:40; Matt 13:14-15; Mark 4:12; Luke 8:10); and Psalm 22, although John selects a different verse (Ps 22:19 in John 19:24 vs. Ps 22:2 in Matt 27:46; Mark 15:34). For all these reasons, it is not surprising that until the twentieth century most interpreters assumed some sort of literary relationship between John's Gospel and the Synoptics. The differences were explained as John's "spiritualizing" the traditions rather than operating from a separate stream (Thompson 2015, 2–5; Brant 2011, 9–10).

Even with these similarities, John's voice comes through with a number of unique features found in this Gospel alone. John includes additional characters, even disciples, who are not mentioned in the Synoptics: Nathanael, Philip, Nicodemus, the Samaritan woman, and Lazarus, among others. The Gospel also presents Jesus differently: he clears out the temple in John 2 rather than immediately before the final Passover; he routinely visits the temple and clearly has three years of ministry in contrast to only one in the Synoptics; he speaks in long discourses rather than short, pithy statements; although he heals, he generally heals individuals rather than crowds (contra Matt 4:23-25; 8:14-17); and he never performs an exorcism on a person. More could be added to this list, such as Jesus' "I am" statements, but this is sufficient to illustrate my point. All these differences led to a rise of opinion in the mid-twentieth century that John's Gospel was more or less independent of the Synoptics, John having crafted his own tradition without concern for the Synoptic parameters (Smith 2001).

As often happens in scholarship, though, the pendulum is now swinging back as scholars acknowledge the complicated history of oral traditions and compositions in the early church (Anderson 2014; Thatcher 2006). Although relatively few will suggest *direct* use of the Synoptics (though see Dodd, Nierynck, and, more recently, Barker), many scholars admit that it is not possible to determine with certainty John's use or dismissal of Synoptic materials. Some, including Anderson (2011, 2014), Mark Matson, and Andrew Gregory, argue that Luke uses elements of Johannine tradition. The difficulty of determining this relationship is, in part, because John's Gospel claims to have been written by an eyewitness to the events of Jesus' life, death, and resurrection (19:35; 21:24-25; cf. 1 John 1:1-4). If John's story is based on an eyewitness account, and so are portions of the Synoptics, then some coherence seems unavoidable.

Neither John nor the Synoptics, however, are simply retelling a set of facts; they are offering interpretations of the person and work of Jesus. Jo-Ann Brant, therefore, concludes that a difference in focus accounts for John's unique form and elaboration of traditions. The Synoptics, she writes, focus on "practical ethical teachings informed by Jesus' proclamation of the reign of heaven," while John's Gospel focuses on "Jesus' proclamations about his identity as the Son of God" (2011, 10). John's Gospel emphasizes Jesus' person, while the Synoptics emphasize his work, although neither element is completely separated from the other. As Marianne Meye Thompson explains, "however one resolves the question of its sources, John bears the distinctive stamp of a creative mind that interpreted received traditions in light of a particular hermeneutical stance," namely that Jesus is "the embodied

Word, the Son of God, through whom God's glory is manifested and God is revealed, and through whom God gives life to the world" (2015, 8).

B. The Gospel and the Letters

The "creative mind" of the Johannine Gospel is also detectable in the Letters. Parsenios notes that the similarities between the Gospel and Letters begin with simple shared vocabulary but continue through the repetition of specific phrases, which appear in common clusters between these works (2014, 5–11). He argues that while it is clear the Gospel and 1 John begin with similar "prologue" sections (John 1:1-18; 1 John 1:1-4), these writings also join with 3 John to offer similar endings that describe why the work was written (John 20:30-31; 1 John 5:13; 3 John 9), including comments that more could have been communicated than has been in the present work (John 21:24-25; 3 John 13; cf. 2 John 12). Parsenios also explores shared theological perspectives in these works, including the emphasis on God's identity as Father, the importance of the Spirit within the community, and Jesus' unique identity as Son as opposed to the believers, who are called "children" (*tekna, teknia,* or *paidia*). He concludes that "the commonalities" between the Gospel and Letters of John "are both broad and deep" (2014, 9, cf. 126–29).

Close reading reveals that the Gospel and 1 John share a number of phrases used by Jesus in the Farewell Discourse in particular (John 13:31–17:26). These phrases are more elaborate in 1 John but are summarized in 2 John as well. Of special importance is the "command" (*entolē*) to "love one another" (*agapate allēlous*), which Jesus gives in John 13:34-35 and 15:12-17. This "command" surfaces explicitly in 1 John 3:11, 23 and 5:3, and it forms the foundation on which the instructions to love the "brothers and sisters" throughout 1 John rest. The verb "to love" (*agapaō*) appears sixty-eight times in the Gospel and Letters, the noun "love" (*agapē*) occurs another twenty-eight times, and the adjective "beloved" (*agapētos*) is used ten times. This accounts for almost a third of the New Testament appearances of these words! The Johannine literature is *very* concerned with love.

The emphasis on *agapē* words does not necessarily come from a specific, inherent superiority of this "kind of love" over and against the verb *phileō*. Rather, the use of *agapē* words reflects their appearance in the two key commandments of the Torah, also captured in a variety of Second Temple Jewish works and in Jesus' teachings in the Synoptic Gospels: namely, Deut 6:4-5 (also known as the *Shema*, "Hear, oh Israel, the LORD your God, the LORD is one. You shall *love* the LORD your God with all your heart and with all your soul and with all your might."); and Lev 19:18b ("You shall *love* your neighbor as yourself."). These two passages encapsulate the heart of the

Torah, sometimes referred to as the "two tables of the law": the love of God (Deut 6:4-5) and the love of neighbor (Lev 19:17-18). When Jesus pairs these passages in his teaching in the Synoptic Gospels, he reflects general Jewish practice of his time, thus leading the scribes and others to agree with him in these exchanges (Mark 12:28-34; Matt 22:34-40). In the Gospels, it is not Jesus' emphasis of these passages that makes him controversial; rather it is the *way* in which he lives them out—they lead him to death on a cross (Myers 2018b).

In the Greek translation of the Old Testament (Septuagint, LXX), the Greek word for "love" in these crucial verses is *agapaō*. When Jesus also uses this verb, and its related noun, he reflects the emphasis on these passages in his theological context. Moreover, John's focus on this verb, and its related words, seems to build on a tradition that began with Jesus. Even though in the Gospel of John Jesus does not quote either the *Shema* or Lev 19:18b, his command for the disciples (and later believers) to "love one another, just as I loved you so that you should love one another" (13:34-35) resonates with these passages. The disciples are called to imitate Jesus' kind of love, a love that extends to his Father *and* to his disciples as well as to the world, even when love for the latter is unreciprocated (John 3:16; 10:17-18; 15:12-17; 1 John 3:16).

First John imitates these Jesus traditions, especially as they are reflected in John 13–17. Not only does the "love" language overlap but 1 John also incorporates language of "abiding" (*menō*), a common theme in the Gospel, especially John 15. The importance of "keeping" (*tēreō*) commands appears, as do the phrases that one is either "in truth" (*en alētheia*), "from God" (*ek tou theou*), "from the world" (*ek tou kosmou*), or even "the evil one" (*ho ponēros*). An emphasis on "having been completed" appears in John 17:23, as well as other places in John (*teleioō, telos*), and is also present in 1 John. Although the connections to the Farewell Discourse are strong, and perhaps especially fitting since it is the speech Jesus gives directly to the audience in the Gospel, 1 John displays similarities to other scenes from the Gospel as well (John 5; 6; 8), valuing "testimony" (*martyreō, martyria*) and "confession" (*homologeō*) of Jesus' name. This does not necessarily mean that 1 John was written *after* the Gospel, but rather that the overlaps demonstrate a *close connection* between these writings because they come from the same community. The speaker of 1 John takes on the voice of Jesus, using the techniques of paraphrase and speech-in-character (*prosōpopoiia*, Myers 2011; Reis, 54) in the letter in order to add authority to the teachings offered. The author speaks as Jesus spoke, encouraging the believers to "abide in" the fellowship rather than "going out" (1 John 2:18-24).

Although 2 and 3 John are not as clearly tied to the Gospel as 1 John, they nevertheless reflect Johannine tendencies. Indeed, the brevity of these letters, 2 John at thirteen verses and 3 John with fifteen, makes a comparative lack of connections understandable; they are simply too short to have as much overlap as the much longer Gospel and 1 John. The similarities that do exist, however, are all the more significant. In addition to further vocabulary similarities (e.g., love, truth, commandment), there are full phrases that appear in the other Johannine writings. In 2 John 5-6, the Elder writes,

> And now I ask you, dear lady, not as writing to you a new commandment, but one which we have had from the beginning, that we should love one another. And this is love: that you should walk according to his commandments. This is the commandment, just as you heard from the beginning, so that you should walk in it.

A quick glance at 1 John 2:7-8; 3:22-24; 4:21–5:3; and John 13–17 makes the thematic connections clear. Third John, while containing fewer overlaps, nevertheless claims the same authorship as 2 John, repeats a concern for "testimony" (vv. 3, 6, 12) that is also found in the Gospel and 1 John 5 but is not present in 2 John. Third John has additional Johannine motifs, such as addressing the audience as "beloved" (and "children"), describing the need to "walk in truth," and emphasizing the importance of love, especially within the community of believers.

The consistent vocabulary, phrases, and rhetoric of the Gospel and Letters of John, therefore, reinforce the traditional link between these works noted in the early church, even as they debated the inclusion of 2 and 3 John in the canon. While we cannot be certain of their composition order, we can be more confident of their similar origins in a Johannine tradition. These writings display a Johannine perspective and, as we will see below, theological concerns that indicate a focus on Jesus' identity and behavior as the core for the fellowship of the community with God, with one another, and with the world.

Key Theological Claims

Narrowing down the theological components of any biblical book is problematic, but this is perhaps even more in the case of the Johannine writings, which are often held up alongside the writings of Paul to form the cornerstone of New Testament theology (Bultmann; Matera; Frey). My goal here is not to encapsulate all of Johannine theology but rather demonstrate consistent areas of overlap between the Gospel and the Letters of John and, in doing so, to highlight some important elements of Johannine theology without claiming to be comprehensive. For those interested in more comprehensive analyses, Craig Koester (2008), Thompson (2001), and, more recently, Dorothy Lee (2012) and Jörg Frey offer a few places to begin.

A. Jesus' Unique Identity and Superior Revelation

The Gospel of John has long been known as a Gospel of revelation. John 1:17-18 contains the claim that "no one has seen God before; One-of-a-kind God (*monogenēs theos*), the one who is upon the breast of the Father, that one showed the way" (cf. 1 John 3:6; 4:20; 3 John 11). This statement contrasts, and even subverts, claims of divine appearances in the Old Testament, especially the theophany Moses experienced on Sinai in Exod 34:5-28 (cf. Elijah's theophany at 1 Kings 19). At the same time, however, the Gospel of John reinforces the validity of Moses' writings as Scripture, arguing that the Scriptures "testify" in support of Jesus' claims (John 5:39-47; cf. 1:45). For the Gospel, then, Jesus' appearance, and indeed his revelation, builds on the revelations previously given through Moses and the prophets rather than undermining them.

The Gospel does not deny the divine sightings by Moses and Elijah; instead it downplays them in comparison to Jesus', the Word's, intimate closeness to God. Particularly important is Exod 33:20, where the Lord responds to Moses' request for a vision saying, "you cannot see my face; for no one shall see me and live" (NRSV). Thus Moses, like Elijah after him, sees only the Lord's back, his presence in the form of a cloud or a voice, but not his *face* (Exod 33:21-23; 1 Kings 19:11-18). In John's Gospel, and in the Letters, Jesus' revelation is in continuity with these previous theophanies, but it is superior since he, as the Word made flesh, is "One-of-a-kind God, the one who *is* upon the breast of the Father," and, therefore, nestled snuggly on the front side of the Lord.

The Gospel and Letters of John are firmly situated on the authority and in the narrative world of the Old Testament while simultaneously claiming a superior revelation embodied and given by Jesus as God's Christ (Myers 2012; Myers and Schuchard). The use of the Old Testament in the Gospel of John, while subtler than the other canonical Gospels, is easy to discern with the opening allusions to Genesis in John 1, the intertwining of the plot to the Jewish liturgical calendar, comparisons between Jesus and Old Testament events and characters or images, and explicit quotations. The use of Scripture in the Letters is more difficult to discern but arguably still present in even subtler ways. First John, in particular, has explicit references to Cain (3:12) but also incorporates Jesus' love command, which is grounded in Deuteronomy and Leviticus.

All these writings also agree on the crucial, and superior, role of Jesus in communicating and embodying God's revelation to the world. Thus, the Gospel repeatedly states that no one has seen God, or ascended into heaven, except for the "one who descended, the Son of Man" (3:13; cf. 1:17-18; 6:36-38; cf. 1 John 4:12). Jesus' alignment with the Father is *so* complete in John's Gospel that when the disciples see him, they have seen the Father (14:9-11). As God's Word made flesh, Jesus is the residence of God's glory, a perfect reflection of God's will (1:16). John, therefore, not only claims that Jesus has done what no other human has, seen God face to face, but also that his revelation shows humans a corresponding theophany.

The Letters also emphasize what the community, or the Elder, has seen, touched, heard, known, and believed, all of which center on the confession of Jesus' identity as God's Christ and Son (1 John 1:1-4; 2:22-25; 2 John 7-11; cf. "the name" in 3 John 7, 15). First John, for example, claims that even though believers do not know exactly what their future will be with God, they *do know* that they will be like Jesus because of the revelation he has provided (2:28–3:3). *Remaining in* (*menō en*) the revelation they received, therefore, is crucial not only in the Gospel, which narrates Jesus' teachings (John 15), but also in the Letters, which are firmly situated after his death, resurrection, and return to the Father (1 John 2:22-25; 3:24; 2 John 9).

B. The World and the Problem of Misrecognition

Jesus' unique identity and his superior revelation are difficult to understand in John's Gospel, and conflict over his words and identity extends to the Letters. Turning again to the Gospel's opening verses, we see that Jesus' rejection is foreshadowed: the Word "was in the world, even the world that became through it, but the world did not know it. It came to what was its own, but its own did not receive it" (1:10-11). Many scholars have compared this description of the Word's coming, and "dwelling" (1:14), to the stories of Wisdom's dwelling with Israel at God's command. Wisdom is sometimes identified as Torah revealed and given as a gift to Israel, and this leads to life when "she" is followed (Sir 24; Bar 3:9–4:4; cf. Wis 7). The partner with God in creation in Prov 8 and Job 28:12-28, in *1 Enoch's* version of the Wisdom story, Wisdom is rejected and ultimately unable to remain in her dwelling on earth, so she returns to heaven (*1 En.* 42). Using Old Testament and Second Temple Jewish theologies, the Gospel of John both explains the Word's unique coming as Jesus *and* his ultimate rejection without detracting from the Gospel's interpretation of his identity (Boyarin; Ringe; Schüssler-Fiorenza).

The rejection of Jesus that plays out in the Gospel is not always straight-forward. As John 1:12-13 indicate, there are some who did (and do) accept Jesus as the Word. Nevertheless, Jesus is rejected by the powers-that-be and the world, which is described as both beloved of God and as that which hates God, Jesus, and his disciples in return (7:7; 15:18-25; 17:14). The crux of this conundrum is the inability of the world to recognize Jesus as God's Christ and Word. Rather than being able "to judge with right judg-ment" (7:24), the world is baffled by Jesus' behavior and audacious claims. In the Gospel, Jesus describes the metaphorical "blindness" that his presence reveals. Those who recognize their own blindness and approach Jesus for light are healed and walk in the truth, while those who claim to see fine on their own continue to walk in darkness (9:39-41; cf. 8:12; 11:10; 12:35; 1 John 1:6-7; 2:6-11; 2 John 4-6; 3 John 3-4).

This situation is complicated by the fact that the Gospel also emphasizes God's role in enabling recognition of Jesus. John (the Baptist) only recognizes Jesus after receiving two divine signs: the auditory revelation of the voice and the sight of the Spirit descending and remaining on Jesus (1:29-34). Everyone else only has John's words. Jesus himself also describes the Father's role in "drawing" those who believe to Jesus as well as his own election of the Twelve disciples, even the one he knows will betray him (6:45, 60-71). As ones chosen and believing, the disciples and the Gospel audience are encour-aged that God will not allow any of them to be snatched from Jesus' hand, except for the one who was destined for destruction, Judas (17:12).

Such rhetoric explains why many scholars have interpreted the Johan-nine writings as "sectarian": that is, as representing the views of a defined and separated group who feels ostracized and threatened by "outsiders" (Meeks; Clark-Soles 2003, Rensberger, 135–50). In this view, these writings have a sharp division between belief and unbelief, between belonging to the commu-nity and being part of "the world." Those who are included are encouraged to remain, and those who are not are provoked either to join or to reject the message. Closer examination, however, shows that the Gospel is not entirely dualistic in this way. There are a number of ambiguous characters who both believe and disbelieve, or whose status is never resolved, such as Nicodemus and the Jews (Conway 2002; Hylen). Defining who and what exactly "the world" is proves to be as much a challenge as recognizing Jesus. The Gospel teaches its readers to be careful about claims of sight.

The Letters repeat the message of the world's rejection and, indeed, hatred of Jesus and his disciples. This is particularly pronounced in 1 John, where the description of the world resonates with Jesus' descriptions from John 15–17. The world contains those whose "desires" are "the flesh . . . the eyes . . . and arrogance" (2:16), it is "passing away" (2:17), and it does not "know" the believers because "it did not know him [Jesus]" and it "hates" the believers as it hated Jesus (3:1, 13). "False prophets" have "gone out into the world" who deny that "Jesus Christ has come in the flesh" (4:1-3). Second John 7 mirrors 1 John 4, explaining that "many deceivers went into the world, ones who do not confess Jesus Christ coming in the flesh; this one is the deceiver and the antichrist!"

Rather than disregarding the world, however, such language is tempered by the consistent descriptions of God's love for the world and God's very identity as "love" in 1 John 4:8. The most famous of these references is John 3:16, but it is echoed elsewhere and lingers behind the entire Johannine confession of Jesus' coming to the world. In these writings, Jesus' coming and his return to the Father that results in his giving the Spirit are demonstrations of God's love for the world. The division between the community and the world begins to diminish when we remember that believers, too, are "in the world" and have no hope apart from God's prior love (John 17). This message is emphasized in 1 John 4:7-10, the same section of the letter quoted above that refers to "false prophets" and the "spirit of the antichrist":

> Beloved, let us love one another because love is from God, and everyone who loves has been begotten from God and knows God. The one who does not love does not know God, because God is love. In this the love of God was revealed in us, that God sent his Son the Unique-One (*monogenē*), *into the world*, so that we might live through him. In this is love, *not that we ourselves loved God, but that he himself loved us, and sent his Son, a means of forgiveness concerning our sins.*

The world may not recognize, or "know," Jesus as God's Word, and it may also hate his followers, but these writings also warn believers against overconfidence in their own abilities to discern who exactly is "from the world" and who is "from God." When we think we can render "right judgment" alone, we quickly find ourselves in darkness, blinded by pride. The verses that encourage Johannine believers, therefore, stand right alongside those that condemn any believer who thinks they can see rightly without the Light of the World. Anyone who "hates" is aligned with "the world," while only those who love are shown to be "from God."

Reading the Gospel and Letters of John Separately

Even though the above connections and history of interpretation encourage
us to read the Gospel and Letters of John together, there are reasons to read
them separately. Just as too much separation of the Gospel from the Letters
can result in their disappearance into the oblivion of the latter portions of the
New Testament canon, so too does an overemphasis on the Letters' reflection
of the Gospel. If we simply assume uniformity among these writings, we
will miss important aspects, distinctive elements that exist because these are
separate writings, written at different times even if not all by different people.
This is the criticism that Lieu levels against many interpreters of the Johannine Letters (1986, 2008, 2014). Although she acknowledges that there are
certainly numerous "and far from simple echoes" between the Letters and
the Gospel, she cautions interpreters from asserting too confidently what
precisely this relationship is and *who exactly* the Johannine "community" was
(2014, 138–40).

Genres

The most obvious difference between our four writings is the presence of
three different genres among the works: (1) the Gospel is a narrative, most
similar to an ancient biography (although it is not entirely similar, as we will
see below); (2) 1 John is called a "letter" but is lacking a number of epistolary
elements, including an opening salutation and a closing, leading a number
of scholars to call it a "homily" or "sermon" instead (Parsenios 2014, 26–28;
Loader, xii); and (3) 2 and 3 John are letters, fitting ancient expectations
of that specific genre. Yet even between 2 and 3 John there are differences.
Third John is the most like other ancient letters, being of appropriate length
(approximately the length of a single sheet of papyrus), informal composition, and including a wish for good health in v. 2 (Lieu 1986, 37–43).
Second John, while also short, nevertheless has a longer greeting than 3 John,
and it includes language similar to a Pauline salutation ("*Grace*, mercy, *peace*
be with us from God the Father and from Jesus Christ, the Son of the Father,
in truth and in love," 2 John 3). For this reason, as well as for its admonitions against those who "are not confessing Jesus Christ coming in the flesh,"
Lieu argues that 2 John is more "consciously constructed" in the apostolic
tradition of authority than 3 John, which is itself a "genuine letter" reflecting
general expectations of the genre common throughout the milieu (1986, 51).

The Johannine corpus, therefore, is a complex and varied collection.
Even the Gospel's genre is debated among scholars. Brant (2004) explores
its connections to ancient drama, including the tendency to feature only

two characters "on stage" at once, showcasing agonistic debates between the protagonist and other characters, and the presence of group characters (such as "the Jews" or "the crowd") who function like a chorus. In the end, however, Brant argues that John's Gospel is an encomiastic biography that employs epideictic rhetoric to praise Jesus as the ideal model to imitate (2011; cf. Neyrey, 3–28; Myers 2012, 35–61). Parsenios likewise notes connections between the Gospel and ancient drama, but uses these parallels to argue that John's Gospel is juridical, acting as a narrative leading up to the single trial of Jesus where Pilate (and the world) misjudges Jesus' identity (2010; see also Lincoln).

Rather than narrowing John's Gospel into a single category, most narrative interpreters build on the work of Harold Attridge, who suggests that John's Gospel "bends" genres. Attridge argues that the Gospel author is not satisfied with a single genre, but blends and bends genres because no single genre is "adequate to speak of the Word incarnate" (2002b, 21). Thus, within the Gospel, whether an epideictic or juridical narrative overall, one finds the use of multiple micro-level genres: recognition scenes (*anagnorisis*) as Jesus encounters a number of characters and they seek to recognize him rightly (Larsen 2008); a hospitality or a marriage type-scene beside a well (Arterbury 2010); rhetorical speeches that employ ancient methods of argumentation (Attridge 2002a; Myers 2013); a dinner scene followed by a lengthy discourse that resembles a philosophical symposium (Engberg-Pedersen 2015); and a speech of consolation from ancient tragedies (Parsenios 2005).

Far from being unique, however, the combination of these micro-level genres, or what ancient rhetoricians would call "exercises" (*gymnasia*), is common in ancient narratives. Aelius Theon, a first-century teacher of rhetoric, explains that "historical writings" (*historia*) bring together a variety of genres, making them ideal for young students because they demonstrate how to weave different types of writing in order to tell a persuasive story (Theon, *Prog.* 61–72, 104P; Myers 2016). John's Gospel, therefore, resembles other "historical" types of writings from its context—historiographies, biographies, legends (e.g., Homer's *Iliad*), or even novels—by using a third-person, external narrator and reflecting other common elements of ancient narratives (Myers 2012, 22–77).

Given the differences between the Gospel and the Letters on the level of genre, therefore, we should be careful to allow each writing room to stand as a complete work. Differences of style are expected among different genres; indeed, the genre employed by a given author will necessarily affect the message communicated. When we elide these differences, we can place either too much emphasis on aspects that are simply reflections of genre (e.g., the health wish in 3 John that is unique in the New Testament but standard in other ancient letters) and too little emphasis on unique elements that distinguish these writings from one another (e.g., the variations on "sin/s" in the Gospel and 1 John).

Authorship and Audiences

Other significant differences between these writings are their authorship claims, or lack thereof, and their audiences. As shown above, the Gospel and 1 John have been associated with John son of Zebedee since the second century (Irenaeus, *Adv. haer.* 3.1.1). Like the other canonical Gospels, however, the Gospel of John is anonymous, never explicitly connecting itself to John of Zebedee. Moreover, there are reasons to doubt such an association, not least because of missing references to his brother, James, in main narratives of the Gospel (Thompson 2015, 18–21).

The Gospel does, however, explicitly associate itself with eyewitness tradition connected to the figure of the "Beloved Disciple," who is never named in the Gospel. In John 19:35 after the soldiers pierce Jesus' side, releasing blood and water, the narrator interjects: "And the one who has seen has testified, and his testimony is true, and that one knows that he speaks truth, so that you also might believe." The disciple in this instance seems to be the Beloved Disciple who, according to this Gospel, is the only disciple who was present for Jesus' death (20:23-25). John 21:23-25 links 19:35 to the Beloved Disciple even more clearly. After Jesus' comments to Peter about the Beloved Disciple ("If I should want him to remain until I come, what is that to you?" v. 22), the narrator explains:

> Therefore this word went out among the brothers and sisters that that disciple would not die. But Jesus said not that he would not die, but "if I should want him to remain until I come." This one is the disciple who is testifying about these things and the one who wrote these things, and *we know that his testimony is true.*

For this reason, most scholars argue that the authority figure behind the Gospel of John is the anonymous Beloved Disciple (Brant 2011, 5–7; Bauckham, 73–91). Although most think that 21:23-25 is a postscript written after his death as an explanation, they argue that the Beloved Disciple seems to be the leader of the Johannine community and the one on whom their traditions about Jesus were based.

Many scholars argue that the Gospel went through several stages of composition and is not, therefore, the product of a single author. Instead, some, like R. Alan Culpepper (1975) and von Wahlde (2010), argue for a communal or even "school" process, where later disciples digested and interpreted the Beloved Disciple's traditions in order to make them applicable to the current situations faced by the Johannine community. Even when scholars disagree on what conflicts lie behind the Gospel and Letters, they agree that some sort of conflict motivated the shaping of traditions to respond to these threats. Consonant with its first-century culture, the Gospel presents not an individualized portrait of a single person's relationship with the Son and Father but rather a communal relationship, where the Spirit resides with all the believers together. It is together, then, that they interpreted and recorded their traditions, probably finalizing the Gospel in the form we have it in 90–110 CE. In this commentary, therefore, I will refer to the Gospel as "John's Gospel," but this is for ease of communication rather than an assertion that the Beloved Disciple is the sole author or that he must be John son of Zebedee.

The importance of eyewitness tradition is also present in 1 John. The audience is told from the outset that the message contained within the homily is based on connections with firsthand experiences, even if those have not been experienced by the audience. Beginning mid-thought, 1 John opens with these words:

> That which was from the beginning, which *we have heard*, which *we have seen* with our eyes, which *we beheld* and with our hands *we touched* concerning the word of life—indeed, the life was revealed and *we have seen* and *we are testifying* and *proclaiming* to you—the eternal life which was with the Father and was revealed to *us*—that *which we have seen* and *we have heard, we are proclaiming* also to you so that you also might continue having fellowship with *us*. And indeed *our* fellowship is with that Father and with his Son, Jesus Christ. (1:1-3)

The firsthand claims of 1 John have encouraged many, including the early church fathers, to identify the author as the same one who wrote the Gospel, whether John son of Zebedee or the anonymous Beloved Disciple. The "we" language, however, is also indicative of a community with shared tradition; the emphasis is on the community rather than on a single individual (Talbert 2005, 14; Lieu 2008, 40–41).

While authorship theories may be enticing, 1 John lacks any explicit authorship claims; we simply do not know the name of its author. Again, Lieu argues that we should not turn to the Gospel to fill in this gap, but rather we should let 1 John stand on its own as an anonymous work (2008,

8). The rhetorical impact of this choice could be significant, particularly in the use of language throughout the letter that strongly mirrors the language ascribed to Jesus in the Farewell Discourse of the Gospel (John 13–17). Rather than emphasizing his own identity, 1 John's speaker takes on the voice of Jesus, paraphrasing and imitating his speech in the sermon, adding to the authority of the message delivered and reinforcing the "fellowship" and "abiding" themes that are so central to the sermon. The speaker *shows* a connection to the Son by disappearing behind Jesus' words. In this way, the audience knows and *hears* that the Word "abides" in this teacher in contrast to those who deny Jesus (2:14; 4:1-3).

Unlike 1 John, 2 and 3 John do ascribe authorship. Both letters claim to have been written by the Elder (*ho presbyteros*, 2 John 1; 3 John 1), but the meaning of this title is not immediately clear. The term "Elder" can simply refer to someone of greater age and wisdom; however, this Elder seems to hold a position of authority over those he writes: "the elect lady" of 2 John and "Gaius" in 3 John. He gives instructions to his "children" and responds to challenges against his authority, particularly in 3 John 9-12. Nevertheless, this elder does not include his actual name as Paul so often does prior to identifying himself by a title ("apostle," "slave of Christ Jesus," etc.), and as was common in the ancient world (Lieu 1986, 52–64). Thus, 2 and 3 John occupy a liminal space of being simultaneously credited to an author *and* remaining anonymous, at least for contemporary readers. In the introduction to the Letters, I will review some theories suggested for the composition of these writings, one of which is that they could have served as different cover letters for 1 John.

Common throughout all these writings is an interest in authority, particularly through a connection to teachings that are "witnessed" or "testified" among the community and trace their lineage back to eyewitness experiences. "Testimony" language (*martyreō* or *martyria*) appears sixty-one times in the Gospel, 1 John, and 3 John, each of which focus on the truthfulness of the testimony offered. In a manner similar to John 19:35 and 21:25 above, 3 John 12 offers its endorsement of "Demetrius," explaining "we ourselves also are testifying, and *you know that our testimony is true.*" Even though 2 John lacks explicit testimony language, it also reflects a concern that the community persevere with traditional stances. They are to continue "walking in the truth" and "walk according to his commandments," and "watch out" for those who do not confess Jesus Christ "is coming in the flesh" (vv. 4-8). Indeed, so close is the language in 2 John to 1 John that even Lieu suggests a literary dependency between the two, although she is unsure which writing precedes the other (2008, 239–40). Parsenios, however, concludes that 2 John is the lynchpin in the Johannine writings; it bridges 1 John, the Gospel, and 3 John, even if the precise authorship, composition order, dates of writing, and audiences cannot be determined (2014, 26–32).

Theological Claims

Finally, although there are many consistent theological motifs across the Johannine writings, there are also diverse elements. In particular, these writings have distinctive soteriological understandings and emphases, especially the Gospel and 1 John. In the Gospel, Jesus' death, resurrection, and return to the Father operate together as his "glorification" and the "completion" of the Father's will. It is through this event that disciples are invited to participate in the eternal life offered by Jesus. Jesus' work enables believers to experience a healing of their blindness so that they can see truly who Jesus is and follow him in the light (9:39-41; 12:37-50). With right sight, these believers come to "judge with right judgment" (7:24) with the aid of the Holy Spirit (16:7-15), so that they no longer "sin" or "miss the mark" with their understandings of Jesus, the Father, and the world around them because they are abiding in the divine unity (17:23). Jesus' return to the Father also makes possible the coming of the Holy Spirit, who is identified as "another Paraclete" (14:26; 16:7) and whose work reminding and teaching the disciples is evidenced in the Gospel itself (2:18-22; 7:37-39; 12:14-16).

First John has several similarities to this soteriological scheme, but it also has significant differences. First, 1 John employs explicitly cultic language in its description that the "blood of Jesus his Son is cleansing (*katharizei*) us from all sins" (1:7) and by describing Jesus as "a means of forgiveness" or "expiation" (*hilasmos* 2:2; 4:10). The use of "sins" plural (rather than singular) is much more common in 1 John than in the Gospel, conveying a perspective of sins as individual mistakes rather than the world's collective inability to recognize Jesus as God's Christ and Word. Second, 1 John does not describe the Holy Spirit as "Paraclete," but only Jesus, emphasizing his role as the ascended advocate before the Father for the believers on earth (2:1-2). While the Gospel shows how Jesus works to emphasize the importance of the Spirit as the guide for the disciples in his physical absence, 1 John (and 2 John) is more invested in underscoring the continued relevance of Jesus' physical existence even after his return to the Father. He has not been eclipsed by the Spirit in the letter; rather the Spirit forms part of the fellowship that is shared between Father, Son, and believers (1 John 1:3-7; cf. 4:2; 2 John 7-11).

Finally, 3 John is alone in its language of "assembly" (*ekklēsia*), the word we most often translate as "church" (vv. 6, 9-10). The scene here is of a public gathering of believers rather than an organized "church" in the contemporary sense. Lieu notes that although this word is common in other New Testament writings, especially other epistles, it is *not* in the Gospel, 1 John, or 2 John. "In 3 John, however, the term appears without comment as the local gathering," and the letter describes additional, rival gatherings in vv. 9-10 (2008, 273). We should not assume formalized structures, or "ecclesiology," in these assemblies, but the language here indicates communal gatherings in a way that is not explicit in the other Johannine writings. The resulting portrait of the community in 3 John is, therefore, different from the dominant imagery of "children" and "beloved ones" in the other letters. Rather than solving these differences, or simply ignoring them, the commentary that follows will explore them, allowing each writing to stand alone in its distinctiveness even while appreciating the relationship between these works.

The Method of this Commentary

Literary-Rhetorical and Sociocultural

This commentary will study the Gospel and Letters of John in their final form. I will not propose a detailed composition history for any of these writings, or of their composition order with respect to one another, even though I find the suggestion that 2 and 3 John could have served as cover letters for 1 John attractive. There are a number of good arguments for reading these writings in canonical order (Gospel, 1, 2, 3 John) or in an alternative order (3 John, 2 John, 1 John, and Gospel; etc.). Explicitly privileging *one* of these perspectives alone risks ignoring the complex compositional debates by assuming that canonical order is chronological order (see Brown) or ignoring the dominant Christian tradition (as well as the interpretive impact of the canon) that has read these writings in canonical order, focusing especially on the Gospel and 1 John. Since no compositional order can be *proven*, I will instead acknowledge a general Johannine tradition in these writings regardless of composition order and process. The commentary, however, will proceed in canonical order both for ease of reference and because the Gospel provides the most robust presentation of Jesus traditions in the Johannine community that are reflected and contrasted in the Letters.

My hermeneutical method is literary and rhetorical in that it will explore the Johannine writings in connection to other literature from the ancient Mediterranean world. This includes other biographies, letters, histories, dramas, novels, Old Testament passages, and Second Temple Jewish literature, but it also incorporates rhetorical handbooks that shed light on various techniques used in these writings, as well as their desired results. My method is also sociocultural in that I do not ignore the social and cultural effects of literature or the information that it reveals about society, including aspects related to the Roman Empire, the interpretation of historical and political events, and understandings of identity (e.g., what does it mean to be "children of God"?). Rather than assuming ancient expectations are the same as our contemporary understandings, I will use ancient Mediterranean contexts to help elucidate the positions put forward in the Gospel and Letters of John, noting the ways in which these writings both employ ancient assumptions and subvert them in favor of a worldview rooted in the unique revelation of Jesus as God's Christ and Son.

Reading the Gospel and Letters Together and Separately

This commentary seeks to balance the connections and independence of the Johannine writings as much as possible. As argued above, each writing has distinct elements that should be explored individually; nevertheless, the connections that link these writings should also not be overlooked. It is fruitful to read these works together as well as separately, in an integrated tension with one another, allowing them to voice divergent views while also exploring similarities that demonstrate a strong association with another text or texts. In this way, I seek to give space for each writing while also noting their connections, with the hopes that such a reading enables greater understanding and theological clarity, or at least conversation. As Jesus beckons his new disciples in the opening chapter of the Gospel, these writings also beckon us both to "come and see" and to linger, "abiding" with the words that have had such a profound impact over the past two millennia (John 1:39). When we listen, and remember well, these writings claim that we too can experience an encounter with God's Word anew.

II. The Gospel of John

A Brief Overview of the Gospel

The introduction to this commentary makes clear the deep debates that run throughout the history of interpreting the Gospel of John. Rather than reviewing these debates again here, I will identify the basic assumptions and perspectives that I bring to reading the Gospel of John. This overview will create a more stable starting vantage point, or road map, as we set out on our journey with and through the Fourth Gospel.

Historical Background

Date

The general scholarly consensus dates the final form of the Gospel to the 90s CE without ruling out the possibility of a slightly earlier or later date. The Gospel itself contains evidence that pushes for a date beyond the destruction of the Jerusalem temple by the Romans in 70 CE, such as the irony of Caiaphas's words in John 11:45-53, the emphasis on synagogues, and the related conversations about worshiping in places other than the temple in John 4, as well as the Gospel's presentation of Jesus as the location of God's dwelling glory (1:14-16; 1:51; 2:13-22; see Coloe 2001). This date means that the Gospel would have been finalized during the reign of Domitian (r. 91–96 CE), Nerva (r. 96–98 CE), or Trajan (r. 98–117 CE). None of these emperors was especially popular among Christians, although Domitian has earned particularly fervent vitriol from later interpreters (e.g., Suetonius, *Dom.*; Cassius Dio, *Hist.* 67; Tacitus, *Agr.*; *Hist.* 4.85–86). Trajan, however, also endorsed the punishment, and even execution, of Christians who were unwilling to denounce their allegiance to Christ (Pliny the Younger, *Ep. Tra.*). Although we should not read this situation too closely to the Gospel's own context, the fact that Christians faced a variety of competing loyalties, particularly between their allegiance to Jesus or to Rome, is significant, especially for a Gospel urging continued abiding in Jesus as God's Christ despite the potential consequences (12:24-26; 16:2).

Conclusions concerning the date of John's Gospel are regularly based on the John Rylands Library Papyrus 3.457, or P[52], which is often dated to around 130 CE. The small papyrus fragment contains John 18:31-33 on the front and John 18:37-38 on the reverse. As Brent Nongbri points out, such dependence on P[52] is problematic given the additional work needed for dating it accurately. Nongbri shows that the scribal hand of P[52] matches papyri that date into the third century rather than being limited only to those from the second (32–48). Additional evidence for an earlier date, however, can be drawn from references to John's Gospel among Christian authors including Hippolytus of Rome's (ca. 180–230 CE) description of an early second-century gnostic teacher, Basilides of Alexandria (ca. 130 CE), quoting John 1:9; Justin Martyr's (ca. 155 CE) reference to Jesus' encounter with Nicodemus (Brant 2011, 4–5); and Irenaeus's discussion (*Adv. haer.* 3; ca. 180 CE). For the Gospel to have been known in Rome and beyond by this time, scholars suspect that the final form must have been completed several decades earlier, at least by the beginning of the second century.

— So still the 90s

Authorship

My perspective on the date of final composition necessarily influences my view of authorship. Rather than interpreting the Gospel as the product of a lone individual, I am more persuaded of a period of development for these traditions within a community, even though the recovery of these precise developments remains a matter of serious debate (see General Introduction). Thus, while I will refer to the author and the Gospel as "John," it is as a matter of clarity in connection to established tradition rather than an argument for authorship. At its heart, the Gospel does claim that these traditions have a connection to an eyewitness or eyewitnesses, who later remember some of the events described in the narrative guided by the Holy Spirit (cf. 19:34-35; 2:18-22; 12:15-16; 14:25-26).

A group of people rather than 1 author (in his opinion)

So how did we get the name "John" than

In John 21:24-25, the trustworthy witness of the Beloved Disciple is outlined as the authority of the Gospel. Nevertheless, the identity of this disciple remains unclear in the Gospel, and the narrative is not limited to a single vantage point. As Jo-Ann Brant states well, "While the narrator tells us that the Beloved Disciple is the authority of the truth of what has been written, the action is not focalized through the eyes of the disciple" (2011, 6). Instead, the Gospel contains scenes that explicitly exclude the disciples (e.g., John 4; 18:28–19:16), as well as those where Jesus himself is absent (1:19-28; 9:8-34; 11:45-57). Rather than emphasizing the authority of this person as the witness of all things, therefore, the Gospel uses his connection to Jesus to substantiate a connection to the Holy Spirit Jesus breathed upon his disciples

So how

"The Beloved" is never confirmed.

after his resurrection (20:19-23). It is not an individual person who "veri-fies" the truth of the Gospel; it is the Holy Spirit who continues teaching and reminding the believers, and who could be "present" even when trusted human witnesses could not (16:4-15). As we will see when we explore the Letters, the role of the Spirit as teacher seems to have been one particularly sticky issue in the community as it debated various interpretations.

Audience and Location

The pervasive, yet allusive, use of Scripture and Jewish festivals in John's Gospel points to its origins in an ethnically Jewish community. The vehe-ment and problematic polemic against the Jews throughout the Gospel also encourages this interpretation. Feeling cut off from previous understandings of their identity, the Johannine believers form their own family, a "household of God" that draws them together on the basis of belief, love, loyalty, and Spirit indwelling, rather than "bloods, the will of the flesh, and the will of a man" (1:13; see Coloe 2007). This same perspective could have enabled the Johannine community to include people from other ethnic backgrounds as well, particularly as they separated from previous synagogues to form one of their own. Indeed, the Gospel itself includes references to Samaritans (4:1-42) and even Greeks (or "Hellenists," 7:35; 12:20) seeking Jesus. A hint at this reality could lie in the narrator's explanation of Caiaphas's unconscious prophecy in 11:51-52: "He did not say this on his own, but being high priest that year he prophesied that Jesus was about to die on behalf of the nation, and not on behalf of the nation only but also so that the dispersed children of God might be gathered together (*synagagē*) into one."

The geographic location of the Johannine community (as well as the later date of Gospel composition) encourages an understanding of Gentile inclusion at some point among these believers (see also the names in 3 John: Gaius, Diotrephes, and Demetrius). Ephesus, the provincial capital of Asia Minor (modern-day Turkey), is the traditional location of the Johannine community thanks to Irenaeus (*Adv. haer.* 3.1.1). Yet, as with other aspects of John's history, scholarly opinion differs largely because Irenaeus's apologetic drives his Ephesian conclusion (Brant 2011, 8). Although many scholars are open to an Ephesian context (Smith 1999, 39–41; Carter 2008; von Wahlde 2010, 1:236), others have suggested Egypt, specifically Alexandria, due to resonances between John and Philo of Alexandria (Ringe, 13–14). Others prefer Palestine due to the Gospel's affinities with Jewish customs and liter-ature, particularly the Dead Sea Scrolls (H. Koester, 138–39; Thompson 2015, 19). Whatever the Gospel's original location, its influence reached Ephesus and Rome by the early to mid-second century CE.

This sentence is TERRIBLE scholarship. [handwritten note]

The Gospel itself encourages allegiance to Jesus as "Lord and God" as well as "the Christ the Son of God" in a context of competing claims, whether imperial or otherwise (20:28-31). Although Romans did not exercise orga-nized persecution of Christians until the third century (Carter 2008, 69–72), the Gospel presents a picture of believers engaging with hostility from various sources, which it coalesces into a single character: "the world." Rather than responding to hostility with fear or violence, however, the Gospel encourages its audience to show love, as Jesus did, and in so doing, to trust in God's love as well.

Nero? the fire? Rome - [handwritten note]

Literary Features

John 2 [handwritten note]

Although the thoughts on John's genre are long and varied, I will treat the Gospel as an encomiastic biography; this means I will approach the Gospel as a story about Jesus' life that is meant to praise him *and* to inspire imitation of him (i.e., John 13:34-35). This is not to suggest that John's Gospel adheres specifically to this genre entirely, or this genre only. Although it is eventually called a "Gospel," meaning that it recounts the life and teachings of Jesus, that shift probably took place later in the second century. Ancient biographies, however, long predate the composition of John. The encomiastic biography of the Greco-Roman world, in particular, serves as a helpful comparison because of its points of connection with John's Gospel and because it reminds us that this story, like any other biblical book, was not written in a vacuum. Rather, it was written in a world full of literature and other means of communication. Thus, it should not surprise us that the author, or authors, utilize a form of storytelling that fits the ancient Mediterranean world, even as they adjust and augment this form in order to tell their own story of Jesus for their own rhetorical and theological ends.

Instead of offering a full articulation of encomiastic biography here, I will only mention a couple of aspects for help with reading. For fuller treatments see Brant (2011), Jerome Neyrey (2009), and Myers (2012, 2016), as well as Talbert (1977, 2005), and Burridge. What is salient here is that John's Gospel, like other encomiastic biographies, is a historical narrative that is biographical in nature. By "historical," I do not mean in the contemporary, Western sense, but in the ancient Mediterranean sense. The Gospel has a third-person, omniscient narrator who stands external to events and offers a post-narrative perspective interpreting the story. It claims to offer truth, specifically in the form of Jesus, but it does not focus on historicity and on *proving* that Jesus did these exact things, said these precise words, or followed this single itinerary. The Gospel, like other ancient biographies, has a broader definition of "truth." John is interested in matters of belief, life, and love

(20:30-31; 21:24-25), and exalts faith without sight (i.e., proof) as more blessed than faith that requires sight (20:29).

The Gospel follows the life of Jesus in a largely chronological, rather than topological, manner although topics could account for some arrangement of materials. John's Gospel includes several common aspects of a person's character provided in ancient writings, especially biographies. These aspects were call *topoi* (lit., "places"). Although some *topoi* are given concerning other characters in John's Gospel, most of the *topoi* focus on Jesus, who is the subject of the biography. These include his "origins, nature, training, disposition, age, fortune, morality, action, speech, manner of death, and what followed death" (Aelius Theon, *Prog.* 78 [Kennedy]). All these elements of Jesus' character are presented, to greater or lesser extent, with the goal of showing Jesus to be "the Christ, the Son of God" and the one through whom "eternal life" is experienced (20:31).

Studying this focus on Jesus closely, Kasper Bro Larsen (2008) argues that the Gospel contains a series of "recognition scenes" (*anagnorisis*). Moreover, the long-acknowledged irony of the Gospel comes from the audience hearing or reading the story knowing so much more about Jesus than the characters within it. Having the opening verses as a foundation, the audience is privileged with knowledge of Jesus' origins, his relationship with Scripture and Israel's story, his ultimate residence "in the bosom of the Father," and his ability to reveal the Father as no one else can because of his unique identity (1:14-18). By highlighting this irony throughout the Gospel, the story repeatedly elevates those listening and reading over those who saw Jesus face to face. Because the audience exists after the resurrection, after Jesus' giving of the Holy Spirit (20:19-23), and has the Gospel as a hermeneutical key, they *can* come to believe and continue believing in Jesus as God's Christ and Son in ways that no one who just saw him could. In this way, the Gospel emphasizes that those who "are believing and yet not seeing" are blessed (20:29).

Gospel Outline

The "classic" outline of John's Gospel breaks the Gospel into two distinct parts, with a prologue (1:1-18) and epilogue (21:1-25) surrounding them. The first half of the Gospel focuses on Jesus' "public" ministry, his performance of and discussion of the signs (1:19–12:50) and is often called the "Book of Signs." In the second half, Jesus focuses on his own disciples (and the later disciples hearing and reading this Gospel), giving instructions for how they should act once he departs and returns to the Father (13:1–20:31). This second book is sometimes called the "Book of Glory," since it details

Jesus' "glorification" through his crucifixion, resurrection, and return to the Father (Dodd; Brown 1966; Smith 1999).

There is nothing wrong with this classic outline. As any outline does, however, the selection of this standard breakdown leads to an emphasis on certain themes to the detriment of others that are just as relevant to the Gospel narrative. Like any other literary text, the Gospel of John can be outlined in several ways. The ways in which it is outlined reveal the foci of the interpreters along with literary elements of the writing. To emphasize themes in John's Gospel that are often overlooked in the more classic breakdown, this commentary will follow the outline below.

Part 1: Introducing the Word's Story (1:1-51)
    The Prologue, 1:1-5
    The Witness, the World, and the Word, 1:6-14
    From John to Jesus, 1:15-51
Part 2: The Beginnings of Jesus' Ministry (2:1–5:1)
    The First Sign at Cana, 2:1-12
    The First Passover, 2:13–3:21
    John's Continuing Confession, 3:22–4:3
    A Samaritan Woman's Confession, 4:4-42
    The Second Sign at Cana, 4:43–5:1
Part 3: Festivals, Confessions, and Confusion (5:1–10:39)
    Sabbath Work at an Unnamed Festival, 5:1-47
    The Second Passover, 6:1-71
    Festival of Tabernacles, 7:1–8:59
    Another Sabbath Work and Festival Teachings, 9:1–10:42
Part 4: Heading toward the Hour (11:1–17:26)
    Delayed Life and Fear of Death, 11:1–12:11
    The Hour Has Come: From Public to Private, 12:12–13:30
    Jesus' Consolation: It Is Better that I Go Away, 13:31–16:33
    Jesus' Prayer: That They Might Be One, 17:1-26
Part 5: Finishing the Father's Will (18:1–21:25)
    The Noble Shepherd Lays Down His Life . . . , 18:1–19:42
    . . . And Takes It Up Again, 20:1–21:25

My division varies from the classic breakdown particularly as it relates to the prologue and epilogue. Rather than dividing these portions from the main story, I have left them integrated for reasons that will become clearer in the commentary to follow. My outline also draws more attention to the transition toward Jesus' departure and return to the Father that begins in

11:1 rather than at 12:50. John 11 comes just after the final mention of John (the Baptist) and initiates the story of Jesus' resurrection of Lazarus. Also significant is the repetition of festival scenes in the Gospel, highlighting the connection of John's story to the Jewish liturgical calendar noted by other interpreters (cf. Hays 2016, 300). Finally, this outline seeks to show the overlap between the various sections of John. When read closely, the Gospel is difficult to divide because of the repetition of words, characters, events, and themes. Instead of seeing these divisions as hard and fast, readers should note how the Gospel flows and builds on itself. Although contemporary readers might be used to a linear progression, the Gospel is not limited to such communication. Instead, it weaves ideas and motifs together in ways that interpreters have compared to a symphony or a tapestry. The artistry of the Gospel stretches far beyond any one method or path of interpretation. This outline, therefore, is only one possible map for the Gospel, but it will act as our road map as we travel through John's story.

Introducing the Word's Story

John 1:1-51

Few passages are considered more important in the Gospel of John than the "Prologue," which is most often defined as the first eighteen verses of the book. While there are certainly interpretive strengths to this division (e.g., Culpepper 1981; Coloe 1997), I have opted for a different one. Focusing on more ancient partitions of the text, as well as the thematic link of the Word's coming as Jesus that unites all of 1:1-51 together, I will treat all of John 1 as the Introduction of the Word's Story (cf. Theobald, 108). John 1:1-5 holds a special place within this chapter, followed by two other divisions at vv. 6-14 and 15-51. Reading John 1 this way enables us to explore not only the length and significance of the Word's becoming (or "happening" as) flesh in the world as a person named Jesus but also the importance of the one "sent by God" to testify about him named John (called "the Baptist" in the Synoptic accounts).

Due to the importance of the Prologue for interpreting the rest of the Gospel, this chapter begins with an extended introduction on the flow of John 1:1-18 before turning to the commentary and ending with a reflection on the main theological threads of this chapter.

What Is the Prologue?

As mentioned above, many English Bibles, most commentaries, and several scholarly works identify John 1:1-18 as the Gospel's "Prologue." In the past, a good deal of discussion has been devoted to the composition history of John 1:1-18, with a variety of theories on when these verses were written and integrated into the Gospel (cf. Ashton). More recently, however, literary studies have focused on how the current content and position of the Prologue establish the theological foundation for the rest of the Gospel as it unfolds (cf. Skinner 2009, 31–41; Culpepper 2016; S. Brown 2017, 8–14). Yet there is a more fundamental observation that all these studies overlook: namely, that for most of the interpretive history of the Gospel, John 1:1-18 has *not* been identified as the Prologue. Instead, P. J. Williams (2011) notes that the earliest manuscripts usually separate only the first five verses from the verses that follow. While they may have another break after v. 14, they do not divide vv. 18 and 19, even though these verses are regularly separated by headings in our modern-day English Bibles. Williams shows that early patristics and church fathers grouped 1:1-5 together, as well as 1:1-13, 1:1-14, or 1:1-17, but the common break we have at 1:1-18 did not gain popularity until the eighteenth century with Griesbach's Greek NT (1777) and began to dominate English translations only in the nineteenth century onward.

Supporting this earlier division is the Greek text of John 1:1-5. When read in Greek, we see that 1:1-5 create a seamless unit. The rhetorical patterns apparent in these opening verses conform to what ancients would have called a "grand style." This type of writing was regularly used at the beginning of ancient dramas, casting the events to follow as cosmically and divinely important as well as divinely ordained (Brant 2004, 17–26). John 1:1-5 reflects these themes as well. It recalls the creation story of Genesis, thus firmly establishing that the cosmic and divine reality of this Gospel is in line with ancient Israel and that this story stretches back even before the beginning of time. These first few verses succinctly, and poetically, summarize who the Word is and what the Word has done and continues to do, and they foreshadow the conflict that will occur later in the Gospel, as well as the Word's ultimate victory.

The rest of the so-called Prologue, however, is more difficult to parse definitively. The style changes from grand to more mixed, or middle, and repetitions appear, leading to a variety of justifiable divisions of the text. The multiplicity of readings should remind us that while we often encounter texts visually first, ancients were aural, encountering texts through their ears rather than their eyes. The links they could make, therefore, need not be limited to a single, linear flow, but could be traced forward and backward as chains of words and sounds linked ideas that were heard.

Many ancient interpreters of John highlighted the repetition of the term *logos* (Word) in vv. 1 and 14, which they argued created an inclusio, or envelope structure, that brought this unit together (Williams, 376–77). John Chrysostom, however, makes a break at v. 13, setting v. 14 off as the climactic moment of the Word's incarnation (*Hom. Jo.* 10–12). Other possibilities include noting the repetition of "it happened" (*egeneto*) in vv. 6 and 14 (e.g., Augustine, *Tract. Jo.*). This division, which I will follow below, sets off John's "happening" (*egeneto*) and the Word's "happening" (*egeneto*) as flesh that surround John (the Baptist's) testimony in vv. 7-13.

Verses 15-18 conclude the Prologue as it is now popularly defined. While most translations and commentators interpret only v. 15 to be spoken by John (the Baptist), most ancient interpreters understood all of vv. 15-18 to be John's testimony (Brant 2011, 26–27). Although there were some who ended his testimony at v. 17, they did not end it at v. 15 as most commentators and interpreters do today. Thus, while Origen goes to great lengths to argue against Heracleon's interpretation that v. 18 came from the evangelist instead of the Baptist, he does not have to argue that vv. 16-17 were part of the Baptist's testimony (*Comm. Jo.* 6.2–3; see also 2.29; Williams, 379). This fact was simply assumed.

The "Prologue" of the Gospel is, therefore, most precisely the first five verses of the Gospel, although a similar style continues to v. 14. In 1:15, however, the Gospel moves to focus on the relationship of John and the now-named Jesus more specifically. This division results in the following outline for John 1:

I. The Prologue (1:1-5)
    A. vv. 1-2: In the Beginning Was the Word
      B. v. 3: All Things Happen through the Word
    A'. vv. 4-5: In the Word Was Life
II. The Witness, the World, and the Word (1:6-14)
    A. v. 6: A Person Named John Happened
      B. vv. 7-9: In Order to Witness about the Light
      B'. vv. 10-13: The Light Was in the World
    A'. v. 14: In the Flesh, the Word Happened
III. From John to Jesus (1:15-51)
    A. vv. 15-28: John's Witness Apart from Jesus
      B/A. vv. 29-34: John's Witness in the Presence of Jesus
    B. vv. 35-51: Jesus Collects John's Disciples

Overall, John 1:15-51 narrates the transition from John (the Baptist) to Jesus, replicating the transition in 1:6-14. The transition occurs in three parts: vv. 15-28, where John (A) witnesses first about himself and then about Jesus before he appears; vv. 29-34, where John (A) now witnesses about Jesus (B) as he approaches; and vv. 35-51, where John disappears from the narrative for a time and Jesus (B) begins collecting his own disciples, two of whom come from John to follow Jesus. The chapter ends with Jesus' climactic promise to all his disciples (and the audience) that "you all will see heaven open and the angels of God ascending and descending upon the Son of Man" (1:51; Gen

28:12). With these words, Jesus claims that he is the place where God's glory dwells on earth (1:14-16).

Commentary

The Prologue (1:1-5)

Dan Nässelqvist notes various technical rhetorical figures in John 1:1-5 that correspond to what ancient rhetoricians called the "grand style"—an elevated level of prose that showcases the power of the speaker and the importance of the topic discussed (36–37; see Quintilian, *Inst.* 12.10.61–62; Cicero, *Or. Brut.*; *De or.* 3). Among these techniques is the chiasm usually noted by commentators in vv. 1-2, but Nässelqvist also finds the use of "climax." This technique involved the "repetition of a word from the preceding line at the beginning of the next line" and created a looping or stair-stepping pattern that amplified the topic, bringing the hearing to the climax of a speaker's thought. In this case, the climax is the revelation of the identity and work of the Word (*Logos*). In addition, Nässelqvist (45–47) identifies three other types of repetition in this passage, all of which amplify the climax (*conduplicatio*, *mesodiplosis*, and *polytopon*). My translation below attempts to communicate these rhetorical figures, despite its awkwardness. Underlined portions show climax, italicized portions highlight the other forms of repetition.

> [1] *In the beginning was* <u>the Word</u>,
>   and <u>the Word</u> *was toward* <u>God</u>
>   and <u>God</u> *was* <u>the Word</u>.
> [2] This one *was in the beginning toward* <u>God</u>.
> [3] All things, through *it, happened,*
>   and without *it, happened* not one thing which *has happened.*
> [4] *In it* <u>life</u> *was,* and the <u>life</u> *was* the <u>light</u> of people,
> [5] and <u>the light</u> *in* <u>the darkness</u> is shining,
>   and <u>the darkness</u>, *it* [the light], it [the darkness] did not overcome.

Nässelqvist ultimately concludes that the John 1:1-18 is an example of middle style (a mix of grand and plain styles) since the number of stylistic figures drops off after v. 5 and then even more sharply after v. 13. As discussed above, however, more ancient readers recognized the first five verses as the Prologue to the Gospel. Perhaps part of this reason is the high concentration of rhetorical figures within these verses; they are written in grand style to set the stage for what follows: the story of the Word's coming into the world.

The main character in these verses is the Word (*Logos*). Although contemporary churches use the phrase "word of God" often to describe the entire Bible, in the Gospel of John (and the rest of the Bible, for that matter) "the Word" has different connotations. *Logos* can be translated as "Word," but it also has connotations of logic, reason, rationality, wisdom, and order. Thus, for Aristotle, the *logos* was an apt description for the element from male sperm that "organized" the matter within a woman's womb to make a child (*Gen. an.* 2.3.737a20–22; Myers 2017a, 48–51). For Neo-Platonists and Stoics, *logos* was also the organizing principle for the world (*kosmos*) and the logic, or reason, with which each person was endowed (Engberg-Pederson 2017). And, as Daniel Boyarin (2001) has aptly shown, the *logos* was a common topic for Jewish reflection as well. It is used by Philo of Alexandria as to describe the means of God's communication with humanity (see also Sturdevant 2014), reflected in wisdom traditions from Proverbs, Sirach, and *Wisdom of Solomon*, as God's instrument for creation (Ringe), and described by prophets who experienced the coming of the "word" (Gk.: *logos, rhēma*; Heb.: *dabar*; Aram.: *memra*) to them and which they then communicated to all who would listen (e.g., Isa 38:4; Jer 1:4; Ezek 1:3; Hosea 1:1; Jonah 1:1; etc.).

The Gospel of John, however, ties its use of *Logos* to the creation account in Gen 1:1 with its opening words: "In the beginning." The Word described in John 1:1, therefore, is none other than the Word which God spoke at the moment of creation, first uttering, "Let there be light!" (Gen 1:3) and then speaking the life of the entire cosmos into being (Gen 1:1–2:3). This Word "was toward God" (*ēn pros ton theon*, John 1:1), positioned, inclined, and part of God as God's desire realized in speech at the moment of creation. To be *toward God* is more than simply to be "with God," as though the Word were separate and standing alongside. Instead, the Word was perpetually *toward God* as a part of who God is, dependent on and yet equal to, rather than entirely distinct. Herman Waetjen suggests that *pros* indicates movement *toward* God as an expression of the Word's union and "participat[ion] in God's essence" (268–69). Such imagery is reinforced in John 1:18, which depicts Jesus "being in the bosom of the Father."

The role of God's Word in creation is re-narrated in John 1:1-5 as the narrator comments that "all things happened through *it*," meaning, through the Word; Jesus is not introduced by name until 1:17. As in Genesis, we learn that the Word communicates life and light, conquering darkness to bring existence to all people or "mortals" (*anthrōpōn*, John 1:4). The verb *phanei* in v. 5 ("shining" or "enlightening") is in the present tense. This means that light (and life)-giving is the perpetual work of God's Word, an ongoing action that cannot be interrupted by darkness (or death). Already in these verses we find the Gospel asserting that God's will, God's Word, will not be undone regardless of the opposition encountered; as in Isa 55:11, God's Word does not return void.

The Witness, the World, and the Word (1:6-14)

John 1:6-14 creates an inclusio with the repetition of the verb "happened" or "became" (*egeneto*). In v. 6, John's "having been sent from God" is narrated, while v. 14 retells the "happening" of the Word as flesh. The transition into these "happenings" resonates with 1:3, which emphasizes the Word's role as the one through which "all things happened" and without which "not one thing happened which has happened" (see above). John 1:10 recapitulates this idea, reminding the audience that the world to which the "True Light came" is the world that "happened through it [the Word]" (*di autou egeneto*).

Within these verses we find more repetitions that hold this group of verses together. Nässelqvist (46–48) notes repetitions of "witness" (*martyria, martyreō*); "the light" (*to phōs*) and "lighting" (*phōtizō*) in 1:7-9; and "the world" (*kosmos*) in 1:10. There is also continued use of the word "was" (*ēn*), and a three-fold repetition of the verb "coming" (*erchomai*) in 1:7-11. These uses of *erchomai* all appear near the preposition "into" or "for" (*eis*), thus tying them even more closely together. References to "the name" (*to onoma*), first for John (1:6) and then for the True Light (1:12), also bracket the passage, facilitating the comparison between John and Jesus that continues throughout the chapter. The verb for "belief" (*pisteuō*) also appears at the beginning of the passage and at its end (1:7, 12), preparing the audience for its importance in the rest of the Gospel (106 more times!).

Although the verses are tightly bound together by these literary devices, John 1:6-14 should not be read or heard in isolation. Continuing from 1:1-5 are uses of a near demonstrative pronoun to emphasize identity ("This one"; 1:2, 7), repetitions of "the light" (1:4-5, 7-9) and "person" (1:4, 6, 8), as well as two additional uses of "all" (1:3, 7, 8). John 1:10-11 repeats the refrain of 1:3 and resembles 1:4-5 in structure (see also 1:1). One effect of this parallelism is drawing out the contrast between the Word and the world. While the will of God, the Word, cannot be overcome, the world fails even to recognize the one through which it was created and by which it is sustained.

Nevertheless, 1:12-13 turns the negative scene of 1:10-11 around, demonstrating the ultimate effectiveness of God's will despite the world's failure. Even though the world did not receive the light, there are some who are "believing in its name," and these have been given a new sort of life: being begotten or born from God (*egennēthēsan*, v. 13). The four-fold repetition in 1:13—*not from . . . not from . . . not from . . . but from!*—builds to the climactic moment of 1:14. Rounding out this section of text is the proclamation that the Word has "happened" in a new way: namely, as flesh (*sarx*) and has "tented among *us*." Switching to first person plural, the narrator draws the audience into the story. What John (the Baptist) previously proclaimed has now come to pass. The True Light's "coming into the world" has now "happened." As "flesh" *we saw* the glory that the Word alone can make manifest; *this flesh* is the embodiment of God's desire to reveal life and love.

From John to Jesus (1:15-51)

The final section of John 1 falls into three major parts: vv. 15-28, 29-34, and 35-51. These sections trace the repeated "testimonies" of John (the Baptist) and their effects. John 1:15-51 forms a hinge in the Gospel of John, one that continues building on and directly referencing what has come before, while also pointing forward into the narrative that follows. The first portion of the hinge is vv. 15-28 (A), encompassing the witness that John provides in the physical absence of the enfleshed Word, whom he reveals as Jesus Christ (v. 17). Verses 29-34 form the connection (A/B), the lengthiest continual witness provided by John up to this point in the Gospel. This is also the first time Jesus' name appears in the Gospel after 1:17. Additionally, it is his first physical entrance into the narrative. Finally, vv. 35-51 form the second portion of the hinge (B) as the narrator turns to focus on Jesus, leaving John behind, at least for now.

A. 1:15-28: John's Witness Apart from Jesus

John first gives witness to the audience in 1:15-18, providing a robust understanding of Jesus and his mission. Interpreting these verses as John's speech, while common among more ancient readers, is less common today; however, it is viable on grammatical and thematic grounds. First, although our English translations have punctuation and paragraph divisions, ancient Greek required none of these, and our earliest manuscripts lack them. Ends of "sentences," therefore, must be determined by ends of thoughts and other grammatical signals. Even though most contemporary translations now end John's speech at 1:16, there is a pattern in the Greek that encourages us to hear his words continue through v. 18: namely, a repetition of three *hoti* ("because," "that") clauses. John's speaking in threes is a trait that also surfaces in 1:19-34, words that have long been recognized as his (Myers 2015, 129–30). As a result, there is no clear transition until the narrator breaks in at 1:19 to describe John's encounter with the priests and Levites.

Paying attention to these grammatical features, we can translate 1:15-18 in the following way:

[15]John is witnessing concerning him and has cried out saying: "*This one* was the one of whom I said, 'The one coming after me has happened (*gegonen*) prior to me, *because* he was before me (*prōtos*), [16]*because* from his fullness we all received even grace upon grace, [17]*because* the law through Moses was given, the grace and the truth through Jesus Christ *happened* (*egeneto*). [18]God, no one has seen before (*pōtote*). Unique-One God, the one being in the breast of the Father, *that one* led the way."

The content of John's testimony is more of a summary of Jesus' completed work rather than an introduction. As Francis Moloney (1983) notes, the present-tense participle in 1:18 (*the one being*) emphasizes Jesus' return to the Father that occurs after his death and resurrection. That John (the Baptist) is the one to give such profound witness, even though he vanishes before Jesus completes his mission, corresponds to John's own divinely commissioned work outlined in 1:6-7: John was sent from God so that "everyone might believe through him." John's words here, then, demonstrate the fulfillment of his own part in God's plan.

John's witness continues to dominate the remainder 1:19-28, which is often divided into two scenes marked by a double introduction of John's interlocutors: the priests and Levites. Introduced as having been "sent" by "the Jews" (*hoi Ioudaioi*, see below) in vv. 19-23, they are reintroduced in v. 24 as having been "sent from the Pharisees." This doubling not only highlights the *three* rounds of questioning that John faces, and the increasing urgency for an answer, but also clouds the identity of his questioners. Although many interpreters suggest that the priests and Levites, as well as those who sent them, have negative motives in this scene, there is nothing in the text itself that requires such a reading. Instead, they seem to have been intrigued by John's ministry and drawn from Jerusalem to him: they want to know *who he is*. Their being sent to John facilitates John's witness to them and, therefore, the enactment of God's will.

John responds four times to his questioners in three rounds of questions. In vv. 19-23, John reverses the well-known "I am" saying that Jesus will use in the rest of the Gospel (4:26; 6:35; 8:12, 58, etc.) in order to deny that he is the Christ (v. 20). He then makes two more denials in vv. 21-23, saying he is neither Elijah nor "the prophet," which is most likely a reference to "Prophet-like-Moses" traditions based on Moses' words that God would send a "prophet like me from among your people" (Deut 18:15-22; Meeks 1967). The Gospel will return to this image later, tying it instead to Jesus himself (John 6:15). In the end, John (the Baptist) describes himself as "a voice crying in the wilderness, 'Prepare the way of the Lord!' just as Isaiah the prophet said" (1:23). John's quotation is from Isa 40:3, the same Isaiah passage associated with John in the Synoptic Gospels (Matt 3:3; Mark 1:3; Luke 3:4). It is in this Gospel, however, that John quotes it about himself and, in so doing, directly claims that God's prophetic activity continues through him.

In John 1:24-28 the priests and Levites again question John, asking if he is this "voice," why is he baptizing? John answers cryptically, pointing out the dilemma to which he will respond in vv. 29-34. John admits to baptizing with water, which is the activity that has drawn these questioners to him from "the Jews" or "the Pharisees." Nevertheless, he explains, that is not the focus of his work. Instead, the real problem is that "among you all stands one whom you yourselves do not know, *the one coming after me*, of whom I am not worthy to untie the straps of his sandals" (vv. 26-27). This title, "the one coming after me," should immediately register with the Gospel audience as a repetition of 1:15. John is baptizing, but only as a means to witness concerning *the one*, which is precisely what he continues to do in vv. 29-34.

A/B. 1:29-34: John's Witness in the Presence of Jesus

In 1:29-34 we learn that not only did John's questioners need a little help recognizing Jesus, but so did John himself. After seeing Jesus approaching, literally "coming" (*erchomenon*, cf. 1:15, 27) toward him, John says, "Look! The Lamb of God, the one taking up the sin of the world! *This one* is the one of whom I said, 'After me is coming a man who has happened prior to me, because he was before me'" (vv. 29-30). John's words are another repetition of 1:15, this time the later portion of that confession. Although the characters in the text may not know it, the audience listening to the Gospel has now heard this testimony concerning Jesus *three* times, which reinforces not only its validity but also John's divine commission: he does what he was sent by God to do (1:6-8).

Despite John's divine appointment, however, he too needed some help recognizing Jesus as the one about whom he was to witness. Again, operating in threes, John emphasizes his inability to know Jesus without divine guidance. In 1:31, 33, and 34 he uses the word *kagō*, meaning "and I myself" or "even I myself." Mirroring his previous conversation with the priests and Levites in 1:19-28, he first gives two negative confessions, followed by a positive one: "And I myself did not know him, but . . ." (vv. 31, 33); "and I myself have seen and have testified that *this one* is the Son of God" (v. 34).

John explains that the purpose of his baptismal mission was to reveal Jesus' identity "to Israel" (v. 31), but what readers often overlook is John's own place among Israel as one also needing revelation. The Gospel of John does not narrate Jesus' actual baptism, but only John's report of it (contra Matt

3:13-17; Mark 1:9-11; Luke 3:21-22). In his testimony, John conveys that it was *his* seeing the Spirit descending and remaining on Jesus that enabled him to recognize Jesus, because this fulfilled what "the one who sent" him said (John 1:33). John, therefore, is not superior to those who came questioning him; rather, he is like they are: he needs divine assistance to see, hear, and know correctly. The question that remains, though, is whether those who hear John will believe his witness.

John's final, and climactic, confession in this scene comes at the end of another triad: the three-fold repetition of "this one is" (*houtos estin*, vv. 30, 33, 34). In v. 34, John reinforces the vision that he "has seen" (*heōraka*) and what "he has witnessed" (*memartyrēka*, see also the perfect tense in 1:15): namely, that "*this one is* the Son of God." The identification of Jesus as God's Son here brings back the imagery of sonship from 1:14-18 with an explicit identification and is the first of another seven times the title "Son of God" is used in the Gospel (1:49; 3:18; 5:25; 10:36; 11:4, 27; 20:31). While a fitting title for Jesus, an alternative reading of this verse found in early and reliable manuscripts suggests John confesses instead, "this one is the *Chosen One* of God" (*ho eklektos tou theou*; see Quek; Skinner 2015). If the "Chosen One" is the earlier reading, it would be a unique use of this title in the Gospel, although it does appear elsewhere in the Bible as a title for Moses (Ps 106:23 LXX), for Israel (Isa 42:1), and for Jesus (Luke 23:35).

B. 1:35-51: Jesus Collects John's Disciples
In 1:35-51 we move into the second link of the chain. The first scene in this section, 1:35-39, begins with an almost verbatim repetition of 1:29. It seems not even John's testimony, with its report of divine visions and auditory revelation, convinced his disciples immediately. Instead, the story starts again: "On the next day again John and two of his disciples stood and when he [John] saw Jesus walking, he said, 'Look! The Lamb of God . . . !'" John's words would seem to have continued into the same confession of 1:30-34 *except* that we learn his disciples "heard him [John] speaking and they followed Jesus" (1:37). In obedience to their teacher, and in fulfillment of 1:6-8, they leave John behind and become Jesus' disciples instead; they turn to the greater, the True Light.

Even though Jesus has been the subject of the conversations and confessions throughout 1:15-37, he does not speak until 1:38, and even then, he offers only two words: *ti zēteite*, "What are you seeking?" The brevity of Jesus' comment here belies the lengthy discourses that he will give later in the Gospel, beginning in John 3. The emphasis on "seeking," however, is fitting. As George Parsenios (2010, 73–82) notes, the contrasting "seeking"

Introducing the Word's Story 47

that happens throughout the Gospel pits those who "seek" Jesus for juridical or legal prosecution against those who "seek" him for light and life. The disciples respond with another key word for the Gospel. After calling Jesus "Rabbi"—which the narrator translates to "Teacher" (*didaskale*)—they ask him their own two-word question: *pou meneis*, "Where are you abiding?" Those familiar with John's Gospel should recognize this "abiding" verb (*menō*) from John 15; however, it is also the verb John (the Baptist) used to describe the Spirit's "remaining" upon Jesus at the moment of his baptism (1:32). These two disciples are the first to "abide" with Jesus in 1:39 and the first to find more followers to "come and see."

John 1:35-51 is a diptych of two collection stories, where Jesus' newly found disciples go to bring more followers to Jesus. The first of these stories progresses smoothly in vv. 35-42. Despite the nearness to sunset ("it was the tenth hour"), Andrew goes to his brother, Simon, and says, "We have found the Messiah!" (v. 41). As in v. 38, the narrator offers a translation of the Hebrew term, explaining that "Messiah" means "Christ" (v. 41). Peter silently complies, is led to Jesus, and is given a new name by his new master: "You are Simon, son of John. You will be called Cephas" (v. 42).

In v. 43 we are set up to expect a similar series of events. For the third time, the scene is introduced, "On the next day" (vv. 29, 35, 43), and a traveling Jesus attracts a new follower, Philip (vv. 43-44). Already the story has shifted, however, since Jesus himself calls Philip rather than relying on John's testimony. This change sets us up for what follows in 1:45-51. Like Andrew before him, Philip also goes to find another to bring to Jesus: Nathanael. Unlike Peter, however, Nathanael is unconvinced by Philip's rather profound (although limited) understanding of Jesus as "the one of whom Moses in the law and the prophets wrote . . . Jesus, the son of Joseph of Nazareth" (v. 45, see below). Rather than silently following, Nathanael offers the first *explicit resistance* to Jesus in the Gospel thus far: "What good thing (*agathon*) is able to be from Nazareth?!" (v. 46; cf. 7:12; Heath).

Nathanael's skepticism, however, does not prevent him from following Philip to "come and see" Jesus (vv. 39, 46). But rather than passively being seen by others "coming" his way, it is now Jesus' turn to see and give testimony: "Jesus saw Nathanael coming toward him and said about him, 'Look! Truly an Israelite in whom there is no deceit (*dolos*)!" (v. 47; cf. 1:29, 35). The irony of Jesus' statement is clear to those who know the story of Jacob, the first one called "Israel," who strove with God and who tricked his father to steal Esau's blessing, a trick Isaac says was done "with deceit" (*dolou*; Gen 27:35). Nathanael's response is still somewhat charged: "How do you know me?!" But Jesus' second statement convinces this hard-won disciple: "Before

Philip called you, while you were under the fig tree, I saw you" (John 1:48). Nathanael answers with a laudatory confession of Jesus' identity: "You are the Son of God, you are King of Israel!" (1:49). Yet Jesus does not praise Nathanael; instead he offers a cryptic promise that is at home among the references to Jacob: "Because I said to you, 'I saw you under the fig tree,' you are believing?! Greater things than these you will see. . . . Truly, truly I saw to you, you all will see heaven open and the angels of God ascending and descending upon the Son of Man" (1:51; Gen 28:12). At Bethel, Jacob watched the angels ascend and descend on a ladder and received a promise of God's provision and protection for himself and his descendants. Jesus promises these disciples will see "greater things" with him, who is the location of God's glory on earth and who will protect them as their shepherd (John 10:1-18).

An often-overlooked aspect of this passage is its parallel in 20:24-29: Jesus' exchange with a skeptical Thomas. In John 20 Thomas resists the testimony of the other disciples who have seen the resurrected Jesus. Thomas wants his own vision and tactile experience. Once he has this, he too is transformed, and offers a profound confession—the most exalted of the Gospel: "My Lord and my God!" (20:28). As with Nathanael, Jesus does not praise his disciple; he changes the conversation and moves to include a larger audience, particularly those listening to the Gospel. "Because you have seen me, have you believed? Blessed are the ones not seeing and yet believing" (20:29). In this way, John 1:43-51 and 20:24-29 form bookends on the entire Gospel. This is part of the larger parallel between 1:29-51 and 20:1-29, where Mary Magdalene follows the role of John (the Baptist), giving testimony of her own vision before Jesus appears to the rest of his disciples. Acknowledging this parallelism highlights the importance of Mary in John 20, and it points to the inclusiveness of Jesus' promise in 1:51. Jesus is promising "greater things" not only to his disciples in the Gospel but also to the Gospel audiences, even though they (and we) cannot see the incarnate Christ. Even here, Jesus assures all his disciples that they are blessed.

Theological Threads

Belief and New Birth

According to John 1:12-13, those who believe the Word is Jesus experience new life; they are born again through their connection to the divine unity (1:4; 5:26). The full development of this union theme comes only later in the Gospel (cf. John 15). In this opening chapter, however, the Gospel mixes images of creation, recreation, and procreation. Although we often separate these ideas in our contexts, Gwynn Kessler (112–15) notes how procreation and creation were intimately intertwined in ancient Jewish thought. Just as God created, and continues sustaining, life in the world, God also creates in each act of conception and birth.

Focusing on 1:12-13 as their starting point, Adele Reinhartz (1999) and Turid Karlsen Seim show that the language surrounding procreative theories resonates with John's language of "the Word" (*ho Logos*). Aristotle, for example, interpreted the *logos* as the organizing principle—and animating principle—that gave life to a developing child within a woman's womb. Such thought was not limited to Aristotle alone but was common, even if adapted by others, in the larger Greco-Roman world. Thus, when the Gospel of John moves on to describe the re-begetting or rebirth of believers by means of the Word in 1:12-13, it does so in a context that would have heard the procreative overtones running throughout. By the time the Gospel goes on to incorporate further imagery of begetting and birthing in John 3, therefore, we have already been prepared to expect the formation of a new family (or household). This family does not rely on blood kinship or ethnic relationships, but rather on a connection to the Word sustained through the abiding presence of the Spirit within believing communities. In this way, believers claim a new kinship as "children of God" (1:13; Myers 2017a, 66–74).

The ability of the Word to create such a family is based on its perfect reflection of God's will and "glory" as described in 1:14. So completely does the Word manifest God's will that it is as though he is a father's only son, a "unique" one, one who was "begotten only" by a father. All these are possible translations of the difficult phrase *monogenēs para patros* from 1:16. The word *monogenēs* repeats as another identification for Jesus in 1:18 and 3:18 as well. Because he completely reflects God's character, the enfleshed Word is, by necessity, "full of grace and truth." When we finally learn his name in 1:17, we are also told that he is the only means to see God's glory, since no human can withstand the sight of God face to face (1:16-18; Exod 33:17-23; 1 Kgs 19:11-13). As the Word made manifest, Jesus is like the tabernacle of the wilderness generation (1:14). Guiding the people through the wilderness, God's glory can light the way, but nearness to it also brings the risk of judgment (cf. John 3:14; 6:49). As the dwelling of God's glory in the Gospel of John, Jesus is a mobile "sanctuary" (*naon*, 2:18-22) who prepares the way for the permanent union of God's people by means of the Spirit rather than through a physical location, or "place" (*topos*, 4:20-24; 11:48; 14:2-3).

The Jews in John
John 1:19-28 includes the first mention of the Jews in John's Gospel. Their characterization, and the polemical language involved in the later portions of

the Gospel, is a topic of much debate among Johannine scholars (Culpepper and Anderson). Reinhartz (2017) explains that this Gospel has a sordid history, a favorite among Nazis and Neo-Nazis, particularly for language in John 8. Keeping this history in mind is crucial when interpreting the Gospel of John, lest we continue incorporating this anti-Jewish stance. John's Gospel was written at a time before the division of Christianity and Judaism that we now know; moreover, it was written seemingly in and for a community that felt threatened by the larger world around them, including what it deemed powerful Jewish religious leaders, even though these religious leaders were themselves marginalized by the much more powerful Roman Empire.

The Jews in this opening scene, however, are not polemicized or negative characters; they are curious ones. They have noticed John's ministry and are interested in what they see God doing through this man. Their questions about his identity are all positive ones; they view his work as divinely inspired (1:20-25). Even though John tells them that they "do not know" the one in their midst who is God's "coming one" (1:26-27), their inability is mirrored by John's own in 1:29-34. They, like John, need some help. That is John's commission: to testify to them so that they can come to believe and know! Thus, while the Jews' exact identity remains nebulous, they are not negative characters in the Gospel at this moment. Rather, they are a group that has roots in Jerusalem and has enough authority to send "priests and Levites" to question John (the Baptist) on their behalf. They are also somehow associated with the Pharisees, a group with historically awkward ties with priests and Levites (1:19, 24; Myers 2017b).

Jesus' relationship with all things Jewish, including the Jews, should not, therefore, be assumed antagonistic. Indeed, the opening of the Gospel relies on the Genesis account of creation, thereby tying its story of Jesus to Israel's Scriptures. As the opening chapter continues, the incarnate Word's consistency with Scripture is reinforced, first in 1:16-17, then by John (the Baptist) in 1:23, by Philip in 1:45, and by Jesus himself in 1:51. John 1:16-17 reads that Jesus' revelation is "grace upon grace"; the first "grace" or "gift" is the "law" given through Moses, and the second "gift" is "the truth," which "happened" through Jesus Christ. John 1 is replete with allusions and references that highlight Jesus' continuation, rather than interruption, of God's scriptural story of revelation and life-giving:

- 1:1-5, 14—allusions to Genesis and Exodus
- 1:16-17—references to Moses (and Exod 33–34)
- 1:23—John's quotation of "Isaiah the Prophet"

- 1:45—Philip's comment that Jesus is the one of whom Moses and the prophets wrote
- 1:47—Jesus' recalling of the Jacob narrative and the reference to the "fig tree"
- 1:49—Nathanael calling Jesus "King of Israel"
- 1:51—Jesus quoting Gen 28:12, another excerpt from the Jacob cycle

Scripture's story will continue to be crucial to John's narrative of Jesus' story in the chapters that follow (see Myers 2012; Myers and Schuchard).

The Revelation of Sin?

The incarnation of the Word is the manifestation of God's glory and God's will among humanity. That Word is life-making, as it was at the moment of creation. This role, and connection to God, is the foundation for Jesus' ministry that follows in the Gospel of John. As noted in the General Introduction, however, people in the world have a difficult time recognizing Jesus, even though he is the embodiment of the very Word by which and through which they live. This inability, often characterized as blindness in John's Gospel, ultimately causes "the world's" *mistake*, its *sin*.

In John 1:29, John (the Baptist) describes Jesus as "the Lamb of God who lifts up the sin of the world." A few things are significant about this verse, beginning with its designation of Jesus as the "Lamb of God." Although not dismissing the broad connotations of "lamb" imagery in Second Temple Judaism, in John's Gospel this image is usually tied to the Gospel's relocation of Jesus' death to the day on which the Passover lambs were slaughtered in John 19 (cf. Brown 1966, 58–63). Those who emphasize the sacrificial aspects of this image, therefore, translate the participle *airōn* as "the one who removes" rather than "the one who takes up" as I have done above. I do not deny sacrificial aspects of John's description; my translation, however, is meant to capture the double meaning of this verb: it means to lift, as in to display, as well as to remove. Jesus' exaltation is a common motif in the rest of the Gospel, as made clear through the double entendre of the verb "to exalt" (*hypsoō*) that foreshadows Jesus' crucifixion (3:14; 8:28; 12:32, 34; Thompson 2015, 85). In the same way, John 1:29 is also open to double meaning.

Jesus' crucifixion lifts up, or displays, the "sin of the world" (*harmartia tou kosmou*) in that it shows the world's mistake: the world has mistaken Jesus as a harbinger of death when, in reality, he is the means of eternal life (cf. 5:24-29; 11:47-53; 12:19). This, I suggest, is why the Gospel of John frequently uses the singular noun *sin* rather than the plural *sins*, a term more common to 1 John. The outcome of this tragic mistake is the crucifixion of Jesus. But the good news of John is that such a mistake is also futile; the world cannot kill Life (10:17-18).

Second, it is also important to remember that all humans are part of the collective of "the world" in the Gospel of John. "The world" is first identified in 1:9-10 as that which "became" through the Word, but it does not recognize or "know" the Word. The world has a vision problem. It needs divine assistance to correct, or heal, its blindness and deafness. Thus, John (the Baptist) relies on visual and auditory signs to help him recognize Jesus so he can proclaim his identity to others. Moreover, the disciples whom Jesus collects are hearing calls to "Look!" and "Come and see!" Although their confessions are not complete—Philip thinks Jesus is the son of Joseph after all—they are shot through with some light (Myers 2012, 82–85). As we will see in the remainder of the Gospel, it is not blindness or deafness in and of themselves that prevent people and "the world" from recognizing Jesus. From the Gospel's perspective, we are all blind and deaf, and we need to be "drawn by the Father" in order to be healed (John 6:45). Rather than metaphorical blindness or deafness, then, it is the false claim that one does not need help that prevents healing. Jesus is the cure for "the world's" affliction, an intrusive revelation of God's will to all. But "seeing" and "hearing" correctly requires humility (cf. 9:39-41).

The Beginnings of Jesus' Ministry

John 2:1–5:1

After Jesus' collection of his disciples and promise to them in 1:51, he begins his ministry in chapters 2–4. Although these chapters do not all take place in Galilee, John brackets this section with narratives of Jesus performing "signs" (*sēmeia*) in Cana, a small village northeast of Nazareth. As the site of Jesus' "first" and "second" signs (2:11; 4:54), Cana is a significant place for Jesus' ministry in John's Gospel even though it is not mentioned in the Synoptic accounts. As in the Synoptics, however, Capernaum also functions as a site of significant teaching in John and may even be depicted as the place where Jesus' mother and brothers reside (2:12; 4:46; cf. 6:17, 24, 59).

Wrapped by narratives of Jesus' first two signs in Cana, turning water into wine (2:1-11) and healing the royal official's son (4:43–5:1), John 2:1–5:1 contains some of the fastest-paced action in the Gospel and sets the stage for later confusion, confessions, and conflicts. In these three chapters, Jesus travels from Cana, north to Capernaum, and then far south to Jerusalem for Passover before returning to Cana via Samaria (a distance of around 162 miles [ca. 261 km], not calculating elevations or actual paths used for travel). No wonder Jesus was tired during the return trip through Samaria (4:6)!

While in Jerusalem, he enters the temple for the first time and has an ambiguous exchange with the religious leaders (2:13-25). During this trip, Jesus also has his famous nighttime conversation with Nicodemus, the first of many extended dialogues between Jesus and another character or group (3:1-21; cf. 4:4-30; 5:9-47). The scene then shifts back to John (the Baptist), who offers his second round of testimony on Jesus' behalf, repeating many of the same ideas that Jesus himself has either performed or referenced in John 2–3 (3:22–4:3). Once rumors of his successful mission begin spreading, Jesus leaves Judea for Galilee, returning through Samaria. It is here where he dialogues with the Samaritan woman, the second half of the diptych with his exchange with Nicodemus (4:4-42). In contrast to the ambiguous reception in Judea, Jesus is welcomed in Samaria and leaves only after "many more believed because of his word" (4:41).

Several significant themes are introduced or continue in this section of the Gospel, including references to "signs" as deeds that point to Jesus' true identity, contrasts between Jesus' physical appearance and his actual identity, and rotations between belief and disbelief. All these themes continue building on the larger focus of the Gospel: namely, the need to recognize Jesus as the Word made flesh, God's Son and Christ, in order to receive life. In spite of the competitions for his loyalty and for him to know his place as a Jewish man from Galilee—a son, a brother, a teacher with disciples, one who is younger and comes after John (the Baptist), and a subject of both Rome and Herod Antipas—Jesus' behavior consistently manifests his embodiment of God's glory (2:11). In this way, he is already fulfilling the promise to his disciples in 1:51, even though more is yet to come.

For John's Gospel, Jesus' true origins are with God, his "Father." But only the Gospel audience, who has heard all the story thus far, knows this. Instead, Galilee is his "homeland" (*patria*, "fatherland") according to human eyes in the story. It is this contrast of who Jesus *appears* to be in person and who he *really* is that the Gospel continually presses in its larger motif of recognition. Even though those who see and interact with Jesus in person would seem to have an advantage over later believers, they often struggle because of Jesus' outlandish words and incomprehensible deeds. When we put ourselves in the shoes of those who meet with Jesus in person, we feel sympathy and empathy, asking alongside them, "What sign are you showing us that you are doing these things?" (2:18).

Commentary

The First Sign at Cana (2:1-12)

The story of Jesus' first sign at Cana can be divided into three parts: vv. 1-2 establish the setting; vv. 3-10 record the sign, although it is never directly "seen"; and vv. 11-12 describe the aftermath. This opening sign is Jesus' first public activity in Galilee, his "fatherland," and could be compared to the Synoptic accounts of Jesus' first actions in Mark 1:21-28; Matt 5:1–7:29; and Luke 4. John's opening action for Jesus is most like Mark's in that Jesus performs an action rather than offering a speech or a sermon; but unlike in Mark, no one directly witnesses his sign and only the disciples respond with "belief." What precisely they believe, however, is unclear.

John 2:1-12 is the first portion of yet another of the Gospel's many diptychs, a coupling of scenes that stand side by side and influence each other's interpretation. John 2:1-12 and 4:43-54 correspond to each other, not only in location (Cana) and as signs ("first" and "second") but also with format, which can be outlined as follows:

- The setting: Cana of Galilee (2:1-3; 4:43-46)
- A request from a parent: the mother and a father (2:4; 4:47, 49)
- Jesus speaks to clarify his control, and his words are obeyed (2:5-8; 4:48, 50)
- The "sign" occurs offstage (2:9-10; 4:51-53a)
- Resulting belief: the disciples; a father and his household (2:11; 4:53b-54)
- Jesus travels to Jerusalem for a festival (2:12-13; 5:1)

In addition to the structural similarities, several themes emerge in these scenes, including the role of signs and faith. For the Gospel of John, signs are important. In John 5, Jesus will mention them as part of the Father's testimony on his behalf. Yet they are also ambiguous, since neither of Jesus' signs in John 2 or 4 are directly witnessed. Instead, as in Jesus' conversation with Nicodemus, one must "see" the results and infer from that evidence the source of the action. One cannot see the Spirit but must look to where it blows (3:8).

A. 2:1-2: The Setting
The first sign begins the contrast between competing loyalties for Jesus that surfaces throughout this section. At Cana, Jesus' loyalty to his mother (and, therefore, to expected familial and kinship responsibilities in first-century Palestine) is contrasted with his loyalty to his Father's will. The opening verses establish this tension with a brief chiasm that sets Jesus' mother in contrast to Jesus and his disciples:

A. [1]On the third day there was a <u>wedding</u> in Cana of Galilee
   B. and the **mother** of *Jesus* was there.
   B'. [2]And *Jesus* was invited, and his **disciples**,
A'. to the <u>wedding</u>.

This contrast is picked up again at v. 11, when Jesus' disciples alone are said to "believe" in Jesus' manifested glory. Jesus then travels with his mother, brothers, and disciples to Capernaum in v. 12, but they "did not remain there many days." Instead, Jesus quickly leaves for Jerusalem without explicit mention of his family (v. 13), while his disciples' presence is indicated at 2:17.

The opening note that the first sign happened "on the third day" (*tē hēmera tē trite*, 2:1) also creates a transition from the previous three scenes, all of which were introduced with the refrain "on the next day" (1:29, 35, 43). Having left these "next days" behind, we are now embarking on Jesus' own ministry apart from John (the Baptist), which will cause some controversy in 3:22–4:3. The reference to "the third day" has sparked a fair amount of comment by scholars, who have noticed that it does not mathematically match the number of days that have taken place so far in the Gospel. Counting the days from 1:19, 2:1 marks the *seventh day* of the Gospel (cf. Brown 1966, 106; Brant 2011, 55). Rather than blaming the author's arithmetic, it is better to explore other possibilities behind the "third day" description. For many commentators, this description immediately points forward to Jesus' crucifixion and resurrection (cf. Brown 1966, 97, Thompson 2015, 61). This view is strengthened by parallels between this scene and Jesus' crucifixion at 19:25-30, the only other interaction Jesus has with his mother in this Gospel.

Nevertheless, "the third day" is also a common marker for significant events in the OT (cf. Gen 22:4; 34:25; 40:18; Esth 5:1; etc., see also Coloe 2007). Of particular note are Exod 19:16, in which Moses brings the people of Israel to the foot of Mt. Sinai where God's glory and will are made manifest, and the description of a purification offering (*tou agniosmou*) in Num 19, in which the people are told to wash with "running" or "living water" (*hydōr zōn*; cf. John 4:10-11) on the third and seventh day after touching a dead body. The mention of purification jars in John 2:6, as well as the connections to Jesus' death between John 2 and 19, makes this a provocative interpretive possibility. Nevertheless, the "purification" in John 2:6 is *katharismon*, a "cleansing" that Leviticus connects to washing in cases of lepers or bodily emissions (Lev 14:32; 15:13), and which Exodus and Numbers use for "cleansing" from sins (Exod 29:36; 30:10; Num 14:18). Written in a context cognizant of ritual overtones that symbolize God's salvation of Israel, the Gospel presents Jesus in light of them. Using the purification jars, Jesus provides wine in John 2 and promises living water in John 4, demonstrating God's intervention and abundance (Thompson 2015, 62–64). These two elements appear again at Jesus' death in John 19: both in the wine that Jesus drinks just prior to his death and in the water that mingles with the blood dripping from his side (cf. 19:28-30, 34-35; 7:37-38).

B. 2:3-10: A Mother's Request

With the setting established, the action picks up in vv. 3-10. Jesus' mother, who is never named in the Gospel, approaches Jesus "after the wine was running out." Jo-Ann Brant suggests this could mean either there was insufficient wine at the wedding or that the wine was of insufficient quality (2011, 56). Either way, the statement made by Jesus' mother ("They have no wine") is not merely an observation but rather a request. Since wedding guests were expected to provide wine or food for the celebration, this could be her hint that Jesus also needed to provide something or else risk not only his honor but also her own (for more on ancient Jewish wedding customs, see Keener 2003, 498–503).

Jesus' response in 2:4 is surprising, though perhaps not outright rude. Certainly his addressing his mother as "woman" would not have the same abrasive overtones that it does in today's context, but it is, nevertheless, an odd way to address one's mother. It is the same address Jesus uses to speak to all the other women characters in John's Gospel, other than when he calls Mary Magdalene by her name in 20:16 (4:21; [8:10]; 19:26; 20:15). The effect of this address, and his entire exchange with his mother, is distancing. Jesus says to her, "What is between you and me, Woman? As of yet, my hour has not come" (v. 4). The phrase "what is between you and me" is regularly used in biblical texts with negative overtones, indicating that the one speaking does not want to get involved (Jdg 11:12; 1 Kgs 17:18; Mark 1:24; Matt 8:29; Luke 4:34). With this statement, Jesus quickly demonstrates that his work is not completed at his (biological) mother's request or urging, but rather according to his Father's desires. His hour will, indeed, come, and it will involve his mother, wine, and water—but it cannot be rushed (cf. John 12:23; 13:1; 16:2-4; 17:1; 19:25-36).

Jesus' answer to his mother is the only answer in the remainder of 2:4-12. From here on out, characters address one another unilaterally, never receiving a verbal response. Rather than responding directly to her son, Jesus' mother turns to direct the "servers" (*diakonoi*), "whatever he should tell you, do it" (v. 5); Jesus himself then instructs these same servers (vv. 7-8). Their obedience to Jesus is also an act of obedience to Jesus' mother (v. 9). Finally, the "leader of the feast" (*architriklinos*), a person tasked with designating the order in which wine and food was consumed (Keener 2003, 514), responds to the groom with either joy or indignation (v. 10). If he is joyful, his comment is one of surprise, highlighting the groom's generosity. It is perhaps better, however, to hear some indignation in his tone, since the late appearance of "the best wine" *(ton kalon oinon*; cf. 10:11, 14) has made it seem like he does not know how to do his job (Brant 2011, 58). We do not hear a response from the groom, which sets the stage for Jesus' own fulfillment of this role in John (the Baptist's) description of him in 3:22-36 as well as in his courtly conversation with the Samaritan woman in 4:4-30. In John 2:1-12, and in these later scenes, we too feel the surprise felt by the *architriklinos*. Jesus is not like any other bridegroom. He provides "the best wine" not when everyone else would (*pas anthrōpos*, 2:10) but rather when his "hour" comes as guided by the Father.

C. 2:11-12: The Disciples' Belief

The narrative ends with two sentences summarizing the results of Jesus' actions. In v. 11 Jesus' work is called a "sign" (*sēmeion*). The designation emphasizes the importance of Jesus' changing water to wine since through it "he revealed his glory and his disciples believed in him." Resonating with 1:14, the narrator reminds the audience that Jesus already possesses "glory" because he is the Word become flesh. Thus, even though prodded by his mother to act in a way that would gain or retain honor, Jesus has no need to participate in social systems of honor and shame. He already has true glory because he manifests "the glory of the Lord" (Exod 33:18-22; 40:34-35; Greek, *doxa*; Hebrew, *kabōd*). As a result, he acts as a bridegroom with different timing by upsetting the usual order of the banquet so that he may manifest God's glory that outshines all human aspirations (2:23-25; 5:41-44).

The disciples, rather than "the mother," "believe" in 2:11, and Jesus' brothers are mentioned only as an afterthought in 2:12. The brothers' ambiguous role resurfaces when they goad Jesus in 7:1-4 to go to Jerusalem and perform signs during the Festival of Tabernacles. Jesus' mother is often highlighted as the first to show faith in John's Gospel because of her trust that Jesus was able to do something to resolve the honor-crisis of wine in 2:3-5 (Brown 1966, 107–109; Moloney 1993, 83–84). While she does trust her son to act, her behavior is socially expected; a mother would have relied on her son to provide on behalf of the family, particularly in the absence of a husband or father (and Joseph is nowhere mentioned in 2:1-12; cf. Dixon 1987). Her role, therefore, does not appear overly negative or positive, but neutral. She is more an emblem of social and familial expectations to be contrasted against Jesus' heavenly prerogatives than a woman with what Craig Keener calls "holy chutzpah" (2003, 504). Moreover, even the disciples' faith is unclear. They may believe (or "trust"), but what they believe about Jesus on this side of Easter is not clear. As we will see in the remainder of the Gospel, they have much yet to learn (2:17, 22).

The First Passover: Zeal for the Father's House (2:13–3:21)

Immediately after the high point of Jesus' self-revelation at Cana in 2:1-12, Jesus leaves his biological family behind to travel "up" (*anebē*, lit., "ascend") to Jerusalem. The language of "ascension" is consistently associated with

travel to Jerusalem because of the topographical climbing of terrain up to
Mt. Zion, or the Temple Mount, as well as the association of going closer
to God's dwelling, thus, literally upward toward heaven. The irony is
subtle but already playing out. Jesus' approach toward Jerusalem should be
bringing him, like any other pilgrim, closer to God. Yet, as the embodiment
of God's glory, Jesus is the "tabernacle" (or "dwelling place," *skēnē*, 1:14)
that is bringing God's glory to Jerusalem in a unique way (1:16-18). He is
fulfilling Isaiah's promise of the Lord's postexilic return to Jerusalem, just as
John (the Baptist) announced in 1:23, but no one can see this yet (Isa 40, esp.
40:5). Jesus' unique identity and relationship to Jerusalem causes conflict
when he makes his debut in the temple at 2:13-22, and in his conversation
with Nicodemus at 3:13 when he says, "Indeed, no one has ascended into
heaven except the one who descended from heaven, the Son of Man." All of
2:13–3:21 should be read together because these events take place in Jerusalem around Passover (2:13, 22, 3:1). Jesus does not leave Judea until 4:3 as
rumors of his successful baptism ministry spread.

A. 2:13-22: Jesus' Defense of his Father's House
John 2:13 is the first mention of Passover in the Gospel. Passover is one of
three pilgrimage festivals in the Jewish liturgical calendar alongside Pentecost and Tabernacles (Exod 23:14; Deut 16:16-17). Passover was especially
significant since, through this festival, Israel remembered and relived their
exodus from Egypt by means of God's mighty deliverance. Although often
assumed to involve atonement, it is important to remember that this is not
the same festival as *Yom Kippur* (Day of Atonement, Lev 16) even though
it does involve sacrifice. The Passover Lamb is not a sin offering since this
festival predates the tabernacle and temple where such offerings would have
been made (see "Jesus and the Temple" below). It is, rather, a "lawful word/
thing" (*rhēma nomimon*, Exod 12:24) kept and a meal shared to reenact
God's "protection" or "covering" (*skepazō*, Exod 12:27) of the people. Passover occurs twice more in John's Gospel (6:1-71; 12–20), and it is during
this festival that Jesus is crucified. Passover and the Jewish liturgical calendar
overall play a significant role in this Gospel. The use of the OT in John is
more subtle than in Matthew or Luke, but it is pervasive, perhaps nowhere
more so than in the careful attention to festivals that accompany, or occasion,
Jesus' actions and words.

Jesus arrives in Jerusalem before "the Passover of the Jews" begins.
This description recalls 1:19-28, where John (the Baptist) was questioned
by "priests and Levites" who were sent by "the Jews from Jerusalem" and
"the Pharisees" (1:19, 24). The Jews are present in 2:14-17, presumably

participating in preparations for Passover, and they witness Jesus' actions before questioning him in 2:18-22. Both 2:14-17 and 2:18-22 run roughly parallel to one another, creating contrasts between the Jews and Jesus, who show "zeal" in different ways (cf. Lappenga), and between Jesus' body, called a "sanctuary" (*naon*) by Jesus in 2:19, and the Jerusalem temple (*hieron*). Each scene begins with a reaction to what is seen and heard (2:14-16, 18-20) and ends with a "remembrance" by the disciples, who recall this story and are able to interpret it in light of Scripture (Ps 69:10) after Jesus' resurrection (John 2:17, 21-22).

Jesus' behavior in 2:14-17 is nothing less than shocking. Jesus displays his "zeal" (*zēlos*) for his Father's house by making a whip (*phragellion*) to herd the animals out of the court, causing their owners to leave in chase (Croy). The temple area would have been full of sacrifices for people to purchase and offer to ensure their ability to participate in Passover, but Jesus sees a different scene. He calls the temple court an "emporium," a marketplace. Unlike John 2:1-12 where Jesus' intervention was coaxed out of him by his mother, this apparent affront to his Father's house causes a public and disruptive response. Moreover, while Jesus' mother drew attention to a situation that would have been immediately visible to the wedding guests, Jesus' own disruption at the temple is in response to a crisis no one else can see. No wine at a wedding is a problem; plenty of sacrifices for ritual purification before Passover is entirely fitting (cf. 11:55).

This context clarifies the Jews' questions in 2:18-22. Their responses seem mild considering Jesus' potential to be a false teacher (as in 5:16-18; 7:32-52; 9:16, 24; cf. Deut 13; 18) or, worse, his ability to gain unwanted Roman attention (John 11:45-53). After all, Jesus would not have been the first prophet to criticize temple practices, particularly in the lead-up to exile (e.g., Isaiah, Jeremiah, Amos). Jesus responds to the Jews with a riddle rather than a clear explanation: "Destroy this sanctuary (*naon*) and in three days, I will raise it" (2:19). Unlike *hieron*, which, along with "place" (*topos*), is consistently used to describe the Jerusalem temple in John, *naon* only appears here. *Naon* means "sanctuary," or the "inmost part of a temple" that housed the "image of the god"; for the Israelites, this is where the ark of the covenant was once kept (LSJ; Hdt. 1.183; 6.19; Xen. *Apol.* 15; 1 Kgs 7:36). The narrator clarifies Jesus' comment for the Gospel audience, but the Jews are left confused. Moreover, Jesus has now planted the idea that he could be a threat to the temple. The last temple was destroyed when the Babylonians swept through and exiled the Judeans. This exchange, therefore, sets the stage for Jesus' final condemnation in 11:47-53 out of fear that "the Romans will come and destroy us and the place (*topos*; i.e., temple) and the nation" (11:48).

Read or heard on their own, Jesus' words *are* strange. Only the Gospel audience learns what he means due to the narrator's post-Easter explanation of the disciples' insights. The reference to the third day describes Jesus' resurrection (cf. 2:1), and the sanctuary (*naon*) of which he speaks is not the temple (*heiron*) but rather his "body" (*sōma*). Even after his death and resurrection, Jesus' body will still matter (20:17, 24-29). As in 1:14, 51 and 2:11, Jesus is the locus of God's glory, and it is to him that those seeking God ought to come. Such a drastic change in worship is impossible for characters to understand at this point in the story. It will come up again in Jesus' conversation with the Samaritan woman (4:16-26), as well as in later, and more hostile, exchanges in Jerusalem (5:39-47) and beyond (6:41-51).

B. 2:23-25: Belief and Unbelief

This short excerpt is a hinge, or pivot, in the Passover sequence from Jesus' public appearance in the temple and city to Jesus' first private dialogue in 3:1-21. In 2:23-25, "many" in Jerusalem for the Passover "believed" or "trusted in his [Jesus'] name because they saw the signs he was doing" (v. 23). These "many" are certainly Jews, not only because Jews were the ones who would be in Jerusalem for the Passover but also because in 1:19 the Gospel described the Jews as being "from Jerusalem." Nevertheless, 2:23-25 does not explicitly include a reaction from "the Jews" (*hoi Ioudaioi*, vv. 18, 20) but rather leaves them wordless after 2:20 when Jesus never answers their question. Their conversation will continue in 3:1-21, when Nicodemus, "a person from the Pharisees . . . a leader of the Jews" (*anthrōpos ek tōn Pharisaiōn . . . archōn tōn Ioudaiōn*) comes to Jesus.

The reaction of these "many" in Jerusalem would seem to be positive at first, and, indeed, it parallels the disciples' belief after Jesus' sign in 2:11. In 2:24-25, however, Jesus' reaction to this trust undermines it. Although the people "believe" in Jesus' name, Jesus doesn't "trust himself to them" (*ouk episteuen*) because he "knows everything" and does not need human testimony (lit., "someone to testify concerning humanity") to recognize human fickleness (cf. 4:43-45). Jesus "was knowing what was in a human" (*eginōsken ti ēn tō anthrōpō*; cf. 3:1); it is people who need help—signs, along with human and divine testimony—to understand who he is. As we will learn in John 5, Jesus has greater witnesses, especially his Father. Jesus is not doing these signs for fame, as his brothers will accuse in 7:2-4 (cf. 5:41-44); he is doing them to point to his Father: "I myself have come in my Father's name," he says in 5:43. Just as Jesus addressed his mother's concern with a sign behind the scenes in 2:1-12, so too does he reject the lure of popularity in 2:23-24.

C. 3:1-21: Jesus' Conversation with Nicodemus

Jesus' conversation with Nicodemus is the first extended dialogue in the Gospel, but Jesus quickly dominates the conversation. The exchange divides into two parts: vv. 1-11 and vv. 11-21, with v. 11 as a hinge. This division uses the words "teacher" (*didaskolos*) and "we know" (*oidamen*) as the markers that shift from a dialogue in vv. 1-10 to a monologue in vv. 11-21. In 3:11, Jesus switches from addressing Nicodemus in the second-person singular "you" to addressing a group as "you all." Just as the Jews disappear in 2:18-22, Nicodemus disappears from the conversation after his last question in 3:9 without giving a final verdict on Jesus.

We Know You Are a Teacher from God (vv. 1-11). Nicodemus comes to Jesus not only as a representative of "the Pharisees . . . a leader of the Jews" but also as a "person" (*anthrōpos*). His introduction connects him both to 2:13-22 and 2:23-25, as well as the opening verses of the Gospel (1:4, 6, 9). In 3:1-11, we learn a bit more about what people were "believing" concerning Jesus' name from 2:23-25 and why Jesus did not trust himself to them. Nicodemus's first statements to Jesus are not hostile. He calls Jesus a "Rabbi" as Jesus' first disciples did in 1:38. He gives an assessment of Jesus based on what he (thinks) "we know": that Jesus "has come from God as a teacher" because of his signs (3:2; cf. 2:18, 23).

Interpreters often highlight the fact that Nicodemus comes at night, "from the darkness toward the light" (Moloney 1993, 108). While the Gospel certainly contrasts darkness and light, and even has Judas go out into the "night" when he goes to betray Jesus (13:30), there is nothing explicitly negative about this time in 3:2. Recalling that Jewish reckoning of days begins at nightfall, this may have been the time Nicodemus was able to come to Jesus since his responsibilities for the Passover would have been complete. Moreover, Nicodemus *comes to* Jesus at night rather than going away from him; he does what he should by coming to the Light (3:19; Thompson 2015, 78). The fact that Nicodemus is coming in from the dark foreshadows the inadequacy of his knowledge, but he is not entirely wrong either. Jesus is a teacher from God, but he is also more, and his lessons are not necessarily the easiest to follow.

In 3:1-11 Nicodemus and Jesus trade statements about "ability," both using the verb *dynatai* (he/she is able) at least once every time they speak (vv. 2, 3, 4, 5, 9). Jesus takes Nicodemus's words and reframes them at each point, thereby taking control of the conversation. In addition to using *dynatai*, Jesus adopts Nicodemus's phrases "unless" (*ean mē*, vv. 2, 3, 5) and "enter into" (*eiselthein*, v. 4, 5), and punctuates his teaching with the phrase "truly, truly I am saying to you" (vv. 3, 5, 11) that will become his trademark in the Gospel (cf. 1:51; used 25 times in John). He finishes the dialogue portion of the encounter in 3:11 by recounting what "we know" in contrast to Nicodemus's statement about what he, the Pharisees, and other people "know" about Jesus. Unlike Nicodemus, Jesus is part of a "we" that testifies from what they "have seen"; the heavenly knowledge Jesus offers is not abstract (1:17-18; cf. 3:32-33; 19:35; 21:24-25; 1 John 1:1-4; 3 John 12).

Although Nicodemus is often interpreted as a bit of a dupe in comparison to Jesus, Brant suggests that he is playing along with Jesus, offering sarcastic repartee rather than ignorant astonishment (2011, 75–76; cf. Whitenton). Keener demonstrates that Jesus' use of "rebirth" imagery was common in discussions of "creation or Israel's redemption" from the time period (2003, 542; see "New Birth" below). As Gwynn Kessler shows, creation and birth (or procreation) were often set side by side in Jewish writings since they were both moments of life bestowed by God alone (112–13). It is not Jesus' metaphorical language that is difficult to understand. What is difficult for Nicodemus is the implication that he needs to change in order "to see" it (v. 3; cf. 3:14). As a teacher, Nicodemus should be providing light and sight to the people. Jesus' challenge is for him to recognize his own blindness, a challenge with which some other Pharisees will also struggle in 9:39-41.

We Know What We Are Saying (vv. 11-21). From here on, Nicodemus disappears from the scene. Jesus' shift to the first-person plural "we" and second-person plural "you all" has led some scholars to argue that 3:11-21 are from the narrator rather than Jesus (see Brown 1966, 149). Keeping in mind that the Gospel would have been performed out loud, however, the blending of Jesus' and the narrator's voices is rhetorically effective. Both Jesus and the narrator share an omniscient perspective, and the "we" of which Jesus (or the narrator) speaks would include the narrator, John (the Baptist), as well as members of the audience, creating a cast of witnesses to which Jesus will add his works, his Father, and Scripture in 5:31-40. The use of "we" language means that Jesus is following the Deuteronomic regulation that testimony should come from at least two or three witnesses (Deut 17:6; John 5:31; 8:13-14). That Jesus *is* still speaking, however, seems justified by the fact that no explicit change of speaker or scene takes place until 3:22.

In 3:11-21, Jesus continues his contrast of heavenly and earthly things from 3:6-8, where the contrast was between "water and spirit" and "flesh." In 3:12-21 Jesus offers proofs that he knows what he is talking about. First, he gives a maxim that would have been understood in the ancient world:

someone who does not understand earthly things cannot understand heavenly things; like is known by like (8:40-44; Keener 2003, 559–60). He then establishes the "Son of Man" as the only one who has firsthand knowledge of "heavenly things" in 3:13 (cf. 1:51). The audience knows that Jesus himself is the Son of Man because of the origin narrative provided in 1:1-18. Jesus' statement that only the Son of Man has ascended into heaven undercuts traditions that Enoch, Moses, and Elijah ascended entirely to God's presence. Their ascents, Jesus indicates, did not penetrate the same heights as those from which the Son of Man descends (on layers in the heavens, see *Mart. Ascen. Isa.*; 2 Cor 12:2). Like in John 1:18, where Jesus is described as the Unique-one (*monogenēs*) who sees God from the breast and face to face, as the "Son of Man" in 3:13 he asserts for himself that he has had a better view.

Second, Jesus gives an argument *from* Scripture by appealing to part of Moses' story as he led the wandering Israelites after Passover during their exodus from Egypt. In Num 21, Moses is dealing with a grumbling group of tired and harassed Israelites as well as his own missteps that have caused the Lord to keep him from leading the people into the promised land (Num 20:9-13). Attacked by serpents because of their complaints over the manna (which they call "empty bread," Num 21:5), the Lord gives life only if the people look upon the image of a bronze serpent set on a pole. The LXX version of 21:8 reads, "And the Lord said to Moses, 'Make for yourself a serpent and put it upon a sign (*sēmeiou*) and it will be if a serpent should bite a person, each one having been bitten who looks at it will live (*zēsetai*).'"

Jesus applies this *sign* to himself and his upcoming "exaltation" upon the cross: "And just as Moses exalted the serpent in the wilderness, thusly it is necessary for the Son of Man to be exalted, so that each one believing in him will have eternal life" (John 3:14-15). Jesus compares himself, as the Son of Man, to the serpent and compares Nicodemus and those he represents to the wandering, grumbling Israelites. Rather than rejected, however, these Israelites are loved, and God's provision is visible when they realize their mistake (Num 21:7). In the same way, Jesus reminds Nicodemus that God continues to act out of love; what is needed is the restoration of sight so that he can see it.

In 3:16-21, Jesus first broaches the topic of judgment, which recurs throughout the Gospel (cf. 7:24). Rather than coming for "judgment" (*krisis, krinō*), Jesus says that God's intervention with the world is out of love—not only in the present but "just as" it has always been (3:14). To experience this love fully, however, one needs to believe or "trust" what Jesus is saying. "The one who is believing is not being judged, but the one who is not believing has been judged already, because they have not believed in the name of the Unique

Son of God (*tou monogenous huiou tou theou*)" (3:18). In language that resonates with 1:17-18, Jesus once again reinforces his superior view. According
to Jesus, judgment has already taken place, or continues taking place, when
people (*anthrōpoi*, 3:19) love darkness rather than the light that is God's love.
In John's Gospel, loving light and "doing truth" means admitting weakness
and failure rather than continuing with a false front of self-sufficiency and
human honor. Those who admit their metaphorical blindness are not left in
the dark but come to the light, and God works through them (3:21).

John's Continuing Confession (3:22–4:3)
After Jesus' description of those who love the light, the narrative shifts to
an example of such a person: John (the Baptist). John 3:22–4:3 contains
John's third appearance in the Gospel (1:6-18, 19-36), this time at some
distance from Jesus, surrounded by disciples who have chosen to remain with
him rather than leaving to follow Jesus. In 3:1-21, Jesus has a conversation
with Nicodemus; in 3:25-36, John has his own conversation with another
Jewish man (*Ioudaiou*) and his disciples. The term *Ioudiaos* could be translated "Judean," meaning a man from Judea, with clear connections to the
Jews/Judeans with whom Jesus had interacted during Passover in 2:13–3:21
and those who first came to question him in 1:19-28. The man's concern
with baptism also shows him to be "Jewish." Like Nicodemus, the man
and disciples call John "Rabbi" and seek clarity concerning what Jesus and
John are doing. John's statements likewise mirror Jesus', including the use
of *dynatai* (v. 27), witness/speech, contrasting things from heaven and from
earth, love, and linking belief with "having eternal life" versus remaining in
wrath or darkness. This is John's last spoken testimony in the Gospel but not
his last mention. True to his own description, Jesus "will increase" as John
"decreases" (3:30), but John does surface again in 10:40-42, the effectiveness
of his witness still ringing out for those who can hear.

In 3:22-24 we learn that Jesus is in Judea, continuing with his disciples
and "baptizing" (*ebaptizen*). It is his baptism ministry that seems to confuse,
or perhaps threaten, the Jewish man and John's disciples in 3:25-26 who
wonder why this latecomer is attracting more followers than their teacher.
John repeats his testimony in 3:27-36, not only summarizing his previous
statement that he "is not the Christ" (3:28; 1:20) but also saying that that he
was "the one sent before that one" (3:28; 1:6, 15, 30). John also reprises the
wedding motifs from 2:1-12, casting Jesus firmly in the role of the groom
while he himself is a rejoicing "friend" (*philos*, 3:29-30; 11:11; 15:14-15). In
3:31-36 he picks up on themes from Jesus' conversation with Nicodemus,
placing himself among the "we" of whom Jesus spoke in 3:11 by reinforcing

Jesus' own words. According to John, Jesus is the one "coming from above/ again" (*anōthen*, 3:31), which recalls Jesus' description of rebirth in 3:3-7 and will describe moments during his trial and crucifixion (19:11, 23). Unlike John, or anyone else, Jesus "testifies what he has seen and heard" even though his testimony is rejected (3:32). While Jesus emphasized God's love for the world, John focuses on the Father's love for the Son, to whom he has given all things "in his hands" (*en tē cheiri autou*). Believing in the Son leads to "eternal life," while rejecting him causes "the wrath of God to remain" or "abide upon" them (*hē orgē tou theou menei ep autou*, v. 36, cf. 15:1-17). John's harsh description parallels Jesus' own in 3:18-21, with "wrath" now explaining "judgment." As before, it is not the Son who is judging, but rather the poor judgment of people that causes them to remain in darkness.

John 4:1-3 problematizes the previous descriptions of Jesus' baptismal ministry in 3:22, 26, and 4:1. Even though the narrator described Jesus as baptizing (3:22; 4:1) along with the Jewish man and disciples (3:26), in 4:2 the narrator offers a correction. The Pharisees may have "heard" that Jesus was baptizing more (*pleionas*, cf. 3:23, *polla*) than John, but we learn that "Jesus himself was not baptizing, but his disciples." Jeffrey Staley argues that the implied author "hoodwinks" the implied reader, causing the reader to "reevaluate his [*sic*] relationship with the narrator and the story" (1988, 98). Ancient rhetorical handbooks strongly urge authors and speakers to maintain a trustworthy stance, particularly in telling narratives, whether as histories and biographies or in legal settings, so that they are believed (Myers 2012, 27–39). Other scholars solve this tension by suggesting that there is an editorial seam at 4:2 (and 5:9) that has not been covered well (Brown 1966, 164–65).

The literary context of John 2:13–4:2, however, includes a number of reactions to Jesus, reports about him, and testimony from him. For the Gospel, only this final category is the most trustworthy (3:11, 32). In 3:22 and 26, we join the cast of "hearers" as the story is told to us, first by the narrator (v. 22) and then in the report to John (v. 26). Staley has a point; we, the audience, are dragged along, caught up in the rumors about Jesus in 3:22, 26, and 4:1 before finding out the truth in 4:2. The effect of this rhetoric could undermine the narrator's authority, but it also reinforces the narrator's point that only hindsight can clarify who Jesus is and what he does. The audience is not above the characters in the story here, but like the Jewish man, John's disciples, and the Pharisees, we too participate in rumors about Jesus that turn out not to be true. Jesus' real baptismal work will not come until 20:22, after his exaltation, when he breathes the Holy Spirit upon his disciples (cf. 1:33; 7:37-39). As in 3:14, the sign that is needed for healing—new birth and new creation—remains in the future.

A Samaritan Woman's Confession (4:4-42)

On his way back to Galilee, the narrator explains that "it is necessary" for Jesus "to pass through Samaria" and situates him in Sychar, a "city" known for having a well "which Jacob gave to Joseph his son" (4:4-5). Although the rumors are of him baptizing, Jesus is doing something else with water in 4:4-30. The scene breaks down in three main parts: (1) an opening scene about "living water" (vv. 4-15); (2) a discussion of worship locations (vv. 16-26); and (3) a closing section of belief among the Samaritans that contrasts Jesus' reception in Jerusalem (vv. 27-42). Throughout this chapter, the narrator plays with expectations, using common literary motifs to show what it means for Jesus to be the location of God's glory no matter where he goes.

A. 4:4-15: An Offer of Living Water

Robert Alter's influential study on this scene illustrates how Jesus' encounter with the Samaritan woman, at Jacob's well, repeats what he calls a "biblical type-scene" of betrothal (51–52). Jacob met Rachel at a well "at midday" (or "the sixth hour," Gen 29:7; cf. John 2:4; 4:6; 19:14), and his own parents' marriage was initiated at a well when Abraham's servant met Rebekah (Gen 24:10-33). Moses, too, who is already referenced in John several times at this point, met his wife Zipporah at a well (Exod 2:15-22). Adding to these intertextual similarities are the repeated references to households and marriage in John 2–3, including the wedding at Cana where Jesus implicitly fills the role of the groom by providing "the best wine" (2:10), a description John (the Baptist) reinforces in 3:29-30 when he casts Jesus as the groom (*nymphion*, 2:9; 3:29) and himself as "the best man" (*philos tou nymphiou*, lit. "friend of the groom"). Mary Coloe explores the role of the "best man" in ancient Jewish traditions, noting that it was this friend who was to "negotiate the amount of the dowry, the down-payment at the time of the wedding, the amount to be received at the time of the wedding and the likely date of the wedding" (2013b, 184). For Coloe, what is significant is that John's role is not simply as a friend but also as a partner who was firmly invested in the success of the wedding. Moreover, he was legally prohibited from marrying the would-be bride himself. Thus, John (the Baptist) is Jesus' forerunner, the voice who prepares his way, and then the one who celebrates the completed marriage, slipping away from the scene rather than occupying center stage (185).

The courtship in John 4, however, is not a normal one. Jesus and the woman do not "marry" literally, but symbolically, restoring the link between Samaria (the northern tribes of Israel) and Judea (the southern tribes of Israel) to bring all of Israel together again. The woman's calling Jacob "our father" in 4:12 points to their shared ancestry in Jacob/Israel, but Jesus is greater than Jacob and "shows the way" to the Father of all (1:18; 4:21-25; cf. Myers 2012, 95–97). Coloe argues that the other persistent symbolism of this scene is Jesus as temple, or the location of God's glory (1:14-16, 51; 2:11, 21). Even though the woman is at first focused on literal water—she has, after all come to collect water for her home—the image of water, especially *living water* (*hydōr zōn*) is commonly associated with the temple in Jewish literature. These traditions "associate the temple with the source of all the waters of creation," so that the temple sits upon the "abyss which is the source of the creative waters in Genesis 2.8" (187; cf. Ezek 47). When Jesus "sits upon" Jacob's well in John 4, he is another temple, sitting on the wellspring of living waters. Although Jacob may have provided water, even a miraculous provision of abundant water (*Tg. Neof.* Gen 29:10), the water Jesus provides is superior because it is eternal (John 4:14; Coloe 2013b, 188).

B. 4:16-26: Supplying Living Water

After the woman's request for the water Jesus provides, the conversation takes on a different tone. While this transition is perhaps jarring for contemporary readers, it coheres with Coloe's analysis above. The woman and Jesus begin discussing "husbands" (*andra*; cf. 1:12-13), which fits the genre of a courtship conversation. Rather than a virginal bride, however, the Samaritan woman is a "woman" (*gynē*), a term that can mean woman or wife but that also meant "a fully reproductive" adult (H. King, 27). Although commentaries have often portrayed this woman as something of a harlot for having five husbands (and now living with a sixth man), Susan Hylen is right to point out that her "sinfulness" is not ever a focus of the story (2009, 42); indeed, she could also be the victim of situations outside her control, such as widowhood or infertility, which could have prompted divorce but not an association with sin (48). Either way, her situation is fruitless, just as it seems Jesus interpreted the situation in the temple to be in 2:14-17.

Rather than defensiveness at Jesus' prophetic words, the woman responds "well" (*kalōs*) and truthfully, pushing the conversation with Jesus deeper than we have thus far seen an interlocutor be able to do. As Coloe writes, this woman is "a perfect dialogue partner with Jesus," and, picking up on the use of marital imagery for covenant relationships with God, she quickly moves to discuss worship outright (191). In this, she shows herself to understand more than her counterpart, Nicodemus, who received chastisement rather than praise from Jesus (4:19). The woman contrasts "the mountain" of Gerizim with "the place in Jerusalem" (*topos*, 4:20), wanting to know which is superior, but Jesus does not choose. Even though he says that "salvation comes from the Jews" (4:22), he does not locate "true" worship in a precise place, but with people: "the ones who worship truly will worship the Father in Spirit and truth" (4:23). In vv. 23-24, Jesus rotates between descriptions of "worship/worshipers" and descriptions of the Father/God to create parallelisms on how "it is necessary to worship" (*proskynein dei*, 4:20; *dei proskynein*, 4:23). Because "God is Spirit," the "place" (*topos*) of worship is not the most important; instead it is a connection to this Spirit, who can blow anywhere (3:8), even in the wilderness of Samaria.

The importance of Spirit recalls not only Jesus' conversation with Nicodemus in 3:5-8 but also the description of Jesus' baptism in 1:29-34. In all these passages, as well as in 4:4-30, the Spirit is connected in some way to water (cf. 7:37-39). The interrelationship between water and Spirit is evocative of creation contexts, when the "earth was unseen and unformed and darkness was above the abyss and the Spirit of God was impending above the water" (Gen 1:2). The verb "impending" (*epipherō*) can mean "laying," but it was also often used in contexts of battle, when an opponent was about to rush upon an enemy (cf. *Il.* 15.743; Thuc. 3.23; Hdt. 8.61, 90). In the context of creation, God's Spirit is about to battle the water and darkness through God's speech ("word," *logos*), causing life (Gen 1:3–2:3; John 1:1-5). Sherri Brown highlights the importance of water in Jewish traditions, including the OT, writing that "it is only God who can control the waters of the earth, and its creative force reveals both the power and presence of God" (2015a, 291). Throughout John's Gospel, Jesus is the one who controls water, repeatedly bringing Spirit into the mix (6:16-21; 7:37-39; 19:34-35). His control of these waters, his relationship with the Spirit, and his ability to give life demonstrate that he is continuing his creative work as God's Word. Indeed, Jesus' revelation to the Samaritan woman culminates with a revelation of his divine identity when he calls himself "I am" (*egō eimi*), the first of the "I am" statements Jesus uses in the Gospel (C. Williams 2000, 257–65).

C. 4:27-42: Sharing the Gift of Water

As with Jesus' conversation with Nicodemus in 3:1-21, Jesus' disciples miss out again in 4:4-26. Having traveled to get Jesus some food, they return and are "amazed" to find Jesus "talking with a woman," but they remain silent (v. 27). The woman herself leaves without a word and without her water jar. Having received the living water Jesus provided through his words, she shares news of her gift in the "city" with the people, who immediately respond by going out to find Jesus (vv. 28-30).

The disciples now have their turn to learn something. Their "amazement" is similar to that expressed by Nicodemus in 3:7 when Jesus told him, "Stop being amazed because I told you, 'It is necessary to be born again/from above!'" He will repeat a similar admonition in 5:20 and 28, reprimanding his interlocutors over their amazement at the works he is doing, including his ability to raise the dead (cf. 11:1-44). The disciples' amazement in 4:27 is a sign of their ignorance; they have missed the point of Jesus' "necessary" travel through Samaria to reunite all the people of Israel by means of his life-giving ministry.

When the disciples command Jesus to "eat" in 4:31, he again shifts from literal to figurative meanings. Rather than literal food, Jesus says, "My food (*brōma*; cf. 4:32; 6:27, 55, *brōsis*) is that I should do the will of the one who sent me and that I should complete his work" (4:34). This work, Jesus explains, is "gathering fruit for eternal life, so that the one who sows may rejoice together with the one who harvests" (4:36). Even though many scholars argue that John does not have parables, Ruben Zimmermann argues that John uses parabolic language throughout in Jesus' teachings, including here in 4:35-38 (2015, 333–39). The definition of a "parable" is much more flexible in the ancient world than we have often permitted based on assumptions from the Synoptics. If John knows the Synoptic tradition, this could be John's version of the Parable of the Sower (Mark 4:1-20; Matt 13:1-23; Luke 8:4-15). In John, Jesus is the Word (*ho Logos*) who has been sent by God, the sower, to be received by the earth (cf. 3:31; 12:23-33; Mark 4:14, "The sower sows the word [*ton logon*]"). As in the Synoptics, this Word is accepted by an unlikely person, the Samaritan woman, and it is she who replicates Jesus' behavior in 4:28-30, not the disciples. In 4:39, "many believed in him . . . *because of the word of the witnessing woman.*" The silent disciples, in contrast, "harvest that for which they did not toil" (v. 38; cf. 4:6). They will "enter into" Jesus' toil, but it is toiling that the woman has already entered into! This same pattern of Jesus commissioning a woman disciple before the male disciples happens in John 20, when the resurrected Jesus first addresses and sends Mary Magdalene (20:1-18).

In John 4:40-42 the belief of the Samaritans shifts as they themselves spend time with Jesus. Like the disciples in 1:38-39, the Samaritans "remain" (*emeinen*) with Jesus, inviting him to stay in their city and thereby undoing the usual pattern of Samaritans and Jews not "coming together" (*synchrōntai*, 4:9). While there, "many believed on account of *his word*" and no longer relied on the woman's testimony. Although perhaps jarring at first—are they discounting what this woman said?—her model demonstrates how testimony on behalf of Jesus should work. The woman is as another, and perhaps more successful, John (the Baptist). Also starting with water, she herself came to understand Jesus' identity in part and witnessed to her city (4:39-41). This testimony is enough to create space for Jesus to sow his own word in their midst, resulting in faith: "We ourselves have heard and know that this one is truly the Savior (*sōtēr*) of the world!" (4:42). The woman, like John (the Baptist), fades from view as Jesus takes his place in the center of the stage. What the Samaritans now *know* is more profound than even Nicodemus, one of the leaders of the Jews, from whom *salvation* comes, could know (*sōtēria* 4:22; cf. *oidamen* in 3:2, 11, and *sōthē* [be saved] in 3:17). From Nicodemus's privileged place, it will take him longer to come to the same conclusion (7:50-52; 19:38-42).

The Second Sign at Cana (4:43–5:1)

The final passage in this section records Jesus' "second sign he did, having come from Judea into Galilee" (4:54). This is not his second sign overall, however, since Jesus performed signs while in Jerusalem during Passover (2:23). Rather, this is his second sign in Galilee, parallel to his first sign at the wedding in Cana in 2:1-12, which is cited in 4:46. Jesus' time in Jerusalem is also blended into this scene in 4:44-45, making this short episode a reprise of Jesus' time with the Jews (or Judeans) generally in contrast to his time in Samaria in 4:4-42 (*Ioudaioi* 2:6, 13, 18, 20; 3:1, 22, 25; 4:9, 22; 5:1).

As in Jerusalem, Jesus is skeptical of the welcome he receives in Galilee. In 4:42, 44, and 45, three statements are set in contrast with one another, all introduced by parallel phrases:

- 4:42 *autoi gar akēkoamen kai oidamen* (For we ourselves have heard and know)
- 4:44 *autos gar Iēsous emartyrēsen* (For Jesus himself testified)
- 4:45 *autoi gar ēlthon eis tēn eortēn* (For they themselves went to the festival)

The Gospel used the same phrase to describe Jesus' reaction to those in Jerusalem in 2:25: *autos gar eginōsken ti ēn en tō anthrōpō* (For he himself knew what was in humanity). It will turn up again in 6:6 and 16:27 to indicate Jesus' superior knowledge. The contrasting structure creates a comparison between 2:23-25 and 4:42-45, leading the audience to join Jesus' skepticism of the Galilean welcome. "A prophet has no honor in his fatherland," Jesus testifies (cf. Mark 6:4; Matt 13:57; Luke 4:24; Keener 2003, 629). True to his earlier statement that his testimony is rejected, the Galileans "welcome" him because of his signs (John 3:11, 32). Jesus' statement, however, already sets the stage for a contrast between welcome and honor. One must look to where signs point rather than remaining satisfied with the signs alone.

Encouraged to hear this sign alongside the first Cana episode, the audience should notice parallels (see above). In this scene, Jesus is approached not by his mother but by a concerned father, who also happens to be a *basilikos*, an official associated with the "king" (*basileus*). Scholars have debated whether this man is Gentile or Jewish because of the ambiguity of this title. Since both Jewish client-kings and Roman emperors could be called "kings," some wonder if this passage is John's version of the healing for the centurion performed in Matthew and Luke (Mead). Focusing on the title itself rather than ethnicity, however, another element comes to the fore. Jesus is here acting out his role as "Savior of the world" from 4:42. In the ancient Mediterranean world, a king's responsibility was to protect and provide for his subjects, particularly his friends and officials, his *basilikoi*. It was from this ability to protect that kings, and especially Roman emperors, used the title "Savior" to describe themselves and maintain loyalty from their subjects (Koester 1990, 665–68). This *basilikos* does *not* turn to his king—regardless if he be Roman or Jewish—he turns to Jesus, the "true Savior of the world" (*alēthōs ho sōtēr tou kosmou*, 4:42).

Jesus' behavior toward the *basilikos* is surprising, but it fits the larger Johannine context. In 2:3-4 we recall that he first rebuffed his mother's implicit request before responding to her concerns. And in 11:1-4 we will again see Jesus delay travel to help a group of friends, Lazarus, Martha, and Mary. Jesus is always emphasizing that his actions are not prompted by anyone else other than his Father (5:19-22). Jesus' rebuke, "Unless you all should see signs and wonders, you all will surely not believe!" is met with persistence by the man, who repeats his request: "Lord, come down before my little son dies!" (4:48-49). Jesus' words seem less directed at the man himself and more toward the Galileans whose sight-focused faith was emphasized in 4:44-45 (cf. 6:22-29 also in Galilee). Jesus' sign, therefore, is performed by *word*; he says to the man, "Your son is living" (v. 50). Trusting this word, the man leaves, walking away from Jesus with faith rather than walking toward him. When he learns from his slaves (*douloi*) that his son is indeed alive and that his fever "released him" at the same "hour" Jesus spoke his word, "he himself and his whole household believed" (v. 53; cf. 2:11). This father, therefore, becomes a model for the Johannine community and all subsequent believers who must learn to trust Jesus based on words rather than sight (20:29).

Theological Threads

Sight, Signs, and Belief

There is a long history of distrusting "signs faith" in NT scholarship. Part of this cynicism is based in the Enlightenment roots of biblical scholarship, which doubted the authenticity of miracles since they are contrary to natural law (Bultmann 1989). Since miracles were not trusted, faith based on such miracles was deemed deficient as well. There are, however, passages in the NT, and John in particular, that seem also to disparage such "signs faith," particularly 4:43-45 and its parallel 2:23-25. Nevertheless, Jesus performs a number of signs in the Gospel of John (*sēmeion* appears 17 times in the Gospel), and counts his "works" (*erga*) among the "witnesses" that reveal his identity (5:36). This leaves readers of the Gospel in a bit of a quandary: are signs good or bad, and is faith based on sight such a bad thing?

Craig Koester argues that signs faith is not in and of itself bad in the Gospel of John. Signs are not bad, because they point toward Jesus' identity and his completion of God's work (2008, 163–64). What is important, however, is how people interpret these signs: do they recognize their significance, or are they inhibited from doing so by other factors? For Koester, "Characters in the Gospel respond to signs with genuine faith if they have already been brought to faith by what they have heard from or about Jesus" (164). In other words, how characters "see" signs depends on the words they hear, or listen to (*akouō*).

As the Gospel continues, Jesus repeatedly talks about the need to *hear his voice* and respond to his words, which have their source in God (5:24-30; 6:45; 10:3-10; 18:37). In John 6:68-69, for example, Peter will say, "Lord, to where shall we depart? You have the words (*rhēmata*) of life, and we ourselves have believed and have seen that you yourself are the Holy One of God." Such hearing does not, however, mean that the characters in the Gospel understand what Jesus is saying. Peter himself will show his confusion by abandoning this Holy One in 18:14-27. These characters still need the final sign: Jesus' exaltation that includes his crucifixion, resurrection, and ascension that precedes the giving of the Spirit. It is only with the aid of this Spirit that the disciples can remember and understand, leading to a deeper level of trust (16:5-15; 20:22). Only after Easter can the disciples' "belief" blend Jesus' words with Scripture so that they come to believe him to be the incarnation of God's Word, spoken at the moment of creation and continuing to communicate God's life-giving will in the present and future to come (1:1-14; 2:22; 5:26). In perhaps its most profound irony, then, the Gospel affirms that it is those who believe without sight, and therefore on the basis of words remembered and taught by the Spirit, who are truly blessed (20:29).

New Birth into a New Household

Another pervasive theme of this section is that of household. "Household" is a better term than "family" because ancient social structures were different from what contemporary Western societies describe as "families." Rather than "nuclear families" consisting of parents or guardians with children living in predominantly single-generation units, ancient Mediterranean societies had households (*oikos, oikia*). A household was run by a main biological family line, at the top of which was the *paterfamilias* (father of the family). In some cases, at the top was a *materfamilias* (mother of the family) if the father had died but the mother had enough resources to remain an unmarried widow (e.g., the famous Roman matron, Cornelia Gracchus). The remainder of the household included all children (and perhaps grandchildren), along with slaves and other properties. Clients, or those loyal and beholden to the household, could also be included, although in a looser sense. The household system represented not only individual family lines but also entire tribes, and even the Roman Empire. Augustus, for example, was honored with the title "Father of your Country" by the Roman Senate (Suetonius, *Aug.* 58.2; cf. Livia Augusta as "Mother of the Country" in Suetonius, *Claud.* 3.2; 11.2; see Myers 2017a, 111–23).

Throughout John 2–4 we encounter contrasting loyalties between various households, particularly for Jesus. In John 2, the wedding represents the merging of households, leading to the continuation of normal social lines. Jesus, however, resists such norms when he rebuffs his biological mother. Jesus' main loyalty is not to his kin, whether his mother, his brothers, or those in Galilee, his "fatherland." Instead, Jesus is loyal to his heavenly Father alone. He is the groom in John 2–4, proliferating his Father's progeny by means of his teaching, sowing the seed of his words. As promised in 1:12-13, those who receive Jesus are "begotten not of bloods, or of flesh, or of the will of a man/husband, but by God." In John 2–4, Jesus rejects the bonds of bloods (his mother), flesh (in his conversation with Nicodemus), and husbands (with the Samaritan woman) to foster children born of "water and spirit." Patterned by God's Word (*logos*) and infused with God's Spirit, rather than those of human fathers and mothers, these children are promised eternal life in this new household rather than temporary existence (14:1-4). As members of God's kingdom, they have God as their Father, not Rome or any other *patria* (fatherland) or *pater* (father, 4:44, 53). These children are to remain loyal to their heavenly Father, even if it means leaving previous households behind (9:1-41; 20:19-25).

Jesus and the Temple

Finally, Jesus is consistently characterized as the location of God's glory in these chapters. This presentation has its roots in 1:14-17, where God's glory is said to "tent" or "tabernacle among us" as Jesus. Jesus' description of his body as the *naon*, or "sanctuary," is likewise provocative. He is not the "temple" in whole, but rather the most sacred part, the holy of holies, where the ark of the covenant was once held, where the glory of God resides (cf. 1 Sam 3:3; 1 Kgs 6:5; 7:36; Mal 3:1; Mark 14:58; 15:29, 38). In John's Gospel, when Jesus arrives at the "temple" (*hieron*), he is a mobile sanctuary ("tabernacle," *skēnē*) containing God's glory. His repeated coming to the temple demonstrates God's promised presence there, even though he is not bound to that place alone. The Fourth Gospel, Coloe notes, shifts the symbolism of God's presence from the temple building to the person Jesus and, finally, to the community of believers among whom the Spirit of God dwells—a transition no doubt influenced by the destruction of the Jerusalem temple in 70 CE by the Romans. Nevertheless, this is not a rejection of the temple or rituals outright; Jesus will instate his own ritual for the disciples in John 13 after all. Instead of rejecting the temple, Jesus has "zeal" for his Father's house and repeatedly travels there to do the Father's work as the embodiment of God's teaching presence.

That does not mean, however, that Jesus' actions in 2:14-22 are not judgmental. They are; but judgment does not mean absolute rejection. Instead, these actions should be viewed within the larger context of John, as well as ancient Judaism. Jonathan Klawans demonstrates that first-century Jews did not all view purity, or the temple, in the same way. According to Klawans, even the OT distinguishes between different types of purity: ritual and moral (2000, 23–32). Ritual purity referred to a person's ritual status, often regarding unavoidable contact with impurities, such as physical discharges or corpses, or even unintentional faults. Such impurities were easily rectified by rituals, hence the presence of merchants to sell offerings before Passover in John 2:14-17 (cf. 11:55; 18:28), or the use of "purification jars" in 2:6. In contrast, moral purity concerned "grave sins" (i.e., sexual sins, idolatry, and murder) knowingly committed. These actions "defiled" the sinner, the sanctuary, and the land even though they did not necessarily render them *ritually* impure. Klawans argues, "Moral impurity is best understood as a potent force unleashed by certain sinful human actions" (29). In contrast to ritual impurities, moral impurity was potentially permanent; even if atoned for, "grave sinners" continued to live in a "degraded" status, and the land also experienced "degradation" (31–32). Such impurity could only be purified by God's miraculous intervention, sometimes as an eschatological promise (cf. Ezek 36:16-25; 39:14-16).

Interpreting the NT generally, Klawans suggests that Jesus did not reject ideas of ritual purity, or even rituals themselves, but that he placed them below moral purity in importance, a move he was not alone in making. Jesus' disruption of the ritual practices in John 2:14-17 could indicate that he, like many prophets *and priests* before him (e.g., Isaiah, Elijah, Samuel, Moses), did not think rituals were sufficient (or perhaps even acceptable) when moral impurity was overwhelming the people, the temple, and the land. In texts criticizing the temple and rituals, Klawans notes a consistent concern with economic exploitation of the poor and with robbery (2006, 87–89). The people are condemned for "stealing" goods and then offering them to God. Their offerings are "robbery," taken from the poor through direct means or by systemic oppression, and thus cost these worshipers nothing but are rather an expression of their moral impurity. Rather than condemning all rituals outright, these writings agree that

> improper ethics render ritual sacrifice ineffectual, not because God doesn't like the idea of sinners atoning through ritual, and not because God would simply prefer to dispense with ritual in hopes that the people would simply seek righteousness apart from the cult. The objection to sacrifice rests [on] the assumption that God detests the facts of the situation at hand. One who has taken unjustly from the poor cannot properly *give* anything, and therefore the "sacrifice" offered by such a person is anathema. (87)

This description resonates with the condemnation uttered in Mal 3, a text quoted in association with John (the Baptist) in the Synoptics and, perhaps, lurking in the background of John 2.

In John's Gospel, Jesus suddenly enters the temple on the heels of John (the Baptist's) testimony. This is not a moment of welcome homecoming but sudden judgment against the exploitation happening in its midst. Malachi 3:1-2 reads,

> "Behold, I am sending out my messenger and he will survey the way before my face. And suddenly, he will come into the sanctuary (*naon*), the Lord himself, the one whom you are seeking. Indeed, the messenger of the covenant, which you wish to behold, he is coming!" says the LORD, the ruler of all. "And who is enduring the day of his entrance or who will survive in his

appearance? Since he himself is entering as fire of a smelting-furnace and as lye of cleaners."

The passage continues, describing the injustice of the offerings, once again, in terms of economic exploitation, particularly of the vulnerable: wives, widows, orphans, and foreigners (3:5-12; cf. 1:6–2:17). Jesus' description of the temple as a "house of emporium" or "house of trade" in John 2:16 resonates with these concerns. It is to the dove-sellers and money-changers that Jesus says, "Take these things away! Stop making my Father's house a house of trade!" Klawans argues that Jesus focuses on these people because their work would have most impacted the poor, who could not afford larger sacrifices and who would be disproportionately affected by any fees and taxes. Instead of paying into the temple, Jesus may have thought the temple should not be a burden for the poor, but rather a place of abundant provision (237). Indeed, Jesus creates such provision in 2:1-11 and 6:1-14.

Jesus' behavior in John 2:14-22, therefore, recalls the prophetic and priestly traditions critiquing the temple out of reverence, or "zeal," especially those leading up to the temple's destruction by the Babylonians. According to Klawans, the exile is presented as the direst time of moral impurity, first for Israel and then for Judea. God's solution for this impurity is punishment, atonement, and then restoration (2000, 26; cf. Ezek 36:16-25). Jesus' command for the Jews to "destroy this sanctuary (*naon*)!" in John 2:19 recalls the Babylonian invasion, but he promises a quick and full restoration. As with the previous sanctuary's destruction, Jesus' death will not destroy God's glory but is the solution to moral impurity: he is the "Lamb of God who takes up the sin of the world" (1:29). Moreover, this sanctuary will not remain in ruins, nor will its worshipers be left as orphans (14:15-31); Jesus will raise it three days later, enabling the children of God to experience God's presence by means of the Spirit dwelling in their midst. In a slight adjustment to Coloe's argument, then, the believers will be God's *sanctuary* in the world, and it will be their responsibility to act like a sanctuary: they should love one another (13:31-35; 17:1-26; 20:19-23).

Festivals, Confessions, and Confusion

John 5:1–10:42

John 5 begins the third major section of the Gospel. In John 5–10, Jesus repeatedly travels to and from Jerusalem, participating in festivals, continuing to perform signs, and engaging in dialogues with groups about his identity and mission. In many ways, John 5–10 continues the pattern of John 2–4: Jesus first travels to Jerusalem from Galilee (5:1-47//2:13–3:21) and then back to Galilee (6:1-71//4:43-54) before returning to Jerusalem again for two additional festivals (7:1–10:21; 10:22-39). What sets these sections apart, however, is (1) that the designation of "signs" now disappears from the narrative, as do references to "Cana of Galilee" (2:11; 4:46, 54; 21:2); (2) there is increasing hostility toward Jesus and a transition to Jesus' speaking before groups rather than with individuals; and, finally, (3) this section is bracketed by another reference to John (the Baptist's) prophetic confession of Jesus (10:40-42; 3:24). The final mention of John reminds the audience of his witness, as well as what he suffered for that witness, prior to Jesus' raising of Lazarus in John 11. Unlike in the Synoptic tradition, it is Jesus' resurrection of Lazarus that ultimately triggers the plot against him (11:45-54).

John 5–10 contains the bulk of Jesus' public ministry in the Gospel: that is, the ministry that he performs before crowds, both in deed and words. Most of his time is spent in Jerusalem, in and around the temple, during festivals that retell Israel's relationship with God and God's repeated deliverance of this people. The series of festivals begins in John 5, where Jesus travels to Jerusalem for "a feast of the Jews" (cf. 2:13). The festival is never named in John 5, which has led to much speculation over which festival it could possibly be. Nevertheless, as Marianne Meye Thompson (2015, 120) and others note, it is the *Sabbath* context that is of primary significance in John 5 (Brown 1966, 207). John 6 recounts the lead-up to and celebration of the second Passover of the Gospel. Unlike 2:13–3:21, Jesus shares this Passover (and tumult) in Galilee with a crowd around the sea and in the synagogue at Capernaum. John 7:1–10:21 focuses on The Festival of Tabernacles and is the longest continuous narrative setting for Jesus' ministry and reactions to him thus far in the story. It includes a controversial buildup to the festival between Jesus and his brothers, a series of teachings from Jesus at the festival that bracket his second Sabbath healing in John 9. This second miracle parallels the first Sabbath cure in John 5:1-18. Finally, John 10:22-42 records Jesus' actions during and after the Feast of Dedication, or Hanukkah, which is Jesus' final time in the temple in the Gospel.

The emphasis on festival time in John 5–10, as well as throughout the Gospel, should not be overlooked. The repeated mention of these times sets John's narrative firmly in Israel's Scriptures and the story of God's faithfulness toward Israel, reinforcing the Gospel's argument that Jesus is a continuation of this faithfulness rather than a threat to it. Jesus acts on and in God's time, operating in concert with the liturgical calendar that is meant to remind the Jews of God's covenant and steadfastness. True coherence of Jesus' actions and words, however, is only gained in hindsight. As a result, these festival settings are also times of increasing tension, where those who do not understand Jesus' confusing behavior and potentially blasphemous words react strongly against him out of their own sense of faithfulness toward God (cf. Sheridan 2012, 2015).

Although reading these scenes in light of their contexts and history of interpretation in the OT and Second Temple Judaism is crucial, Warren Carter also highlights the importance of festivals in Hellenistic and Roman contexts (2011; cf. 2008, 52–89). Focusing on Ephesus in particular, Carter argues that we can at least be certain that the Gospel was read and interpreted there, even if we cannot prove its composition in that city. He notes the regularity of festivals in the city, particularly in honor of Artemis, whose temple in Ephesus was one of the seven wonders of the ancient world, as well as in honor of the empire, whose good will enabled Ephesus to flourish as the provincial capital of Asia Minor (2011, 2–3). Although we often focus on the spiritual aspects of religious festivals, Carter explores the social and economic impacts—impacts that any of us during Christmastime can certainly appreciate. For Carter, the broader criticism of Jesus is not against Judaism, or the Jewish festivals as celebrations and reminders of God's faithfulness, but rather the religious leaders' alliances with Rome that would have facilitated economic and social advancement in the Roman Empire, whether that be in Palestine (Jerusalem) or Ephesus (2011, 5–6). Those who fear the empire and love glory from other people rather than God's glory have the wrong priorities and are missing out on the life that God desires to provide. Jesus' confrontations in these festival scenes illustrate this clash of perspective: what one who operates only in line with God faces when encountering those who "trust themselves to people" instead (2:24-25). Rather than demonizing those whom Jesus encounters, however, we ought to recognize our own faces in those crowds and among the leaders. What Jesus is living out and what he is asking for are not easy to do, and they will result in his death.

Commentary

Sabbath Work at an Unnamed Festival (5:1-47)

John 5 records Jesus' first trip back to Jerusalem since 2:13–3:21. The passage builds on themes begun there, although this time, Jesus eventually faces open hostility from the Jews. In this chapter, therefore, the Jews continue their characterization as those aligned in some way with power structures in Jerusalem. It is this association that has led several scholars to argue that the Jews are simply the "religious leaders" of Jerusalem (CEB; NET; de Boer 2001, 141–42; Bennema, 88–89), many of whom would have allied themselves with Rome to keep the peace as Carter notes above.

Even though Jesus travels to Jerusalem for "a feast," the identification of the feast is unclear and may just serve as an explanation for Jesus' going to Jerusalem (Keener 2003, 635). The real focus is on the Sabbath and how one should behave on this holy day of rest. Without undermining the Sabbath as a whole, Jesus' actions on that day demonstrate his unity with God as the embodiment of God's glory. Even though first-century Jews saw the observation of the Sabbath as a universal law, and sometimes even the most important law, God's relationship to this law was unique (Gen 2:2-3; *Jub.* 2). Just as exceptions to Sabbath rest were made in cases of life and death, God also continued in creating and sustaining life on the Sabbath (1 Macc 2:41; Philo, *Alleg. Interp.* 1.5, 18; *Cher.* 87; see Keener 2003, 641–47). Indeed, if God were to cease such activity, all life would also end. Jesus' activity on the Sabbath, therefore, shows him to be God's life-making (*zōopoieō*, 5:21, 26) Son who imitates his Father's never-ending work.

This chapter can be divided into two major sections, with shorter subsections in each. The first main section is Jesus' curing activity and its immediate response in 5:1-18. In 5:19-47, Jesus offers his first major public defense. This speech is a monologue, prompted by the exchanges in 5:10-18, and ends without a definitive response from Jesus' opponents (cf. 2:18-22; 3:1-21). As we will see, their response is rendered unnecessary by Jesus' speech in which he transitions from defendant to judge, declaring "my judgment is just!" (5:30). Jesus' judgment in this chapter resonates with his knowledge from 2:24-25: "he knew what was in humanity." What is "in humanity," it turns out, is not God's word or God's love, but vainglory. Jesus knows that one cannot receive God's glory (namely, himself) if one is caught up receiving and trusting the glory received from other people. When we seek our own glory, we lose sight of "the One God" who alone is Glory (5:41-44).

A. 5:1-18: Work on the Sabbath

A Miracle at the Sheep Gate (vv. 1-9). As after his "first sign" in Cana of Galilee at 2:13, Jesus again travels to Jerusalem for a festival after his second in 5:1. John 5:2 repeats the setting from 2:23 by situating Jesus "in the area of Jerusalem" (*en tois Ierosolymois*; cf. 10:22). The setting prepares the audience for the sustained parallels between Jesus' first time in Jerusalem and this second appearance. Unlike 2:14-22, however, Jesus does not immediately enter the temple. Instead, the narrator describes his location at a pool "by the Sheep Gate" (*probatikē,* 5:2). The description foreshadows Jesus' speeches in John 10, where he calls himself the "noble shepherd" and "the door for the sheep" (10:7-9, 11, 14). These connections are reinforced by the emphasis Jesus will place on hearing his "voice," which, in John 10, only his sheep are able to do (10:2-5, 25-30; cf. 5:25-29). In a move opposite to the usual translation of Hebrew into Greek (1:38, 41; 4:25), the narrator here moves from Greek to Hebrew, identifying the pool as "Bethzatha" with "five porticos" (*pente stoas,* 5:2; cf. *stoa* at 10:23; on "Bethzatha" see Brown 1966, 206–207; Brant 2011, 101–102). The next time in the Gospel that the narrator will do this is at 19:13, 17, and 20—during Jesus' crucifixion. Significantly, 5:18 is the first time anyone expresses a desire to "kill" Jesus (*apokteinō*; cf. 7:1, 19, 20, 25; 8:22, 37, 40; 11:53; 12:10; 16:2; 18:31).

Working again in parallels, Jesus' Sabbath works in John 5 and 9 follow a similar pattern, although with different outcomes for the ones made healthy (cf. 2:1-12; 4:43-54). In both scenes, Jesus initiates interaction with the impaired person to cure their medical conditions, either an unnamed "illness" (*astheneia,* 5:5) or blindness from birth (*typhlos ek genetēs,* 9:1). Both cures also involve a pool. In John 5, Jesus' ability to cure by a word belies the need for the ill man to descend into its waters for life (cf. 4:53). Instead, acting out his teaching from John 4, Jesus demonstrates that those desiring "living water" need only come to him. Jesus' command, "Rise up (*egeire*), take your mat and walk/live," also foreshadows his speech in 5:21 where he affirms the Son's ability to "raise" (*egeirei*) the dead just like the Father. It is only after the man begins walking (or "living," *peripatei*) that the narrator mentions that it was the Sabbath day. Not only is this another surprise for the audience, perhaps prompting a gasp from those listening, but it also sets the context for the tension that follows (cf. 4:2). Jesus' actions are rightly understood to be a profound claim: he is *the* Son of God.

A Series of Reactions (vv. 10-18). In obedience to Jesus' words, the cured man continues walking until he is stopped with a reprimand from the Jews, who seem to have enough authority to confront the man as a Sabbath-breaker. The importance of the Sabbath for first-century Jews should not be underestimated. To work on the Sabbath was to claim superiority to God's law and design for creation (Exod 20:8-11); that this also took place during a festival contributes to the potential audacity of the man's stroll with his mat. In response, the man points to his healer, whom he describes as "the one having made me healthy" (*ho poiēsas me hygiē*), since he does not know Jesus' name. The man's ignorance coheres to the Gospel's repeated characterization of human beings' lack of knowledge in contrast to Jesus' complete knowledge (1:48; 2:25; 4:1; 5:6, 42). Unlike the cured man in John 9 who will offer extensive testimony on Jesus' behalf, these are the last words spoken by this man in the Gospel.

Jesus "finds" the man in 5:14, and we also learn that "the place" described in 5:13 is "the temple" (cf. 4:20; 6:1-15). Jesus' comments are troubling because they can imply some sort of connection between sin and illness, an issue that will emerge again in 9:4 (see "Sin and Impairment" below). He warns the man, "Look, you have become well! Stop sinning lest something worse should happen to you" (5:14). What the man's "sin" is precisely, the Gospel never clarifies. Nevertheless, Jesus' comment reminds the audience of John (the Baptist's) witness in 1:29 that Jesus is "the one who takes up (*arōn*) the sin of the world." While the man has been caught carrying his mat, Jesus will carry the world's "sin," or mistake. Although the Gospel may imply some individual "sins" or "mistakes," overall it prefers the singular use of this noun—"sin"—emphasizing the prime mistake people in the world make: namely, accepting human glory rather than God's glory, particularly as it has been manifested in Jesus (1:16). As we will see, 1 John terms this sin in classic Jewish terms: it is idolatry (1 John 5:21).

One part of the irony in John 5:16-18 is, therefore, that the Jews are pursuing (*diōkō*) Jesus because they think he is an idolater. He is "doing" or "making" (*poieō*) on the Sabbath, a time when God alone creates and sustains life. Jesus explains his unique ability to do such work in 5:17: "My Father until now is working, and I myself am working." In other words, Jesus is God's life-giving and sustaining will on earth. For the Jews in John 5, however, Jesus' work and words are not proof that he is God's Son, but rather that he is doing another work: "making (*poiōn*) himself equal to God" (v. 18). They have missed the message to which Jesus' work, or sign, points. Jesus' lengthy speech in 5:19-47 will morph from defense to judgment as he turns the tables on his accusers and occupies his place as judge. According to

Jesus, they are the idolaters, and the laws they are breaking are nothing less than the first through third commandments (Exod 20:1-7) communicated by the *Shema*: "Hear, O Israel, the LORD our God, the LORD is one. Love the LORD your God with all your heart and all your life and all your power" (Deut 6:4-5).

B. 5:19-47: Jesus' Defense and Accusations

In 5:19 the chapter turns to Jesus' monologue, his first public speech in the Gospel. The speech is given in the temple, making its claims even more startling for those who consider Jesus an idolater. His words do little to refute this concern. Rather than explaining away his behavior, Jesus argues that it is justified on account of his unique identity as God's Son. Indeed, this work on a single Sabbath during a festival in Jerusalem is only a precursor to the works he will continue to do during his ministry and in the eschaton, where his voice will raise the dead to face judgment (5:24-30).

The organization of this speech can be a bit confounding for contemporary readers unaccustomed to ancient rhetorical styles. Yet the argumentation coheres to expectations established not only in rhetorical handbooks but also in Scripture, such as the need for two or three witnesses on one's behalf (Attridge 2002a; Myers 2013). The speech has three sections: in 5:19-30, Jesus gives his defense; 5:31-40 includes his witnesses and also begins the transition to accusation; 5:41-47 renders Jesus' judgment against his opponents, complete with pithy statements full of rhetorical figures (Brant 2011, 105–109).

Jesus' Defense: I Am Just because of Who I Am (vv. 19-30). Jesus' defense is not a denial of his behavior but rather a demonstration of his righteousness, or innocence (*dikaios*, 5:30; 7:24; 17:25; cf. 1 John 1:9; 2:1, 29; 3:7, 12). This is what Pseudo-Cicero calls a "juridical issue with an absolute cause" (*Rhet. Her.* 2.13.19) and Quintilian describes as an issue of "quality" (*Inst.* 3.6.10). A common example of this sort of case in Greco-Roman sources is the slaying of Clytemnestra by her son, Orestes, at the behest of the god Apollo. Rather than denying his act, Orestes is defended by Apollo himself who argues that Orestes' behavior was just in light of Clytemnestra's murder of Agamemnon, her husband and Orestes' father (Aeschylus, *Eum.* 574–680; Quintilian, *Inst.* 3.11.1–8; Cicero, *Mil.* 3.8). Jesus' work in John 5 is about causing life rather than death, but the type of argument is the same. Jesus' behavior is justified because it is done at God's behest. It is even more just than Orestes' since Jesus' imitation of God is the outworking of his identity; he needs no prodding and shows no hesitation (Aeschylus, *Cho.* 895–906).

As God's Son, Jesus is the manifestation of God's will; by definition, he *cannot* act or speak in ways contrary to who God is (5:19, 30).

The structure of this first portion of Jesus' speech is chiastic as well as climactic. He begins by describing a son-father relationship that would have been easily recognizable in the ancient world. For this reason, Ruben Zimmermann counts this episode as one of Jesus' parables in the Gospel of John (2015, 336; cf. Dodd, 386 n. 2). The introduction of the speech in 5:19 builds to 5:30, which repeats the beginning of 5:19 but includes first-person pronouns and verbs, reinforcing Jesus' claim to be God's Son. The chiasm is illustrated as follows:

A. v. 19a, The Son Can Do Nothing without the Father
   B. vv. 19b-20, Greater Works for Your Amazement
      C. vv. 21-23, Life-Making and Judging
         D. v. 24, Hear My Word and Live
      C'. vv. 25-27, Life in Oneself and Authority to Judge
   B'. vv. 28-29, Do Not Be Amazed!
A'. v. 30, I Myself Can Do Nothing without the One Who Sent Me

The major themes of Jesus' defense are life and judgment. These themes resonate with the "work" of "raising up" the ill man in 5:1-9, where Jesus provides a type of resurrected life to the man (Brant 2011, 104). In 5:10-18 judgments are passed both against the cured man for carrying his mat on the Sabbath and against Jesus who is the one guilty of working by giving life. The judgments rendered, however, are both unjust (*adikia*, 7:18; 1 John 1:9; 5:17) in contrast to Jesus' just (*dikaios*) judgment (John 5:30). In this way, John 5 anticipates Jesus' comment in 7:24 when he admonishes the crowd: "Stop judging according to appearance, rather judge the just judgment (*tēn dikaian krisin*)!" Indeed, Jesus' Sabbath healing is still the topic of debate in John 7–8.

Of course, judging Jesus justly is difficult to do because he behaves in ways no other human being has before (cf. 7:46; 9:32). This, however, is the foundation of his defense: he is the unique Son of God. Moreover, Jesus shows his unique relationship with God by doing what no other human can, life-making and just judgment, *on the very day that God alone works* (Keener 2003, 641–45). Jesus' performance of these same works leads the Jews to "be amazed" or "marvel" (*thaumazō*), but this posture is not a positive one in John's Gospel. Rather, those who "marvel" are not found praising God but are dumbfounded by Jesus' behavior. Their "amazement" stuns them and they are unable to render a "just judgment" concerning his true identity

(4:27; 5:20; 7:15, 21). For this reason, Jesus commands them to "stop being amazed!" (3:7; 5:28; cf. 1 John 3:13); one would think those well-versed in Scripture and so rigorous in their observance of the Sabbath ought to recognize God in action.

The center of the chiasm is John 5:24: "Truly, truly I am saying to you: the one who hears (*akouōn*) my word and believes (*pisteuōn*) the one who sent me has eternal life, and they are not coming to judgment, but rather they have departed from death to life!" (cf. 1 John 3:14). The participles Jesus uses in this verse are in the present tense and, therefore, have an ongoing aspect: the one who continues hearing, listening to, and obeying as well as the one who continues believing, trusting, and being faithful to the one who sent Jesus is the one who has already departed from death (judgment) into life. Jesus has not come to issue judgment but instead to save the world from the "wrath" in which it already finds itself (John 3:16-18, 36). Jesus' presence, however, *causes* judgment because he is the light who shines in the darkness, revealing the mess to which humanity seems blind. Hope is not lost because Jesus is able to heal blindness (John 9), even creating sight where it has never been before (cf. Gen 1). When his light shines upon people, penetrating and rectifying their blindness, they experience an eternal connection to him and to the Father in life that begins now and continues forever (8:51).

Jesus' Proof: Witnesses, Human and Divine (vv. 31-40). Jesus' speech shifts in 5:31 where he begins listing witnesses as evidence in his favor. In this section, however, he also shifts from defense to accusation, revealing the "just" judgment his presence exposes. In 5:31-47 Jesus' accusation against his opponents is that they are the true idolaters because they accept glory from other human beings rather than God. Focusing on 5:31-40, Jesus begins his list by contrasting human witness, which the Jews accepted, and divine witness, which they are rejecting.

In 5:31-35, Jesus describes John (the Baptist's) witness, introducing him into the narrative for the fourth time, although this time he is not physically present. Jesus and John, therefore, have completed the switch begun in John 1 and 3, where John (the Baptist) witnessed concerning Jesus in his absence (1:15-28; 3:22-36) and proclaimed his desire to decrease, making room for others to hear the groom's "voice" (*phōnē* , 3:29; 5:25, 28, 37; cf. 10:3-5). In 5:31, Jesus repeats the common forensic maxim that one cannot issue believable testimony for oneself (Num 35:50; Deut 17:6; 19:15; *Rhet. Her.* 4.1.2), even though he will contradict this statement in 8:14 because of his unique identity. Disregarding his own testimony, then, Jesus describes that of John, a "human" (*anthrōpos*, 5:34), but one whom his opponents have recognized as special, meriting their sending of delegates to question him in 1:19-28 (5:33; on human testimony see Quintilian, *Inst.* 5.7; Aristotle, *Rhet.* 1.15.13–17; Cicero, *Top.* 20.78). Indeed, Jesus says, they "rejoiced for an hour in his light" (5:35; cf. 8:56). While their temporary acceptance of John *should* have enabled them to see the "true light" to which he pointed, it seems they may have been satisfied with the harbinger.

Even though John offered true and good testimony, Jesus again repeats that he "is not receiving witness from a person" (*anthrōpou*, 5:34; 2:24). This comment is jarring at first, but it should not be read as a rejection of John or his words. Instead, it is a restatement of Jesus' superior knowledge of humanity, as well as the fact that he does not need human endorsement to prove his identity or require "glory" to be given to him from people; he is the manifestation of God's glory (1:14-16; 2:11, 24-25). The witness Jesus accepts is divine: his works that the Father has given him to do and which demonstrate the Father's testimony on his behalf (5:36-38). Since Jesus only says and does what the Father gives him to say and do, his actions and words show his acceptance of this witness, and the glory that is alone God's. Ancients, likewise, valued "divine testimony" over human (Quintilian, *Inst.* 5.11.37–42; Cicero, *Top.* 20.76–77; cf. McConnell, 47–52), yet valuing divine testimony and being able to recognize it are two different things (cf. *Apol.* 31c–32a).

Jesus demonstrates the inability of his opponents to interpret divine testimony rightly, not only with their rejection of his miraculous work in 5:1-18 but also in their use of Scripture that formed the basis of that rejection. The command to "keep the Sabbath holy," repeated throughout Scripture, comes from Exod 20:8-11 and is explicitly connected to God's creating the world in six days and resting on the seventh. Their valuing of Scripture is, therefore, apparent in their reaction against Jesus' behavior on this holy day; it is in Scripture that they are "seeking eternal life" (John 5:39). While they interpret their behavior as just, Jesus reveals their misunderstanding: Moses' writings, including Exodus, as well as all the Scriptures are "the ones witnessing" (*hai martyrousai*) about Jesus. Like John's testimony, these writings point to Jesus as God's Word, the Light and Life of humanity. But they have missed out on the revelation.

Jesus' Judgment: You Are the Idolaters (vv. 41-47). Finally, in 5:41-47 Jesus explains how such rejection and misunderstanding could happen: his opponents, *like all people* who do not have direct help from God, are believing wrongly and accepting the wrong type of glory. This section divides into two shorter sections: 5:41-44 and 5:45-47. Each section begins with a statement, then moves into a parallelism before ending with a rhetorical question, "How?" The implied answers to each question are explanations for why these opponents cannot believe and, therefore, do not experience the life they so eagerly seek.

In 5:41-44 Jesus continues his contrast of human and divine, moving into the real topic of his concern: not testimony, but glory. For Jesus, the rejection of divine testimony is a symptom of a much bigger problem: the rejection of God's glory. In 5:41-42 Jesus states his rejection of "glory from people" (*doxan para anthrōpōn*) and his knowledge that "you do not have the love of God in you" (cf. 1 John 4:7–5:3). In other words, Jesus does not need honor or glory from people because such glory is meaningless since they do not have the love of God. In John 5:43 Jesus contrasts himself to his opponents with antithetical parallelism:

A. I myself have come in the name of my Father,
    B. and you are not receiving me.
A'. If another one should come in his own name,
    B'. that one you will receive.

Jesus' emphasis on "the name" reflects the Gospel's emphasis on belief or trust that "the name of the Christ the Son of God is Jesus" (20:31; cf. 1:12-13; 3:16-18; 15:21). It also connects back to the Ten Commandments of Exodus 20 where the Lord commands the people not to "receive his name in worthlessness (*epi mataiō*)" (20:7). This is the commandment prior to the Sabbath command, perhaps suggesting that the focus on the Sabbath is misguided if one cannot decipher the Lord's work on that holy day.

The possibility that Jesus is making an appeal to Scripture in John 5:43 is strengthened by his reference in his rhetorical question in 5:44. Jesus asks, "How are you yourselves able to believe when you are receiving glory from one another and the glory from the One God you are not seeking?" As Lori Baron suggests, this is an allusion to the *Shema*, Deut 6:4-5, quoted above. Baron argues that the confession of the *Shema* was crucial to first-century Judaism, as it continues to be in Jewish contexts today (2010, 53–54). The confession of the *Shema* declared Israel's monotheism as well as their loyalty to *this God*, the one who delivered them from Egypt (Deut 6:3). The "love of God" is not, therefore, a sentimental feeling, but rather loyalty, a promise to act in the best interests of God's glory over and against the claims of anyone else, be they human, divine, or demonic (57–58). When Jesus says his opponents "do not have the love of God" in them, he is setting the stage for his comment in 5:44: even though these religious leaders claim to adhere to the law revealed in Scripture, they reject it at its core because they are disloyal to

God, fearing one another and accepting glory from one another rather than from God alone.

In 5:45-47 Jesus rounds out his argument, coming full circle and picturing a courtroom different from the one envisioned by his opponents. Instead of being the defendant, prosecuted by Moses, Jesus occupies the judge's seat given to him by his Father (5:22). His opponents find themselves in the defendant's position, prosecuted by Moses, the traditional authority of the law. In v. 46 Jesus underscores his relationship with Moses with another parallelism that centers on Jesus' identity (matching portions are emphasized):

A. <u>For</u> if **you would have believed in** <u>Moses,</u>
   B. **You would have believed in** *me.*
  B'. <u>For</u> about *me*
A'. <u>That one</u> wrote.

The combination of literary features in this verse emphasizes the importance of Jesus' comment: he is not in competition with Moses, but rather his work is in continuity with God's work begun at creation and described by this prophet (Harstine, 117–18).

The final line of the speech in 5:47 drives his point home:

A'. Now if <u>that one's writings</u> (*grammasin*) you are not **believing**,
   B". how in *my words* (*rhēmasin*) will you **believe**?

As in 2:22, Jesus' words are equivalent to Scripture; to believe in Scripture is also to believe in Jesus' words. Indeed, the Greek highlights this point further by switching from *logos* (word) to *rhēma* in 5:47, creating assonance and consonance that blend writings (or Scripture) with his words: *grammasin*, *rhēmasin*. In John 6, Jesus continues using *rhēma* to describe his words after reenacting Moses' provision of manna in the wilderness. Again figuring Moses' work as a precursor to the Father's work in himself (3:14), Jesus' words are "spirit and life" (6:63, 68).

The Second Passover: Bread in Galilee (6:1–7:1)
After Jesus' dramatic second trip to Jerusalem, he returns again to Galilee, making his third appearance there. The location in Galilee recalls Jesus' two previous experiences with the Galileans in John 2 and 4. Jesus' acceptance by the crowds is contrasted with Jesus' lack of trust in their belief, and the disciples, too, are left in a state of some confusion in 2:18-22, needing help to understand Jesus' words (cf. 4:31-38). In John 6, this confusion comes

to a head as both the disciples and a large crowd are challenged by Jesus' "hard word" (*sklēros . . . ho logos*, 6:60). Although most scholars focus on the possibility of Eucharistic overtones in this passage, Jan Heilmann argues that the passage is about Jesus' election of the Twelve (2018, 496). Heilmann's thesis is supported by the fact that episodes with the disciples are interspersed throughout John 6 (vv. 5-13, 16-21, 60-71). Jesus' final statement in 6:70 is the climax: "Have not I myself chosen you, the Twelve?"

In this reading, the crowd and the Jews act as foils for the disciples who are undergoing an elaborate "test" (*peirazō*) Jesus initiates in 6:5-6 when he lifts his eyes and notices the large crowd spread out before him on the mountain. The test not only challenges the disciples' belief that Jesus can again make miraculous provision (2:1-11) but also if they understand his words from 4:31-38 that the fields are ripe for a harvest. Jesus' harvest is not the large crowd but the Twelve, who endure the testing by following Jesus' twisting metaphors in 6:25-59. Privileged also to Jesus' theophanic crossing of the sea in 6:16-21, these disciples confess through Peter, "we have believed and have known that you are the Holy One of God" who has "the words of life" (6:68-69). This collection includes eleven given to him by the Father and one devil, who completes the Twelve (6:70-71) but who is also the "son of the destruction" (17:12).

A. 6:1-15: Eating at the Mountain

John 6:1-4 contains the first mention of the Sea of Galilee in the Gospel of John (cf. 21:1, 7). Jesus' continued curing of "the ill" (6:2; cf. 5:3, 7) has attracted a "large crowd" who follows him and his disciples "to the mountain" (6:3; cf. 4:20-21). In 6:4 we learn that "Passover, the feast of the Jews, was near." This phrase is a combination of 2:13 and 5:1, bringing Jesus' first two Jerusalem experiences to bear in Galilee. While Jesus' absence from Jerusalem for this festival is surprising at first, it furthers motifs from his conversation with the Samaritan woman in 4:20-26 that worship is not about "the mountain" or "the place" but rather about recognizing and receiving God's glory when he comes.

The mountain location in John 6 is also significant because it contributes to the extended comparison between this Passover and the events surrounding the first Passover, undergirding the misunderstandings that happen in 6:25-59. This rhetorical move is called a *synkrisis* (Theon, *Prog.* 112; Quintilian, *Inst.* 5.10.86–93; *Rhet. Her.* 1.6.10; Aristotle, *Rhet.* 1.9.38–41). John uses *synkrisis* to compare Jesus to events and figures from the OT, always showing his superiority (e.g., John 1:50-51; 3:13-14; 4:12; 6:58; 8:53; Myers 2012, 47–49). According to John's Gospel, OT figures and events are themselves signifiers that, when rightly understood, point to Jesus, whose existence as the Word precedes them all (1:1). As Jesus said in 5:45-47, Moses wrote about him.

The feeding episode is an inclusio with a parallelism in the middle that emphasizes Jesus' interaction with his disciples. The structure can be divided as follows:

A. vv. 1-4, A crowd follows Jesus to the mountain because of signs
  B. vv. 5-6, Jesus looks up, sees the crowd, and initiates a test
    C. vv. 7-9, The disciples respond
  B'. vv. 10-12, Jesus feeds the crowd
    C'. v. 13, The disciples harvest the abundance
A'. vv. 14-15, A crowd has seen signs and Jesus departs for the mountain

Unlike the Synoptic accounts, Jesus does not express emotion at the sight of the large crowd following him; instead, the crowd's presence prompts the test for the disciples sitting with Jesus on the mountain. Jesus' "lifting his eyes" in 6:5 repeats from his parable in 4:35 when Jesus told the disciples, "Do not you yourselves say, 'Still there are four months and the harvest comes'? *Look! I am saying to you, lift your eyes and see the fields that are white for harvest!*" The reference to "barley loaves" in 6:9 and 13 reinforces this connection, since barley turns a white color when ready to harvest (Theophrastus, *Caus. plant.* 3.21.3; Plutarch, *Nat. Q.* 15; *Mor.* 915d; *p. Pe'ah* 2:5; cf. Keener 2003, 625). Its use in the five loaves demonstrates that it is already time for a harvest (cf. the Samaritan woman's "five" husbands, 4:18). In 6:13 the disciples have their own harvest when they "gather together" (*synagō*, 4:36) the abundance (*perisseuō*, 6:12-13), for which they did not work (cf. 6:26-27). They do not yet realize that they are in the process of being harvested by Jesus as well.

The crowd wants to make (*poiēsōsin*) Jesus king in response to his signs (6:15). The ability to cure and to provide food are two qualities associated with ideal kings in the ancient Mediterranean world. Ancients constructed ideal kings as special men who had a unique connection to the divine and were able to adjudicate heavenly justice upon earth. More than legal justice, ideal kings provided complete justice and order. All those who demonstrated loyalty (or love) to the king were given protection and provision in return—this was how a king showed his (and his god's) love for the faithful people (J. Smith, 86–89, 170–72). Jesus' signs in the Gospel of John resonate with this construction: he represents God's perspective in words and deeds (2:13-22; 5:19-20), his judgment is just (5:30), he cures the ill (4:46-54;

5:1-9; 6:2), he provides drink and food (2:1-11; 6:5-13), and he protects his own (10:1-18).

Jesus' provision of manna around the time of Passover places him in continuity with the other great prophet-king of Israel's past: Moses. In Jesus, the crowd believes it has discovered "the prophet who is coming into the world" (6:14), the one who was promised by Moses to follow in his footsteps. This prophet should be heard and obeyed (*akousesthe*), while other false prophets are to be rejected (Deut 18:15-22). Even in Deuteronomy the people fear not recognizing the prophet promised to them. They are told to test the prophet's words based on truthfulness: if his words come true, he is from God. In John 6, the crowd recognizes Jesus as a prophet, but they do not "hear" Jesus' words because he is more than a prophet (6:25-40). While Jesus is similar to Moses, the crowd's chronology is all wrong: Jesus does not follow and imitate Moses, but Moses communicated the Word told to him, and when Moses obeyed God, he followed this Word (John 1:15, 30; 8:56; 12:41; cf. Philo, *Vit. Mos.* 1.155–62). By focusing on the human imitator, this crowd misses the full vision of the divine before them. In a hint at the theophany that is to come, John describes Jesus' solo time upon the mountain, writing that "he went up again into the mountain, himself only (*monos*)." The adjective *monos* was used in 5:44 to describe God's glory in a reference to the *Shema* (Deut 6:4-5). That Jesus, too, can be described in similar terms reinforces his identity as God's glory made flesh while also emphasizing a key point of conflict in the narrative: his unique relationship with God, his Father.

B. 6:16-24: Sea Crossings

The next episode records two sea crossings, one begun by the disciples alone but during which they are joined by Jesus (vv. 16-21), and one the following day by the crowd (vv. 22-24). Jesus' miraculous stroll upon the turbulent waters of the Sea of Galilee could be compared to Moses' crossing of the Red Sea, which continues the exodus themes of John 6 (Brown 1966, 255–56). This is also, however, a theophanic scene: that is, one in which the divine appears. The sea, or any large body of water, was considered an emblem of chaos in the ancient world; it was unstable, unfathomable, and uncontrollable for any mortal, often leading one into danger and death (Job 9:8; Ps 77:16-20; 78:11; see Brant 2011, 118). Thus, in Genesis, God's Spirit roams above the chaotic waters before God speaks order and life into existence. It is God's order, and God's control, that tames the chaotic waters. In the same way, the disciples suffer when they depart from their Lord in John 6:16 and head out, alone, into the waters.

Rather than a spirit, it is a "great wind" (*anemou megalou*) that begins "stirring up" the waters around them in the dark (6:17-18). Some distance from the shore, the disciples are at the mercy of the chaotic darkness; it is in this moment that they "saw Jesus walking upon the sea" coming "near" their boat. In a reenactment of the Light's victory over primordial chaos, Jesus strides upon the waters to meet his lost disciples, even though they left without him! Recognizing the theophanic scene before them, the disciples do not fear the waters, but they fear Jesus, who overcomes the darkness (cf. 1:5; 8:12). Jesus speaks his second "I am" statement in 6:20, this time also incorporating the command to "stop fearing!" that resonates with angelic and divine appearances as well as prophetic utterances from the OT (Gen 15:1; 21:17; Deut 1:21; 20:3; Isa 35:4; 40:9; cf. Tob 12:17). The disciples, then, "want" to take him into their boat, but Jesus has other plans. In a moment that parallels the formation of earth from the waters in Gen 1:9-10, the disciples' boat suddenly "happens upon the earth" as though the earth rose from the deep to meet them. Just as God "gathered together" (*synagagō*, Gen 1:9) the waters and the sky in Genesis to make room for life, Jesus repeats such a gathering in John 6, showing that his harvest still leads to life (cf. *synagagō*, John 4:35-36; 6:13).

The second crossing comes the following day when the crowd arrives to find that Jesus and his disciples have left. Jesus' departure from the crowd suggests that the narrative is still focused on the disciples' ongoing test rather than the fate of the crowd (6:5-6). The crowd realizes something miraculous has again happened, however, since Jesus was not with his disciples when they left and he did not have access to another boat for the journey (6:22). When another "small boat" comes near their location "at the place where they ate the bread after the Lord gave thanks," they also "embarked" for Capernaum "seeking Jesus" (6:23-24). The crowd's crossing is ambiguous. Their response to go to Jesus is positive, since he is the source of life (5:40), yet the association with the feeding miracle again reminds us of their misunderstanding of Jesus in 6:14-15. Their "seeking" of Jesus continues their behavior from 6:14 when they were "about to come and to seize" Jesus in order to "make" him king. Jesus, however, will not be seized by anyone else's agenda other than his Father's (2:4; 4:34; 5:30). When the crowd finally finds Jesus in 6:25-40, Jesus explains that "one coming" to him must accept the Father's will rather than what they may "want" (*thelō*; cf. 6:11, 21, 67; cf. 5:6, 35, 40; 7:17, etc.). What we want is simply too meager compared to what the Father gives.

C. 6:25-59: Teaching in Capernaum

Although we are not told until 6:59, the crowd eventually finds Jesus in a synagogue in Capernaum, where they and the Jews engage Jesus in a lengthy conversation. This is Jesus' only appearance teaching in a synagogue in John's Gospel. Craig Koester argues that the synagogue location explains the unique form of Jesus' rhetoric in John 6; his exposition of biblical texts may reflect actual synagogue practices of his day (2017, 68–72; cf. Luke 4:14-30). Peder Borgen's monumental study also shows extensive similarities between Jesus' exposition in John 6 and practices outlined by Philo of Alexandria.

The synagogues were important religious and social locations for Jews in the ancient Mediterranean world, particularly after the Babylonian exile (even if they existed in some form prior to this time), which left most Jews dispersed from Palestine. As Erich Gruen shows, Jews continued worshiping and learning in these synagogues, which were diverse as well as pervasive "from the Black Sea to North Africa, and from Syria to Italy," even after the temple was rebuilt (105–13). Believing God to be the one Lord of the whole world rather than one bound to a particular physical location, the synagogues did not compete with the temple but preserved Jewish traditions valued by specific communities and also facilitated participation in aspects of Roman culture (113–32). Jesus' time in both the temple and this synagogue in Capernaum resonates with these beliefs of God's ability to manifest glory in any place. The challenge for people remains the ability to recognize that glory. Moreover, continuing the themes of the chapter, Jesus' presence in a place of "gathering together," a *synagōgē*, shows him "gathering together" (*synagō*) or harvesting in a place fit for harvest; this is his field (4:35-36). Later in the Gospel, however, Jesus' harvested ones will face opposition in these fields. While Jesus is not forced from the Capernaum synagogue, his "hard" words result in the departure of most of his disciples (6:60-71). The "going out" from Jesus in John 6, therefore, sets the stage for the later expulsions from the synagogue (*aposynagōgos*, 9:22; 12:41; 16:2) in the narrative to come (6:37; 9:34-35).

The synagogue setting also raises the possibility that Jesus is teaching on the Sabbath, thus continuing his working on this holy day from John 5 (cf. Mark 1:21; Luke 4:14-16). In John 5, the Gospel audience is not told that it was the Sabbath until after Jesus cures the man; in the same way, the Gospel audience does not learn of Jesus' location in the synagogue after his teaching is complete in 6:59. In John 7, Jesus' Sabbath behavior continues to be the subject of debate, especially his cure of the man in 5:1-9, which Jesus mentions explicitly in 7:19-24. Jesus also reportedly teaches "on the great day" of the Festival of Tabernacles in 7:37, perhaps also a Sabbath day (cf. 9:14). He will then follow this teaching with another Sabbath cure in 9:1-7. If John 6 is set on a Sabbath day, even implicitly, it participates in a larger section of the Gospel devoted to Jesus' work on this holy day: "My Father until now is working and I myself also am working" (5:17).

Jesus' discourse in 6:25-59 contains a number of literary structures. Its intricacy is evidenced by the variety of chiasms and parallelisms found within it by interpreters. As Jo-Ann Brant shows, Jesus repeats words throughout his speech, building parallelisms that create meaning, as long as one can follow all the twists and turns (2011, 120; cf. Brown 1966, 288–89). Heilmann argues that the key to understanding Jesus' speech is knowing the "basic conceptual metaphor" Jesus uses: namely, that when Jesus says "whoever *eats* of the living bread that came down from heaven will live forever" he means, "whoever receives the incarnated word and believes in it will live forever" (487). Jesus uses a variety of metaphors to help clarify what he means by "food" (*brōsis*, 6:27, 55; cf. 4:32; 6:13), "eternal life," and "seeking" to create symbolic networks that one must follow to their end rather than being scandalized by the literal definitions of Jesus' words and abandoning him midway. "Food that remains for eternal life," for example, is linked to bread, true bread, bread from heaven, manna, bread of life, bread descending from heaven, the one descending from heaven, flesh, and words. As we will see, it is when the crowd, the Jews, and the disciples get stuck on their own expectations that they stumble: the crowd is hung up on literal food, wanting more literal "manna" (6:25-40), the Jews think Jesus is lying about his origins and is trying to get people to commit cannibalism (6:41-58), and many of Jesus' disciples are likewise "scandalized" by Jesus' teaching (6:60-66). Only those who remain with Jesus the whole way through the teaching can come to confess that Jesus "has the words of eternal life" (6:69).

John 6:25-59 breaks into two major portions: 6:25-40 in which Jesus speaks with the crowd, and 6:41-59 where Jesus speaks specifically to the Jews who also seem to have been present for 6:25-40 at the synagogue (v. 59). The topics covered in these sections create a larger chiasm in vv. 25-51, leading to a climax in vv. 52-58, where Jesus blends the metaphors of food and resurrection.

A. 6:25-35, Bread and Drink
   B. 6:36-40, Resurrection on the Last Day
   B'. 6:41-47, Resurrection on the Last Day
A'. 6:48-51, Bread and Drink
A/B. Climax: 6:52–59 Bread, Drink, and Resurrection

Further parallels and chiasms are also present in these smaller divisions, often building to a climactic statement in each one as Jesus takes a single word or idea from either the crowd or the Jews and develops it, teaching via metaphors about his life-giving words.

In John 6:25-35, for example, Jesus and the crowd debate the phrases *ergazomai* ("working") and "bread from heaven," which the crowd equates with manna in the wilderness (6:31; quoting Ps 78:24; cf. Exod 16:4, 15). Jesus, however, declares, "I am the bread of life!"—a gift currently given by God that is superior to the manna (John 6:35). In vv. 36-40, there is an inclusio between vv. 36 and 40, both of which describe seeing and believing, although in antithetical terms. In the middle, Jesus describes his mission as doing "the will of the one who sent me," his "Father," the same God who is giving "bread from heaven" from v. 33 (6:38-40).

In vv. 41-47, the Jews take over as interlocutors, focusing on Jesus' origins, which he clarifies in v. 46. In this section, Jesus explains the rejection he faces in terms that are disturbing to modern sensibilities but that were common in the ancient world and in all four canonical Gospels: those who believe were chosen by God. They did not *do* anything to merit belief nor could they discern God's actions on their own. In vv. 48-51, Jesus returns to his food metaphor, once again highlighting the inadequacy of the "manna" comparison as a foundational understanding of his work (cf. Myers 2012, 104–12).

As the tension builds from "grumbling" (*gonguzō*, cf. Exod 17:3; Num 11:1; 14:27-29; 17:6, 20; Pss 57:16; 105:25, LXX) in v. 41 to "quarrelling" (*machomai*) in v. 52, Jesus likewise ratchets up his language. In these verses, Jesus combines the food metaphor with resurrection themes, but he describes them both in hyperbolic terms. Now the elect do not simply eat his flesh but "chomp" (*trōgō*) it, and they "drink" (*pinō*) his blood. The combination of flesh and blood in John 6 makes sense because *sarx* is not the word for dead flesh, or meat, but for living flesh (Heilmann, 491). If someone were to "chomp" flesh literally, they would, necessarily, also drink blood. The consumption of blood is explicitly forbidden in Lev 17:10: "And any person of the sons of Israel, or any of the proselytes worshiping with you, whoever should eat any blood, indeed I will set my face against the life that is eating the blood and I will destroy it from all its people." Leviticus 17:14 explains the reason for such a drastic response: "You will not eat the blood of all flesh *because the life of all flesh is its blood*; all who should eat it will be utterly destroyed" (cf. Gen 9:4-7). Jesus risks a lot by using this metaphor; it *is* a difficult word (John 6:60). If people were not ready to hear Jesus' words before, 6:52-58 almost guarantees their abandonment of Jesus' teaching. As Heilmann concludes, Jesus' frankness leads to his rejection and, eventually, his death (493). The irony is that in rejecting Jesus, people reject life and continue seeking perishable and destructible things, even though it is precisely destruction that they fear (cf. 11:45-53; 12:24-26). Nevertheless, the Gospel of John is also clear that to believe—to eat and drink—Jesus fully is a daring and divinely aided gift.

D. 6:60–7:1: Going Back or Remaining with Jesus

In 6:60–7:1 the focus suddenly shifts back to the disciples. Although we may anticipate that Jesus' words were not readily accepted by most of his conversation partners from 6:25-59, the narrative never tells us definitively what their reaction to Jesus was after his teaching. John 7:1 reports that Jesus continues "walking around in Galilee" because it is Judea where the Jews (or Judeans) are seeking his death, not in Galilee, even though "the Jews" debated with him there in 6:41-58. For this reason, the Jews as a character remain ambiguous, like Nicodemus, one of the leaders of the Jews and a Pharisee (3:1-2). The turn to the disciples, however, shows that they are the focus of the action and teaching in John 6: *this* is the end of the test begun in 6:5-6. The results might surprise us as readers, but the narrator is careful to reiterate that it was no surprise for Jesus, who "already knew from the beginning who they are who are not believing and who it is who will betray him" (v. 64b).

The scene with the disciples can be divided into two sections, each of which contains chiastic components that emphasize Jesus' knowledge, his paradigmatic teaching in 6:63-64a, and the Twelve's confession uttered by Simon Peter in 6:68-69.

Scene 1: 6:60-65
    A. 6:60, Many disciples question: Who is able?
        B. 6:61-62, Jesus knows and questions: Are you scandalized?
            C. 6:63-64a, Jesus' words are life-making
        B'. 6:64b, Jesus knew from the beginning
    A'. 6:65, Jesus answers: Only those given by the Father are able.
Scene 2: 6:66–7:1
    A. 6:66, Many disciples go back and stop walking
        B. 6:67, Jesus questions "the Twelve": expects a negative answer
            C. 6:68-69, Confession: Jesus has the words of life
        B'. 6:70-71, Jesus questions "the Twelve": expects a positive answer
    A'. 7:1, Jesus keeps walking in Galilee

The final interactions of John 6, therefore, demonstrate the truth of Jesus' teaching: namely, that no one can come to Jesus without divine assistance (6:45). Even though Jesus has attracted a large following through his signs, he knows that not all of them truly believe or trust him. The test of John 6 reaches a climax in 6:61-64: the word (meaning Jesus' teaching) has scandalized "many" of his disciples. Even though they have seen Jesus feed the multitude and collected the abundance, and seen him tread over the stormy sea, his words offend them. In 6:62 Jesus knows that "even if you should see the Son of Man ascending to where he was before," they would not believe (1:51). In John, sight is important and signs are helpful, but only when one is able to see. For John, our visual impairment must be rectified by God's divine love first, and continually, through Spirit-infused remembrance (2:22; 12:15-16; 15:26–16:15).

In contrast to the "many" who turn back, "the Twelve" remain (6:67, 70). Peter's confession in 6:68-69 is unique among the canonical Gospels. He first summarizes Jesus' teaching from 6:63 that Jesus' words (*rhēmata*) communicate eternal life and then adds a dramatic profession of faith: "We ourselves have believed and have known that you yourself are the Holy One of God" (cf. 1 John 2:20). The use of the perfect tense, *have* believed and *have* known, shows the durative quality of their belief. These are the ones who have been believing since 2:11, and at least three of them have been with Jesus since 1:35-51: Philip (6:7), Andrew (6:8), and Simon Peter (6:8, 68-69), all of whom were from Bethsaida of Galilee. In John's Gospel, the adjective "holy" (*hagios*) is also used to describe the Spirit (1:33; 14:26; 20:22) and the Father (17:26; cf. 1 John 2:20). That all three are described as "holy" shows their unity and connection, which Jesus will describe in his Farewell Discourse (14:26; 15:26; 16:13).

This profound and confident confession in John 6:68-69 is also tinged with ambiguity since it comes from *Simon* Peter, the one who will challenge, disobey, and walk away from his Lord in the story ahead (13:36; 18:10-27). Moreover, even though Peter speaks for all the disciples, "Judas of *Simon* Iscariot" also stands among them, "the devil" whom Jesus already knows (6:64, 70-71). The combination of the two "Simons" in John 6 sets the stage for their later comparisons in John 13 and 18 that record their differing betrayals. Persevering through this one test, therefore, is not the end; regardless of whether one confesses belief or turns back, there is more to come as Jesus heads toward his "hour" of glorification through the crucifixion, resurrection, and return to the Father (16:16-33). His "flesh," his words, are life-making only when they are continually chewed, swallowed, and incorporated into one's being. Indeed, ancients believed that food eventually became flesh as it was processed and refined by the body (Aulus Gellius, *Noct. att.* 12; Aristotle, *Part. an.* 2.4.651a14; cf. Flemming, 98). Good food made the best people, giving them vitality and even shaping their souls. Jesus offers the best "food," food that not only sustains but also re-begets, reforms, and rebirths those who consume it so that they become "children of God" (1:12-13; Myers 2017a, 91–95).

Festival of Tabernacles: Water and Light (7:1–8:59)
The next large portion of the Gospel is set during another festival, "the festival of the Jews, the Tabernacles" (*hē skēnopēgia*, cf. 1:14). Tabernacles or *Sukkoth* is another pilgrimage festival associated with the exodus narrative, the return from Babylon, as well as with the yearly harvest (Deut 16:16). According to Deuteronomy, every seven years the law was to be read to the gathered Israelites, as well as all those dwelling with them, during Tabernacles, "so that they should hear and so that they should learn (*mathōsin*) to fear the LORD your God and hear to do all the words of this law (*logous tou nomous toutou*)" (Deut 31:12). These associations made Tabernacles a time that "could arouse hopes for subsequent deliverance," making the questions that surface about Jesus' messianic identity in John especially fitting (Thompson 2015, 164). The importance of learning the law, and "these words," during Tabernacles continues themes from John 6, where Jesus described those who are able to hear his words as ones "taught by God" (6:45; Isa 54:13). The subsequent discussions of Jesus' own education (*memathēkōs*) in John 7:13-15 and the debate over the interpretation of the law in 7:19-24 continue to develop these themes, setting Jesus in contrast to the religious leaders who oppose him (cf. 9:39–10:21).

Occurring in autumn (15th of Tishri; September–October; cf. Lev 23:39; Deut 16:13), the Israelites built "tabernacles" or tents (*skēnai*) to dwell in for seven or eight days. Still celebrated today, *Sukkoth* is a time for the faithful to reenact their years of wandering in the wilderness and depending on God's miraculous deliverance, guidance, and provision. It was also during Tabernacles that the first temple, Solomon's Temple, was dedicated (1 Kgs 8:2). Tabernacles, therefore, is a time for Jews to remember their utter dependence on God for life in the past, present, and future.

The book of Zechariah captures the future hopes associated with Tabernacles, all of which are built on its depiction of God's faithfulness to Israel in the past and present. In Zech 9–14, Raymond Brown explains, the "day of the Lord" takes place during Tabernacles, a day when "the messianic king comes to Jerusalem" riding on a donkey (Zech 9:9), and God

pours out a spirit of compassion and supplication on Jerusalem (12:10);
He opens up a fountain for the house of David to cleanse Jerusalem (13:1);
living waters flow out from Jerusalem to the Mediterranean and Dead Sea
(14:8); and finally, when all enemies are destroyed, people come up year
after year to Jerusalem to keep Tabernacles properly (14:16). . . . [E]very-
thing in Jerusalem is holy, and there are no more merchants in the Temple
(14:20-21). (Brown 1966, 326)

These images from Zechariah especially resonate with the Gospel of John,
which explicitly quotes Zech 9:9 in John 12:15 and Zech 12:10 in John
19:36, thus bracketing the Johannine Passion Narrative (cf. Bynum). The
connections with this same portion of Zechariah during Jesus' final scenes
in the Jerusalem temple set the stage for the culmination of Jesus' messianic
work in John 12–20.

A. 7:1-13: Boldness in Secret?

The Tabernacles sequence begins with an exchange between Jesus and his
brothers, who urge him to travel to Jerusalem openly so that his "disciples
will also see your works which you are doing (*poies*)" (7:3). Mention of Jesus'
brothers immediately brings to mind John 2:12, when Jesus traveled to Capernaum with "his mother and his brothers and his disciples" after changing
water into wine. Although nothing negative is said of Jesus' brothers in John
2, they form part of the contrast between Jesus' biological connections and
his heavenly loyalties to his Father. In John 2, Jesus emphasizes his obedience
to his "hour" rather than to his mother's request and the implied opportunity
to gain honor or glory from the people at the wedding. A similar scene plays
out in John 7:1-13 when Jesus' brothers voice their misunderstanding of his
mission. The ambiguity of their own stance is clarified, however, when the
narrator reports that their comments are based on unbelief (v. 5).

   Rather than believing in Jesus' words, the brothers believe he desires to
gather more disciples, and they press for him to travel to Jerusalem for Tabernacles in a way that will gather attention, "for no one who does in secret (*poies
en kryptō*) also seeks to be in openness (*en parrēsia*). If you are doing (*poieis*)
these things, reveal yourself to the world!" (7:4). The antithetical parallelism
of the first part of this verse showcases the brothers' confusion. They assume
that Jesus is doing works in order to gain attention; this is the sort of "openness" or "frankness" (*parrēsia*) they believe Jesus desires (7:4, 13, 26).

   In classic Johannine fashion, the brothers express truth in their misunderstanding: Jesus is *not* seeking the same type of openness or attention that

his brothers describe—glory from people—but rather, Jesus is speaking and acting with boldness to show that he seeks his Father's glory alone. Indeed, "seeking" (*zēteō*) remains a key theme in the discourses that follow in John 7–8 as some "seek" Jesus for violent ends while Jesus warns them that their time to "seek" him for life is drawing to a close (7:1, 11, 18-20, 25, 30, 34–36, etc.; cf. 5:44; 13:31-35). Because Jesus does not seek human glory, his going up to Jerusalem "in secret" in 7:10 is not deceptive but further illustrative of his priorities (cf. 8:59). It is revelation, just not the revelation the world recognizes or wants.

The dialogues and debates in John 7–8 also show that it is in seeking God's glory that Jesus encounters the most hostility, precisely because he rejects the human glory that the world so treasures. When Jesus boldly rejects "glory from people," he effectively disempowers the world (or the existing power structures) around him (cf. Parsenios 2016, 261–66). Brant suggests that John 7–8 contains examples of an *agōn*, "a debate that imitates the standard oratorical and rhetorical features of the debates heard in courtrooms and political assemblies" and that were often included in Greco-Roman writings. An *agōn* showcases the rhetorical ability of the protagonist, in this case, Jesus, enabling him to put forward a "dissenting voice" that would otherwise be "silenced in actual public life" (2011, 133). Jesus' dissenting voice in John 7–8 continues his discourse from John 5:40-47, where he prioritized God's glory over human glory, thereby removing the power of the authorities around him to pass judgment against him. Because Jesus does not value human perceptions, since "he knows what is in humanity" (2:25), he is not beholden to the status quo of the world.

As the religious leaders will note in John 11, this makes Jesus a threat. Even though the Jewish religious leaders are often interpreted as jealously guarding their authority, in John's Gospel it is not the loss of their own authority they fear; it is Rome. If the religious leaders cannot control the Jewish crowds, they know that Rome will quell any rebellion with astounding violence. Recalling that the final composition of the Gospel of John is *after* the Roman siege and destruction of Jerusalem and the temple, such a fear is understandable. The audiences of John's Gospel knew well the overwhelming political and military might of Rome. What the Gospel challenges them (and us) with, therefore, is real. To live like Jesus, that is, as "one seeking the glory of the one who sent me," means to invite the wrath of the world because it exposes the limited power of the world in spite of its claims of control (7:18). It unmasks the world's idolatry (cf. 1 John 5:21). As Jesus will explain, such living is the only way to experience true freedom (John 8:32).

B. 7:14–8:59: The Christ or a Deceiver? Division at Tabernacles

Jesus arrives in Jerusalem and spends the last half of the festival teaching in the temple, prompting a variety of reactions from those who hear him: crowds (7:12, 20, 31, 32, 40, 43, 49), Jerusalemites (7:25), Pharisees (7:32, 45, 47, 48; [8:3], 13), and Jews or Judeans (7:1-2, 11, 13, 15, 35; 8:22, 31, 48, 52, 57). The winding repetition and quick back and forth of this section makes it difficult to outline with precision, but the effect is clear: Jesus sparks controversy and creates tension in Jerusalem. His openness (*parrēsia*) gets him attention, but not the glory that his brothers thought he desired in 7:3-4. Instead, Jesus' speech eventually prompts the most violent reaction thus far in the Gospel narrative when even those who had been believers pick up stones after Jesus says, "before Abraham was, I am" (8:58-59).

Focusing on the violence of John 7–8, Ruth Sheridan (2015) explores the requirement for "two witnesses" in trials leading to capital punishment described in Deut 17:6; 19:15; Num 35:30 and their surrounding OT contexts (cf. Deut 13). Alluded to already in John 5:31-40, these passages also surface in the discussion of testimony (*martyria*) in 8:12-20 when Jesus describes his own witness and the requirements of Torah saying, "and in your own law it has been written, 'the witness of two people is true.'" Also significant is the fact that such trials, at least according to Deuteronomy, were to take place in or near the temple (Sheridan 2015, 172–73). Jesus' presence in the temple is emphasized repeatedly in John 7–8, where Jesus teaches and "cries out" in the temple, and even teaches in the "temple treasury" (7:14, 28; [8:2], 20, 59).

In her reading, Sheridan notes that the requirement for multiple witnesses was meant to protect the accused as well as the community. Even though apostasy, idolatry, perjury, and murder were crimes punishable by death, false conviction was itself murder and "pollut[ed] the land with blood-guilt" (Num 35:33-34; Sheridan 2015, 177–80). Sheridan argues that all of John 7–8 centers on questions from these trial settings—idolatry, blasphemy, murder, perjury, and apostasy—since Jesus makes claims that closely align himself with God (John 5:16). Not only is Jesus himself potentially committing idolatry and blasphemy if he is lying (cf. 7:20; 8:48, 52; 10:21), but he is also a danger to others if he successfully leads them astray (Deut 13). Jesus does collect believers at different points in these debates, and it is at these moments that the religious leaders react against him (7:31-32, 40-52). The Pharisees, and other leaders who oppose Jesus, see their role as protecting the crowds from this false prophet. From the Gospel's perspective, however, Jesus' opponents are conducting a poor trial as they convict an innocent man, a "man sent from God" who boldly speaks the truth to them, while they seek his death (Sheridan, 182). The question at the center of John 7–8, then, is which capital offense is being committed: Is Jesus a falsely accused, potential murder victim? Or is he one "who deceives the crowd" to commit idolatry and is therefore justly punished to prevent further apostasy (Deut 13:6-10; 17:1-3)?

In the following analysis, I have divided the passage into four major sections: 7:14-52; 7:53–8:11; 8:12-29; and 8:30-59. Because of the interruption of 7:53–8:11, however, some of the structures in John 7–8 are obscured, which will cause some backtrack in the analysis of light and water (7:37-39; 8:12-29). In 7:14-52 the topic shifts from Jesus' education to his origins as the crowds and religious leaders debate with themselves Jesus' messianic status. The tone shifts in 8:12-29, when the Pharisees begin to address Jesus directly. Jesus' frank speech does earn believers, but as with his testing of his disciples in John 6, Jesus seems also to test these believers with even more frankness in 8:30-59. As in 6:60-66, the results are a loss of potential followers for Jesus, yet Jesus is not perturbed. He simply leaves the temple "in secret" because it was not his "hour" (7:30; 8:20; 8:59).

The episode, therefore, turns full circle back to the beginning of 7:1-13. The brothers had accused Jesus of operating in secrecy out of fear, but Jesus speaks boldly before the crowds in the temple. This is a claim he will make explicit during his trial before the high priest in 18:20: "I myself have spoken with boldness (*parrēsia*) to the world; I myself taught always in a synagogue and in the temple, where all the Jews are coming together, and in secret (*kryptō*) I spoke nothing" (cf. Parsenios 2016). Jesus' bold speech leads to the misunderstanding and even violence that makes his movement secretive. Because those around him do not understand who Jesus is, or the one whose glory he seeks, they cannot "see" him rightly (9:39-41).

Jesus is Taught by God (7:14-52). The temporal and thematic links in 7:14-52 create a parallelism made up of three pairings:

    A. 7:14-24, Jesus Teaches in the Temple
        B. 7:25-31, Mixed Reactions among the Masses
            C. 7:32-36, Judgment from the Religious Leadership
    A'. 7:37-39, Jesus Teaches in the Temple
        B'. 7:40-44, Mixed Reactions among the Masses
            C'. 7:45-52, Judgment from the Religious Leadership

The first sections (A, A') begin with a temporal marker, noting when the encounter takes place during the festival, midway through or at the end. These sections also include Jesus' teaching, in which he interprets Scripture

(Mosaic Law and a psalm) and issues a command. The second sections (B, B')
include the mixed reactions of those listening. Rather than speaking to Jesus,
these groups react among one another, demonstrating the fear described in
7:12-13 in contrast to Jesus' boldness. The asides in these sections center on
the question of Jesus' identity as the Christ (Messiah), which is debated by
means of scriptural interpretation and in ways that recall the crowd's identification of Jesus as "the prophet" because of his signs in 6:14. Finally, the
third sections (C, C') describe the reactions of the religious leadership who
are concerned about the belief emerging in the crowds (7:31, 48-49). The
repetition in this section contributes to the increasing tension of the chapters, which will only continue in 8:12-59.

Beginning with 7:14-15, we notice the focus on Jesus' education, literally his ability to interpret Scripture even though they assumed he "does not
know letters (*grammata*)" (i.e., that he is illiterate; Keith 2009, 152–57).
Although Jesus' knowledge of Scripture was demonstrated in his exposition
in the Capernaum synagogue in 6:25-59, the Jews in Jerusalem are nevertheless "amazed" when they hear him teaching in the temple (cf. 3:7; 5:20,
28; 7:21). Their amazement stems from the fact that they cannot trace Jesus'
educational pedigree; he has no human teacher, or at least not one they
recognize (cf. Neyrey 1991, 446–47). He should not know Scripture, or how
to interpret it, as well as he does. Without proper instruction, Jesus is not
vetted and is potentially a false teacher. Jesus' response does not calm their
fears, however, as he claims to have been taught "by the one who sent me"
(7:16). The Gospel audience knows this "one" to be God, but those listening
to Jesus in John 7 could easily be baffled; moreover, how does one *prove* they
are from God anyway? Proof requires clear sight, and sure hearing, from
those observing—two traits that have nothing to do with actual physical
ability (9:39-41; 12:39-41; Isa 6:9-10).

These comments are about Jesus' authority and his origins. The mention
of "instruction" (*memathēkōs*) in John 7:15 recalls Jesus' words from 6:45
that only those "taught by God" will come to Jesus as believers. It also resonates with the Tabernacles tradition of reading the law to the gathered so that
they "should learn (*mathōsin*) to fear the LORD your God and hear to do all
the words of this law" (Deut 31:12, see above). When Jesus mentions Moses
specifically in his response to the Jews' amazement, he likewise reflects this
tradition: "Moses has given you the law, hasn't he? But no one from you is
doing the law! Why are you seeking to kill me?" (John 7:19). As in 5:39-47,
Jesus presents Moses (and all of Scripture) as revelatory and explanatory for
his identity and behavior, but only if it is interpreted correctly; that is, only
if one *hears* his words.

Jesus' interpretation of Scripture is directly contrasted with the Jerusalem-ites' and crowd's confusion in 7:25-31 and 7:40-44. In 7:19-24 Jesus presents a logical argument justifying his curing of the paralyzed man in 5:1-9. His argument moves from a point of well-known agreement. As Craig Keener notes, "That some commandments must override some other command-ments is a well-attested principle of rabbinic ethics and undoubtedly reflects a long-standing tradition" (2003, 716). In other words, it was not possible to fulfill *literally* every commandment; some had to take precedence. Debate, therefore, centered on *what* took precedence and why. Jesus' emphasis on healthfulness as the basis for his "breaking" Sabbath law to "make a whole person healthy" prioritizes life; it moves from the lesser (circumcision, for the health of one part) to the greater (curing of a whole person) (Brown 1966, 313). This type of argument is also called *qal vahomer* (light to heavy) and is common among rabbinic writings and Greco-Roman works, which call it *a minori ad maius* or define it in discussions of comparisons (e.g., *synkrisis*).

Jesus plays on the assumed relationship between health and rationality in his question to the crowd in 7:23. As Brant notes, Jesus' question—"why are you angry?"—literally means "why are you filled with black bile (*cholate*)?" This statement comes from the common understanding of the body being full of four humors that needed to be in balance for one to be healthy (2011, 157). Jesus' question, therefore, accuses the crowd of being unhealthy and out of balance, their rage against him contrasting with his restoration of the man to health in 5:1-9. The accusation of being *cholate* can also imply insanity or "mania," a state often associated with demon possession and explicitly mentioned alongside it in John 10:20-21. In Aristophanes' comedy *Clouds*, for example, Phidippides responds to his father's frenzied pleas for him to learn philosophy by saying, "Have you come to such mania (*manion*) as this that you are persuaded by black-biled men (*andrasin . . . cholosin*)?!" (line 833). If one is full of black bile, righteous judgment becomes impossible to render (John 7:24) because one loses their mind. In John 7:19-24, there-fore, Jesus turns the tables on his accusers and the confused, fearful crowd around him. Based on the logic of the Gospel, Jesus is not demon-possessed or insane for healing the man or knowing the machinations against him; rather those who reject him are because their rejection of Jesus is a rejection of life (3:31-36; 5:40). Jesus' own accusations become more explicit as the conflict progresses (8:39-47).

This section also includes the second appearance of Nicodemus, whom our narrator reminds us is "the one who came to him [Jesus] before" (7:50). Nicodemus appears along with the religious leaders, the lead-priests and Phar-isees, as well as the "soldiers" (*hyperetai*) who had been sent out to "capture"

Jesus (*piazō*, 7:32). His location in Jerusalem coheres with his characterization from John 3, but while his speaking may show his leadership position,
it also distinguishes Nicodemus from the group character that is "the Pharisees." Nicodemus's statement comes on the heels of the Pharisees' response
to the soldiers' failure to arrest Jesus. They speak in unison, "No one from
the leaders believed in him or from the Pharisees, did they? But this crowd,
who does not know the law, they are accursed!" The irony of the Pharisees'
statement is that it condemns themselves and the lead-priests who were to
teach the crowd the law. Moreover, Nicodemus's statement that follows raises
the possibility that at least *one* from the Pharisees has believed: Nicodemus.

Nicodemus responds with his own rhetorical question: "Our law does
not judge a person unless it should first hear from him and know what he
is doing, does it?" This tactical question is deferential and also revealing. It
assumes the rest of the Pharisees will agree with him; Nicodemus is assuming
they know the law (unlike the crowd whom they have condemned). As Sheridan notes above, the law was stringent in requiring testimony from multiple
witnesses before passing judgment, particularly capital punishment, against
the accused. Nicodemus, however, is silenced with another rhetorical question: "You yourself are not also from Galilee, are you? Search and see that
from Galilee, no prophet is raised up" (7:52). The Pharisees' answer, rather
than agreeing with Nicodemus, is cutting. They have made their judgment
based on different Scriptures: Jesus is not a prophet because he is from Galilee
(7:28-29, 40-44). Their words imply Nicodemus's ignorance of Scripture and
include him in the insult against the Galileans, who had "believed" in Jesus
in 4:43-45 and 6:1-14. Even though, as Thompson notes, several prophets
did originate from Galilee, the "prophet-like-Moses" was not associated with
the region (2015, 178). Enacting the behavior described by Jesus in 5:39,
the Pharisees have "searched the Scriptures," but rather than seeing them
testifying on Jesus' behalf, they focus on Jesus' apparent origins from Galilee
and condemn him. Caught up in Jesus' physical appearance, these Pharisees
miss the Gospel's central claim: Jesus is God's Word made flesh. While many
interpreters have condemned the Pharisees for this reaction, their response is
entirely logical and, indeed, largely unavoidable in the timeline of the Gospel
narrative.

Jesus' Type of Justice (7:53–8:11). Although scholars have long recognized
that John 7:53–8:11 is a narrative inserted sometime later into the Gospel
of John, Chris Keith argues that we should not dismiss its importance, or
its connection, to the story of John 7–8. John 7:53–8:11 does not appear
in our earliest manuscripts for the Gospel of John, while it does appear in
other locations in NT manuscripts, including in the Gospel of Luke (Keith

2009, 120–21). Nevertheless, the earliest manuscript in which the passage is included, and its most often appearance, is in the location of John 7:53–8:11. This explains its placement in our contemporary English Bibles, although it perhaps does not alleviate anxiety about its inclusion. If this story was not part of the earliest Gospel of John, why should we read it at all?

Textual variants are as common in the NT as they are in all ancient literature; this is simply a fact of hand-copied texts, and no text is so copied as the Bible, particularly the NT (Aland and Aland). That 7:53–8:11 was added to the Gospel of John is not a secret among NT scholars, nor is it an issue unique to this passage (cf. Mark 16:9-20). Although later, this passage is found in its present location as early as the fourth century and Keith counts at least 1,427 manuscripts where it appears in the same location (120–21). This does not include the additional NT manuscripts that have the passage in an alternative location as part of the Jesus tradition. Thus, while we *cannot* be certain why this story was added later, we *can* see that Christians recognized its value as part of the Jesus tradition, communicating significant aspects of Jesus' identity, particularly in ways that resonate with John 7–8.

Reading the passage in its current location, we find a number of motifs consistent with John 7–8, including the importance of judgment, particularly by means of the "Law of Moses" (8:5; cf. 1:17; 7:19). In 7:14-15, the Jews communicate their astonishment at Jesus' teaching, which Jesus then demonstrates in 7:19-24 and again in 7:37-39. The conflict turns to knowledge of the law in 7:45-52 when the Pharisees condemn the crowd and Nicodemus challenges them to use the law in their indictments against Jesus. John 7:53–8:11 is an outworking of this challenge, as the Pharisees and scribes—the keepers of the written and oral Torah—"test" (*peirazontes*) Jesus in order to find a way to accuse him legally (8:6; cf. 6:6; 7:1). When they bring forward a woman "caught in the act of adultery," they present someone who has broken the Decalogue, the laws considered to be at the core of God's commands for Israel (Keith 2009, 149).

For Keith, the real challenge in John 7:53–8:11 has little to do with the woman herself; rather, it is a moment meant to expose Jesus' supposed Galilean ignorance. After all, no prophet will arise from Galilee (7:52; cf. Keith 2018). Jesus' dramatic and drawn-out response silences his opponents. Jesus does not simply answer them verbally, but he writes in the earth, not once but twice. As Keith observes, the verbs used to describe Jesus' writing (*katagraphō, graphō*) correspond to those used in the LXX of Exodus to describe God's writing the Decalogue on the stone tablets with his "finger" (*daktylō*) before giving them to Moses (Exod 31:18; 32:15-16). Jesus' writing twice corresponds to the two stone tablets given to Moses, further reinforcing the allusion. According to Keith, then, the insertion of 7:53–8:11 is fundamentally about demonstrating Jesus' superiority to Moses by presenting him as Scripture's author (2009, 181–90). The scribes and Pharisees may trace their educational lineage back to Moses, but Moses traced his own back to the Word himself, now embodied as Jesus. Unfortunately, then, these teachers of the law have not understood correctly what their own teacher taught.

Nevertheless, we should not overlook the compassion demonstrated by Jesus in this passage. Jesus' movement in this passage—from sitting (8:2), to bending (8:6), to rising (8:7), to bending again (8:8), to standing and addressing the woman herself (8:10)—rotates around the woman even as it draws the shaming gazes of the crowd away from her and back onto themselves. Jesus' writing on the ground may showcase his literacy (7:15), but it also draws the attention of the eyes around him—especially those of the scribes and Pharisees who, presumably, had a greater chance of being literate than the average Jewish person gathered in the temple (Keith 2009, 150). Rather than staring at the woman, these individuals find themselves looking to the ground. Jesus' words that "anyone who is without sin" should throw the first stone cause them to look longer still, but this time at their own actions rather than those of the woman. Slowly, those gathered—scribes and Pharisees among them—realize their inadequacy to judge others while simultaneously revealing Jesus' ability to occupy that role.

Unlike the Pharisees in 7:45-52, Jesus needs no reminder from a Nicodemus to hear from the woman; he addresses her in 8:10 and hears her response in 8:11: "No one, Lord." When Jesus replies to the woman, "Neither am I myself judging against you. Go, and from now on, sin no longer" he demonstrates the messages conveyed in John 3:31-36; 5:30; and 8:15-18 (cf. 5:14). While Jesus is perfectly suited to judge, it is his presence that reveals the world's current state in darkness and wrath. In John 8:11 Jesus is shown to be merciful and loving toward a woman he could have condemned; in his presence, she experiences new life. In the same way, the world experiences unearned love from God through Jesus (3:14-18; 1 John 4:7-21).

Jesus Is Not Alone (8:12-29). Jesus' public teaching in the temple resumes in 8:12-29, which originally followed immediately after 7:52 before 7:53–8:11 was added by our later editor. This means that Jesus' teaching in 8:12-29, and all the way through 8:59, still happens on the last, great day of the Festival of Tabernacles. The tension builds in 8:12-29 when the Pharisees and the Jews question Jesus directly. Jesus continues to offer his words to a more general "they," which would seem to include a larger crowd alongside the religious leaders (cf. 7:14-52).

The section can be divided into two parts, which expand upon the stair-step parallelism in 7:14-52 outlined above. In 8:12-20, Jesus makes another proclamation of his identity, this time imitating the other "I am" statements uttered in the Gospel (4:26; 6:35, 41, 48, 51). In 8:21-29, Jesus repeats his statement from 7:33-34 that he is "going away" where "they" will not be able to come. As in 7:35-36, the Jews are confused by his statement, suggesting perhaps that he is going to kill himself, thus making the place they "cannot come" death. Jesus' departure, however, means a return to his Father. This fact will become clear in John 13–17, but it is already discernable to the Gospel audience who knows Jesus' true origins (1:1-14). Using imagery especially significant to Tabernacles, Jesus reinforces his identity as life in contrast to the world's residence in darkness and death around him. The hope God provides comes as it has always come, through trusting the Word (8:24).

Calling himself "the light of the world," Jesus evokes John 1:1-5, which describes the Word of God as the light of life that is not overcome by any darkness, as well as the "true light" who was coming into the world (1:9). A common metaphor for Jesus' identity and work in John's Gospel, this image is rooted in the OT beginning with Genesis. It was also a commonly used symbol for life in the larger Greco-Roman world, thus making it decipherable to people from a number of backgrounds (Thompson 2016). Nevertheless, as Koester notes, "light" had a particular importance during the celebration of Tabernacles, when priests lit lamps in the women's court each night and young men attended them so they would not go out (2003, 157–58). Jesus claims to be the real light, the light these lamps imitated in the darkness, who lights not just the temple precincts but the entire world.

The image of Jesus as "light of the world" works in tandem with 7:37-39 when Jesus promised "rivers of living water" for those who come to him to drink. Recalling his conversation with the Samaritan woman in John 4, this image of "living water" also combines other scriptural motifs, explaining Jesus' description of it as a quotation even though scholars struggle to identify precisely what passage Jesus means. It is likely that Jesus is here paraphrasing several traditions, such as God's provision of water in the wilderness (Exod 17:1-6; Num 20:2-13; Ps 78) and descriptions of the law or wisdom as living water (Prov 13:14; Ps 40:8; Sir 24:30-31; Koester 2003, 194–95). Water manipulation also played a significant role during the celebration of Tabernacles, when a priest drew water from the Pool of Siloam (John 9:7, 11) and brought it into the temple, pouring it into a bowl upon the altar as a "visible petition that as God provided water for the people in the past, he would send the rains again and grant prosperity to his people during the coming year (*m. Sukkah* 4:9)" (Koester 2003, 197).

Jesus' teaching in John 8:12-29, therefore, picks up where he left off in
7:37-39 with an image crafted from a combination of scriptural and liturgical motifs that fit the festival setting. This setting, moreover, reinforces the
audaciousness of Jesus' claims. Standing in the midst of this celebration of
God's unique faithfulness to Israel, Jesus declares himself to be the embodiment of that faithfulness in the past, present, and for the future. He claims
that it is by coming to him that Israel, and all people, will experience the
salvation and life promised to them as described in Ps 36:7-9: "How precious
is your steadfast love, O God! All people may take refuge in the shadow of
your wings. They feast on the abundance of your house, and you give them
drink from the river of your delights. For with you is the fountain of life; in
your light we see light" (NRSV).

A Bold Word to Believers (8:30-59). In spite of Jesus' contentious encounters in 7:14–8:29 he, once again, gathers believers through his bold speech.
In 8:30 we learn, "While he was saying these things, many believed in him."
This response seems to satisfy Jesus' instruction from 7:37-38 and 8:24: these
people have believed and are coming to Jesus for water, light, and life. If the
episode had ended here, we would think Jesus had a successful trip to Jerusalem, gathering disciples in spite of his brothers' sarcasm from 7:3-4. This is
not, however, how things end. In 8:31-59 Jesus proceeds to teach "the Jews
who had believed in him," not with consoling and praising words but with
more frank speech. As in John 6, Jesus provides for the believers around him
a bounty of words meant to nourish them and give them life, but it is a bitter
meal, and one that sparks an especially negative response.

Interpreters *must take special care* when reading and teaching John
8:30-59 because of its harsh language and horrible history (Reinhartz 2001).
The rhetoric of 8:40-47, in particular, has been used by explicitly anti-
Semitic groups and has been incorporated in anti-Jewish bias in a number of
Christian contexts as well, both intentionally and unintentionally (Sheridan
2017, 2019). The larger context of the Gospel of John, as well as the rhetorical context of the first century, however, helps us to understand more about
the exchange.

As we have seen thus far in the Gospel, Jesus does not shy away from
offensive words. He "tests" his own disciples in John 6 in ways that cause
"many" of them to leave him behind. In John 8, we encounter a similar
scene. While the narrator has told us in John 2 and 4 that Jesus did not
"believe" those who "believed" in him, John 8 shows Jesus putting these
festival believers to the test. He says, "If you should remain (*meinēte*) in my
word truly, you are my disciples, and you will know the truth and the truth
will free you" (8:31-32). Jesus here challenges the Jews gathered around him

with similar words he will use in 15:7 for his disciples: "If you should remain (*meinēte*) in me and my words in you remain (*meinēte*), whatever you should wish, ask, and it will happen for you." In other words, true disciples remain with Jesus even when he speaks boldly to them, when he challenges their current lives and pushes for them to reprioritize their pursuits of glory. They also remain with Jesus and listen, allowing for him to define his own identity rather than thrusting presuppositions upon him (cf. 6:14-15; 7:12, 25-31, 40-44).

Belief of this sort is not easy. Jesus says outlandish things in 8:31-59, not least his description of the Jews around him as both descendants of Abraham *and* "children" of the devil. He also claims to be greater than Abraham and the prophets, able to give unending life, that he is "before" Abraham, and that Abraham "saw" his day and "was glad"! In addition to Abraham's reception of the three strangers at Mamre in Gen 18, Mary Coloe notes that *Jubilees* presents him as the first one to celebrate Tabernacles (1999, 6–7), and later traditions also attributed to him visions of the future (*Apoc. Ab.*; *T. Ab.*; cf. Arterbury 2005, 59–71). These traditions make the Jews and Jesus' appeals to Abraham in John 8 fitting for the context, while also showing that the Jews understand the identity implied by Jesus' words. Jesus' bold words work on several cultural assumptions along with the Abrahamic traditions, especially that one demonstrates "true" parentage through one's behavior. Because Jesus says the Jews "are seeking to kill" him, he regards their "true" father to be the devil, who is a "murderer from the beginning" in spite of their literal lineage from Abraham (8:44; cf. 1 John 3:11-17). For a group of Jews sympathetic to Jesus' words in John 8:30-31, this is—understandably— too much. When Jesus finally claims, "before Abraham was, I am" the crowd grabs stones to throw because they themselves have become the witnesses of what they perceive to be Jesus' blasphemy and idolatry. They determine him to be a deceiver and seek to fulfill the law (cf. Sheridan 2015).

The judgment rendered by the crowd of Jews brings us back to Jesus' statement in 7:24, "Stop judging by appearance, but judge the right judgment!" For those gathered in Jerusalem, Jesus' appearance is the first thing they would have noticed. He appears to be a Jewish man from Galilee, with a history of causing trouble in the temple and in Capernaum, less than fifty years of age. He has no recognizable, formal theological training to support his interpretation of Scripture, and he causes division whenever he speaks, driving away even those who would seem to support him. Focusing on Jesus' appearance, then, it is no wonder that the Jews determine Jesus is "a Samaritan and demon-possessed" (8:48)!

Again, instead of returning judgment of these Jews with our own, we should render a "just judgment" similar to Jesus' from 8:10-11. As we have seen, the Gospel repeatedly prioritizes its audience by giving us more information than any character in the story itself can have. Indeed, the Gospel will end with a blessing for those who believe without having seen Jesus, which seems in part to be because of their access to the Spirit, to the community, *and* to the Gospel (20:30-31). Before Jesus' glorification, gathered in Jerusalem and under the thumb of the Roman Empire, John's Gospel shows us what our reaction to Jesus-in-the-flesh would have been then, and still could be today. Bitter words are not easy to swallow, and even Scripture can be used for injustice (Myers 2011, 2017b).

Another Sabbath Work and Festival Teachings (9:1–10:42)

After Jesus "is concealed" or "secreted" out of the temple in 8:59, he strolls through Jerusalem, still on the "last" and "great day" of Tabernacles. In 9:14 we will learn that this is a Sabbath day, paralleling the late identification of this day in 5:9 when Jesus cured the paralyzed man. The confrontation begun in John 5 has continued to spark debate in John 7–8, and it is repeated in John 9 as Jesus again cures on this Sabbath day (cf. Brant 2011, 98). In contrast to the cured man from chapter 5, however, this man resists the temptation to acquiesce to the judgment of the Pharisees and Jews who question him (and his parents) in 9:13-34. As a result, the man is emphatically "cast out outside" (*exebalon auton exō*, v. 34) the Jewish community of which he had formerly been a part. In many ways, this story foreshadows a time *after* Jesus' glorification, hinted at in 7:37-39 as well as in Jesus' statements about his coming departure, when believers would need to act as his "witnesses" in the physical absence of their Lord. The result of faithful witness, at least in John 9, is expulsion from previous kinship and communal groups. For this reason, John 9 is the key text in reconstructions of the Johannine community that focus on division within Jewish communities over the identity of Jesus as the Christ (Martyn; Culpepper and Anderson).

Jesus not only cures on this Sabbath day; he also teaches. In 10:1-21 Jesus offers his final discourse of Tabernacles, a festival during which he has spoken repeatedly, causing division, belief, and rejection because of his bold words. His speech continues almost unabated in 10:22-42, even though it is set during a later festival, that of Dedication (or Hanukkah). The continued confusion of those around him is apparent in 10:1-42, a speech often referred to as "The Good Shepherd Discourse." Jesus focuses this discourse on his own identity in contrast to the existing religious leadership in Jerusalem. Coming on the heels of John 9, Jesus describes his faithful leadership as the "noble shepherd" who sacrifices himself for the sake of his sheep against those whom he describes as hired hands, weak shepherds who abandon the sheep at the threat of wolves. Replete with Roman imperial and scriptural imagery, this discourse reflects on and summarizes all of Jesus' teaching thus far in the Gospel, building to a climax with themes of his chosen mission of love and his unity with the Father (10:17-18, 30). Even if what he says seems impossible, he nevertheless encourages these divided crowds to believe (10:34-39).

A. 9:1-41: Curing the Man Blind from Birth

John 9 is a narrative unit made up of three major parts: 9:1-7, 8-34, and 35-41. The narrative is bracketed by Jesus' speech and works (vv. 1-7, 35-41), thus demonstrating that, in spite of his departure from the majority of the story (vv. 8-34), he is still the main actor even offstage. In 9:1-5 Jesus speaks with his disciples, building to the thesis statement of the story: "Whenever I am in the world, I am the light of the world" (9:5; cf. 8:12-19). Jesus exercises his role as light by enabling the light to come to a blind man's (*typhlos*) eyes in 9:6-7. Speaking in Jesus' absence, the blind man—who continues to use this title for himself! (9:25)—offers three rounds of testimony explaining how he "received sight": first to his neighbors (vv. 8-12), then to the Pharisees (vv. 13-17), and finally to "them" (presumably a combined group of Pharisees and other religious leaders described as "the Jews," vv. 24-34). The dramatic interaction between the blind man and these religious leaders results in his separation from his religious and kinship groups; even his parents disassociate with him as a result of their fear (vv. 18-23). Not one to let this lonely sheep become lost, however, Jesus returns to him in 9:35-41, enfolding him into his own flock.

   Sin, Disability, and a Revelation (vv. 1-7). The narrative as a whole is prompted first by Jesus' sight of the "blind-from-birth person" (*anthrōpon typhlon ek genetēs*) and second by his disciples' question: "Rabbi, who sinned, this one or his parents, so that he was born (or begotten) blind?" (vv. 1-2). The disciples' assumption, that disability is the result of sin, was a common one in the ancient Mediterranean world among Greeks, Romans, and Jews. Ancients, like contemporary people, assumed that they *could* judge a book by its cover. A person's physical characteristics, abilities, beauty, etc. were taken as indicators of positive and negative traits. These beliefs were even formalized in writings devoted to deciphering such associations, called *physiognomy*, literally "physical knowledge," which gives us some insight into the biases of the ancient world (Gleason, 3–54; Parsons, 17–66). Blindness was a particularly significant disability in the ancient world, as it is today. Working on the assumption that eyes were literally the lamps of the soul, however, blind individuals were often portrayed as darkened, unable to access the light in the world around them as well as unable to contribute light to that world (Sophocles, *Aj.* 69–96; Homer, *Il.* 16.805; Plato, *Resp.* 7; *Tim.* 45–47; Philo, *Abr.* 150–53; cf. Hartsock, 53–124). Nevertheless, that ancients too knew the limits of physiognomic thinking is demonstrated in the commonplace of the "blind seer," a blind prophet or wise individual endowed with superior wisdom or access to the divine (e.g., Tiresias).

The disciples' question to Jesus, therefore, sets up the Gospel to engage in its own ways with these cultural assumptions, using them and subverting them in the service of its theology. Jesus' response in 9:3-5 has often been used to make an argument for instrumental suffering: that God allows (or even causes) suffering in order to be glorified through it (cf. 11:4). While a theological option in the ancient world, this is not what Jesus says in John 9:4. Remembering that all punctuation is a later addition to our NT manuscripts, there is no reason to include a period at the end of v. 3; instead v. 4 completes the thought begun in that verse. The resulting translation is "Jesus answered, 'Neither this one sinned nor his parents, but so that the works of God might be revealed to him it is necessary for us to work the works of the one who sent me while it is daytime. Night is coming when no one is able to work.'" Jesus is *not* saying that God allowed this man (and his parents) to suffer in order for God to be glorified; instead, he flips the disciples' focus. They are focused on the man and his parents' potential shortcomings; Jesus tells them, instead, to focus on the work they should be doing. Jesus does not offer a rationale for the suffering endured, but he acknowledges it and clearly says that it is *not* the result of these individuals' sins. Instead, they, like everyone else, should be given the revelation sent by God: namely, the chance to encounter the Light of the World.

Even though the man cannot see, he does show exceptional ability to hear. In an act that resembles God's creation of Adam with the earth in Gen 2, Jesus "makes clay" and smears it over the man's eyes before commanding him to go and wash (John 9:6). Jesus seems to make the man new eyes, or working eyes, by means of this clay and his words. Jesus' use of spit in this healing is similar to Mark 8:22-26, a story that some suggest is being reinterpreted by John in this passage (cf. Brown 1966, 378–79). Joel Marcus notes that spit was often understood to have healing and magical qualities in the ancient world, a common ingredient in medicinal potions and cures (2000, 473–74). It is not Jesus' spit, though, or even the clay alone, that effects the cure; covered with mud, the man still cannot see until after he washes himself in the Pool of Siloam in obedience to Jesus' words.

Testimony from the Seeing Blind Man (vv. 8-34). Returning "seeing," the man sits himself again in the same spot where he was accustomed, and he begins hearing other words—this time from his neighbors and onlookers who are debating his identity in ways that mirror the fast-paced exchanges concerning Jesus in John 7. Unlike Jesus, who addressed the man in 9:6, these individuals gossip about the man rather than speaking to him directly. The man interjects his first testimony in 9:9: "I am he!" The statement parallels Jesus' claims throughout the Gospel, but especially in 8:24-29 where he tells those gathered around him, "Unless you should believe that *I am he*, you will die in your sins" (v. 24) and "Whenever you should lift up the Son of Man, then you will know that *I am he*, and from myself I am doing nothing, but just as my Father taught me, these things I am speaking" (v. 29). The use of the phrase "I am he" in 9:9, therefore, establishes the man as a proxy for Jesus.

The question the neighbors ask him in 9:12 reinforces this role. The neighbors want to know *where* Jesus is, but the man does not know. Fulfilling Jesus' prediction in 7:33-34 and 8:21, these people are seeking Jesus, but even the cured man cannot find him. Foreshadowing Jesus' departure, and return to his Father, John 9 portrays the cured man as an ideal disciple; one who endures the questioning from neighbors and onlookers, religious leaders, and lack of protection by parents but continues witnessing to the truth. Like Jesus, the man expresses wisdom that transcends his social position and dearth of formal education, teaching even the teachers with rhetorical proofs and scriptural insight (9:34; cf. 7:14-15).

As in John 5, the religious leaders rely on Moses as their "hope," but the man (like Jesus before) shows Moses to be their accuser. He says, "We know that God does not hear sinners, but if someone is devout and doing his will, this one he hears" (9:31). The man's description, "we know," includes himself as an equal to those "reviling" him (9:28). It also shows that the man believes his cure is God's will, cohering with the larger scriptural depiction of God as the source of light and life. Since Jesus has done God's will, he must be "from God." The fact that he has again done so on a Sabbath day (9:5, 14) is not evidence against him, but rather in his favor; as in John 5, it shows Jesus has a unique relationship with the Father. In spite of the man's repeated testimony, his logic, and his scriptural interpretation, the religious leaders render judgment against him and throw him out (9:34). Although Jesus was unwilling to cast blame for the man's disability, these religious elites do not shy away from offering their own verdict, one that condemns both the man and his parents who had attempted to avoid negative repercussions in 9:21-23.

From Light to Shepherd (vv. 35-41). Even though the man, religious leaders, and neighbors were unable to find Jesus, Jesus "finds" the man after he is cast out from his community. Asking the man if he "is believing in the Son of Man," Jesus again evokes 8:28-29 and foreshadows the confession of believers after his glorification. In the exchange, Jesus resumes his role as the key speaker of the Gospel, accepting the "worship" of the man in 9:38. In 9:39-41, Jesus shifts from a private exchange to a proclamation, once again summarizing his work and recapitulating themes from John 7–9. Jesus declares, "I myself came into this world for judgment, so that the ones not seeing should see and the ones seeing should become blind ones" (9:39). It should be noted that Jesus does not say he himself judges when he comes into the world, but rather that his presence causes judgment by revealing one's state: "seeing" or "not seeing." His comment is sometimes associated with Isa 6:9-10, which the Gospel will quote in John 12:40 (Lieu 1988), and can seem cruel: why would Jesus rob someone of sight?

Keeping in mind his role as "Light of the World" helps make sense of his comment. In 3:19-21, Jesus summarizes the reaction he faces as the light coming into the world:

> Now this is the judgment: that the light has come into the world but people loved the darkness more than the light, for their works were evil. For everyone continuing to practice wickedness hates the light and does not come to the light, lest their works should be shown. But the one continuing to do the truth comes to the light, so that his works might be revealed because they have been worked in God.

As the true light, Jesus' presence evokes a response: either one will be drawn to him, or they will recoil from his shining intensity. In John 9:3-5, Jesus encourages his disciples to keep on doing God's works in the daylight so that they can been seen. Having experienced this light, therefore, the cured man remains in it, allowing himself to be a sign of Jesus' identity as the Light of the World.

Jesus' challenge in 9:39-41, therefore, is a call for the world to admit its blindness and its need for him. The cured man submits to Jesus' words and, like the Samaritan woman before him, comes to a greater understanding of this Light. Even after he is cured, the man continues to call himself blind, therefore admitting he still needs Light. In 9:25 he says, "Even though I am a blind man, now I am seeing!" The Pharisees, however, much like Nicodemus, have a lot more to lose. If they admit blindness, they show weakness and vulnerability; thus, they continue to say "we are seeing!" Like the Jews who would not admit their slavery in 8:31-36 but were adamant of their free status, these Pharisees make the same mistake, or "sin" (*hamartia*). Jesus has not come to condemn, but the world condemns itself and reveals its condemnation by refusing to let go of pride, confidence in human glory and perceptions, in order to receive the Light and Life God gives.

B. 10:1-42: The One Shepherd

Jesus' exchange with Pharisees begun in 9:39-41 immediately transitions into another discourse in 10:1-21 with Jesus' characteristic phrase, "Truly, truly I am telling you . . ." (10:1; used 25 times in John). Jesus' teaching in 10:1-21 is on the same day as the events of 7:37–9:41 (see 7:53–8:11 above): that is, the "last" and "great day" of Tabernacles, a "Sabbath day" (9:14). The setting for 10:22-42, however, changes to the Festival of Dedication, which is more commonly known as Hanukkah today. This festival celebrates the rededication of the temple of Jerusalem after Antiochus IV Epiphanes' desecration of it with a statue of Zeus, as well as the victory of the Maccabees that facilitated this rededication. The miraculous story of the Maccabean revolt against the Seleucid king is told in 1–4 Maccabees, which are not included in many Protestant Bibles. Their exclusion does not diminish their importance for first-century Jews, as well as later Jews and Christians, who likewise suffered under foreign oppression (Romans rather than the Seleucids). Moving from Tabernacles to Dedication in this way, the Gospel of John sets Jesus' actions and words in a festival that recalls an ancient example of deliverance (exodus) as the warrant for their hope in future restoration (Tabernacles) and connects it to a festival that recounts a more recent deliverance from foreign rule (Dedication). During the brief period of the Hasmonean Dynasty (ca. 164–63 BCE), Israel was ruled by Jewish leadership as a united nation in ancient Palestine.

As Carter has shown, these festivals are especially poignant for a first-century population living in the midst of the Roman Empire (2008). The Maccabees' ability to overthrow the foreign, pagan, and oppressive rulers in the past could be referenced as support for resisting Roman power in later centuries, as indeed it was during the First and Second Jewish Revolts (ca. 68–73 CE, 132–35 CE; Sharon, 242, 251–53). Jesus' claims of unity with the Father during *this* festival in particular are at once fitting for the Gospel as well as unthinkable. For those who fear Rome, his words threaten the tenuous alliance between the religious rulers and Roman authorities. For those who fear God alone, his words threaten the *Shema* that declares God's oneness. Either way, Jesus' claims to be Israel's "One Shepherd" of prophetic traditions

(Ezek 34–37) earn him quick castigation in spite of Jesus' appeals for belief, even if it is only in the proof garnered from his works (John 10:34-39).

Metaphorical Speech at Tabernacles (10:1-21). Jesus' speech begins in 10:1-21 with metaphors the narrator describes as "figures of speech" or *paroimia* (10:6; see also Parsenios 2016). *Paroimia* can be classified among other types of figurative speech in rhetorical handbooks, including with parables, similes (similitudes), and metaphors, which are all forms of comparisons (Quintilian, *Inst.* 5.11; Pseudo-Cicero, *Rhet. Her.* 4.45–47). Brant notes, however, that *paroimia* are allegorical short fables or proverbs rather than just comparisons (*parabolē*) and that they are often meant to "veil offensive or hurtful speech" (2011, 160). Zimmermann, nevertheless, argues that although different from the parables given by Jesus in the Synoptic accounts, Jesus' *paroimia* in John still have the marks of parabolic speech (2015, 335–39; cf. 2008). This is particularly true if compared to the longer, allegorical "Parable of the Sower" that appears in all the Synoptics (cf. Mark 4:1-20; Matt 13:1-23; Luke 8:4-15). Whether specified as a *parabolē* or a *paroimia*, both John and the Synoptics present Jesus using common imagery to communicate, and obfuscate, his meaning. In John 10, he appeals to the image of a "shepherd." Well known in agricultural contexts, this image was also common in political, prophetic, and historical works from throughout the Greco-Roman world, Jewish and otherwise (Carter 2008, 185–88). Scholars have noticed resonance between John 10 and Ezekiel's prophecies of eschatological restoration, where God promises to set "one shepherd" over all of Israel, reuniting the fractured people and saving them from foreign rule (Ezek 34–37; Manning; Baron 2017).

Also significant is the transition from Jesus' "bold speech" (*parrēsia*) in John 7–8 to *paroimia* in John 10. Unpersuaded by Jesus' frank words before, he switches to figurative language in John 10:1-21, resulting again in division among the Jews listening (7:40-44; 8:12-59). As in John 8, Jesus returns to bold speech in 10:22-42, this time at the explicit request of those "encircling" him (10:24). They believe they are able to hear Jesus' bold words; they think that these words will enable them to understand Jesus finally! Once again, however, Jesus' words are too hard to swallow. These would-be sheep chase their shepherd out of the pen. Their in-gathering must wait until the Shepherd lays down his life *and* takes it up again (8:28-29; 10:17-18).

Jesus' speech in 10:1-21 falls into two main parts: 10:1-6 and 7-21. In 10:1-6 Jesus lays out the main metaphors of thief/rebel, shepherd, and doorkeeper, creating a chiastic structure full of repetitions. Jesus' *paroimia* is not only the metaphors but also the entire statement, which is full of rhetorical figures.

A. v. 1a, The Opening: Truly, Truly I Am Telling You
    B. vv. 1b-2, Identity Revealed through Entrance: Thief vs. Shepherd
        C. v. 3, An Open Gate
    B'. vv. 4-5, Whom the Sheep Follow: Shepherd vs. Stranger
A'. v. 6, Conclusion: Ignorance of the Pharisees.

Further contrasts complement this chiasm. Within 10:1b-2 a doublet contrasts the "thief and rebel" and the "shepherd" by means of how they enter the pen. John 10:4-5 repeats this contrast but begins by describing the shepherd and then moves to the "stranger" (*allotrios*) as another description for the "thief and rebel" who enters from "another way" (*allachothen*).

Verse 3 is the center of the chiasm and describes the work of the shepherd in terms of his relationship to his sheep, as well as to the door-keeper. The repetition of this verse can be diagrammed as follows:

A. For this one, the door-keeper opens,
    B. and the sheep,
        C. his voice (*phōnēs*), they hear
    B'. and his own sheep,
        C'. he calls (*phōnei*) according to name and he leads them out.

The repetition of "voice" and "calling" fits Jesus' previous emphasis on the power of his voice and the importance of hearing his words (3:8, 29; 5:25-30, 37; cf. 8:43-47). Jesus reinforces hearing in the rest of 10:7-42 (cf. 11:43; 12:28-30; 18:37). Jesus' sheep recognize and follow him as the One Shepherd because in him they recognize the Father.

The image of the "one shepherd" (*heis poimēn*) in John 10:16 resonates with language from Ezek 34:23-24, which reads, "And I will raise up over them one shepherd (*poimena hena*) and he will shepherd (*poimanei*) them, my servant David, and he will be their shepherd. And I myself, the Lᴏʀᴅ, will be their God, and David [will be] a ruler in their midst. I myself, the Lᴏʀᴅ, spoke." The promise for "one shepherd," from the lineage of David, appears right after a prolonged description in Ezek 34:11-22 of God as the shepherd of Israel. God is the one who "will search for my sheep," who will "rescue" them from all their "scattered" (*diasperō*) places, who will "feed" them, and "judge" between them "the fat sheep and the lean sheep. Because you pushed with flank and shoulder, and butted at all the weak animals with your horns until you scattered them far and wide" (34:21, NRSV). In Ezekiel, God is the real shepherd of the sheep. The Davidic servant is but an extension of God's provision, only initiated after God's own saving action. Jesus' claim, therefore, to be this "one shepherd" is a claim that he is enacting God's promise of restoration, even though it seems like his words scatter the flock. According to Jesus, it is not he who has scattered them; rather, the "wolf" has scattered the sheep who were abandoned by the hired hand. The symbolism here draws on the larger context of Ezek 34, where the religious leaders of Jerusalem are criticized for their selfishness. Rather than caring for the sheep, these "shepherds" feed themselves, becoming fat and leaving the sheep to starve or, worse, "slaughtering" (*sphazete*) them for themselves (34:1-3; 1 John 3:12, *sphazai*; John 10:10, *thysē*). When wild animals approached in the form of other nations, these shepherds saved themselves, leaving the sheep to be food and scattered (Ezek 34:5-10). Jesus' reference to a "wolf" in John 10:12 is also symbolic, since the wolf was one of the traditional images for Rome. Romulus, the founder of Rome, was said to have been reared with his twin brother by a she-wolf, drinking in her milk and thus taking on her strength and ferocity (Livy, 1.4). The message of John 10:1-21 is offensive as *paroimia* often are. In this allegory, Jesus continues chastising the Pharisees from 9:39-41, blaming them and their fear for the scattering of God's sheep.

In contrast to their selfishness, Jesus acts as the "noble shepherd" (*ho poimēn ho kalos*) who values the sheep both because they are "his own" (*ta idia*) and because the Father has commanded him to "lay down his life" on their behalf *so that* he might take it up again (10:11-18). Jerome Neyrey argues that "noble" is a more fitting translation than "good" for *kalos* not only because it alleviates the confusion that perhaps the word *agathos* ("good"; cf. 7:12) is used here but also because it better describes the virtue of Jesus' actions, especially with traditions of a "noble death" (*kalōs apothanein* or *euthanatos*) that were common in Mediterranean antiquity (2009, 283–307). Alongside other general commonplaces used in characterization, "manner of death" and "events after death" could be used to describe a person as either noble (*kalos*) or wicked (*kakos*). Noble actions were those that benefited others, even more so if they were for the good of everyone, if they were done with "toil" or contrary to expectation, if their effects were long-lasting, if they were chosen and were unique, being done for the first time, alone, or only able to be accomplished by this certain individual (Myers 2012, 91; cf. Quintilian, *Inst.* 3.7.12–18; Theon, *Prog.* 110–13; Cicero, *Top.* 69–70).

A quick glance at Jesus' portrayal of himself as the "noble shepherd" shows its reflection of these criteria for praise. Jesus' actions are for the benefit of his own sheep, rather than for his own bodily preservation. He "lays down his life on behalf" of the sheep, an action that is fitting for a shepherd but also contrary to the behavior of the hired hands currently occupying that role. Jesus' suffering is also apparent. He repeatedly "toils" in his speeches with and actions for others. Even though he works for life, he repeatedly has to defend himself and explain his deeds. He also claims the ultimate effect of his mission, the laying down of his life in order to take it back again, is eternal life. Moreover, in 10:17-18, Jesus is emphatic that his actions are entirely his choice, just as they are also God's "command" for him. As has been stressed by various interlocutors and witnesses, Jesus' abilities are utterly unique and have not been done before. Indeed, the Gospel argues, it is only through him that life is possible; after all, he is the *monogenēs*, the Unique-one (1:18; 3:16).

Rather than the "not knowing" of the Pharisees in 10:6, the Jews are again "divided" by Jesus' statements (10:19-21). They understand the audaciousness of his speech; the question is whether or not they can trust it. Only those who focus on what Jesus has done, his work of curing the blind man, are able to resist the identification of Jesus as "demon-possessed" and "manic" (10:19-20). Like the seeing-blind-man of John 9, these Jews cling to Jesus' "words" (*rhēmata*, 10:21; cf. 5:47; 6:63-71), knowing that what he has done is proof of what he says. The uniqueness of his works corresponds to the uniqueness of his words (9:32-33).

Bold Speech at the Feast of Dedication (10:22-42). Suddenly 10:22 informs us that a new festival is underway, that of Dedication (*egkainia*) when Jews celebrated the restoration of the Jerusalem temple for the worship of God alone after Antiochus's desecration (see p. 117 above). For this reason, Dedication was a time when crowds would be especially sensitive to claims of divinity that could infringe upon the *Shema*, the declaration that Israel's God is "One" (Deut 6:4-5; cf. Exod 20:4-6). It is, however, also a perfect festival for Jesus' proclamation of his unity with the Father (John 10:30). As the manifestation of God's glory on earth, Jesus' declaration to be *part of* God's Oneness, rather than in competition with it, fits the moment of Dedication as he calls on those around him to believe or trust, even if they do not yet understand.

John 10:22-42 picks up from 10:21 almost seamlessly; the question asked by the encircling crowd of Jews summarizes the main question that dominated Jesus' dialogues throughout his appearances at Tabernacles: is he the Christ (7:26-27, 31, 41; 9:22)? The vividly described scene is *ekphrastic* in character, enabling the audience to visualize Jesus walking through Solomon's portico, a stretch of the temple lined with columns, or *stoa*, named for the king who built the first Jerusalem temple (1 Kgs 6–8; on *ekphrasis* see Myers 2012, 49–51). Jesus is "encircled" by Jews present for the festival but also still divided by their previous encounters with Jesus during Tabernacles.

Unlike Jesus, who affirmed that "no one removes it [my life] from me (*oudeis airei autēn aph emou*), but I lay it down from myself" in 10:18, the Jews ask Jesus, "How long will you keep removing our lives (*heōs pote tēn psychēn hēmōn aireis*)?! If you are the Christ, tell us with boldness (*parrēsia*)!" (10:24). The request for "boldness" contrasts the *paroimia* Jesus spoke in 10:1-21, which he used to criticize the religious leaders but also to encourage understanding. In 10:7 Jesus uses more *paroimia* because the Pharisees "did not know what he was saying to them." When he returns to *parrēsia* in 10:25-39, he does not start a new way of speaking. Rather, he resumes the boldness that he previously showed, at Tabernacles (7:1–8:59) and previous festivals (5:19-47; 6:26-71). Jesus highlights the fact that he has spoken frankly throughout his ministry in 10:25, telling the Jews, "I spoke to you and you are not believing!" Jesus' comment here parallels his previous statement in 8:25, "What am I saying to you since the beginning?" He repeats this sentiment again before the high priest in 18:20 as well: "I have spoken boldly (*parrēsia*) to the world, I always taught in a synagogue and in the temple, where all the Jews gather together and in secret (*kyrptō*) I spoke no thing." Jesus' bold speech is not the problem; instead, it is difficulty of hearing, recognizing, and understanding truth (18:38).

Jesus is not ignorant of this difficulty. That, he explains, is why he is doing works. His behavior demonstrates, or testifies (*martyreō*), to the truth of his words (10:37-38). As ancients knew, actions and words revealed the character of individuals. Making sure these traits matched was a key then, as it is now, in determining believability (Myers 2012, 51–61). Yet the divided Jews around him are unable to recognize the coherence of Jesus' works and his words because they are so unique and audacious. When Jesus now returns to bold speech in 10:25-39, this incomprehension increases and the crowd once again turns to stones in an attempt to silence Jesus' frank words (8:59).

In 10:25-39 Jesus first explains the *paroimia* of 10:1-21 and then interprets Scripture to reinforce his argument. Returning to themes from 6:45-71, Jesus says the inability of these Jews to trust him is because they are not his sheep. Just as Jesus' character is revealed through his behavior, so is the identity of his sheep: his sheep will follow him as the One Shepherd (10:26-28). Jesus has not stolen these sheep, like the thieves and rebels before, but his Father has given the sheep to him. Jesus' ownership of the sheep parallels that of the Father. As in 8:34-36, Jesus portrays himself as the inheriting son who embodies and continues a father's will. Indeed, Jesus' Sonship is so unique, and so complete, that he is unified with his Father in ways no human son could ever be. Thus, he claims, "I myself and the Father are one" (10:30).

As Baron notes, Jesus' claim here is an adjustment of the *Shema* (2017, 167–70). Rather than "the Lord your God, the Lord is one," Jesus says, "I myself and the Father are one." Again, during the Festival of Dedication in particular, *and* in the temple itself, this was an incredible thing to claim. The Jews' reaction to reach for stones is entirely understandable based on their context and scriptural interpretation (Num 35:30-34; Deut 13:6-10; 17:1-7; 19:15-21). How could Jesus say such a thing?!

Jesus, however, justifies himself based on his own interpretation of Scripture, this time quoting Ps 82:6 (Myers 2012, 122–24). The description of this quotation as from "the law" has troubled some interpreters, but calling all of Scripture "the law" was not uncommon in the Second Temple period. Moreover, it fits the focus on the law and Moses that pervades all of John 5–10 (see pp. 101–106, 112–15 above). Jesus' argument moves from the lesser to the greater (7:19-24). He says, if God is willing to call your ancestors (and, therefore, you all) "gods" because you have been privileged with the gift of God's Word, how much more should I call myself "a son of God"? Like a true son, Jesus explains, he does the works his Father gives him (cf. 8:37-47). Even if they cannot recognize Jesus by sight, therefore, he says they should recognize him by his works. Based on their descent from Abraham, Jesus calls on these Jews to see him as a divine messenger and welcome him, even if they cannot completely understand his words. Nevertheless, they are unable to do this. As Jesus has said in 8:28-29 and 10:17-18, there is still work for him to do: he must lay down his life, be lifted up, and then take his life back again.

In 10:40-42, Jesus retreats for the last time "across the Jordan," traveling to the "place where John was baptizing." Rather than returning all the way to Galilee as he had in chapters 4 and 6, Jesus instead travels to Perea, outside Judea but remaining in closer proximity. His remaining near to Judea raises the tension of the narrative; the audience can sense that Jesus' "hour" and "time" is drawing near (2:4; 7:6-8, 30; 8:20).

The reference to John (the Baptist) in these verses also recalls his previous witness on Jesus' behalf in 1:15-36 and 3:25-36, and Jesus' appeal to him in 5:33-35. As in all the earlier descriptions of John, his inferiority to Jesus is again emphasized, this time because he did not do any signs in contrast to Jesus' ministry. In spite of this, however, "many" still recognize that "everything John said concerning this one was true!" (10:41). No longer speaking himself (presumably because he had been arrested and killed, 3:24), John's desire to decrease from 3:30 has happened, but the value of his testimony remains.

Even so, another contrast is created between the Jews in Jerusalem and the "many" in Perea. The many are able to believe because of Jesus' works/

signs and the testimony of John, without explicit reference to Jesus' own words. Whether or not this belief will last remains unknown, however, since Jesus has gathered believers before only to lose them the moment he speaks (8:30-59). The test for sheep remains the ability to hear and obey Jesus' voice.

Theological Threads

Sin and Impairment

Jesus' curative signs in John 5 and 9 explicitly raise questions of how impairments, ailments, and disabilities relate to sin, a question that is an outworking of theodicy: why bad things happen to good people. A simple, and common, answer to this question is to suggest that the people suffering are not good—they have somehow merited the bad thing happening to them. "Bad things," according to ancient and contemporary societies, can include impairments, whether physical, cognitive, or both. Often we assume impairments are "bad" without any explicit conversation about the implications of this conclusion on the lives of those impacted by disability, which to varying degrees is all of us (Clark-Soles 2017, 334).

Many Christians have used Scripture, either consciously or not, to reinforce such a view. After all, does not Jesus demonstrate his "saving" power by healing individuals plagued by demonic possession, disability, and death throughout the Gospels? John's Gospel, in particular, has been used to reinforce this association since Jesus tells the recently cured man in 5:14, "Stop sinning, so that nothing worse should happen for you!" Doesn't that mean he was sick because he was sinning? In John 9, Jesus' disciples ask who is to blame for the man's blindness, and many translations of 9:4 have encouraged an instrumental view of his suffering: the man and his parents may not have sinned, but he suffers (and so do they) for the sake of God's future glory (cf. 11:4).

I have addressed the translation issue in John 9:4 above and will discuss this issue again in 11:4, but I focus on the larger question of sin and disability here. The burgeoning field of disability studies has alerted many to the problems of assuming sinfulness or something less-than humanness for those who have disabilities (as well as for those who birth, parent, and care for them). In her recent analysis of disability in the Gospel and Letters of John, Jaime Clark-Soles makes a distinction between "healing" and "curing." Use of "healing" often implies that one can only be a whole person when they are able-bodied, however that is so defined. She offers an alternative definition. "Healing," she writes, "refers to a person who has experienced integration and reconciliation to self, God, and the community" (2017, 334). Thus, we all need "healing," regardless of perceived abilities or impairments. In contrast, a "cure" is "the elimination of impairment and is experienced on the individual level" (334). In John 5 and 9, she argues, Jesus "cures" both men, but only the man in John 9 experiences anything close to a "healing" (340–54). Moreover, his healing reveals the need for the Pharisees' own; even though they can physically "see," they are "blind," like all the rest of us, in need of God's light (9:39-41).

Although the Bible certainly employs physical impairment as a metaphor for spiritual waywardness, contemporary readers need to take care when interpreting these passages. In biblical texts, this metaphor is often used to correct those who interpret themselves as able-bodied to reveal their own ignorance and self-deception rather than to shame those who are living with impairments. In the Gospel of John, for example, characters deceive themselves when assuming superiority to others, including when assuming full ability—physical, cognitive, and spiritual—to discern truth in the world. The Gospel pushes back against the myth of normativity, revealing all of us to be in need of healing. As often as not, those whom the able-bodied deem "inferior"—whether because or gender, race, or perceived ability—have more insight (4:1-54; 9:1-41). According to Jesus, we must acknowledge our own need for healing rather than pointing fingers and diminishing the value of those around us. God, John 3:16-18 tells us, loves the whole world, not only the parts that are "able-bodied."

Predestination and Free Will

This section of the Gospel also raises questions about belief: is one predestined to be one of Jesus' sheep, or can one choose to hear and follow? As is often the case with NT writings, we can make arguments for both sides of this equation. On the one hand, Jesus emphasizes that only those whom he has chosen and whom God has given him can hear and follow (6:43-71; 8:30-59; 10:1-39). Jesus will not lose these sheep. On the other hand, however, Jesus also holds accountable those who do not recognize him. He may say that they are not his sheep, but he still calls on them to start believing and to remain with him (10:38-39). Why would he waste the effort if there was no room for choice and change?

Brant (2011, 129–30) and Koester (2008, 78–80) rightly emphasize the importance of acknowledging our perspective versus that of the Gospel, and its audience, when answering this question. Remembering that John's Gospel was probably written for people already believing in Jesus as the Christ, the Son of God, helps to clarify the Gospel's presentation (20:30-31; cf. Talbert 2005, 267–68). Presenting believers as God's chosen and Jesus' sheep helps to encourage them to continue on in faith. At the same time, however, this narrative explains Jesus' rejection, as well as the rejection faced by his followers, regardless of how that was historically experienced in the Johannine community (15:18-25; see General Introduction).

Also playing a part in this question is the Gospel's presentation of "sin" and the state of "the world." According to the Gospel, the world is beloved by the God who created it, but it is nevertheless in darkness, full of people who love darkness more than they love light. As described above, people are convinced that they do not need assistance to decipher God's activity. This unwarranted confidence maintains their distance from God while also revealing their fear of other entities, such as Rome. In spite of this situation, God continues to reach out, sending the Word as Jesus, the True Light to enlighten the world. Jesus' presence reveals the shadows, but it also provides access to the Father in a new way. As Reinhartz notes, though, newness can be threatening; the incarnation is not an easy thing to recognize and believe (2015).

Overall, while the Gospel may not answer our question of predestination or free will as clearly as we would like, what it does emphasize is the world's need for God's intervention. Whatever the conclusion, it is clear that "faith is not self-generated" (Koester 2008, 78). Instead, all the world needs revelation and assistance; we cannot claim to be authors of salvation any more than we can claim authorship of life. When we claim such authority, or act in ways that give that authority to ones other than God, we commit idolatry. Rather than solving the riddle, therefore, the Gospel encourages believers to keep on believing, in spite of the confounding nature and difficulty of Jesus' words. God, John assures us, is still reaching out with love—the same "complete" love that was revealed in Jesus' crucifixion, resurrection, and return to the Father that enabled the giving of the Holy Spirit. Our role, therefore, is humbly to remain in it.

Heading toward the Hour

John 11:1–17:26

The fourth portion of the Gospel begins at John 11. In this chapter, Jesus moves from the safety among believers "across the Jordan" (10:40-42) back to the region of Judea for the sake of his friend (*philos*, 11:3, 11), Lazarus, and Lazarus's two sisters, Martha and Mary. From this point on, Jesus remains in Judea, even if he does not walk "openly" (*parrēsia*, 11:54) among the Jews (or "Judeans") until he enters Jerusalem again to cries of "Hosanna" in 12:12-13. Although some commentaries keep John 11 in the section about Jesus' public ministry, stretching from John 2–12, I have chosen to focus on its transitional role. Unlike the Synoptic Gospels, which present Jesus' clearing of the temple as act that instigates the religious leaders to move against him, in John's Gospel it is his raising of Lazarus. In John, it is clear that the leaders are not jealous, but afraid; they are concerned that Jesus' attraction of followers would eventually provoke the Romans to crush the Jews ("the nation," 11:48, 50-51) and its holy "place" (*topos*), the temple, thus forcing the people into another exile—*if* they survived the onslaught of the Roman forces (11:45-54; 12:19; 19:15).

The power of the Roman legions, as well as the horrific realities of siege warfare, are ably laid out by Caryn Reeder (2018). Romans squashed rebellions with sieges, overtaking those who resisted their rule. Sieges were costly for the besieged as well as for the army camped outside, not only financially but also physically, psychologically, and spiritually. When an army prepared to encamp around a city, those in the countryside often fled into the stronghold instead of away from it, since the soldiers would vent their wrath upon any civilian they found outside the city gates. Once besieged, there was little chance of escape for those in the city, unless they surrendered early on or won the final battle. Women, children, and elderly participated alongside men, often preparing weaponry and traps for the entering army, fighting from rooftops, and dealing with limited supplies, starvation, and the disintegration of social structures. They also counted among the casualties and captives when an army attacked.

The destruction of Jerusalem in 70 CE is in the future from the narrative perspective of John's story, but it is a past event for the Gospel audience. Enraged by the length and cost of the Jerusalem siege, the Roman army was especially cruel in their slaughter and rape of the inhabitants, and the destruction of the city, when they finally overtook its defenses. They crucified those who tried to escape and, according to Josephus, "made the whole city run with blood, to such a degree indeed that the fire of many of the houses was quenched with these men's blood" (*J. W.* 5.11.1; 6.8.5). The fear expressed by the Jewish leaders, and those who ally with them in John's Gospel, is understandable. If the Romans think Jesus is a revolutionary who could raise an army (no matter how meager) to oppose them, the Romans will come, and they will destroy, just as they do in 70 CE.

In John 11–17, therefore, Jesus repeatedly faces the fears of those around him, countering this darkness with the light that he offers. As the narrative continues, it becomes clearer that his mission will eventually result in his death, as this noble shepherd lays down his life on behalf of the sheep so that he might "take away" their sin: their mistake of fearing Rome that blinded them to the gift of life standing among them. Indeed, Jesus' choice to die so that he might rise again and return to the Father is the greatest demonstration of his, and God's, love for the world, even though it has rejected them.

In John 13–16, Jesus turns his attention to his disciples, retreating from the public crowds but also noting that his disciples, too, will be "scattered" (*skorpisthēte*, 16:32; cf. 11:52). Jesus' final speeches to his disciples are focused on consoling and encouraging them as ones left behind but not abandoned. The Spirit, "another *paraklētos*," will come to teach, remind, and testify among the disciples while also convicting the world concerning its disbelief in Jesus (14:26; 15:26; 16:7-9). So sure is his victory that Jesus says, "Take courage! I have overcome the world!" (16:33). Jesus ends this section with a prayer for these disciples as well as for all those who believe in him, asking God to keep them in the world as witnesses and to make them one, not only with God and Jesus but also with one another (17:1-26), as the location of the Spirit's presence in the world.

Commentary

Delayed Life and Fear of Death (11:1–12:11)

One of the best-known stories from in the Gospel, John 11 contains Jesus' raising of his "friend" or "loved one" (*philos*), Lazarus. This story not only foreshadows Jesus' resurrection but also precipitates his death, creating an inversion of death and life motifs throughout the narrative. The "dead man" (*tethnēkōs*, 11:44), Lazarus, will end up living; and the living Jesus will soon die. References to Jesus' coming death bracket the narrative. The story begins with the proleptic description of Mary's anointing Jesus in 11:2 (12:1-11) and the disciples' concerns about Jesus being stoned to death when he returns to Judea (11:8-16); it ends with plans for Jesus' death, orchestrated "on behalf of the nation" so that they might avert Roman wrath (11:45-54).

The story does not end with Lazarus's resurrection, but continues into 12:1-11 and beyond. The prolepsis in 11:2 points toward 12:1-11, inviting these verses to be read alongside John 11. The entirety of the story arc creates an inclusio that is explicitly marked at 11:2 and 12:1, and can be outlined as follows:

A. 11:2, Mary, the one who anointed Jesus
   B. 11:3-57, Story of Lazarus's resurrection
   B'. 12:1, Lazarus, whom Jesus raised
A'. 12:2-11, Mary anoints Jesus for burial

In 11:2, the narrator points toward Mary's anointing Jesus, writing about the event in the past tense: "Mary was *the one who anointed* the Lord with myrrh and *wiped* his feet with her hair." In 12:1, the evangelist recapitulates Lazarus's resurrection by writing, "Six days before the Passover, Jesus came to Bethany, to the house of Lazarus, whom *he raised* from the dead." Lazarus is described with this same phrase in 12:9 and 17, which detail his precarious position in spite of his recent resurrection (11:25-26; cf. Lee 2013, 200). Having been raised by Jesus implicates Lazarus, and his own death is also orchestrated as part of the larger plot against Jesus.

Although I have separated sections for ease of reading here, the connections between John 11–13 create a series of inclusios that form chain-links that reach forward and backward in the narrative. As Bruce Longenecker shows, chain-links were a common literary structure used in ancient writings at points of transition (Lucian, *How to Write History*; cf. Talbert 2005, 186). One set of these links in John 11–13 is diagrammed below, where "A" references Lazarus's resurrection and "B" Mary's anointing and foot-washing:

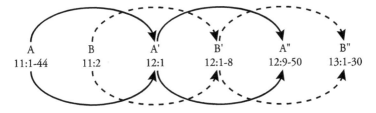

A	B	A'	B'	A"	B"
11:1-44	11:2	12:1	12:1-8	12:9-50	13:1-30

The hoops linking As and Bs, create tension and form a hinge in John 11–13 as the Gospel proclaims the arrival of Jesus' hour and shifts to narrate his return to the Father.

A. 11:1-16: News of Lazarus and Jesus' Delay

The first portion of the narrative outlines the crisis at hand. As in John 5, Jesus encounters a "weak" or "sick" (*astheneia*) man. This time, though, it is not because he found him but rather because he received word. Moreover, this is not some nameless man, sitting without friends beside a pool waiting to be lowered into its depths to receive a cure (5:1-9). Instead, it is Lazarus, who has Jesus himself as a "friend." If anyone should expect a quick cure, it is Lazarus. That, it seems, was at least the thought of his sisters, who emphasize their relationship to Jesus in their implicit request to him: "Lord, behold! The one whom you are loving (*phileis*) is sick" (11:3). Like his mother in 2:3, these women do not ask anything outright, but insinuate Jesus' obligation to respond. Jesus, again, demurs and delays his departure.

Jesus' delay is not the only curious element in 11:1-6. Elizabeth Schrader explores textual variants that center on the character of Martha here and elsewhere in John, noting that there is surprising evidence of her *absence* in early versions of the Gospel (385). Schrader's careful analysis brings her to the conclusion that Martha could have been a second-century addition to John's Gospel rather than part of the original tradition. As we have seen, later additions surfaced in this Gospel (and other NT works) as it was collected and preserved (7:53–8:11; 21:1-25). The addition of Martha could be the result of influence from Luke's Gospel, but it also reduces the role of Mary, who would otherwise dominate John 11–12. Moreover, Schrader writes, "a Johannine text form without Martha would create a strong textual implication that Mary of Bethany was Mary Magdalene" (388), particularly since the name "Magdalene" could be an honorific title ("Mary the Tower" or "Mary the Great") rather than a geographical reference (Beavis, 286–87). Given Mary's role in what would become heretical Christian traditions (cf. *The Gospel of Mary*) alongside other gnostic and docetic concerns in John (see General Introduction), the later addition of Martha is a possibility, even if it is a startling one for contemporary readers.

As the story now stands, however, Mary *and* Martha send word to Jesus concerning their brother, Lazarus, and seem to expect a prompt response. The disciples, although also said to be friends of Lazarus in 11:11, do not learn of his illness or death until after Jesus shares it with them, two days past when he first learned of his predicament. This creates a contrast of perspectives between vv. 1-6 and 7-16, which can be outlined as follows:

A. 11:1-6, Private Communication
vv. 1-3, Family Introduction and Situation
v. 4, Jesus' Response
vv. 5-6, Jesus' Love and His Delay
B. 11:7-16, Telling and Traveling
vv. 7-10, After this, Jesus Said, "Let Us Go"
vv. 11-15, After this, Jesus Said, "Let Us Go"
v. 16, Thomas Says, "Let Us Go"

The first six verses pivot at v. 4, where Jesus offers a response to the news he received from Lazarus's sisters. The communication is oral, although a messenger is never identified (compare 4:43-54). Reading *autē* as a dative, feminine, singular noun rather than as a near demonstrative pronoun "this" (Schrader, 374–75 and 11:40 below), 11:4 can be translated as "And having heard, Jesus said *to her.* 'The sickness is not for death (*pros ton thanaton*), but on behalf of the glory of God so that the Son of God might be glorified through it.'" This verse, much like 9:3-4, can have troubling implications. Unlike in 9:3-4, however, the issue is not resolved with punctuation. If the clause in 11:4 begins a new sentence with "but," the sentence is incomplete ("But on behalf of the glory of God so that the Son of God might be glorified through it . . ."). This is certainly not unheard of in John—6:62 is also an incomplete sentence—but the move here would be driven by uncomfortable theology rather than necessitated by grammar. Jesus does indeed seem to be saying, "The sickness is not toward death (*pros ton thanaton*), but [it is] on behalf of the glory of God so that the Son of God might be glorified through it." What are we to make of such a statement?

As with all interpretation, context is the key. Of particular note is the use of *pros ton thanaton*, which roughly means "to/toward/unto/for death" (cf. 1 John 5:16-17). The Gospel often notes that something, or a person, is *pros.* For example, in 1:1-2, the Word (*Logos*) is said to be *pros ton theon*, "toward God," from the beginning. The use of *pros* connotes some sort of movement or disposition: the Word was, from the beginning, inclined toward God. Everything the Word does is in line with God's will. Thus, throughout the Gospel, Jesus questions, to whom are people *pros* (cf. 3:20-21)? In John 11, Jesus says that the illness from which Lazarus suffers is *not* inclined toward, or benefiting, death. In other words, it is not a loss. Instead, it is "on behalf of the glory of God."

The "glory of God" is the glory that Jesus himself manifests as well as the glory for which he works throughout the Gospel. Jesus repeatedly casti-gates people for working for the wrong glory, but Lazarus's illness is "on behalf of," *hyper*, God's glory. In John, the preposition *hyper* is most often used to describe Jesus' dying "on behalf of" others, including most recently in 10:11-18 when Jesus described his work as the noble shepherd (cf. 6:51; 15:13; 17:19; 1 John 3:16). This is also the preposition Caiaphas uses to justify Jesus' dying "on behalf of the nation," and that the narrator expanded to "not on behalf of the nation only, but also so that the children of God, the ones having been scattered, might be gathered into one" (11:49-52; cf. 18:14). Jesus says in 15:12-14 that the greatest love is dying "on behalf" of friends. This is the love that Jesus shows, and at least unwittingly, this is the love that Lazarus shows to Jesus as well. His death is a precursor to Jesus' own, greater death, just as his resurrection is a demonstration of Jesus' coming resurrection. Unlike Lazarus, Jesus goes into his suffering and death with eyes wide open. But Lazarus's suffering, as well as that of Mary and Martha, is also testimony. By dying "on behalf" of the glory of God, Lazarus, acts as a model, if not an entirely aware, disciple. His sisters do as well.

Jesus' disciples come into focus in 11:7-16, and they continue with their characteristic misunderstanding (e.g., 4:27-38; 6:1-9; 9:2). Jesus must command them twice, "Let us go" (11:7, 15), before Thomas utters the assenting response and they head out as a group (11:16). In the conversation with his disciples, Jesus explains three times, moving from metaphorical to more literal language, why they must go to Judea despite the potential danger. Jesus' statement in 11:9-10 resembles his previous teaching from 9:3-5 by emphasizing that he is the one who brings light into the world: "Are there not twelve hours in the day? If someone should walk in the day, they do not stumble, because they see the light of this world. But if someone should walk in the night, they stumble, because the light is not in them."

The disciples' confusion continues even after Jesus' next metaphor: "Lazarus, our friend, is asleep, but I am going that I might wake him" (11:11; on health and sleep see Brant 2011, 173). Finally, Jesus must speak "boldly" (*parrēsia*) that, "Lazarus died" (11:14), yet, as in 11:4, Jesus does not focus on the death (*apethanen*) but rather on the eventual outcome: "I am rejoicing on your account so that you might believe *because* I was not there" (11:15). Since the Light of the World was not present, darkness and night had a chance to creep into frame (1:5; 9:5); but Jesus' coming will show the victory of Light and Life with the resurrection of Lazarus and with "belief" for some of those who witness it (11:45; cf. 2:11). Even then, however, Thomas shows the disciples' continued confusion. His comment, "Let us go that we might die with him," is ambiguous. Does he mean so that they, the disciples, might die with Jesus? Or that they, the disciples and Jesus, might die with Lazarus? Either way, the disciples have missed the point: Jesus said this illness was not "toward death." Whereas the group resisted Jesus' two commands to go, they now respond to Thomas; Jesus' disciples are following, but without clear sight.

B. 11:17-57: Resurrection and Reactions

When Jesus arrives near Bethany, he has several quick exchanges before resurrecting Lazarus in 11:38-44. The following analysis is divided by his primary dialogue partners in each scene: 11:17-27, 28-37, 38-44, and 45-57.

Martha's Confessions (11:17-27). Jesus arrives in Bethany in 11:17, and the narrator takes special pains to emphasize his proximity to Jerusalem (v. 18). As Jo-Ann Brant observes, the nearness both heightens the tension of the scene with the potential danger to Jesus and invites comparisons between Lazarus and Jesus that will become more apparent in hindsight (2011, 174). It is also significant that Martha and Mary were not abandoned in their grief. Rather, as Jews themselves, they also were "comforted" or "consoled" by other members of the same religious and ethnic community. This scene rightly problematizes the interpretations of those who vilify the Jews in the Fourth Gospel or, as Susan Hylen argues, those who divide the Jews into subgroups: believers vs. unbelievers. Hylen suggests that we are more faithful to the Gospel's presentation when we recognize that the Jews are a mixture of both/and. She writes, "The portrayal of the Jews suggests a conflicted or divided character, perhaps even a contradictory one, one who believes in Jesus and also seeks to kill him" (118).

In 11:20-27, the action centers on the sisters: Martha goes out to meet Jesus and Mary remains at home. The sisters' actions are both acceptable responses. Brant notes (2011, 171) that the social conventions for women loosened during periods of grief, when they were permitted to express their sorrow and, indeed, were often the chief mourners (cf. Standhartinger). Mary's staying at home is a description of her "sitting in the house" (*en tō oikō ekathezeto*) and is often tied to her similar behavior in Luke 10 (Lee 2013, 209); however, it also corresponds to contemporary Jewish practices of "sitting *shivah*" in which those who are grieving sit, or remain in the home, for the first seven days after an immediate family member dies. Visitors come to console and care for the family, but they are the caretakers; the family is not required to acknowledge these visitors' presence as they mourn. The tradition of seven days of mourning has ancient roots (Gen 50:10; Ezek 8:14; Sir 22:11; 4 Ezra 5:20; Gen. Rab. 3.6; 15.7; 27.4; 32.7; *t. Sanh.* 2.3), although some traditions advocate for a shorter period of time (Sir 38:17-20 suggests only three days) and also include trips to the tomb (*Gos. Pet.* 12.50; Achilles Tatius, *Chaer.*; Corbeill, 67–106). Jesus' arrival on the fourth day after Lazarus's burial means he arrives in the middle of an intense time of mourning.

Meeting Jesus alone, Martha has a short but profound exchange with him. Gail O'Day argues that Martha is confident throughout her conversation with Jesus (2013, 491–502). Martha approaches Jesus and states the facts that also demonstrate her faith ("Lord, if you had been here my brother would not have died," 11:21); twice she uses language of knowledge (11:22, 24) and once of belief (11:27). Unlike the Gospel audience, Martha does not know that Jesus has purposefully delayed his travel, but she does know that Jesus has the power to cure illnesses. Moreover, she anticipates not only Jesus' prayer in 11:41-42 that God will give to Jesus whatever he asks but also Jesus' teaching to his disciples in the Farewell Discourse (14:13-14; 15:7, 16; 16:23-26). Martha also expresses her knowledge (and belief) in the resurrection, a belief that was not universally shared in first-century Judaism, but about which Jesus has repeatedly spoken in his teaching thus far (cf. 5:19-30). Martha may not understand that Jesus means to raise her brother on this day, but she agrees that Jesus *will* raise him (11:25-26). Indeed, Martha's confession in 11:27 mirrors closely the narrator's hope for the Gospel from 20:30-31. In response to Jesus, she states, "I myself have believed that you yourself are the Christ, the Son of God, the one coming into the world!"

Mary and the Jews Come to Jesus (11:28-37). The next scene is also initiated by Martha's actions. Returning home after her confession, she "called" (*ephōnēsen*) her sister aside privately. She says to Mary, "The teacher is calling (*phōnei*) you." The repeated use of the verb *phōneō* resonates with previous uses of this verb, and its related noun *phōnē* (voice), particularly in 10:1-39 where Jesus used these words to describe his "calling" of his sheep and their ability to hear his "voice" (10:3-5, 16). Martha's mimicry of Jesus' call, therefore, not only makes her similar to the disciples from 1:35-51 who brought their brothers and friends to Jesus (1:48) but also implies her participation in Jesus' sheepfold. She, too, is a disciple. Mary's "immediate" (*tachu, tacheōs*; cf. 13:30) response, leaving her mourning posture to see her "teacher" and "Lord," also shows her to be one of Jesus' own. The privacy of Martha's words needs not imply secrecy, since mourners were not obligated to converse with visitors. This could also explain why the Jews do not question Mary but simply assume her travel is to Lazarus's tomb (11:31). Rather than initiating conversation, as Martha was permitted to do as Mary's sister, the visitors remain rightly silent and continue attending Mary.

When Mary comes to Jesus, the text says she "fell at his feet." She then repeats the same statement Martha spoke in v. 21: "Lord, if you had been here, my brother would not have died" (11:32). The repetition creates unity between Mary and Martha, blurring their characters and also contributing to textual variants that may suggest Martha's later addition (Schrader, 381–83; cf. Tertullian, *Adv. Prax.* 23). Mary's statement of fact is accompanied by prostration rather than words of confession like those of her sister. In John 11–12, Mary is more a woman of action than words. Again in 12:1-8 she will remain at Jesus' feet, washing and wiping them, preparing his body for burial rather than her brother's. One should be careful, however, not to assume that Mary is a "better" disciple than Martha. Instead, both women show devotion, simply in different ways. Martha makes clear her faith in 11:17-27, and she enables her sister's coming to Jesus. Mary is like Martha: they both have faith in Jesus, but Mary shows her faith with postures of submission. Rather than putting these models in competition, it is better to see the larger picture of these disciples in unison: words *and* actions make a more complete disciple of Jesus (cf. 1 John 3:16-18).

Instead of repeating his conversation with Martha, Jesus' response to Mary moves the plot forward while also showing his love. Jesus matches Mary's physical display of devotion with one of his own. He observes her "weeping" (*klaiō*, cf. 20:11-15) along with the "weeping" of the Jews around her, and he is "deeply moved in spirit and stirred in himself," so much so that he himself "cried" even though he knows that he has come to "wake up" Lazarus (11:11, 33-34). The suffering that Martha, Mary, *and* the Jews experience is not insignificant to Jesus, or to the Father, whose will and perspective Jesus manifests. Jesus becomes a mourner alongside Mary and the Jews regardless of the end of the story and Lazarus's rising from the dead. In other words, Jesus shows that God is not only focused on the ends, but God also sees the journey and recognizes the reality of the pain that happens along the way. Indeed, it is this sight and this behavior on Jesus' behalf that help explain why God sent his Son into the world even though it results in his death (3:16). First John 4:9-10a reads, "In this the love of God was revealed to us, that God sent his unique Son into the world so that we might have life through him. In this is the love, not that we ourselves loved God, but that God loved us!" Love means sharing not only in joy but also in sorrow (16:19-24). Jesus does both.

It is also significant that it is here that Jesus is "deeply moved in spirit and stirred" and not in his own Gethsemane. John's Gospel seems to refute the Gethsemane tradition of the Synoptics, particularly in Mark (cf. Anderson 2006, 104–10; 2011, 126–52). In Mark 14, Jesus struggles with what is to befall him, asking for prayer from his disciples, and alternatives from God, before ultimately surrendering to his Father's will. Jesus' behavior in Mark is also profound, but different from his behavior in John's Gospel. For John, Jesus is the Word of God made flesh, and he does not ever hesitate to fulfill the Father's will. In John 12:27, Jesus says, "What shall I say, 'Father, save me from this hour?' But for this reason I came, for *this hour.*" Jesus' statement rephrases, and refutes, Mark 14:35, where *Jesus* falls to the ground and prays "so that if possible the hour might pass him by." John displaces Jesus' distress from being over his own approaching death to being over the death of Lazarus. Jesus retains the characteristics of a noble shepherd; he would rather die than lose one of his sheep.

Finally, 11:28-37 reports an interaction between Jesus and the Jews who are comforting Mary and Martha. Again, these Jews are acting as community, joining Martha and Mary in mourning and caring for them in their grief. In 11:28-37 they continue this role, never addressing Mary directly, but attending her and taking over the role of communicating with Jesus so that Mary will not have to do so (11:35). Moreover, their divided response to Jesus is entirely logical, just as the divided reactions to him have been in the past (cf. 7:43; 9:16; 10:19-21). They continue to wonder at the man before them who does miraculous things, and makes incredible claims, but whom they cannot predict or understand. The question, "This one who opened the eyes of the blind man could have made it so that also this one would not have died, couldn't he?" implies a positive answer (11:37). They, like Martha and Mary, know that if Jesus had been there, Lazarus would not have died. The Jews, therefore, join with all of Jesus' disciples (those who traveled with him as well as Martha and Mary) as witnesses in 11:38-44. In this way, they too are ones for whom Jesus rejoiced that he was not present "so that you all might believe (*pisteusēte*)" (11:15).

Lazarus, Come Out! (11:38-44). The story comes to its climax in 11:38-44. Resuming the narrative progression, Jesus is again "deeply moved in himself," a shortened version of his emotional state from 11:33. Locating the tomb, Jesus commands the stone to be taken away. Martha protests, albeit implicitly: "Lord, already it smells, for it has been four days." Martha is often criticized for this comment, which has been seen by some to undercut her confession in 11:27 (cf. Brown 1966, 433). As O'Day explains, it is unclear how much Martha knows; as in 11:21, she is here again stating a fact (2013, 501). The Gospel audience knows that Jesus is aware that it is the fourth day since Lazarus's burial, but only because the narrator reported it in 11:17. From Martha's perspective, it appears that Jesus simply wants to continue his mourning in the tomb.

Jesus' corrective in 11:40 brings the miracle full circle. He tells Martha, "I told you that if you should believe, you will see the glory of God, didn't I?

Therefore, take away the stone." O'Day ties this statement back to Martha's conversation with Jesus in 11:21-27, suggesting that she saw Jesus' "glory" in his self-revelation: "I am the resurrection and the life" (11:25). Jesus' words, however, are closer to 11:4 when Jesus responded to the initial request: "And Jesus said to her, 'The sickness is not for death, but on behalf of the glory of God so that the Son of God might be glorified through it.'" In 11:40 Jesus tells Martha that this is now the time he will fulfill his promise to her, which is beyond what she can immediately imagine.

Jesus continues in 11:42-43 with an audible prayer to the Father. The words of Jesus' prayers are reported only three times in John's Gospel: 11:42-43; 12:27-30; and 17:1-26. In 11:42-43 Jesus is clear that the prayer is not because he doubts his Father's response but so that it can act as testimony for those watching "so that they might believe that you have sent me" (11:43). Jesus expresses this same hope in 12:27-30 and 17:1-26: believing that Jesus has been sent by God is the necessary lens for *seeing* God's glory, that is, for seeing that Jesus himself embodies the glory of God "as one from a father alone" (1:16). Indeed, throughout the Gospel *this* is the crux of the conflict and confusion. In 9:31-33 the formerly blind man says, "We know that God does not hear sinners, but if someone is devout and doing the will of God, this one he hears! From eternity it was not heard that someone opened the eyes of one having been born blind. If this one were not from God, he would not be able to do anything!" Seeing Jesus' origins means seeing Jesus' glory (12:41).

Jesus, again, enacts this paradigm in 11:42-44. He knows God is hearing him and that is why he does what no one else can. If he could open the eyes of one born blind, how much greater is the miracle of raising Lazarus from the dead? Jesus' counterargument to those who do not believe is not words directed toward them but words to his Father that result in action. Jesus calls to his sheep, Lazarus, with a "loud voice" (*phōnē megalē*). This is the same type of voice that the Synoptics have Jesus shout with from the cross prior to his death (Matt 27:46, 50; Mark 15:34, 37; Luke 23:46; cf. Acts 7:60). In John's Gospel, however, Jesus' shout is before the tomb of one of his sheep. His cry is for this one's life. He calls Lazarus by name: "Lazarus, come out!" And Lazarus comes. Rather than being cast from his religious community like the blind man was in 9:34, Lazarus is cast outside of a tomb. Like the man who is still called a "blind man" after he sees, Lazarus is still called "dead" even after his resurrection, demonstrating that, like the rest of the world, he is still need of life. Lazarus needs unbinding in order to be "let go" so that he can "depart" (11:44).

Belief or Fear? (11:45-57). The scene suddenly shifts after Lazarus's resurrection. Not only do we never hear from the "dead man," but his sisters' reactions are also missing, delayed until 12:1-8. Instead, attention returns to the Jews, who were the focus of Jesus' conversation in 11:34-37. In 11:45-46 we learn,

> A. Many, therefore, *from the Jews,*
>> B. the ones who *went* to Mary and saw
>>> C. *the things which he did,* believed in him.
> A'. But certain ones *from them*
>> B'. *went* to the Pharisees and told them
>>> C'. *the things which Jesus did.*

The parallelism reinforces the division that remains among the Jews concerning Jesus. The implication of "the certain ones" going to the Pharisees is that they continued not believing in Jesus, that is, they did not believe that God sent him. If Jesus' actions are not from God, they reveal him to be a threat.

John 11:47-57 outlines the rationale for the plot against Jesus' life. As mentioned in the introduction to this chapter, the fear expressed by these religious leaders *is* logical. If Jesus is not from God, and if he does gather followers as a result of his raising Lazarus as he seems to be doing (11:45; 12:17), then he is dangerous. In this light, their desire to protect "the nation and the place" (the temple) is a good desire; they are acting as shepherds. The perspective of the Gospel, however, regards these shepherds as misinformed. Their desire to protect God's people and place results in the unwitting destruction of them.

Throughout the Gospel, the word "place" (*topos*) is used as a stand-in for "the temple" (4:20; 5:13), meaning the "place" where God's glory resides, as well as Jesus' location. According to the Gospel, the Word's becoming flesh as Jesus means that God's glory is now more completely manifested in the place that is his flesh (1:14). The word *topos* is also used in 11:30 when Mary comes to Jesus, who "was still *in the place* where Martha met him." The contrast in uses of *topos* between 11:30 and 11:48 is telling. Like the Samaritan woman in 4:20 who asks in which "place" (*topos*) is it necessary to worship, the religious leadership is focused on the "place" of the temple in Jerusalem, and with good reason. But the challenge of the Gospel is the radical claim that the place of worship is now in the person of Jesus, because through him followers experience unity with the Father (14:1-14; 17:20-26). For the Gospel, when people see that Jesus is from God, they will recognize the "place" where God resides, regardless of whether or not the temple remains standing. Although a plot is enacted against Jesus, the narrator assures the audience that all of these events are according to God's plan. In 11:51-52, the narrator describes the nature of Caiaphas's prophecy: he may have spoken rightly about Jesus dying "on behalf of the nation," but his speech is limited and ironic. God will not fulfill this prophetic word in the way Caiaphas expects (Reinhartz 2013, 531–34). After all, Jesus has repeatedly spoken about his hour as well as his choice to "lay down his life" from himself rather than having it taken from him (10:17-18). Jesus' departure from Judea in 11:54 delays the plot so that it occurs during the third and final Passover of the Gospel (11:55). The events of this Passover bring together themes from all of the festivals described in the Gospel, creating a climax around Jesus' "hour." As in John 7, the Jews gathered for the festival in 11:56-57 wonder about Jesus' arrival, still puzzling about his identity. But Jesus will not be coaxed into coming early (2:3-4; 7:30; 8:20); instead, he will arrive only when his hour does (12:23; 13:1; 17:1).

C. 12:1-11: Burial Anointing: Food, Feet, and Betrayal (Part 1)

The final segment of the larger inclusio of the Lazarus episode, John 12:1-11, recounts Mary's anointing of Jesus. An episode that appears in each of the Gospels, this scene was famously harmonized in a sixth-century sermon by Pope Gregory the Great with remarkable staying power. In reality, each Gospel's version of Jesus' anointing is different, even though they share elements. John's telling takes place during a meal, six days before Passover, when Jesus comes to Bethany in Judea. Jesus' presence in Bethany outside of Jerusalem contrasts with the travelers from the Judean countryside who traveled to Jerusalem, to the temple, "so that they might purify themselves" before Passover (11:55; 12:1). As in John 2:13-17, early arrival in Jerusalem is not unusual since many Jews would need to participate in sacrifices to become ritually pure before the Passover celebration. Jesus' decision not to come to Jerusalem but rather to go to his friends' home continues the contrast between Jesus as the residence of God's glory versus the temple.

It also creates a point of conflict that becomes more apparent in 12:9-11. While in the temple, some Jews continue to wonder about Jesus and think he may not travel to Jerusalem for the festival (11:56). Nevertheless, "a great crowd of the Jews" knew that Jesus was in Bethany and they *leave Jerusalem* in order to see him *and* in order to see "Lazarus, whom he raised from the dead" (12:9-10). Seeing the threat they feared in 11:45-54 begin to materialize, the lead-priests—the ones who would have been involved in the temple performing the purification rites—decide also that they must work to kill Lazarus along with Jesus, "because many of the Jews, *on account of him*, departed and began believing in Jesus" (12:11). From the perspective of these priests, a large crowd is amassing around a single man as well as the man whose life is a sign of his power, just outside the city limits as the Passover draws near. That Jesus, and Lazarus, have such an ability to draw people away from purification rites to celebrate the Passover, for which they may have traveled many miles, is startling. The problem will only get worse in 12:12-19 when this crowd welcomes Jesus into Jerusalem with songs meant for a king and start testifying on his behalf because they were "with him when he called Lazarus out of the tomb" (12:17). What will Rome think?

Sandwiched between the crowd's interactions with Jesus and Lazarus is Mary's anointing, an act that occupies only one verse but elicits a strong reaction from Judas Iscariot. This private mealtime contrasts the public events that surround it in 11:55-57 and 12:9-36, while also foreshadowing Jesus' final meal (*deipnon*) with his disciples before his death in 13:1-30. It begins with a report about each member of the household. Martha's service is, again, often tied to Luke 10 and, not surprisingly, is rife with textual variants. There is, however, nothing negative implied by her service, or ministry (*diēkonei*), in John 12:2. Lazarus, the dead man, is now "one of the ones reclining" with Jesus, participating in the meal. His eating reinforces the reality of his resurrection; he reclines alive at a meal that could have otherwise been one to mark his passing. Mary's actions, though, are striking, emphasized by the parallelism of 12:3:

> A. Mary, therefore, having taken a **jar of myrrh nard**, genuine and costly,
>   B. <u>anointed</u> the *feet of Jesus*,
>   B'. and <u>wiped dry</u> with her hair *the feet of him*.
> A'. And the house was filled from the **fragrance of the myrrh**.

The focus on Jesus' feet repeats Mary's prostration from 11:32. It is also significant given the upcoming role of Jesus washing his disciples' feet in John 13. Preceding even Jesus' own actions, Mary acts an ideal disciple.

Mary, however, does not "wash" Jesus' feet; she "anoints" (*ēleipsen*) them, a preparatory action setting Jesus apart for what is to come (12:3, 7). Anointing not with water but with "genuine and costly" myrrh nard, she abases herself by bending to the floor behind where Jesus would have reclined and wiping his feet with her hair. This not only would have required a closeness between Mary's face and Jesus' feet but is also fraught with intimacy since a woman's hair was often sexualized in the ancient Mediterranean world, as were men's "feet" (Martin, 79–82). Married women wore veils in public, including some Jewish women, which was the mark of a matron, a woman not available for other men's attentions (Ilan, 129–32). Mary's uncovered hair would have been normal since she was in her home and therefore only around family and close friends; however, using her hair to wipe Jesus' feet is shocking, and it is open to critique according to ancient mores because she and Jesus are not husband and wife.

Recalling patristic traditions, Dominika Kurek-Chomycz highlights connections between this scene and the Song of Songs because of their unique imagery surrounding the pleasant aroma of nard (Sol 1:12; 4:13-14). She notes the specific role that aroma has in "association with the lover's identity" in Songs 1:2-3, when the bride proclaims, "Let him kiss me with the kisses of his mouth! For your love is better than wine, your anointing oils are fragrant, your name is perfume poured out" (342). Kurek-Chomycz argues Songs 1:12-13 is even closer to the scene in John 12:3. In both stories the "fragrance" (osmē) of the nard pours out while the king, or Jesus, reclines (anaklisei) at the table. For Kurek-Chomycz, even though modern-day readers are uncomfortable with associations with Songs because of the potential for sexual imagery, the overlap between John and Songs is an important part of John's characterization of Jesus as king (343). It should also be noted that erotic language was commonplace in conversion narratives and depictions of philosophical and religious devotion in the ancient world, which is why patristic authors do not avoid the allusion (Lipsett). Characters in John's Gospel have previously described Jesus as "king" (1:49), even though Jesus himself resisted such an identity in 6:15. He does not, however, shy away from Mary's royal anointing in John 12, nor will he resist the title during his entrance in Jerusalem (12:13) or before Pilate in 18:33-38. The difference is one of context. Rather than a kingship that mirrors that of earthly kings, Jesus' kingship becomes most apparent in his exaltation upon the cross that ultimately leads to his return to the Father.

Judas's reaction to Mary's behavior highlights neither the social transgression nor the royal connotations but rather the monetary investment. He is astounded at the cost of the perfume, asking, "Why was the myrrh not sold for three hundred denarii and given to the poor?!" (12:5). The extravagant amount even exceeds that mentioned by Philip in 6:7, "Bread worth two hundred denarii is not sufficient" for the crowd gathered at the mountain. Judas's concern, the narrator tells us, is not the poor but rather his own pockets since he was a "thief who used to take from the things cast into the money-box" (12:6; cf. 10:8-10). The characterization of Judas as an intentionally duplicitous disciple in John contrasts that of other Gospels, most notably Matthew, which offers a pitiable Judas killing himself out of remorse (Robertson). In John, however, Judas is consistently a negative and deceptive character (Wright). He is among the believing disciples in 6:67-71, but Jesus already knows his true identity as a "devil." The scene in John 12 foreshadows the next meal Jesus will share with his disciples in John 13, where Judas's role of keeping the "money-box" is again recounted and where he, after Jesus' instruction, begins enacting the plan of betrayal (13:26-30). Judas's behavior, while appearing righteous on the surface, is a dramatic contrast to Mary's own faithfulness, which appears inappropriate. Once again, Jesus' admonition to "stop judging by appearances but with just judgment" rings true (7:24).

The Hour Has Come: From Public to Private (12:12–13:30)
John 12:12 begins five days before Passover, the third and final Passover of the Gospel, with Jesus' final entrance into Jerusalem. His public entrance contrasts the private meal he will have with his disciples in 13:1-30, just before Judas Iscariot leaves to initiate his betrayal. In both settings, the arrival of Jesus' hour is emphasized (12:23; 13:1). Although Jesus no longer walked "openly" (*parrēsia*, 11:54) in Judea before, with the coming of his hour he enters boldly as the "great crowd" welcomes him as "King of Israel" (12:13; cf. 12:9-11). This dramatic scene is followed by one last dialogue between Jesus and a "great crowd" of worshipers, which includes his disciples as well as some "Greeks" who have come to Jerusalem for the festival (12:19-21). These final public moments before Jesus' crucifixion end with his implied rejection by the same crowd who welcomed him moments before. The narrator recounts Isaiah's prophetic "word" from Isa 6:10, a version of which appears in each of the canonical Gospels as well as Acts as an explanation for Jesus' rejection that results from the crowd's misunderstanding (John 12:40; Matt 13:14-15; Mark 4:12; Luke 8:10; Acts 28:26-27; cf. Evans). In John 13:1-30 the scene moves to a private encounter between Jesus and his disciples, who are also not immune from the charges of the narrator in 12:37-43 or Jesus' summary in 12:44-50. Wrestling with Jesus' washing of their feet as well as his description of the "one" who will betray him, Peter's reactions epitomize the confusion among Jesus' closest companions. The coming of Jesus' hour, in both public and private settings, may be an hour of glorification, but it is glory in ways that the world cannot yet recognize.

A. 12:12-19: The King's Entrance
This first portion of 12:12-50 begins Jesus' final time in Jerusalem and continues rehearsing the aftereffects of his raising Lazarus. In 11:45-53 the Pharisees and lead-priests gathered in a council and decided, after Caiaphas's

prophetic word, to orchestrate means for Jesus' death. John 12:9-11 tells of the lead-priests' decision to extend this plan to include Lazarus's death as well, since many Jews were leaving Jerusalem to find Jesus because of him. Lazarus is mentioned for the third time in 12:17, described as the one whom Jesus "raised from the dead" (12:1, 11, 17). The Pharisees then react to the lead-priests' plan from 12:9-11, highlighting its futility. Despite their desire to kill Lazarus and stem the tide of those seeking Jesus, the "great crowd which came for the feast" welcomed Jesus into Jerusalem as a king, forming an inversion of a Roman Triumph and declaring Jesus' victory (12:12-13). The Pharisees' words are also unknowingly prophetic in v. 19: "Look, you can do nothing! See, the world went after him!" As Jesus has emphasized throughout the Gospel, and will continue to demonstrate now that his hour has come, nothing can thwart God's will.

John 12:12-19 has three parts: vv. 12-14a, 14b-16, 17-19. Like 12:1-8, it is a single scene interrupted, this time by the narrator in 12:14b-16. The scene is vividly presented by the narrator: the "great crowd" who traveled to Bethany to see Jesus and Lazarus now gathers to bless Jesus' arrival in Jerusalem. Andrew Brunson notes that the psalm quoted by the crowd is Ps 118, which is a Hallel psalm, praising God for victory and sung at festivals. The image of welcoming a king with a procession at the gates is not only well attested in OT and Second Temple Jewish literature but was also practiced by the Romans (Brant 2011, 189; cf. Polybius, *Hist.* 30.25; Josephus, *J.W.* 7.132–57). When a general, or emperor, succeeded in a conquest, he entered Rome dressed in purple and crowned, showcasing his captives and treasures as he paraded through the city before arriving to offer a sacrifice at the temple of Jupiter. In John's version (and that of the other Gospels), Jesus imitates the Roman Triumph and subverts it, coming into the city with hails of blessing upon a young donkey, as Solomon did in 1 Kgs 1:32-40. Solomon's humble entrance contrasts Adonijah's parade of chariots, to demonstrate his succession of David (Coloe 2013, 213). Like Solomon, Jesus does not conquer with an army, but through his submission. Nevertheless, any image of conquest could be seen as a threat to Rome.

The narrator explains Jesus' actions in 12:14b-16, using a scriptural introduction found three other places in the Gospel: "just as it has been written" (2:17; 6:31, 45). The connection to 2:17 is especially significant, because like 12:16, John 2:17-22 emphasizes the disciples' ignorance of the events they saw in the moment. They needed reminding after Jesus "was glorified," a reference not only to his death but also to his resurrection and return to the Father, after which Jesus comes back to give the Holy Spirit in 20:22. The reminder helps the disciples associate Jesus' behavior, as well as that of the crowd, with Scripture, specifically Zech 9:9 (cf. Zeph 3:14-15; Isa 44:2; Coloe 2013a, 212). As in John 7, Zech 9–14 tells the story of the messianic king arriving in Jerusalem during Tabernacles to declare the day of the Lord. Even though Jesus was in Jerusalem for Tabernacles in John 7–8, the narrator repeatedly told the audience that it was not Jesus' "hour"; indeed, the entire story begins with Jesus telling his brothers, "My time (*kairos*) is not yet, but your time (*kairos*) is always here. . . . I myself am not going up to this feast, because my time (*kairos*) has not yet been fulfilled" (7:6-7). The fulfillment of Jesus' time (*kairos*) comes only in John 12 onward, when he chooses to enter the city not at Tabernacles but just before the third Passover.

The Tabernacles resonances, however, should not be overlooked. As Brunson notes, Tabernacles is a more fitting context for the use of palm branches in John 12:13, which would have been used for constructing booths for Tabernacles but are not called for in Passover celebrations (215–22). Rather than suggesting John's ineptitude, it seems better to notice how he brings together various motifs from all the festival contexts from John 2–10 into John 11–21: this is Jesus' time, his hour, when he will draw all things to himself (12:32). Aspects of the previous festivals now collide under Jesus' orchestrated and chosen actions that fulfill Scripture. Even the unwitting actions of others fulfill Scripture, therefore cohering to God's design (Myers 2012, 156–57). By reenacting Ps 118, the crowd works with Jesus to create a double testimony of his identity as God's chosen King, bringing to life not only the thanksgiving psalm but also Zechariah in the first of three double-quotation scenes that punctuate John's Passion Narrative (12:37-41; 19:36-37).

B. 12:20-36: We Want to See Jesus

The Pharisees' comment that "the world went" to Jesus is reinforced in 12:20-36 as a crowd of Greeks joins the "great crowd" going up to Jerusalem to worship. This could be a reference to Hellenistic Jews, that is, Jews who speak Greek rather than Aramaic as their primary language (Thompson 2015, 264). Such an identity fits the previous reference to "Greeks" in John 7:35 as the Jews wonder if Jesus means to depart to the "Dispersion" (outside Palestine) in order to teach Greek-speaking Jews. Mary Coloe (2013a) suggests that these Greeks are Gentiles, coming to Jesus to demonstrate the realization of his eschatological and "cosmological" kingship in contrast to the "nationalistic" hopes of the crowd gathered around him. If Coloe is correct, the inclusion of Gentiles in John 12 continues the reach of the Gospel, which already included a royal official's household and Samaritans in the fold.

The specific identity (Jewish or Gentile) of this group is not clarified, perhaps because the Gospel assumes its audience will know the ethnic identity of these Greeks already. The emphasis in the story is that they come to see Jesus. Their arrival illustrates not only "the world" going after Jesus but also that Jesus' departure does not mean he is leaving for the Diaspora in order to teach Greeks there (7:35). Instead, Jesus, the noble shepherd, gathers his sheep around him when they hear his voice. Their coming to Jesus is part of the larger collection of motifs from previous scenes in the Gospel that coalesce in John 12. Some of the other repeating images include the phrase "on the next day" (*tē epaurion*, 1:29, 35, 43; 6:22; 12:12), requests to "see" Jesus (1:39, 46; 4:29; 12:21), and the appearance of Philip and Andrew as well as the information about their hometown being Bethsaida (1:44; 12:21). The scene also brings to mind John 6, where these two disciples approach Jesus to feed the crowd. Jesus' description of grain in 12:24-26, and its implicit association with food, reinforces this connection and brings in imagery from 4:35, where Jesus described the disciples' need to harvest that for which they did not labor. Jesus will talk again about light and darkness, walking/living, the Son of Man, and glorification, and he will pray a prayer for the sake of the crowd rather than for himself, all of which repeat from previous sections in the Gospel. While the exact identity of the Greeks, therefore, remains ambiguous, the literary function of John 12 does not: the chapter brings together references to Jesus' teachings and signs, creating a climactic moment of transition. It is here that everything has been brought together, and the collision demonstrates Jesus' dramatic proclamation, "The hour has come that the Son of Man should be glorified!" (12:23).

Jesus' conversation with the crowd of worshipers can be split into three parts: vv. 20-26, 27-33, and 34-36. In 12:20-26, Jesus declares the arrival of his hour and offers another *paroimia*, or parable, to describe the necessity of his own death (cf. Zimmermann 2015, 340–44). Jesus' death is a constant theme of 12:20-36 as part of the "hour" of his glorification. As noted above, Jesus' speech resembles the previous *paroimia* in 4:35-38 and so involves those who come after the sower to harvest the "fruit" grown from the seed's death. This work will not necessarily be easy. The sacrifice of the servant points ahead to Jesus' words to his disciples in John 15–17 that they will have to cope with the world's hatred, just as Jesus did, even as he saved it. By mimicking Jesus' priorities, the servant will experience "eternal life" and "honor" from the Father rather than death and fickle "glory from people" (12:25-26, 43, 50).

In 12:27-33 Jesus continues with the theme of his coming death, recasting Gethsemane traditions from a dark moment of solitude between

Jesus and his Father to a public pronouncement before a great crowd that is endorsed by "a voice from heaven." In the Synoptics, the "voice from heaven" speaks during Jesus' baptism (Matt 3:17; Mark 1:11; 3:22). In John, however, the voice speaks here as direct divine testimony: "Indeed I have glorified it [my name] and I will glorify [it] again!" (12:28). The voice's immediate response to Jesus' devotion and use of the first person shows that *God hears Jesus,* an unambiguous proof supporting the formerly blind man's testimony from 9:31-33 and Jesus' own claims from 11:38-44. The crowd is again divided; even a voice from God did not help them recognize Jesus. This does not mean that God's testimony has been deflected. Instead, Jesus explains, "Now is the judgment of this world; now the ruler of this world has been cast out outside! And I myself, when I am exalted from the earth, I will draw all things to myself." (12:31-32). God's statement in 12:28 is a statement of reality, covering the past, the present, and the future glorification of God's name. The misunderstanding crowd is a revelation of the world's spiritual deafness that corresponds to its metaphorical blindness (9:40-41; 12:37-41; Isa 6:9-10). Rather than abandoning the world to darkness and wrath, however, God's Son will be "exalted"—crucified, resurrected, and returned to the Father—to reveal God's love for the world.

Jesus and the crowd complete their exchange in 12:34-36, repeating scenes from John 6, 7, and 10 where parties quote Scripture to one another in an attempt to understand Jesus' identity and claims. The source of the crowd's quotation is open to debate, since there are several locations where God promises an unending reign to David's successors (2 Sam 7:12-16; Ezek 37:25; cf. John 7:40-44). The language of 12:34 is close to Ps 89:36 (88:37 LXX), which is part of a psalm recounting God's unending covenant with David. In Ps 89:36 the psalmist writes, "his seed will remain forever" (*to sperma autou eis ton aiōna menei*); compare to John 12:34, which reads, "The Christ remains forever" (*ho christos menei eis ton aiōna*). If the crowd is alluding to this psalm, they are repeating Jesus' language from John 10:34 when he cited a psalm as coming from "the law." In John 12:35-36, Jesus responds to the crowd's confusion, not with another scriptural reference (contra 6:32) but with a command in the form of another *paroimia*: "Walk (or Live) while you have the light!" This command repeats Jesus' teaching before a Jerusalem crowd in 8:12 and before his own disciples in 9:3-5 and 11:9-10 (cf. 1 John 2:10-11). Now is not the time for more scriptural debates; rather, these are the last moments that the light will be on the earth. As in 8:59, Jesus suddenly disappears from the crowd, being "concealed" (*ekrybē*, a passive verb, implying divine involvement rather than Jesus "hiding" himself) from them without hearing their answer (12:36).

C. 12:37-50: Who Can See the Glory of God?

John 12:37-43 is a narrative aside that describes the crowd's disbelief as a fulfillment of Isaianic prophecy. Even though the form of John's Isa 6:10 quotation differs from any known form of the text, its use resembles quotations of Isa 6:9-10 elsewhere in the NT. John also quotes from Isa 53:1 immediately beforehand, tying these two passages together as a single explanation for Jesus' rejection. The appeal to Isaiah at the end of Jesus' public ministry parallels the initial quotation from Isaiah by John (the Baptist) just prior to Jesus' first appearance. In John 1:23, John (the Baptist) quoted Isa 40:3 to characterize himself as the Isaianic voice "crying in the wilderness" and *not* as the Lord or the Christ. Jesus also quotes from Isaiah once during his own ministry, in 6:45 (Isa 54:13), but he does not mention Isaiah by name—something that only happens in 1:23 and 12:37-41. In this way, the narrator highlights Isaiah specifically at the beginning and end of Jesus' public ministry, creating an inclusio that casts Jesus' ministry in light of Isaiah's own.

This reading is reinforced by the quotation of Isa 53:1 in John 12:37: "Lord, who believed in our message (*akoē*)? And the arm of the Lord, to whom was it revealed?" The larger context of Isa 53 recounts the work God's servant—Isaiah and Israel but, from the Gospel's perspective, also John (the Baptist) and most especially Jesus—through whom God has spoken and revealed his word (Isa 55:1-11). Rather than arguing for a fully articulated Suffering Servant reading of Isa 52–53, the Gospel's readings resemble interpretations of Isaiah from the Second Temple period, during which Isaiah was recognized as a faithful prophet whose message was nevertheless rejected by kings and the people in spite of the signs he performed (cf. Isa 7–9; John 12:37). Indeed, when God commissions Isaiah, God tells him that he will be rejected. After Isaiah volunteers to be sent, the Lord tells him,

> Go and say to this people:
>> "Keep listening, but do not comprehend;
>> Keep looking, but do not understand."
> Make the mind of this people dull,
>> and stop their ears,
>> and shut their eyes,
> so that they may not look with their eyes,
>> and listen with their ears,
> and comprehend with their minds,
>> and turn and be healed. (6:9-10, NRSV)

When Isaiah responds, "How long, O LORD?" God is unrelenting: "Until the cities lie waste without inhabitant, and houses without people, and the

land is utterly desolate" (6:11). The prophecy in Isaiah refers to Judah's
exile to Babylon as an explanation for Judah's destruction that ultimately
led to the people's return (Isa 40–66). Nevertheless, the image of a prophet
whose message was rejected had staying power in the Second Temple period,
including for early Jesus followers who saw in their Messiah the same pattern
repeated.

In the book of Isaiah, the prophet's understanding, like John (the
Baptist's) in the Gospel of John, is not based on his own virtue but rather
on divine intervention. Upon seeing God's glory fill the temple around him,
Isaiah recognizes his "unclean lips" (Isa 6:5). Rather than condemning Isaiah,
God purifies him and gives him revelation. John (the Baptist), too, requires
divine patience and revelation to understand Jesus' identity, the glory of God
in the flesh (John 1:29-34). Isaiah's vision is alluded to in John 12:41 as
the explanation for Isaiah's understanding, even about Jesus himself: "Isaiah
said these things because he saw his glory and he spoke about him." Catrin
Williams suggests that the narrator means that Isaiah saw Jesus, rather than
God directly, just as Abraham "saw his [Jesus'] day and was glad" (John 8:56;
Williams 2005, 112–13). Indeed, the Aramaic version of Isa 6:1 says just
that: "Isaiah saw the glory of the Lord" (*Tg. Ps.-J.*). Like Abraham, Isaiah
was also said to have seen future events in Second Temple Jewish and early
Christian writings (Sir 48:22-25; *Mart. Ascen. Isa.* 3:14–4:22; 6–11). The
Gospel may, however, simply be equating God's glory with God's Word, as it
does in the opening chapter (John 1:14-18). Even if Isaiah did not see Jesus
himself, the message is that he would have recognized him because he is the
manifestation of God's glory, a sight he was not able to forget. In this way,
Isaiah too is a member of the Johannine community, as a part of the "we"
who "saw his glory" (*etheasametha tēn doxan autou*, 1:14).

In contrast, the world reacts more like the Judeans (*Ioudaioi*) to whom
Isaiah spoke during his ministry: they have blinded eyes and hardened hearts.
According to John, the "many" who believed in Jesus, even "from the rulers,"
did not confess their faith "because of the Pharisees . . . so that they might
not become *aposynagōgoi*," that is, ones cast out of the synagogue (12:42-43).
The fear of these believers makes sense in the narrative, since the blind man
was "cast out outside" by the Pharisees after he confessed that Jesus must be
"from God" (9:31-34). This fear is misplaced fear, idolatry, because it reveals
that "they loved glory from people more than the glory of God" (12:43).
This summary repeats Jesus' condemnation of the Jewish leaders in 5:41-44
that they prefer glory from one another rather than "the glory from the one
who alone is God" (cf. 7:45-52). The leaders are not alone in this behavior,
however, as the narrator also finds this inappropriate fear and desire among

others (2:23-25; 4:43-54; 7:18; 8:50-54). As in Isaiah's day, God's glory is in competition with idols (Isa 8:16-22; 40:18-20; 42:14-20; 44:9-20).

This is also the key criticism in John 12:44-50, where Jesus says that his appearance and his words are the manifestation of the one who sent him. These verses have often troubled interpreters who wonder why Jesus suddenly "cries out" after having been concealed in 12:36 (cf. 1:15; 7:28, 37; Brown 1966, 490). Jesus' statement, however, creates a parallel to the narrator's telling of Isaiah's words in 12:37-43. Both Isaiah and Jesus "spoke" (*elalēsen*) what they were given to say (12:36, 41, 48-50), and rather than undermining them, the rejection each faced reaffirms their divine commission. This section also concludes motifs from John 11 onward of opportunities to "see" God's glory and to "see" Jesus (11:40; 12:9, 21, 40-41, 45). Even though the great crowd, disciples, Pharisees, lead-priests, Greeks, and "the whole world" saw Jesus physically in the story, our narrator concludes that they did not compre-hend his glory. Rather than speaking to any of these characters, in 12:44 -50 Jesus speaks directly to the Gospel audience, summarizing his teaching from John 1–12 while also foreshadowing elements of the Farewell Discourse (cf. 14:1-31). Hearing the Word of God who is no longer is physically present with them, the Gospel audience is still invited to "see" his glory made flesh in the speaking of these words.

Finally, the association between John, Jesus, and Isaiah here and elsewhere could further explain the Gospel's insistence on the term *Ioudaios* (Jew or Judean), since Isaiah's ministry was primarily based in the southern kingdom of Judah. *Ioudaia* (Judea) is used twenty-eight times in Isaiah, twenty-five times in Isa 1–40 alone (Isa 1:1; 2:1; 3:1, 8; 5:3, 7:1, 6, 17, etc.) and the specific term "the Judeans" or "the Jews" (*tōn Ioudaiōn*) appears in Isa 19:17. The term is common in postexilic writings, especially in the stories of the Jewish revolt against Antiochus IV in 1–4 Maccabees (see also Ezra-Neh; Est; *1 Esdr.*). By calling Jesus' interlocutors *Ioudaioi*, the Gospel further connects Jesus' ministry to Isaiah's. Like Isaiah, Jesus speaks to Jews who are fearful of foreign nations more powerful than they, leading them to make compromises that both the writers of Isaiah and John consider idolatrous. Jesus knows that he, his message (*akoē*), and his words (*rhēmata*) will be rejected, just they were when spoken by Isaiah. This does not mean, though, that all is lost. Instead, God remains faithful and loyal, loving the world, even through another "exile." In John 2:19, Jesus commands the *Ioudaioi* to "destroy this sanctuary, and I will rebuild it in three days." As I suggested in chapter 2, Jesus' language recalls the Babylonian invasion, and it also ends with a promise of restoration. Jesus' death, the temporary destruction of his *sōma* (body), the sanctuary of God's glory, does not destroy God's glory—such a thing is not possible. Rather, it is the solution to the moral impurity of the world and enables the dwelling of God's Spirit among believers.

D. 13:1-30: Another Private Meal: Food, Feet, and Betrayal (Part 2)
John 13:1 is the classic break between the Book of Signs and the Book of Glory used by many to outline the Gospel (Brown 1970, 563; Keener 2003, 899; Thompson 2015, 279–80). There is good reason to begin a new section here. In 13:1 the narrator starts with another temporal reference and high-lights Jesus' knowledge of the arrival of his hour, taking the time to define this "hour" with greater precision than has been done up to this point. Leaving 13:1-30 as part of the previous section, however, acknowledges the hinge structure outlined above, made of various chain-links that begin in John 11. Viewed in this way, John 13:1-30 marks the end of the transitional hinge, where Jesus participates in his final meal with his disciples and instigates the betrayal by Judas with the coming of night (13:30; cf. 9:3-5; 11:9-10; 12:35-36). It also creates several contrasts, the most apparent between Jesus, who "loved his own into completion" (13:1), and Judas Iscariot, who is demonically inspired to betray the one who loves him (13:2, 27-30).

John 13:1-30 can be broken down into three sections: vv. 1-11, 12-20, and 21-30. The center is Jesus' teaching concerning the foot-washing as well as the coming betrayal by Judas (vv. 12-20). Both teachings are enacted by Jesus, first when he washes the disciples' feet as an "example" (*hypodeigma*) for them to imitate (vv. 1-11), and second when he dips the piece of bread and gives it to Judas (vv. 21-30). Jesus' teaching pivots at 13:17-18 as he transitions from the foot-washing to the betrayal proper. Although Judas's role is emphasized throughout the episode, he is mentioned explicitly only at the beginning (v. 2) and end of the section (v. 27), along with his demonic connections, to create an inclusio that brackets the passage along with Peter's appearances (vv. 6-11, 24-26).

Jesus remains in control of the entire scene, even though it anticipates his departure and betrayal. Jesus' hour has come, but he is not a victim of circumstance. Instead, in laying down his outer garments (*tithēsin ta himatia*, 13:4; cf. 19:2, 5, 23-24), he demonstrates to his disciples that he lays down his own life on their behalf because he has chosen to do so. Even though he lays these garments down, he also "receives" or "takes" (*labōn*) them back again in 13:12, just as he will his life. In this way, Jesus models more than just hospitality with foot-washing; he shows his disciples how to be noble shepherds and sheep (10:17-18; cf. 13:36-38).

The Foot-washing (13:1-11). John's Gospel does not have a "Last Supper" meal celebrating Passover like the Synoptic Gospels. John situates Jesus' death on the same day that the Passover lambs were slaughtered, the Day of Preparation, rather than on Passover itself (John 18:28; 19:14; cf. Mark 14:12-16; Matt 26:17-19; Luke 22:15; see Brown 1970, 555–58). Because Jesus dies *before* the Passover meal is eaten in John, he cannot participate in that meal with his disciples. This difference has caused concern over what happened during Jesus' final meal, as well as when it was; these issues, however, are not John's primary concern (cf. Keener 2003, 901). It is not that ancient authors did not care about historical accuracy; they did—and they could be criticized if they veered too far from traditional memories (Theon, *Prog.* 78)—but all good historians (ancient and modern) are motivated to communicate the "truth" as they see it. Aelius Theon writes that credibility is a narrative's "most special feature," valued above conciseness or clarity, the other two key virtues of the genre (*Prog.* 79–85; cf. Aristotle, *Rhet.* 3.16.4–7; Quintilian, *Inst.* 4.2.36–53). For ancients, achieving credibility had greater flexibility since no one could expect verbatim accounts of events or words (Lucian, *How to Write History*; Thuc., *Hist.* 1.22.1). It is important to remember that John's focus is primarily theological and christological. He is writing a biography (focusing on a particular person), not a historiography (focusing on events), and, while there are overlaps between the genres, John makes clear that the Gospel's aim is to show his audience that Jesus is the Christ, the Son of God (20:30-31). For this Gospel at least, that means Jesus is the ultimate Passover Lamb, whose death on the Day of Preparation showcases both God's love that seeks to deliver as well as the world's mistake or sin in killing God's gift of Life (cf. 1:29). This is the truth that John communicates (for more, see General Introduction).

Instead of a Eucharistic scene, in John's Gospel the ritual Jesus reshapes is that of foot-washing, an act precipitated by Mary's anointing in 12:1-11. Jesus interprets the foot-washing in 13:12-17, where it is described in terms of purity (*katharos*) rather than hygienic cleanliness. After their washing, Jesus declares that the disciples are "wholly pure" (*katharos holos*), although not all of them (13:10-11; cf. *katharos* in 15:2-3). In John's Gospel, Jesus' final meal reinterprets not the Passover meal but rather the purification of those who would participate in Passover in the days to come. John 11:55 describes the crowd coming "so that they might sanctify themselves" in Jerusalem; in 13:1-11, Jesus provides an act of purification for his disciples, one that centers on his own model of love "to completion" (13:1).

John 13:1-5 emphasizes Jesus' knowledge and deliberate actions. Jesus is motivated to act upon the knowledge that "the Father gave to him all things in his hands and that he came from God and is departing to God" (13:4). Jesus' knowledge contrasts that of Judas Iscariot, whose motivation is diabolical rather than heavenly. In 13:2, the narrator explains the devil's role, writing, "the devil, having already thrown (*beblēkotos*) into the heart that he, Judas of Simon Iscariot, should betray him" (cf. 13:5 where Jesus "throws," *ballei*, the water into the basin). The Greek is emphatic about the betrayer's identity, just as it was in 6:70-71, the first time Judas was introduced. The demonic connections also resurface from 6:70 in 13:2 and 13:27, where the narrator explains, "after the dipping, then Satan entered into *that one* [Judas]." The Gospel and Letters of John consistently associate diabolical activity with murder, as laid out in John 8:44 where Jesus says, "You are from your father, the devil, and you desire to do your father's desires. *That one* was a murderer (*anthrōpoktonos*) from the beginning and the truth does not stand in him, because the truth is not in him" (cf. 1 John 3). God "commands eternal life" (12:50), while the devil desires murder and death.

Those who work for death, therefore, are aligned with the devil's activity in the Gospel and 1 John (John 6:70; 8:44; 13:2, 27; 1 John 3:8-10). This does not imply that people are aware of this activity, since those working against Jesus do so out of fear of their own deaths and the destruction of the temple (11:45-53). They wrongly think Jesus brings death rather than life and thus accuse him of demonic possession (7:20; 8:48-52; 10:20-21). Judas, likewise, may not realize his submission to demonic forces. Nevertheless, this does not release Judas from the responsibility of his choices any more than it will prevent Jesus' own death. Instead, the good news is God's enduring love to resolve the world's misrecognition. As Jesus says in 12:31, "Now is the judgment of this world; now the ruler of this world was cast out outside!" While John's Gospel may not present Jesus as performing a variety of exorcisms, it does depict Jesus' demonstration of God's love through his death, resurrection, and return to the Father as a type of exorcism. It is by means of Jesus' obedience that he declares victory over the world (16:33).

Judas is not the only disciple ignorant of Jesus' actions, even if he is the only one identified as Jesus' betrayer. Simon Peter makes another appearance in John 13, the first time he has spoken since his confession in 6:69 that Jesus is "the Holy One of God." Although he has confessed faith in Jesus' words in 6:68 ("You have the words of eternal life!"), he nonetheless challenges Jesus' words in 13:6-11 and 13:36-38, resisting what Jesus knows with his own ignorance. In both instances, Peter is rejecting the same thing: that Jesus will "lay down" his life on Peter's behalf. As Peter knows, it is not socially acceptable for a superior to be humiliated before his followers (on foot-washing, see Keener 2003, 902–907), yet Peter's public challenges to Jesus (twice!) also disrupt the hierarchy. Peter may call Jesus "Lord," but his behavior exposes rebellious instincts (13:13). In 13:38 Jesus reveals just how wrong-headed

Peter's complaints are: "*You* will lay down your life on my behalf!? Truly, truly I tell you, surely the rooster will not call (*phōnēsē*) until you should deny me thrice!" As Jesus knows, *he himself* will lay down his life, as well as take it back, for the sake of his disciples. They will not be equipped to follow his lead until after the Father's work is finished (19:28-30; 20:20-23; 21:15-19).

Jesus' Teaching (13:12-20). Having washed his disciples' feet, Jesus "took" his garments again and now rejoins his companions, reclining at the table. He explains his actions, beginning with a question: "Do you know what I have done for you?" (13:12). Rather than waiting for an answer, Jesus continues in vv. 13-17: if he, who is their Lord and Teacher, has inverted the usual hierarchy by washing their feet, how much more should they be willing to do so for one another? Jesus says he has given them an "example," a *hypodeigma*. Alan Culpepper (1991, 142) argues that while this may mean that disciples are to wash one another's feet, or serve one another, in John's Gospel it also means they should be "ready to die for one another" (John 15:13; 16:2; 21:19). Looking at the term *hypodeigma* in particular, Culpepper notes its use in contexts that "mark an exemplary death" (142–43; cf. 2 Macc 6:28, 31; 4 Macc 17:22-23; Sir 44:16). For the Johannine community, therefore, living according to the example of Jesus means showing concrete love in words and deeds, even when the cost is one's life (12:24-26; 13:31-35; 1 John 3:13-18). It is fitting, then, that Jesus ends the first portion of his teaching with the Gospel's first statement of blessing in John 13:17: "If you all know these things, you are blessed if you all are *doing* them." Knowledge cannot remain abstract; true knowledge is shown through deeds.

In 13:18-20, Jesus shifts the teaching back toward the identity of his betrayer, just as he did in 6:70-71 and 13:10-11. In 13:18 Jesus repeats his words from 6:70, although they are now a statement rather than a rhetorical question: "I know whom I chose." He will again emphasize his role in choosing in 15:16 and 19, using the same aorist middle form of the verb *eklegō* (*exelexamēn*, "I chose for myself"). That Jesus selected the Twelve reinforces his knowledge of his betrayer in contrast to his disciples' ignorance. Stephen Voorwinde argues that Jesus chose Judas in spite of his knowledge that he was "a devil." He suggests that Jesus also loved Judas as "one of his own" even "to the end" (13:1). Nevertheless, he chose Judas because he knew "from the beginning . . . who will betray him" (6:64). In 13:18, Voorwinde writes, "at last the reason for this mysterious choice is divulged": namely, that Judas's selection and betrayal fulfills Scripture, Ps 41:9 (214). In John 17:12 Jesus also says Judas's perishing (*apōleto*) was to fulfill Scripture, probably another reference to Ps 41:9 (103, n. 100; cf. Myers 2012, 129).

Jesus' citation of Ps 41:9 (LXX Ps 40:10) in John 13:18 also links this passage back to John 6. Jesus says, "I know the ones I chose for myself, but so that the Scripture might be fulfilled, 'The one *chomping* my bread lifted his heel against me'" (*ho trōgōn mou ton arton epēren ep eme tēn pternan autou*; cf. John 6:54, 56, 57, 58). Jesus emphasizes his quotation with a fulfillment formula, but the quotation itself does not match any known version of the psalm (LXX: "The one eating my loaves exalted his heel against me," *ho esthiōn artous mou emegalynen ep eme pternismon*). The changes made, however, fit the larger context of John's Gospel, especially John 6. In 6:53-58 Jesus offends his listeners by calling on them to "chomp" (*trōgō*, 6:54, 56, 57, 58) his flesh, which is "bread" and "true food." In John 6:31-58, Jesus regularly uses the singular form of "bread" (*arton*, 13 times) rather than the plural that appears in the LXX version of the psalm (*artous*). For the audience listening to the Gospel, these connections again emphasize Judas's identity as the betrayer; at the same time, however, they reveal the continued ignorance of the disciples who do not notice the resonance with Jesus' previous words.

Studying the use of the Psalms in John, Margaret Daly-Denton explores thorough, albeit implicit, comparisons between Jesus and David in the Gospel (193–95). The use of the Psalms to describe Jesus' suffering is especially striking, surfacing in John 2:17 (Ps 69:10); 13:18 and 17:12 (Ps 41:9); 15:25 (Ps 35:19 or 69:4); 19:24 (Ps 22:19); 19:28 (Ps 69:21); and 19:36 (Ps 34:20). For Daly-Denton, there are marked connections between Jesus' suffering and betrayal and that of David, who was betrayed by a son, Absalom, as well as key advisors, including Ahithophel. In 2 Sam 15, David is forced to flee from Jerusalem across the Kidron Valley, which is explicitly referenced in John 18:1, just prior to Judas's arrival. Other connections include plots against the king at night (2 Sam 17:1; John 13:30) and a servant's desire to be with his king. Following him in his escape in spite of the risks, David's servant says, "In the place where my lord may be, if for death or for life, there your servant (*doulos*) will be" (2 Sam 15:21 LXX // John 12:26; 14:3). Finally, sounding much like Caiaphas's prophecy in John 11:50-51, Ahithophel's counsel is highly regarded, "as if one asked for a word of God" (2 Sam 16:23). Like Caiaphas, he advises Absalom saying, "You seek only the life (*tēn psychēn*) of one man and all the people will be at peace" (17:3). In John's Gospel, Jesus emphasizes the "peace" that he alone gives after his death and resurrection (John 14:27; 16:33; 20:19, 21, 26). As in 2 Samuel, one man is to die for the benefit of the whole. David, however, does not die; this is Jesus' role as the superior shepherd-king. Even though not as overt as in the Synoptics, Jesus is still characterized in Davidic terms in John's Gospel.

Bread and Betrayal (13:21-30). At 13:21, Jesus transitions to discuss his betrayer directly. Being "troubled in spirit" again (11:33), Jesus says clearly to the Twelve, "one from you will betray me." Rather than troubled by his coming death (12:27-28), Jesus is instead troubled by the betrayal that is about to take place and the sorrow that will result. In 11:33, Jesus was also "troubled in his spirit" after seeing Mary and the other Jews "weeping" over Lazarus's death. In 14:1 and 27 he will command the disciples not to be "troubled" over his own departure, which includes his death that will cause them to "weep and mourn" (16:20). Even though they will weep, he promises that their "pain will turn to joy." Jesus' being troubled, therefore, appears in contexts that include his "friends" and those whom he "loved" (11:4-5, 11; 13:1; 15:12-15); he is troubled because he loves them and knows the realities of suffering.

In contrast to Jesus' clarity, the disciples are all confused. In 13:22-30 they remain in the dark about the identity of Jesus' betrayer, even after his explicit prophetic enactment of Ps 41. Brant's observation that all the disciples "reluctantly had to make this gesture" of lifting their heels against Jesus when he washed their feet makes sense of the disciples' ignorance in 13:22; from their perspective, any of them could be the betrayer (2011, 203). Peter's curiosity ultimately provokes him to question Jesus, but after his last exchange in 13:6-11, he takes an indirect approach, using the unnamed "Beloved" (*ēgapa*) Disciple as his intermediary (13:23-26). The identity of this disciple is the topic of much debate in scholarly literature with John of Zebedee (Bauckham), Lazarus (Stibbe), and Mary Magdalene (E. de Boer) being among the best-known suggestions. The Gospel, however, leaves this disciple nameless, perhaps because his (or her) identity was known to the community or so that this disciple could act as an example for other believers.

This disciple's particular location next to Jesus, reclining "in his bosom" (*en tō kolpō*), mimics the description of Jesus' location "in the Father's bosom" (*eis ton kolpon*) from 1:18. Many scholars suggest that this description identifies the Beloved Disciple as the Johannine community's founder, the one who has inherited teaching from Jesus just as Jesus received it from his Father (19:25-27, 35-37; 21:24-25). Jesus' closeness, his imbibing from the Father's bosom, enables him to offer superior revelation of the Father so that, in comparison to his understanding, it is as though "no one has seen God before" (1:17).

In John 13:23-30 itself, however, the Beloved Disciple does not display superior understanding (Culpepper 1991, 145–46). In spite of his closeness, this disciple is among those who "did not know" why Jesus commanded Judas, "What you are doing, do immediately" (13:27-28). Incorporating further allusions to John 12, the disciples again associate Judas's actions with care for the poor because of his administration of the "money-box" (13:29-30; 12:4-8). Just like the other disciples, the Beloved Disciple needs the fruits of Jesus' return to the Father—the work of his death, resurrection, and giving of the Holy Spirit who will teach in Jesus' physical absence—in order to interpret Jesus' teachings and actions (14:26-31).

In John 13:30, the narrator ends the scene, writing, "and it was night" immediately after Judas's departure. The transition from day to night not only means the narrative has now shifted into another day, which we will learn is the Day of Preparation, but also communicates that the plot against Jesus will now begin. The darkness of night will seek to overcome him, but as it was unable to do so before, so too will it fail now (1:5). The references to day and night bring Jesus' teachings of himself as the "Light of the World" to a climax as well as remind the audience of those who work at night. In the symbolic world of John's Gospel, work at night is done blindly because one "cannot see where he is going" (12:35; cf. 1 John 2:11). The ambiguity of this phrase means they can neither see where they themselves are going *nor* see where Jesus is going (7:33-36; 8:21-22; 13:33). Judas's departure into the darkness confirms Jesus' words from 3:19, "Now this is the verdict (*krisis*): the light has come into the world and people loved the darkness more than the light, for their works are evil (*ponēra*)." Disappearing into the darkness, Judas goes to do an evil work, but blindly; unbeknownst to him (or to his diabolical influencer), this is part of the ruler of the world's exorcism (12:31; 16:33). God is at work to bring eternal life.

Jesus' Consolation: It Is Better That I Go Away (13:31–16:33)

Convincing his disciples that it is better that he departs from them is a key part of Jesus' message in his final discourse of the Gospel. They may not know that this is all part of God's plan of love, but Jesus does. Better known as the Farewell Discourse (FD), John 13–17 has a complicated interpretation history because of its redundancy, awkward transitions, and jarring false stops (13:31; 14:31; 16:5). This has led a number of scholars to posit a history of redaction as editors compiled Jesus' sayings but left seams in the text, especially at 14:31 (Brown 1970, 581–604). George Parsenios suggests that this is not a satisfying solution, especially since Jesus' delayed departure at 14:31–18:1 resembles other literary genres in the ancient world, particularly the exit to death in ancient dramas (2005, 6–7). According to Parsenios, the FD incorporates a variety of ancient genres: testimony (Gen 49; Deut 34; *T. Ab.*; *T. Mos.*), commission (Deut 31; Josh 1; 1 Kgs 2), literary symposium (*Symp.*; *Phaedr.*), consolation literature (Plutarch, *Exil.*, *Ad Apol.*, Seneca, *Helv.*, Cicero, *Ad Marc.*), and exits to death in tragedies (Euripides, *Tro.*; Sophocles, *Phil.*; Aeschylus, *Ag.*). Blending these genres, the Gospel consoles the audience about Jesus' death while also encouraging them that Jesus' death, unlike that of the dramatic characters they know so well, is far from tragic.

A number of scholars, including Parsenios, argue that 13:1-30 should be included as part of the discourse because it is the narrative scene that serves as the foundation for what Jesus says in 13:31–17:26. Certainly, there is merit to this observation since Jesus' actions often prompt a discourse in the Gospel of John (e.g., 5:1-18; 6:1-15; 7:1-13). I have sectioned 13:31–16:33 off here because it marks the departure of Judas Iscariot at 13:30 and differs from 17:1-26, which is Jesus' prayer to his Father. This intervening section, then, is Jesus' final speech to his disciples, "his own" who have remained with him to this point even though Jesus knows that future betrayals will also come (18:2-9, 25-27). As an extended scene with limited narrator interruptions, this speech also reaches out from the confines of the Gospel to the audience listening. When gathered to hear the Gospel of John, the audience hears directly from Jesus in 13:31–16:33, and they too receive encouragement and consolation. They may not have seen Jesus in the flesh, but they hear his words through the flesh of others and through the Paraclete who already resides in their midst.

A. 13:31–14:31: Commandment to Love
The first section of the FD stretches from 13:31–14:31 and lays out a number of themes that recur in 15:1–16:33, including Jesus' commandment to love (13:31-35; 14:15, 22-24), his return to the Father as a reason not to be troubled (14:1-7, 27-31), the unity between himself and believers that enables them to ask in his name (14:8-14), the coming of "another" Paraclete who is the Spirit of truth (14:15-21), and his gift of peace (14:25-31). According to Brant, this speech showcases the Gospel's "epideictic nature," its goal to motivate action based on praise and shame rather than logical arguments. Brant suggests that all of 13:31–17:26 "bolster[s] the beliefs and values of the audience, elaborating on, and interlacing four assertions about Jesus' death": his departure is a return to the Father; his death is a paradigmatic act of love; he lives on in the community when they love and recognize the Paraclete; and his "death is a revelation of God's glory" (2011, 210). In this way, the audience is encouraged to imitate Jesus' love and be consoled about his departure, which includes not only his death but also his resurrection and implied ascension (20:1-18).

John 13:31–14:31 can be outlined as follows:

13:31–35, Love Command
13:36–14:24, Explanations for Confused Disciples
    13:36–38, Jesus and Peter
    14:1–14, Jesus, Thomas, and Philip
    14:15–24, Jesus and Judas (not Iscariot)
14:25–31, Another Paraclete

The key section of this opening portion of the FD is 13:31-35. These verses set the tone for all that will follow in 13:36–17:26, from Peter's adamant confession of loyalty to Jesus' final prayer on behalf of *all* his disciples—past, present, and future. Because of the overlap in themes, as well as its importance, I will focus most of the commentary here on 13:31-35.

After Judas's disappearance into the night, Jesus makes a bold announcement: "*Now* was glorified the Son of Man, and God was glorified in him; and God will glorify him in himself, and *immediately* he will glorify him!" The Greek of these verses is as messy as the English translation but also as emphatic. The repetition makes the point clear: this is the hour of Jesus' glorification. The verses are two parallel phrases: the first with a chiasm (ABBA) pivoting on "the Son of Man and God" surrounded by the same verb *edoxasthē* (he was glorified), and the second with a repeating ABAB pattern that resumes the immediacy of v. 31, "now" (*nun*) and "immediately" (*euthys*). Jesus also emphasizes the transition to his hour by repeating his teaching from 7:33-34 and 8:21: "A little while I am with you; you will seek me, and just as I said to the Jews, 'where I am going you are not able to come,' also I am saying now to you" (13:33). Even though the remaining disciples are Jesus' "little children," they too will endure the sorrow and frustration of his departure. He does not, however, leave them without hope.

In order to experience the continued presence of Jesus in spite of his physical absence, the disciples must imitate him; specifically, they must love as he loved. Jesus summarizes this key teaching, or "commandment" (*entolē*), in 13:34-35, using parallel phrases once again to highlight their importance:

A. A new commandment I am giving to you:
    B. That (*hina*) you should love one another,
        C. just as I loved you
    B'. so that (*hina*) you should love one another.
A'. By this everyone will know that you are my disciples,
    B". if you should have love for one another.

Close readers of the OT and other Gospels (Mark 12:29-31; Matt 22:37-40; Luke 10:27-28) will see that Jesus' command is not entirely new. John 13:34-35 resembles commands to love God (Deut 6:4-5) and love neighbor (Lev 19:18) that were commonly combined in first-century Judaism as a summary of the Torah (Marcus 2009, 843; Ruzer; Stern). What *is* new about Jesus' command in John, however, is his emphasis on imitation: *just as I loved you.* The disciples are to learn from Jesus' model of love, the laying down of his own life (13:1; 15:12-14; 19:28-30), which embodies both his love for his Father (10:17-18; 14:31; 15:9-10) and his love for the world (6:54; cf. 3:14-18).

Jesus' command to love is shorthand for all that follows in his FD because it is the core for the abiding unity that Jesus describes as existing between himself, his disciples, and the Father. As Lori Baron explains, love, whether *agapē* or *philos*, carries connotations of loyalty rather than just feeling (2010, 57). This is true in the contemporary world as well as the ancient world: we expect those who love us to show that love through faithfulness, just as we show our love through faithfulness. The one who loves is loyal to their beloved, fulfilling their desires. Jesus, however, commands even deeper love; he commands complete love (*telos*, 13:1; *teleioō*, 17:4; 19:28; cf. 1 John 2:5; 4:12-18). As he will explain, such love not only means a willingness to die for loved ones, or friends (*philoi*, 15:12-14), but also to live in unity with them so that one's thoughts and actions imitate those of the beloved, the most beloved being Jesus and the Father. Jesus has shown this type of love for God by speaking only the words his Father gave him and by doing the works he gave Jesus to do. This is why Jesus says to Philip, "The one having seen me has seen the Father" (14:9). Jesus not only invites his disciples into this relationship by their unity with him; he *commands* it. If they are his disciples, they will participate in this unity through love.

The disciples, however, need some help to understand and follow Jesus' teaching. Starting a chain of interruptions, Peter first insists that *he himself* will model complete love by dying on Jesus' behalf first (13:36-38). Peter has misunderstood his role. He cannot show complete love *until* Jesus first models it, which requires his death and resurrection as part of his return to the Father. Trying to usurp Jesus' role will lead Peter to betraying him, once again proving the validity of Jesus' words (18:25-27). Thomas and Philip follow with interruptions of their own. In his characteristically pragmatic tone, Thomas notes the obvious: "Lord, we do not know where you are going. How are we able to know the way?" (14:5). There is truth to what Thomas is saying: the disciples do not understand that Jesus is returning to the Father. Jesus highlights this in his response: "If you all had known me, you all would also have known my Father" (14:7). My translation reflects a textual variant that creates a "contrary-to-fact conditional statement." Even though most English translations do not include it, this translation is probably closer to the original, given Jesus' continued conversation in 14:8-31 where he (1) promises, "Indeed, from now you all know and have seen him" (v. 9); (2) chides Philip for not believing that "I am in the Father and the Father is in me" (v. 10); (3) tells Judas (not Iscariot) that he will remain manifest to the disciples because of their love for one another (i.e., the keeping of his word) (vv. 22-24); and (4) uses another contrary-to-fact conditional statement, saying "if you all had loved me, you all would have rejoiced because I am going to the Father, because the Father is greater than me" (v. 28; cf. 13:19). Even though the disciples have been with Jesus "from the beginning," they cannot understand until his revelation is complete.

The commands of the FD, therefore, can only be followed *after* Jesus' death, resurrection, return to the Father, and giving of "another Paraclete," the Spirit of truth (14:17, 26). A "Paraclete," meaning an advocate, encourager, and comforter, is one who comes alongside, calling and helping. The Spirit, according to Jesus, is "another Paraclete," continuing his own ministry, which is an extension of God's will. The Holy Spirit, Jesus explains, "will teach you everything and will remind you of everything which I said to you" (14:26). The work of the Spirit is evidenced in the Gospel with the "remembrance" passages in 2:13-22 and 12:15-16 where the disciples are said to have "remembered" and interpreted Jesus' actions and words in light of Scripture only after the fact; they needed the Spirit to "believe the Scripture and the word which Jesus spoke" (2:22; cf. 13:7). With the Spirit's teaching, the community can understand the extent of Jesus' revelation, that when they saw him they saw the Father, and they can have joy even in his physical absence. Only then do they receive Jesus' peace (14:27; 16:33; 20:19, 21, 26). This gift, as Jesus says, is why it is better if he should go away, even though his departure is painful (16:7).

B. 15:1-27: Metaphors of Love and Endurance
Even though 14:31 ends with the command, "Rise, let us go hence," Jesus continues with his speech in John 15. It is primarily this apparent contradiction that has led many scholars to argue for an editorial seam here in John's Gospel. Parsenios, again, asserts that Jesus' delayed departure to death in John's Gospel is far from an uncommon literary device. Instead, key characters and legendary figures offer one final "Big Speech" before they die, especially in Greek tragedies. Given John's other similarities to Greek dramas—the tendency to have Jesus appear alone with one other character in dialogue,

to have group characters similar to choruses, the beginning Prologue that mirrors dramatic prologues, and the extensive use of irony—Jesus' delayed departure continues the Gospel's dramatic elements (Brant 2004). This is not to suggest that John *is* a drama, just that it incorporates elements of drama in its literary style. Parsenios notes that before characters depart to meet their deaths, they repeatedly delay, not only once as Jesus does here, but even five times! Cassandra, the prophetess who knows of her impending murder by Clytemnestra in Aeschylus's *Agamemnon*, bemoans her fate, pausing five times before walking off stage to her end. The chorus interacts with her during this delay, asking her questions about why, if she knows she is to die, she does not prevent her death. Cassandra, however, knows she cannot escape the prophecy given to her by Apollo and so, ultimately, faces her death (Aeschylus, *Ag.* 1070–1341).

For Parsenios, Jesus' delay at 15:1–17:26 may surprise modern-day readers, but it would not have been confusing for an ancient audience. They would recognize this technique from other well-known stories and dramas. Jesus' delay not only reinforces the inevitability of his death once he does depart and the action resumes in 18:1 but also heightens the tension during Jesus' speech. This is his final speech to his disciples; this is information they *really* need to hear and obey. And yet Jesus' speech does not have the tragic qualities of many departure speeches in dramatic literature. As Parsenios notes, John's Jesus does not bemoan his own fate like Cassandra, nor does he fear his coming death (2005, 75). Instead, his death is a return to the Father. The ones who need comforting are the disciples, which is what requires him to linger a bit longer to continue explaining how they are to live in his coming absence.

John 15:1–16:4 has three sections: in 15:1-8 Jesus offers an organic *paroimia*, a metaphor concerning the vine; in 15:9-17 Jesus explains the *paroimia*, tying it back to his love command from 13:34-35; and in 15:18–16:4 he gives warnings about the disciples' relationship with the "world." The entire section contrasts love, as the reflection of God's nature, and hate, the reflection of the world and its "ruler" (14:30; 16:11; cf. 12:31). At the same time, however, the section remains focused on how to continue experiencing Jesus' presence in spite of his departure and return to the Father. The key, Jesus says, is to remain, or abide (*menō*), in him.

The Vineyard (15:1-8). In one of the most well-known metaphors from John's Gospel, Jesus describes his relationship with his Father and the disciples in terms of a vine in a vineyard. The vineyard was a common image used for Israel, God's chosen people, in the OT (Isa 5; Ps 80; Hos 10; Ezek 17; Jer 2:21) and is developed in a parable in each of the Synoptic Gospels (Matt

20:1-16; Mark 12:1-12; Luke 20:9-19). In John, however, the parable shifts from describing an absent owner and hired hands to describing an intimate relationship between the "true" Vine, the "true" Vine-dresser, and multiple Branches. The image of a vine-dresser caring for a vine by pruning, that is, cleaning (*kathairei*) to promote growth, would be easily understood in Jesus' context, just like his *paroimia* of the shepherd in John 10. Craig Koester writes, "Across the Mediterranean world, vines dotted fields and hillsides, thriving on dew and the occasional rains that moistened the coarse soil in which they took root" (2003, 272; cf. Cicero, *De senectute* 15.52–53). Jan van der Watt (2000, 52) focuses on the Jewish elements of this metaphor in particular, noting the similarities between John 15 and Ps 80:8-19 (LXX 79:8-19). In Ps 80, Israel is described as a vine "removed" (*metēras*) from Egypt and planted by the Lord in a new land (v. 8). The psalmist prays for the restoration of this vine, which was once great but is now destroyed by the removal of its hedge. Rather than Israel, or its king as God's son and vine, the Gospel of John interprets Jesus in that role, making him not only the focus of God's care as the vine-dresser but also the means of the branches' connection to God. Branches cannot grow apart from the vine (15:4-5).

The vine metaphor is only the latest in a series of metaphors used by Jesus in the Gospel. The shepherd and sheepfold in John 10 are perhaps the other most obvious examples, but Jesus also regularly appeals to the image of a household (*oikia, oikos*) or what we would call a "family" (van der Watt 2000). "Household" is a better term for the first-century Mediterranean world because their families looked different from our own. Led by the *paterfamilias* (father of the family), households not only contained biological family members in a hierarchy dependent upon age and gender but also all property: houses, land, household goods, and slaves. Also connected to households were clients, other kin, and friends of various sorts who showed loyalty (and, therefore, love) to the household and to whom corresponding loyalty was owed. The household metaphor in John's Gospel begins in 1:12-13 when the narrator describes those who "believe" or "trust" in Jesus as becoming the "children of God" (13:33, *teknia* "little children"). As God's children, it is as though these people are born "again" or "from above," and their primary loyalty is to their heavenly Father, a loyalty and love that Jesus himself exemplifies. The metaphor continues, not only in John 3 but also anywhere the Gospel mentions a father and the Father (ca. 136 times! cf. Thompson 2001), sons (8:34-36; 12:36), children (4:49; 16:21; 21:5), slaves (8:34-36; 13:16; 15:15, 20), and friends (11:11; 15:13-15). Jesus' metaphors in John 14–15, therefore, although different on the surface, continue to build on previous examples, especially with his descriptions of a "place" and "dwelling places" (*monē*) in 14:2 and 23. He will offer one more in 16:20-23a.

In 15:1-8 Jesus' image illustrates how one remains in him *and* how one can be separated from him. Healthy branches produce fruit while dead vines are cut off and burned. Koester emphasizes that the branches are not killed by God, nor separated prior to their death, but are only removed once they have cut themselves off from life (2003, 273). The image remains startling, however, like the previous language of judgment in John's Gospel (3:36; 9:41). Nonetheless, the image is consistent with the Gospel's opening lines that nothing exists without the involvement of God's Word. This does not mean that one should prioritize their individual life over all else; it means the opposite. Drawing also on language of "fruit" (*karpos*) used in 12:24, Jesus' instruction in John 15 reminds the disciples and Gospel audience that "unless a grain of wheat falls into the earth and dies, a single one it *remains* (*menei*). But if it should die, it bears much fruit (*polyn karpon pherei*)" (cf. 15:8). To "remain" or "abide" (*menei*) in Jesus, the Vine, these branches need to imitate him as mini vines who transmit his Life and Love to others, the "fruit" waiting in the fields for harvest (4:35-36).

The Love of Friends (15:9-17). Jesus continues in vv. 9-17 explaining the vine metaphor from vv. 1-8, ultimately returning to and rephrasing the key command of love from 13:34-35. John 15:9-12 summarizes Jesus' teaching with parallel structures and a restatement of his command from 13:35. Once again, his role as the model—example (*hypodeigma*, 13:15)—is highlighted as well as his role as the connection between the disciples and the Father. Verse 9 contains a chiasm that reinforces the parallel Jesus makes between himself and the Father:

> A. Just as he loved
> > B. me,
> > > C. the Father,
> > > C'. I also,
> > B'. you,
> A'. I loved.

The overall structure of 15:9-10 is even more complex, with looping phrases that knit together love and remaining with vine-like tendrils.

> A. Just as (*kathōs*) he loved me, the Father, I also (*kagō*) you, I loved:
> > B. Remain in my love.
> > > C. If my commandments you should keep,

B'. you will remain in my love.
A'. Just as (*kathōs*) I myself,
   C'. the commandments of my Father, I have kept,
B". I also (*kagō*) remain in his love.

The layered parallelisms build on Jesus' organic *paroimia* from 15:1-8, verbally illustrating the interdependence of Jesus, the Father, and the disciples. Such revelation is meant to give the disciples "joy" even as they suffer through Jesus' departure. Jesus' leaving is the demonstration of his profound love, the same love that connects them to the Father (v. 11). Recapitulating his command from 13:34-35, he says again, "This is my commandment: that you should love one another, just as I loved you" (15:12).

Jesus begins to clarify that he is talking about his coming death in 15:13-17. Returning to the household imagery from John 14, Jesus explains, "Greater love than this no one has, that someone should lay down his life on behalf of his friends" (15:13; cf. 10:17-18; 13:36-38). Friendship was a common topic among authors of the ancient Mediterranean world, Jewish as well as Greco-Roman. Speaking frankly (*parrēsia*) to offer criticism or praise was a mark of true friends, as was desiring the best for the sake of a friend, even at the cost of one's own benefit and life (Seneca, *Ep.* 3.2–3; Plutarch, *Adul. amic.*; cf. Engberg-Pederson 2014). Although so-called "ideal friendships" existed only between social equals—largely because we only have writings from noblemen who wrote to and for one another—friendships also extended to those of different social standings as well as between groups (Culy, 38–84). Friends, as "loved-ones" (*philoi*), knew more than slaves (*douloi*) because they were assumed to have some agency in showing loyalty or love, but they were not necessarily of equal standing. As we will see in 19:12, one could also be a "friend" of a political leader, which was displayed through loyalty rather than open conversation.

Jesus, therefore, both uses and subverts ideas of friendship so commonly debated in his world. As a true friend, Jesus speaks frankly, or boldly (*parrēsia*), to his disciples as well as to anyone he meets throughout the Gospel. Indeed, it is his frank speech, his display of friendship toward the world, which eventually causes his rejection and death. Nevertheless, Jesus continues to show friendship by suffering for the sake of others and securing for them a greater future. Jesus also subverts expectations by revealing the Father's will and dying on behalf of his friends, even though he "outranks" them. Instead of demanding his friends die for him (contra Peter's expectation), Jesus himself will "lay his life down" on their behalf. According to Jesus, it *must* be this way because the world does not know how to love. Those in the world have no model to follow until Jesus himself loves. As 1 John describes, it is "not that we have loved God, but that he loved us and sent his Son" (4:10).

The Hatred of the World (15:18–16:4a). The tone of Jesus' comments changes in 15:18–16:4a even as his household metaphor continues. Rather than focusing on love, Jesus shifts to discuss "hatred" (*miseō, misos*). Love and hate were considered opposites in the ancient world as they are in our modern-day contexts, but they are also set side by side in another important OT passage that resonates with the FD: Lev 19:17-18. These verses form part of the Torah summary with Deut 6:4-5 described above (John 13:34-35). Although many are familiar with the final portion of Lev 19:18b, "You shall love your neighbor as yourself," the passage as a whole should be read beginning with 19:17. In its entirety, Lev 19:17-18 (LXX) makes clear the contrast between hatred and love:

A. [17]You shall *not* hate your brother in your mind,
   B. with reproach you shall reproach your neighbor,
      C. and you shall *not* receive sin on account of him,
A'. [18]And your hand shall *not* avenge,
      C'. and you shall *not* rage with the sons of your people,
   B'. and you shall love your neighbor as yourself. I am the LORD.

According to Lev 19:17-18, if someone wrongs you, you are to reproach or reproof (*elegmos*) them rather than seek vengeance with your hand. You are to love "your neighbor as yourself." Moreover, the authority behind these verses is the Lord, whose identity, "I am the LORD," is the cornerstone for this command just as it is for all of Lev 19 (vv. 2, 3, 10, 12, 14, 16, 25, 28, etc.).

Jesus' shift to discuss hatred, in contrast to the love that a "friend" shows, is supported by Lev 19. Rather than reciprocating Jesus'—and God's—love, Jesus argues that "the world" (*ho kosmos*) hates both him and his Father (John 15:20-25). Because of their hatred for Jesus' words and his works they have heard and seen, they no longer have a "valid excuse" to escape consequence; now they have "sin" (*hamartia*, v. 22). This "sin," or mistake, is their misrecognition of Jesus. Instead of seeing the light and life that he offers, they perceive him to be a threat and orchestrate his death. Indeed, Jesus *is* a threat to "the world" in a sense, but only to its status quo of being ruled by one who is not God and so does not desire life (8:40-44; 1 John 3:7-16). Jesus has come to "cast out outside" the "ruler of this world" in order to restore God's proper dominion (John 12:31; 14:30; 16:11). Even though the world's ruler tries to destroy Jesus through death, it is that same act that causes the ruler's own exorcism. In spite of the hatred shown him, Jesus satisfies God's will by modeling the true love that God has for the world.

John's Gospel has often been read as distancing its community from the world, which is regularly interpreted as another shorthand for the Jews who have expelled them from synagogues (16:1-2; Meeks; Rensberger, 135–54). This "sectarian" reading of John has led some to argue that John's Gospel is not concerned with "the world" of nonbelievers but is only focused on the perseverance of the believers' own community in the midst of oppression. Such a reading relies heavily on Martyn's hypothesis of the Johannine community's origins (see General Introduction) and has also contributed to the argument that John's Gospel is largely devoid of ethics (see p. 174–75 below).

While John's Gospel does offer encouragement to disciples facing opposition, we need also to remember the larger context of this story. In John, it is *God's love for the world that motivates all the action* in the narrative and, indeed, in creation (3:14-18). The world may have "sin" because it rejects the Son, but that does not negate God's will or God's love. In this passage, Jesus says that "the world" hates, but he never gives permission for his disciples to do likewise. Jesus assures them that they will face hatred, but their role is to be witnesses, speaking the words the Paraclete gives them (15:26-27). When wronged by being cast out of the synagogues, cut off from kinship networks or biological families, or even if they are killed (16:2; cf. 21:18-19), believers are *not* to retaliate and "avenge" with their hands; nor are they to remain silent, removed from the world and never facing it (17:13-19). Instead, they are to be like Jesus: they are to love.

C. 16:4b-33: Final Consolation

John 16:4b-33 records Jesus' final words to his disciples before the resurrection. Other than the Beloved Disciple, these disciples will not hear Jesus teach them again until they experience the fulfillment of these promises in 20:19-29. John 16:4b-33 resumes the disciples' interjections from 13:36–14:31 after a long stretch from 15:1–16:4a of unbroken speech from Jesus. This means that the "yous" (all plural) were heard by the Gospel audience as directed at them along with the disciples in the story; for a moment the past, present, and future dissolve and the audience joins the disciples in hearing these words from their Savior (O'Day 1991). In 16:5, however, Jesus reinstates narrative time with an implicit reference to the disciples, who enter the scene again in vv. 17-18 and 29-30. Repeating their pattern of misunderstanding, they sound much like Peter from John 13: first by demonstrating their ignorance (13:6-11, 24; 16:17-18) and second by offering an overconfident claim of faith (13:36-38; 16:29-30). Coming on the heels of Jesus' discussion of "the world," the actions of his disciples also remind us that we should always be careful about what we claim to know and believe about God's plan. Speaking as a group, the character of the disciples merges with the Gospel audience listening to the story as they, too, reflect on Jesus' teaching. After living in the time after Jesus' departure, do they truly believe it was better for him to go away?

Summary: It Is Better that I Go Away (16:4b-18). In this section, Jesus summarizes his discourse and emphasizes the truth of his consolation: It is better that I go away (16:7). This is a hard word for the disciples (as well as for later believers) to hear (cf. 6:60). Nevertheless, Jesus repeatedly explains the *reasons* he has said "these things" to his disciples in the FD, using speaking terms twenty-eight times in 13:31–16:33. These verbs appear fourteen times in John 16 alone, bringing to a climax not only Jesus' encouragement, warnings, and consolations from the FD but also his teaching and works from throughout the Gospel. After all, this is the Gospel where Jesus repeatedly says, "Truly, truly I am saying to you."

Jesus contrasts the disciples' real feelings and the truth of his departure. "I said these things to you from the beginning," he explains, ". . . but *now* I am going to the one who sent me" and "pain has filled your heart" (16:4b-6). He acknowledges the disciples' pain (*lypē*), just as he also wept over the death of his friend, Lazarus, in 11:35. Jesus tells them, "I am speaking the truth to you! It is better for you that I should go away!" (16:7). This is a rephrasing of his consolation from 14:25-31, especially vv. 28-29. Rather than primarily pain (*lypē*), Jesus' departure is an occasion for rejoicing (15:11; 16:24). He is departing for a time, but his departure is not abandonment: he is sending a Paraclete and he himself will return. Jesus again makes clear that the Paraclete's work is a continuation of his own, which is the furthering of God's will (16:8-11). It is this long view that informs Jesus' admonitions for joy in spite of the pain of his present departure, both for the disciples in the narrative and for those listening to the Gospel.

Jesus' comment about the disciples' failure to question him in 16:5 has often been a point of contention in the interpretation of this passage (cf. Segovia 1983). Nevertheless, no disciple asks the question Jesus phrases, "Where are you going?" The closest is Thomas's question, but it is first an assertion: "We do not know where you are going. How can we know the way?" (14:5). Indeed, looking back through the Gospel, *no one asks Jesus* where he is going when he discusses his departure. In 7:35 and 8:22, the Jews offer possibilities, either the Diaspora to teach the Greeks or suicide. They come closer in 8:19 when they ask Jesus, "Where is your Father?"

The disciples, in contrast, do not ask these questions because they seem to think they already know the answers, so they make assertions instead: I will lay down my life on your behalf; we do not know the way; show us the Father. Rather than asking Jesus for clarification, they question each other in 16:17-18, exasperated because they "do not know what he is talking about!" (v. 18). All of their misunderstanding again reinforces their need for the next Paraclete whom Jesus will send. In 16:13, Jesus finally answers Thomas's question from 14:5: "How can we know the way (*tēn hodon*)?" They will know because "the Spirit of truth will show the way (*hodēgēsei*) in all truth" (16:13). It is for this reason, Jesus asserts, that he must depart in spite of the pain it causes.

Pain, Joy, and Victory Assured (16:19-33). The final portion of Jesus' speech is divided by two rhetorical questions he poses to his flustered disciples (16:19, 30b). In v. 19, the narrator tells of Jesus' perceptiveness: the disciples cannot hide their flurried questions from vv. 17-18. Even though they did not ask (*erōta*, v. 5) him, Jesus answers, but with a question of his own: "Are you seeking with one another because I said, 'a little while and you will not see me, and again a little while and you will see me'?" (v. 19). Again, rather than asking Jesus where he is going, the disciples are focused elsewhere; and, like Peter in 13:24, they do not want to show their ignorance to Jesus (even though he already knows it and has told them about it!). Instead of speaking to Jesus, they huddle among each other, just like the crowds and other Jews with whom Jesus interacts throughout the Gospel. Nevertheless, Jesus does not leave them yet; he gives them one more round of teaching and one more *paroimia* to help make his message clear.

In 16:20-23a Jesus gives his final *pariomia* in the Gospel; this time it focuses on a woman who is in the midst of labor. Not only is the image of a woman in labor common in eschatological and apocalyptic writings (e.g., Isa 26:16-21; 66:8-14; Hos 13:13; Matt 24:8; 1 Thess 5:3; cf. Keener 2003, 1045–46); it is also particularly fitting in John's Gospel, which uses birth imagery to describe believers' becoming the "children of God" (1:12-13; 3:3-8; 13:33). In John 16, however, the image shifts from the disciples being children to the disciples being the mother. Although perhaps surprising, the transition makes sense given the location of this discourse and Jesus' preparation for the disciples to continue his ministry. In 17:18 he prays, "Just as you sent me into the world, I also sent them into the world." With Jesus' departure, the disciples will take over Jesus' maternal role (19:34; Fehribach), delivering his words and abiding with the Spirit in his physical absence. In so doing, they will also suffer, just as any woman does in childbirth. Instead of passing over this pain, Sheridan (2016) acknowledges that memories of such suffering are real and *do* linger; Jesus' repeated descriptions of the disciples' pain make this clear. The Gospel audience, too, may feel as though they are in labor *now* as they wait for Jesus' return. But the promise is also important. Unlike pregnant and laboring mothers, who exist at a precarious juncture of life and death in the ancient and modern world, the disciples are assured that the life within them *will* be born; they *will* birth new life into God's household, just like Jesus (20:23).

The disciples' connection to the Father is reinforced in 16:23-28 as Jesus turns from the image of labor to the time of the disciples' joy. When their "joy" comes, Jesus says, they "will question him about nothing" but instead, "whatever you should ask for from my Father in my name, I will give you." These promises parallel Jesus' teaching in 14:12-15 and 15:16, but in 16:25-28, Jesus goes further. When "the hour" comes, the disciples will no longer have to rely on Jesus as an intermediary but will have direct access to the Father because "the Father himself loves (*philei*) you, because you have loved (*pephilēkate*) me and have believed that I came from the Father" (16:27). The verb used here is *phileō*, which is the verbal form of the word *philos*, or "friend," used in 15:12-14. This is no inferior type of love; rather, because of Jesus' example and friendship, the disciples will also become friends of God, able to hear the bold words God speaks as well as able to speak boldly to God because their wills align (*parrēsia*, 16:25; cf. 1 John 2:28; 3:21; 4:17; 5:14).

In 16:29-30, however, the disciples want to skip over the pain and jump straight to joy. They claim to understand Jesus' words, calling the *paroimia* he has just given them "plain speech" (*parrēsia*). They also refuse to question him, saying, "You have no need that anyone should question you" (*ou chreian echeis hina tis se herōta*, 16:30), thereby repeating the mistake Jesus already identified in 16:5: "and no one from you questions me" (*kai oudeis ex hymōn herōta*). Rather than correcting them directly, Jesus asks another rhetorical question and predicts their upcoming betrayal. "Now you believe?! Look, the hour is coming and has come that you will be scattered!" (v. 32). Despite their desires, the disciples cannot avoid the pains of labor, yet the fulfillment of God's promise does not rely on the disciples' comprehension. Instead, so sure is God's plan that Jesus ends with a proclamation of victory: "I have spoken these things to you so that in me you might have peace. In the world you will have affliction (*thlipsis*, cf. 16:21), but be courageous! I have conquered the world!" (v. 33).

Jesus' Prayer: That They Might Be One (17:1-26)
Having finished his speech to his disciples, Jesus "lifts his eyes to heaven" and says a prayer to his Father in 17:1-26. Although Jesus' intimacy with the

Father is a major theme in the Gospel, this intimacy is most often demonstrated through Jesus' works and stated in his discourses. We hear of Jesus praying in 6:11—more precisely, he "took the loaves and gave thanks"—and again in 11:40-42, where he offers another thanksgiving prayer: "Father, I thank you that you heard me. And I know that you always hear me, but for the crowd standing I spoke, so that they might believe that you sent me." In 12:27-28, Jesus has an exchange with the Father, calling on him to "glorify" his name before the "voice from heaven" responds with affirmation in v. 28. In 12:30-33, Jesus again says that this voice spoke for the benefit of the crowd, rather than fulfilling any need he himself had, in spite of the troubling of his life or soul (12:27).

John 17:1-26 brings together elements from all these previous prayers and goes a step further. Jesus lifts his eyes to heaven (4:34-35; 6:5; 11:41), expresses concern that others will recognize he has been sent by the Father (cf. 3:17, 34; 5:36-38; 6:29; 7:29; 11:42), and commands glory be given (12:23, 38; 8:54; 11:4; 13:31-32; 16:14). The prayer is also for the benefit of the audience, who listen in not on thanksgiving for requests already satisfied (as in John 6 and 11) but on requests Jesus actively makes to the Father. In what is often called the "high priestly prayer," Jesus intercedes for his disciples across all time and space, asking for God's protection, sanctification, and unity (Attridge 2013). The prayer is also another model for the disciples to imitate (cf. 13:15). Jesus shows all disciples *how* to ask the Father in Jesus' name (16:23-28; 17:9, 15, 20). Each time they read this prayer, or hear it out loud, it is prayed again by the disciples, who take on Jesus' voice and make these requests; here, they become one with him. In this way, the Gospel shows the disciples' transition from "slaves" to "friends"; they can now hear and speak Jesus' desires that they did not know before. It is here that they learn most clearly "what the Lord is doing" (15:15).

A. 17:1-8: Glorify Your Son

In the first portion of the prayer Jesus begins with a similar request as 12:27, "Father, . . . glorify." This time, however, the glory is not for the Father's "name" (that will come in 17:6, 11-12, 26) but for his "Son, so that the Son might glorify you" (17:1). The Son is Jesus himself, but speaking in the third person here both incorporates the sonship language used by Jesus throughout the Gospel and creates a contrast between two sons: the Son of the Father and "the son of destruction" in v. 12 (see below). In 17:1-3 Jesus builds his prayer in ways similar to 1:1-18, moving from an unidentified "son" to the revelation of his name. John 17:3 is crucial because it defines eternal life as knowing "the only true God and the one whom you sent, Jesus Christ." The refrain of "sending" and knowing Jesus as the one "sent" by God continues throughout the prayer as the requirement for receiving God's glory, knowing his name, and experiencing his love (vv. 8, 18, 20, 23, 25). Jesus is emphatic that God "has given" (*dedōkas*, vv. 2, 9) him all that he has, using the verb *didōmi* fifteen times, all while asserting that everything remains God's own (v. 10). The unity that exists between Jesus and the Father does not erase their distinctiveness, but they are one; whatever is the Father's has been given to Jesus, who relies on his Father as the source of all he does. His prayer is to extend this unity to his followers, those who "believe that you sent me" (vv. 8, 25-26).

In 17:4-5, Jesus switches to emphatically personal and repetitive language:

A. [4]I myself glorified you upon the earth,
    having completed the work which you have given me that I should do.
A'. [5]And now, you glorify me, Father,
    B. from yourself (*para seautō*)
        C. with the glory which I used to have (*eichon*)
        C'. before the world existed (*einai*)
    B'. alongside you (*para sou*).

In v. 4 Jesus explains why the Father should listen to him: he has fulfilled his filial duty of love by completing the Father's work (cf. 19:28-30). In 17:5, therefore, he resumes his first request for glory, but now he is explicit that *he* is the Son. Jesus' request for glory should not be seen as a selfish or idolatrous prayer. Not only is this clear in v. 5 with the chiastic parallelism that emphasizes Jesus' glory is *from* the Father, but it also coheres with Jesus' teaching throughout the Gospel. The desirable glory is God's glory, not human praise. With language similar to 5:44, in 17:3 Jesus stresses God's oneness, again bringing in allusions to the *Shema* (Baron 2017, 170–72). Eternal life is knowing the *One* True God. This knowledge should lead to actions lived in accordance with God's will, allowing one to participate in God's glory, love, and unity. This is the revelation of Jesus' life, death, resurrection, and return; he is the one who makes clear what human priorities should be, even though people do not always live up to them.

B. 17:9-23: On Behalf of Believers
This next section divides at vv. 9-19 and 20-23. In both vv. 9 and 20, Jesus begins modeling how to "ask" (*erōtaō*) God in prayer, starting with the words,

"I myself concerning them, am asking you." The "them" are the ones God has given Jesus "from the world" described in vv. 6-8. Verse 9a is a transition to Jesus' list of requests on their behalf, acting as the foundational statement for vv. 9-23. In v. 9b, Jesus clarifies the identity of the ones for whom he prays with a digression: "Not concerning (*ou peri*) the world am I asking, but concerning the ones whom you have given to me." Jesus asks for God to "keep them in your word which you have given me, so that they might be one" (v. 11). The "keeping" of these followers is parallel to their "keeping" of God's word described by Jesus in vv. 6-7. Not only has Jesus shown loyalty, but so have his followers. As friends of Jesus, they are also friends of God, and as such they can count on God's protection (cf. 1 John 5:18-21). Such "keeping" does not mean that God will rescue these believers out of the world, but that God will "keep them from the evil one" (a refrain that sounds much like the Lord's prayer from Matt 6:13). Rather than being tainted by evil, Jesus prays for their sanctification, or that they should be made holy, even as they are sent out into the world (17:15-18). Just as Jesus "sanctifies [him]self on their behalf," disciples too are to be "sanctified in truth" for the sake of others (17:19-23).

Jesus repeats the phrase "not concerning" (*ou peri*) again in v. 20, extending the number of those for whom he prays: "But not concerning these ones am I asking only, but also concerning the ones believing in me through their word." Explicitly including all believers, especially those among the Gospel audience, Jesus makes his prayer for unity particularly emphatic in 17:21-23. Jesus repeats this request three times, with growing intensity, interspersing with comments about his own unity with the Father and the believers. The redundancy can be overwhelming, but it is also effective. Jesus is clear with his desire: he wants believers to "be completely one" with him, the Father, and one another so that the world might also come to believe. Jesus' prayer may not be directly for "the world" (v. 9), but it *does* include benefits for the world alongside believers. Rather than isolating themselves off from the world, John's Gospel encourages believers to imitate Jesus while they are in the world, so that the world might also learn of God's love and revelation through Jesus his Son and Christ.

C. 17:24-26: Culmination
In vv. 24-26 Jesus rounds out his prayer with two direct addresses to his Father (*pater*, vv. 24, 25). The repetition of "father" in quick succession changes the pattern of address from vv. 1-23, summarizing Jesus' prayer in two final statements that repeat much of his earlier words. First, in v. 24 he explains his desire to be with the ones whom God "has given" him. This request coincides

with Jesus' promise from 12:26 for the one "serving" (*diakonē*) him: "where I am there also my servant will be." Second, he returns to the motif of his glory (*doxa*). Jesus' prayer began with requests for glory in 17:1-5, and in 17:22 he explains how he "has given" his glory to those who believe in him. In 17:24, he explains his desire that they also "behold" his glory, just as Isaiah in 12:41. The beginning of the Gospel claims that this prayer has been answered when the narrator explains, "And the Word became flesh and dwelled among us, and *we beheld his glory*, glory as an only son from a father, full of grace and truth" (1:14). That this glory is from "before the foundation of the world" also reminds the audience of the prologue and Jesus' identity as God's Word.

Another significant element of these final verses is the relationship that Jesus creates between glory (*doxa*) and love (*agapē*). God's love for the believers was already described in 16:27-28, but in 17:24-26 the verb shifts from *phileō*, with its resonances with ideals of friendship (*philos*), to *agapaō*. Again, this is not because *agapaō* or *agapē* are necessarily "better" types of love than *phileō*; rather *agapaō* is the verb used in the double-love command from Deut 6:4-5 (love of God) and Lev 19:18 (love of neighbor). Returning to this verb, Jesus again reminds the audience of living out these commands and, as such, following his superior example. Jesus also unites this idea of love with God's glory. Again, the connection is not new to the Gospel; in 5:42, during his first acrimonious exchange with the Jews, Jesus already demonstrated the overlap of love and glory, saying,

> I do not receive glory from people, but I know that *you do not have the love of God in yourselves*. I have come in the name of my Father, and you do not receive me. If another should come in his own name, that one you will receive. How are you able to believe while receiving glory from one another, but you do not seek glory from the one God? (5:41-44)

According to Jesus, one cannot have the love of God and receive glory from other people. Seeking God's glory is a demonstration of one's love for God; rather than pursuing fickle and impermanent glory from people, true glory comes from the One God (Deut 6:4), the only one who has glory in himself to give.

The connection between love and glory also reinforces Baron's point that love is about *loyalty* as well as feeling (2010, 55–56). Seeking God's glory, and glory from God, shows one's love and loyalty to God alone. God is also faithful and, as Jesus says in 17:25, "righteous" or "just." That means God, unlike people, can be counted on to reciprocate our love. Moreover, Jesus reminds us in this prayer that God is the one who initiated the relationship.

God is the one who "loved" the Word and gave him glory "before the foundation of the world." It is this *first love* that Jesus makes available to those who follow after him, believing, trusting, and therefore imitating his example. Jesus concludes (17:25-26), "Righteous Father, indeed the world does not *know* you, but I *know* you and these ones *know* that you sent me. And I made *known* to them your name, and I will keep making it *known*, so that the love which you loved me might also be in them as I am in them."

Contrasting "the world" first with himself, Jesus summarizes his ministry of making God known (cf. 1:18; 15:15). His ministry does not end here with his death, but he says that he *will* continue revealing this knowledge. This continual ministry of Jesus is especially significant when reading 1 John. The goal of this revelation, Jesus says, is so that God's initial love—the love that prompted the creation of the world, God's continual intervention throughout Israel's story, retold in the festivals celebrated throughout John's Gospel and in Jesus' own work—might be "in" believers. His desire is God's desire: that people know they are loved.

Theological Threads

Johannine Ethics

Although surprising for some readers of John, this Gospel has traditionally been considered largely devoid of ethics (Skinner 2017, xix–xxv). Of course, it does have fewer overt ethical commands than Matthew, where Jesus delivers his Sermon on the Mount (5:1–7:29), or Luke, with its own version, the Sermon on the Plain (6:17-49). Recent scholars, however, have pushed back on this conclusion, building on the flood of character and characterization studies in John to argue that the Gospel has thorough "implicit" ethics (van der Watt and Zimmermann). Ancient authors often constructed characters in their writings in order to help form the ethics of their readers. Plutarch says this explicitly in his prologue to the *Life of Aemelius Paulus*, writing, "I began writing my 'Lives' for the sake of others, but I find that I am continuing the work and delighting in it now for my own sake also, using history as a mirror and endeavouring in a manner to fashion and adorn my own life in conformity with the virtues depicted therein" (1.1 [Perrin, LCL]). According to Plutarch, the depiction of characters in his biographies had the goal of encouraging one to imitate the good and to be repulsed from evil, even without explicit admonition (1.2–5).

It is in this light, then, that John's Gospel is *ethical,* offering "implicit ethics" through the emphases on the works of God, love, and in the presentations of various characters—good, bad, and ambiguous (van der Watt and Zimmermann; Brown and Skinner). The clearest example of ethics in the

Gospel comes in the FD, where Jesus does command his disciples on how they should behave: they are to love one another, just like Jesus loves them (13:34-35). This love, however, is not "sectarian," cut off from the world, but it lays the foundation for loving the world as well. As seen above, Jesus' mission to the disciples is a mission to the world, and it does not end with his return to the Father. Instead, his example of love should inspire similar love, a love that travels outward, extending the unity of the Father and the Son to the world "so that the world might believe you sent me" (17:21). Even without a Sermon on the Mount, Jesus does give ethical instruction in the Gospel of John. His ethic is his example, his *hypodeigma*, that extends far beyond just the foot-washing; it is his entire life, death, and return to the Father that brings about the sending of the Holy Spirit so that his disciples can be inspired to live a life that is abundant and full of the love of God (cf. Trozzo).

The Holy Spirit

The Spirit (*pneuma*) is mentioned throughout the Gospel, often tied to imagery of water, but it is in the FD that Jesus defines the Spirit and the Spirit's work most clearly: the Spirit is "another Paraclete" (14:26). The word "paraclete" (*paraklētos*) is notoriously difficult to interpret because of its flexibility. In legal contexts, it can mean "Advocate," as in one who defends a defendant before a judge (cf. Keener 2003, 955–62). It can also mean "comforter" or "encourager," as one who literally "calls alongside" a person in any situation (*para* = alongside; *kaleō* = call). Instead of getting lost in this flexibility, however, Jesus gives the audience clarity with the adjective "another" that precedes this title: the Spirit is "*another* Paraclete." Understanding the Spirit as *another* Paraclete means the audience must only look to the first Paraclete it was sent: Jesus. The Spirit continues Jesus' work, that is, the work of God, by explaining, reminding, and teaching the disciples about Jesus' words *and* by convicting the world of its mistake in rejecting Jesus. Noticing this connection, Koester writes, "If Jesus himself is the way, the truth and the life (14:6), the *pneuma* leads believers into an understanding of the truth that Jesus embodies (16:13)" (2016, 243).

Although there are certainly resonances between the Gospel's understanding of Spirit (*pneuma*) and the larger Greco-Roman context from which it comes, including philosophical contexts (cf. Engberg-Pedersen 2015, 2017), Koester argues that the Spirit in John is contextualized by Jewish categories, reframed by its own christological perspectives (2016, 249–50). This means that, rather than inherent to the world, God's *pneuma* is a gift given by Jesus, who asks for and sends the Spirit, breathing on his disciples after his resurrection (John 20:22). This gift causes new birth and new creation for the disciples and all believers, who become God's children (cf. Weissenrieder). Such an understanding resonates with both Greco-Roman and Jewish literature, which incorporate "spirit" into procreational theories. Jewish contexts in particular focus on *God's Spirit* rather than human spirits as the source of all life. Just as God created the world, breathing spirit into Adam at the moment of creation (Gen 2:7), so too is God's Spirit needed for the procreation of all human beings, who cannot be truly animated apart from God's involvement (Kessler). In this way, Jesus' gift of the Spirit of truth, made possible by his return to the Father, causes a new creation moment at John 20:22. This new creation and new birth means the disciples can experience life as God intended, so long as they remain "in" the Father through Jesus (15:1-8, 26-27; 16:7-16). In Jesus' physical absence, this connection is only possible by means of the Spirit. Even though the Gospel does not have a fully articulated Trinitarian perspective, it is no wonder that later church fathers found within it the beginnings of what they later termed "Trinity."

Finishing the Father's Will

John 18:1–21:25

The final portion of John's Gospel brings us to the moment of Jesus' hour, as well as its beginning aftereffects. Events start happening in quick succession in John 18, picking up the action after the long pause of chapters 13–17. Jesus has worked to prepare his disciples, but now his departure and return to his Father is underway. This means Jesus must endure the betrayals of Judas and of Peter. Peter continues his inappropriate responses to Jesus' words; he still does not believe Jesus completely, and so tries again to lay down his life on Jesus' behalf at his arrest, though he quickly turns to deny him a few verses later. Jo-Ann Brant suggests that Peter fits the ancient character mold of a *mōros*, who is "the secondary character who imitates the principal character and misunderstands or reacts inappropriately" (2011, 233–34). In this case, Peter keeps thinking he is the noble shepherd *or* that he knows the best way for Jesus to die. Jesus is still revealing the Father's will to Peter, and all his disciples, by fulfilling his mission and showing them the work of the true noble shepherd (10:1-18; 19:28; 20:22-23). Jesus must do this before he can appoint others to take up the work of feeding and caring for his sheep (21:15-19).

Peter is not the only foil for Jesus in John 18–21. Indeed, the only one not taken aback by the events is Jesus, who exerts control at a time when he would seem to be at the mercy of others. He surrenders himself in the garden and rebukes Peter's rash behavior, and then he testifies "well" or "nobly" (*kalōs*, cf. 10:11-14) before Annas (18:19-24). Shuttled to Pilate's praetorium, Jesus again remains steadfast, speaking boldly to Pilate, who tries unsuccessfully to exert his control over Jesus and the Jews outside the praetorium. Pilate, in contrast, scurries from Jesus to the Jews in seven short scenes, rushing in and out of his own quarters like a servant, because the priests and Pharisees refused to enter Pilate's home for fear of being defiled before Passover (18:28). Jesus even remains in control on the cross, watching the soldiers divide his clothing, appointing a new home for his mother, and fulfilling Scripture with his words before he "hands over" (*paredōken*, 19:30) his spirit at the moment of death. As Brant writes, in these chapters, the "indecisive folly of those who seem to be agents of action" sharply contrasts "the constancy of Jesus," thereby reinforcing his heroic characterization and casting his death as an honorable one *in spite* of all appearances to the contrary (2011, 231).

Jesus' death, however, is *not* the end. Much to the surprise of his disciples—Mary Magdalene, Peter, the Beloved Disciple, and the well-known "doubting Thomas," along with the others gathered in fear and the Gospel audience—Jesus lives. Appearing first to Mary, Jesus comforts her in the garden and also gives her a commission. She is not to cling to him, but to let him continue his return to the Father while she tells the disciples of Jesus' resurrection (20:17-18). It is only later that Jesus appears among the other disciples and fulfills his promise by giving the Holy Spirit in a scene that replays the creation story of Genesis.

Despite the climactic moment of 20:19-23, John's Gospel remains acutely sensitive to the position of the Gospel audience, who has not seen the Risen Lord and was not present for this giving of the Holy Spirit. How can they believe? And how are they included in Jesus' promises? Can they also receive this Spirit? Both Thomas's "killjoy" attitude in 20:24-29 (Brant 2011, 272–73) and the story of Jesus' third appearance to this group in John 21 answer these concerns. Jesus declares a blessing upon those who believe in spite of "not seeing" him in 20:29, and 21:1-25 reminds us again that even disciples who have seen the resurrected Jesus still need nudging and correction. There is still work to be done, it seems, in order for Jesus' prayer of unity for his disciples to be realized.

Commentary

The Noble Shepherd Lays Down His Life . . . (18:1–19:42)

Even though there is good reason to divide Jesus' arrest, interrogation, and trial scenes from his crucifixion and burial, doing so risks dividing a narrative that is tightly bound together. These events happen quickly, all on the same day, and are connected to one another through thematic and semantic links. Contemporary readers may overlook that these events occur on the same day because we forget that according to Jewish reckoning of time, days are measured from sunset to sunset. When the sun goes down in 13:30, a new day has begun. In 19:14 the narrator reports that is it the Day of Preparation, the day before Passover when the lambs were ritually slaughtered by priests in the temple (Lev 23:5; Num 9:2).

On this busy and holy day, when the priests should be occupied with preparations for the Passover, they are focused instead on Jesus' death. As

Brant notes, this is another example of Johannine irony (2011, 242). The priests are orchestrating the death of someone just before Passover, under false charges (Num 35:33-34; John 7:14–8:59; Sheridan 2015, 177–80). This is a crime that not only defiles an individual but, recalling the distinction made by Jonathan Klawans in the discussion of 2:13-22, is also a sin that causes "moral impurity" (2000, 23–32). Unlike "ritual impurity," which was often incidental and unavoidable, moral impurity included culpability and could not be rectified by ritual cleansing alone; it defiled both the land and the temple, requiring divine intervention for purification. At the same time, however, Jesus' suffering *is* that divine intervention, since, as priests should, they here enact the killing of *the* superior Passover Lamb, namely, Jesus.

In John 18–19, therefore, Jesus fulfills the role of both the noble shepherd (10:1-18) *and* the "Lamb of God" (1:29). He is God's lamb, willingly submitting to the desires of God, his Shepherd, regardless of the cost (cf. Gen 21; Huizenga, 75–128). Jesus is the demonstration of God's love for the world (3:14-18), a sacrifice that certainly costs something from Jesus but also from God, whose love for Jesus is also emphasized in John's Gospel (3:35; 10:17-18; 15:9; 17:23-26; cf. Klawans 2006, 87). He is also the noble shepherd who shows his own sheep *how* to have life. He protects and preserves them, fulfilling his word that he did not lose or destroy (*apōlesa*) any of those whom God gave him (18:9; cf. 3:16; 6:39; 10:28; 17:12). In this series of events, Jesus, the *true* noble shepherd, faces down the imposters who surround him: from the midst of his disciples (Judas and Peter, 18:1-27), the Jewish elite who rally against him (18:15–19:22), and Rome as personified in the person of Pilate (18:28-42). Despite every temptation to abandon his sheep, Jesus remains steadfast, standing at the center of the storm swirling around him and focused on finishing the will of the Father.

A. John 18:1-27: Jesus' Arrest and Interrogation

John 18:1 resumes the action paused at 13:31. In 13:30, Judas disappeared into the night and Jesus followed with extended instruction for his disciples. Even though they did not yet understand, Jesus continues with God's will, which brings him to the garden in 18:1. The scene divides into two portions: vv. 1-12 recount Jesus' purposeful and powerful surrender in contrast to the foolishness of all those around him, especially Judas and Peter; vv. 13-27 describe Jesus' transportation to and interrogation by Annas, Caiaphas's father-in-law. Even though Peter and the other disciple follow Jesus, Peter's interrogation differs from Jesus' own. While Jesus speaks "well" and truthfully, Peter fulfills Jesus' words by denying him three times. Peter's cowardice reveals the limits of his rash confession in 13:36-38; Jesus, not Peter, is the noble shepherd of this story.

A Powerfully Peaceful Surrender (vv. 1-12). In 18:1 Jesus travels with his disciples to a place across the Kidron Valley. Jesus selects a location known by his disciples, including Judas, "because Jesus used to gather there frequently with his disciples" (v. 3). Jesus' choice of this location shows that he is not hiding or seeking escape from his hour (comp. 7:4, 10; 8:59; 12:36; 18:20). It is now time. This location is not explicitly named in John, but as "the other side of the Kidron Valley" it is the Mount of Olives described also in Synoptic accounts (Brant 2011, 101). Margaret Daly-Denton (193–95) suggests that in focusing on the Kidron Valley, the Gospel reinforces its comparison of Jesus and David, who fled across the Kidron Valley when he was betrayed by his son, Absalom, and his close advisor, Ahithophel (2 Sam 15–17). Unlike David, however, who left Jerusalem to avoid his death, Jesus travels there to facilitate his own death. Jesus is not victimized by Judas's betrayal; he has known about it and he submits, not to Judas but to the Father, whose revelation of love comes through Jesus' death. Indeed, once Judas arrives with a superlative force of Roman soldiers (a cohort, which is 600 soldiers) *and* armed men (*hypēretas*) from the lead-priests and Pharisees, his work is done. This ridiculous crew of Roman and Jewish elite allies has come for a battle, but Jesus steps forward in v. 4 to assume full control of the scene.

Jesus does not wait for the army before him to approach, nor does he cower in fear of their massive show of force in the garden; instead he takes initiative because, as the narrator explains, he "knew everything that was coming against him" (v. 4). Jesus does not need an army to show his power. Verses 4-9 proceed in an ABAB pattern that underlines Jesus' control of what unfolds, as well as Judas's location with those rallied against his former teacher.

A. vv. 4-5, Question and Answer: "I am."
    B. v. 6, The Power of Jesus' Words: Army's Retreat
A'. vv. 7-8, Question and Answer: "I am."
    B'. v. 9, The Power of Jesus' Words: Release My Followers

In response to Jesus' self-revelation, "I am he" (*egō eimi*) in v. 5, the gathered forces, hands full of lanterns, torches, and weapons, immediately fall backward and to the ground in a forced retreat (v. 6). The scene is at once compelling and comedic. Powerful soldiers that the ruler of this world has mustered stand gathered, menacing before Jesus, with one of his own disciples at their head. Jesus, however, does not hesitate. As the embodiment of

God's Word, he speaks and they falter. Their involuntary submission before Jesus' words shows his true kingship and his choice to die. He is no victim.

Peter, however, does not seem to understand the power of Jesus' words. Brant suggests that when Peter attacks Malchus, he has one of two aims in mind: either he is trying to die on Jesus' behalf, fulfilling his promise from 13:36-38, *or* he is trying to die alongside Jesus, as Thomas said they all would in 11:16 (2011, 236). If it is the former, perhaps Peter is trying to prompt Jesus to flee, although his flailing attack certainly pales in comparison to the power Jesus has just displayed in his words (18:5). If it is the latter, Peter is not only acting in accordance to the wrong person's words but is also trying to force the type of death that Jesus will die. Capital punishment was shameful, bringing dishonor to the one killed and to all who were associated with that person. For this reason, stories of people committing suicide before they could be convicted or captured, and certainly before they were executed, were not uncommon (e.g., Plato, *Crito*; Valerius Maximus, *Fact.* 9.12.4–7; Livy, 1.58; Josephus, *J. W.* 7.9.389–406; 1 Sam 31:1-6). By killing themselves, these people (women as well as men) looked to retain their honor as well as the honor of their households. Building on the work of Jennifer Glancy (2006, 2010), Brant notes that heroic deaths in the Roman world were active deaths, deaths in battle, where one's body was scarred with wounds on the front rather than marked with beatings on the back. Crucifixion, as the most shameful type of death, meant not only a back marked with scourging (John 19:1) but also pierced hands and feet, and a body displayed naked for all to see as life slowly drained from the victim. Powerful men did *not* die this way, and Peter, it seems, cannot imagine the Christ suffering such a fate; better for him to die in battle, like a real man (Glancy 2010, 30–33).

Jesus rebukes Peter by paraphrasing his words from 12:27: "Put your sword in its sheath! The cup which the Father has given to me, shall I not drink it?!" (18:11). Once again, the portrait of a reluctant Jesus from Mark's account is undermined (Mark 14:36). Moreover, unlike in Luke's story, Jesus does not heal the slave's ear after Peter's assault (Luke 22:51). Instead, the slave, ironically named "Malchus," which means "king," remains deformed. This could impact his service to the high priest, and it also demonstrates the inability of the high priest to protect him. Jesus and his followers are the ones who were surrounded by armed men, but they leave corporally whole; Jesus' words secure their safety, just as he said they would (18:9; 17:9-12). Already, Jesus is acting the part of the shepherd, the real king, by protecting his sheep from the wolves and thieves who threaten them.

When we recall that Rome was personified by wolves, having been founded by Romulus who was nursed with his brother by a she-wolf, the image becomes even more striking (Livy, 1.4). Malchus's deformity opens him to ridicule in a first-century world that regularly evaluated character on the basis of physical appearance and ability (Parsons 2011, 17–66). As Glancy explains, however, it *also* reflects back upon his master, the high priest, since slaves stood in the place of their masters, often as "surrogate bodies" (2006, 24–25). Peter's attack on Malchus is an attack on the high priest himself, and it leaves "him" deformed. Malchus's injury would have diminished his ability to hear; indeed, in the scene to follow the high priest will show himself deaf to Jesus' words. Jesus' ability to shield Peter from repercussions is, therefore, all the more astounding, particularly in light of the blow Jesus receives when speaking to Annas in 18:22.

   Speaking Nobly or Wickedly: Jesus and Peter (vv. 13-27). Jesus is then bound and taken to Annas, who is Caiaphas's father-in-law (v. 13). The trip first to Annas, rather than Caiaphas, is somewhat surprising, particularly because of the narrator's reminder of Caiaphas's role in plotting Jesus' death (v. 14; 11:45-53) and because Annas has not yet featured in the Gospel. Annas, however, *was* high priest from 6–15 CE, when he was deposed by the Roman procurator Gratus. Brant (2011, 237) and Keener (2003, 1089) emphasize that Annas would have continued to exert considerable influence because of his position. Indeed, Num 35:25-28 states that high priests were appointed until death, regardless of what Rome might say. Annas, moreover, remained connected to the men Rome recognized as high priests, being the father-in-law of Caiaphas as well as the father of five sons, all of whom were high priests at some point. Arrival before Annas, therefore, meant connection to one recognized as God's authority without this being an official trial, which would require Caiaphas's participation. As it was the Day of Preparation, Caiaphas could have been otherwise occupied before Jesus was eventually taken to him in John 18:24. Even then, Caiaphas does not appear in the story. His words from 11:49-50 are paraphrased in 18:14, and stand on their own as his judgment: "it is better for one person (*anthōpos*) to die on behalf of the people (*laou*)." He not only fails to protect his slave, Malchus, but also hands over one who—according to the world's perspective—was supposed to be his own sheep to die, rather than standing to suffer punishment himself.

   Verses 15-27 set side by side the interrogations of Jesus by Annas and of Peter by various slaves in the courtyard. This is not an official trial scene; again, differing from Mark's account, Jesus only has one trial in John's Gospel—his trial before Pilate. The Romans and Jewish leaders are already working together in John 18:1-3, when Judas arrives with a mixed army to take Jesus. Warren Carter emphasizes that, in these scenes, the Jewish leaders and Pilate are allies, not enemies: "Roman troops could not have been deployed without Pilate's command. It seems, then, that the narrative assumes a previous meeting or meetings at which Pilate heard the Jerusalem elite's concern about Jesus as a major threat" (2008, 301). Perhaps the sending of an army aimed to spark a response similar to that of Peter in 18:10; if Jesus (and his followers) were killed attacking Roman and Jewish soldiers, the problem would be solved. Moreover, they could frame Jesus' crime as sedition, a revolutionary rebellion against Rome, without ever needing the pretense of legal proceedings. Things, however, do *not* go as planned, and the interaction between the Jerusalem elite and Pilate reveals their deep mistrust of one another—both sides act out of fear rather than friendship (contra 15:12-14; 16:26-28).

The side-by-side interlacing of 18:15-27 creates an ABA pattern that causes us to read these events as "simultaneous action" (Brant 2011, 238).

A. vv. 15-18, Peter in the Courtyard: First Denial
   B. vv. 19-24, Jesus before Annas: Speaking Boldly
A'. vv. 25-27, Peter in the Courtyard: Second and Third Denials

The overlaying of action raises the tension of the scenes while also reinforcing the contrast between Peter and Jesus. Peter continues in his missteps while Jesus continues to speak boldly and truthfully.

In v. 15, Peter's response to Jesus' arrest is to follow him, along with an additional anonymous disciple. John 18:15-19 picks up the noble shepherd motif again with several key words from John 10 that form a contrast between Peter and this disciple. In 18:15, the anonymous disciple enters into the high priest's "courtyard" or *aulē*. This the same word that Jesus used in 10:1 and 16 to describe the "fold" or "pen" where his sheep reside. In 10:1, he explains that the shepherd enters through the "gate" (*thyra*) of the *aulē*, in contrast to the thieves and predators who sneak in another way. Like Jesus, the unnamed disciple enters through the *thyra*, but Peter hesitates. He needs the other disciple's help in order to enter. This disciple speaks with the "gate-keeper" (*thyrōnōs*) to secure Peter's entry. In doing so, the disciple again imitates the shepherd's actions from John 10:3 where Jesus said, "For this one [the shepherd] the gate-keeper (*thyrōros*) opens." Notably, this model disciple remains unnamed for the Gospel audience, but he is known to the high priest. His recognition not only enables Peter's (belated) entrance into the courtyard but also opens him up to risk; known to the high priest, this disciple comes anyway, and orchestrates the entrance of another of Jesus' followers! He could have certainly been seen as a threat, but he trusts Jesus' promise: Jesus said he will not lose any of those whom God has given him. Peter, in contrast, has not learned this lesson—or he does not trust it (yet).

Peter's lingering outside the courtyard, therefore, already associates him with those who would try to enter the *aulē* by other means: the thieves and those who come to destroy (10:1). The last thief who associated with Jesus was Judas Iscariot (12:6; 13:29), the "son of destruction" (17:12) and the only one from among Jesus' disciples who perished, left in the garden beyond the Kidron Valley. Already the audience should anticipate that Peter is still acting according to a different plan than Jesus: is he here to steal Jesus away or to destroy those who threaten him? Maybe this is what Peter had initially planned, but soon he finds himself fulfilling a different one of Jesus' promises. When the gate-keeper, a slave girl, addresses Peter, he denies Jesus. Her question is far from threatening in tone; she expects a denial, and she receives it: "You are not also a disciple of this person, are you?" Peter's response is the exact opposite of Jesus' words from 18:5 and 8. Rather than Jesus' truthful word of power, Peter responds, "I am not" (*ouk eimi*). The phrasing, "you are not *also*," perhaps indicates that the other disciple did *not* deny his association. Peter, however, is unwilling to be so bold; he hides himself among those who just seized his Lord, warming himself with them beside a fire (18:18).

At the same time, the narrator explains, "the high priest questioned Jesus about his disciples and his teaching" (18:19). Instead of hearing the entire interrogation, Jesus' words dominate the scene: he does not deny teaching but rather emphasizes the openness with which he taught. "Why are you asking me?" he says, "Ask the ones having heard what I said to them. Look! These ones know the things I said" (18:21). Jesus is already turning the testimony over to others, gesturing even to people in the room with him when he commands Annas to "Look!" In the courtyard, however, Peter is simultaneously failing at this very task. Jesus is slapped, or struck in the face, for the boldness of his answer, but he does not cower. He replies, "If I spoke wickedly (*kakōs*), testify about the wickedness (*kakou*). If I spoke nobly (*kalōs*), why are you beating me?" (18:23). The audience knows that Jesus has spoken nobly, or truthfully, because they have heard the story of his bold teaching in the synagogue and temple throughout the Gospel (2:13-22; 5:19-47; 6:26-59; 7:14–8:59; 10:1-39). Jesus' response exposes the wickedness of the soldier (*hypērta*) while also showing his authority. The scene ends when Annas sends Jesus off to Caiaphas without a word of his own (18:24).

Peter's interrogation continues during this time, and he persists in his wicked speech of denial (18:25-27). His unwillingness to speak nobly on Jesus' behalf seems to belie Jesus' response to the high priest noted above. Peter, it seems, *could have* helped Jesus if he would have been willing to be truthful. He could have been one of those questioned on Jesus' behalf to share the world Jesus had so boldly proclaimed to him; but, as Jesus well knows, Peter is not willing to do that—he is not willing to die *this* way. Peter, the narrator reports, "denied" (*ērnēsato*, 18:25, 27; cf. 1 John 2:22-23) Jesus two more times: once in answering another question that anticipated a negative answer ("you are not also one of his disciples, are you?" v. 25), and again in answering a more difficult questioner, an eyewitness and relative of Malchus. His question expects a confession from Peter: "I did see you in the garden with him, didn't I?" (v. 26). Peter's foolish behavior in 18:10 opened him up to genuine testimony against him, unlike the false accusations Jesus faces in 18:28–19:16. This man "testifies to the wickedness" that Peter has done, but Peter will not be the one who ends up dying for it. Peter denies his Lord for a third time, thereby fulfilling Jesus' prophecy from 13:36-38 just as the cock sounds its call (18:27). Just as Judas is left in the garden, Peter is—at least for a time—left here, apart from his shepherd, a lost sheep in need of rescue (cf. John 21).

B. John 18:28–19:16a: Jesus on Trial

When Jesus arrives at Pilate's headquarters, the praetorium, his trial begins. Many scholars note the seven-scene progression through 18:28–19:16a marked by Pilate's quick scurrying out of and into his quarters (Brown 1970, 857–59; Bond, 168–69; Brant 2011, 242). Pilate accommodates to the desires of the Jewish elite who have brought Jesus to him; these devout leaders do not want to risk defilement before Passover (18:28-29). Indeed, Brant notes that with priests among the group bringing Jesus, their defilement could risk postponing the celebration of Passover by an entire lunar month according to Num 9:9-12 (2011, 234). The larger context of Num 9 emphasizes the need to "keep the Passover at its appointed time" (NRSV) or "according to its *hour* (*hōra*)" (9:2, LXX). The word "hour" is especially significant in John's Gospel, as Jesus' preferred term to describe the moment of his death as well as his return to his Father (John 12:23; 13:1; 17:1). Even though the Jewish leaders want to avoid defilement, and may think they are controlling the situation in John, it is Jesus' obedience to the Father that ensures *this* Passover is celebrated at the right time.

Carter observes that Pilate's behavior in this scene is a further indication that he is allied with these Jerusalem leaders (2008, 301). The image of a Roman governor rushing around the praetorium is comedic and contributes to the contrast between Jesus' stability and the instability of those around him. Rome, represented by Pilate, joins the cast of characters—alongside Annas, Caiaphas, and a number of unnamed lead-priests and Pharisees, as well as Judas and Peter—who are unable to comprehend either Jesus' identity or his mission. Pilate's willingness to meet the Jewish leaders outside does not mean that he will completely surrender to their will. Instead, what follows is a tug-of-war between Rome (Pilate) and the Jewish religious leadership, each one seeking to show its superiority.

The seven-scene chiasm proceeds as follows:

A. 18:28-32, Pilate Comes Out: Refuses to Execute
  B. 18:33-38a, Pilate Enters to Question Jesus
    C. 18:38b-40, Pilate Goes Outside: Barabbas Not Jesus
      D. 19:1-3, Jesus Is Flogged and Crowned
    C'. 19:4-8, Pilate Brings Jesus Out with Him
  B'. 19:9-11, Pilate Enters to Question Jesus Again
A'. 19:12-16a, Pilate Comes Out: Agrees to Crucify

The debate between Pilate and the Jewish lead-priests is best understood as a power struggle between Roman and Jewish rule as well as between Rome's gods (including the emperor) and Israel's God, "the One True God" (17:3). The fear the Jerusalem leaders expressed in 11:45-53 still dominates this scene; they are hoping to stop Jesus and his movement before the Romans think he is starting an uprising. Helen Bond argues that Pilate's backstory might explain his odd behavior as well, whether or not John's is a precise recounting of events. Stationed over a "relatively unimportant province," Pilate was a middle-rank Roman nobleman (9). He was, however, a nobleman who had risen enough in rank to be appointed provincial governor even though he was born in the *equestrian* order. Pilate was well equipped to play the game of seeking glory for himself and for Rome (10). Rather than a shaky and weak pawn, then, Bond understands Pilate to be cynical and conniving, a "victor" who succeeds in forcing the Jewish leaders to forsake God's kingship and submit to Caesar's rule instead in 19:14 (177, 191–92).

Taking an alternative view, however, Brant follows the tradition that connects Pilate to Aelius Sejanus, a Roman general with a particularly powerful hatred for the Jews (on the rise and fall of Sejanus, see Tacitus, *Ann.* 3–6). According to this reading, Pilate was a known client of Sejanus, who tried to overthrow Tiberius in 31 CE (Brant 2011, 243). When Sejanus was convicted and executed for this crime, Pilate was also associated with his seditious offense. Pilate, therefore, needed to prove his loyalty to the emperor. He needed to keep the peace in Judea by enforcing Roman rule and controlling a Jewish populace who had a reputation for rebellion, particularly around festival times (Josephus, *J. W.* 2.169–77; *Ant.* 18.55–62; Philo,

Embassy 38.302). He also needed no one to question his commitment to the emperor, especially not a group of Jewish priests in Jerusalem (18:35). What follows, then, is a back-and-forth built on fear: Pilate's fear of being executed and torn to pieces like his old friend Sejanus, and the priests' fear of a Roman legion destroying Jerusalem; neither, according to the Gospel, is fearing the God who sent his Son into their midst.

False Charges: Sedition (18:28-40). The charge leveled against Jesus is sedition (that he is usurping Roman rule by setting himself up as a king), but it does not stick. When Pilate asks the leaders for their "charge" against Jesus, they reply instead with a question: "If this one were not one doing wickedness (*kakon poiōn*), we would not have handed him over to you" (18:30). The accusation of Jesus as one "doing wickedness" recalls Jesus' exchange with the soldier who struck him in 18:20-24: "If I speak wickedly (*kakōs*), then testify to the wickedness (*kakou*)." The soldier remained silent, and Annas, likewise, silently sent the bound Jesus to Caiaphas, who also never even appears to question Jesus. The lack of testimony against Jesus is, thus, testimony that Jesus has spoken "nobly" or "well" (*kalōs*), just as is fitting for the noble shepherd (*ho poimēn ho kalos*, 10:11). In contrast, the Jewish leaders' words in 18:30 are wicked because they play a part in the death of an innocent man (Num 35:33-34; Deut 17:6).

As the exchanges continue in John 18:28-40, Pilate hurries in and out again, confirming that he finds no charge to bring against Jesus. Even after asking Jesus directly if he is a king, Jesus deflects: "*You* are saying that I am a king" (18:37). Jesus' responses are indecipherable to Pilate and are instead meant for the Gospel audience who eavesdrops on the exchange. With no disciple of Jesus present, the content of this conversation is privileged for the audience alone. They, and not the disciples who walked with Jesus during his ministry, witness how Jesus speaks to the Roman governor—and they are instructed by his boldness. Pilate may ask, "What is truth?" but he seems entirely uninterested in Jesus' answer. As Bond notes (179), Pilate does not wait for Jesus to speak but goes back outside to give his own evaluation of truth to the waiting Jews: "I myself find no motive in him" (*egō oudemian heuriskō en auto aitiman*). According to Pilate, Jesus is not a threat. The Jews, therefore, should not fear taking him back; Rome is not going to attack Jerusalem or the temple because of this man.

The concerns in 11:45-53 are rendered irrelevant, at least it seems. Pilate, according to Josephus, was prone to violent outbursts and threats against the Jews on a number of occasions in the past. Rome was a fickle ruler, as the Jerusalem leaders well knew. They, understandably, do not trust Pilate's words. Still fearful of the movement Jesus could spark, they choose to take back Barabbas when Pilate offers to release a prisoner. In contrast to Jesus, Barabbas was a man who was recognized by Rome as an insurrectionist (*lēstēs*) and, therefore, a potential reason for Rome to attack Jerusalem (18:40)! So great is the priests' fear of Jesus' potential that they take Barabbas over him. Nevertheless, such a choice would not alleviate Roman concerns of rebellion; the Jerusalem leaders have freed a rebel and have left the one without kingly aspirations in Roman custody. By welcoming back a rebel, the Jerusalem leaders expose themselves (as well as all of Jerusalem) to Roman suspicion of hidden nationalistic ambitions. The Gospel audience, situated on the other side of the Roman destruction of Jerusalem during the First Jewish War, would be well aware of the results of harboring insurrectionists in the holy city and even in the temple itself (Josephus, *J. W.* 2.409–10, 422–25; 4.151; Regev).

Making Himself a Son of a God (19:1-12). The narrative moves quickly on after the crowd calls for Barabbas; we never hear if Pilate released him or not since he is not the protagonist of the story. Instead, 19:1-3 records Jesus' mock coronation as "King of the Jews" or "Judeans." Crowned with thorns and a purple robe, Jesus is supposed to be a mockery of a Judean king. Romans enjoyed crafting punishments they believed fit the crimes committed, and they regularly dressed condemned prisoners in the garb of defeated generals or tragic figures, forcing them to reenact legendary battles or mythical death scenes as they died (Marcus 2006). These scenes reinforced Roman power, displaying for the crowds gathered around not only entertainment but also a gory lesson in what awaited those who challenged Rome and the gods who sanctioned its rule. This scene is the crux of the chiasm in 18:28–19:16a and is full of more Johannine irony. Jesus, after all, is not only the King of the Jews/Judeans but also of the world as the Son of the One True God.

The scourging or flogging that Jesus endures is not a frivolous display of Roman violence. Rather, Romans considered confession under torture admissible in trials (Glancy 2005, 118–25; *Dig.* 48.19.15.41; 48.19.28.2; Suetonius, *Tib.* 61). Since Pilate could not secure a confession from Jesus through his first round of questioning, it seems likely that he is now seeking it through torture. Such a move also indicates that he does not trust the Jerusalem leadership's evaluation of Jesus either; he does not take their word on Jesus' seditious intent. The "slap" or blow that Jesus receives from the Roman soldiers repeats the abuse he faced before Annas (18:22; 19:3). The parallel is poignant; Jesus fares no better with the Jewish priests than he does before Rome. These rulers, although distrustful of one another, form a unified opposition to Jesus. Controlled by fear, both are in favor of retaining the status quo that seems to benefit them, although in different ways.

When Pilate emerges again in 19:4, he explains that the torture has also failed to force a confession from Jesus. Pilate continues to "find in him no motive." Displaying Jesus' beaten and humiliated body before the priests gives evidence of Pilate's torture, showing the Jews gathered that he has interrogated Jesus further. The sight, however, sparks seemingly irrational rage; the priests and soldiers shout (*ekraugasan*), "Crucify! Crucify!" Brant argues that the verb *kraugazō* means "howled," the same verb used to describe the baying of dogs (2011, 247). In John's Gospel, however, Jesus has also "howled" or "shouted loudly" (*ekraugasen*) when raising Lazarus (11:43) and the crowd who welcomed him into Jerusalem also "shouted" repeatedly (*ekraugazon*), "Hosanna, blessed is the one coming in the name of the Lord, *the King of Israel*" (12:13). Rather than dogs baying, then, John's contrast is between those who welcomed Jesus with shouts that identified him as king and the lead-priests and soldiers who now call for his death. Jesus is not a "blessed" king in any recognizable sense, but he remains King anyway.

In John 19:7, the Jerusalem leaders articulate a charge against Jesus for the first time, carefully phrasing it in ways that Pilate will understand: "We ourselves have a law and according to the law, he ought to die, because he is making himself a son of a god." By avoiding definite articles in their description, the Jewish leaders avoid strict monotheism and invite Pilate to think through the implications. After all, Pilate knows others who are recognized as "a son of a god," not only the demigods of mythical fame (e.g., Aesclepius, Hercules, and Aeneas) but also the Roman emperors. During Pilate's lifetime, the title *divi filius* (son of a god) was reserved as a posthumous honor bestowed by the Senate to affirm the reign of a past emperor (Suetonius, *Aug.* 53, 100; *Claud.* 45; *Vesp.* 23; *Titus* 10). Eventually some emperors began to take the title even while alive as an attempt to secure loyalty when the Senate opposed them (Suetonius, *Cal.* 22; *Dom.* 13). The Jewish leaders' clarification means that if this one makes himself a son of a god, he is a threat to the emperor himself. No wonder Pilate reacts with "fear" (19:8).

Pilate returns inside and questions Jesus again; this time, however, Jesus is a less amiable witness and he refuses to tell Pilate "where he is from" (19:9; cf. 18:37). Pilate correctly interprets Jesus' silence as an affront to his—and, therefore, to Rome's—authority and he seeks to remind him of his subordinate place in 19:10. Even after Pilate's threat, Jesus does not submit but instead reminds Pilate of his own place: "You would not have authority over me at all except if it has been given to you from above. For this reason, the one who handed me over to you has a greater sin" (19:11). Jesus' response is ambiguous and could be interpreted in at least two ways. First, the ultimate authority to which Jesus refers is God's authority. The audience knows this is his intent because of his use of "from above" (*anōthen*), which recalls Jesus' conversation with Nicodemus in John 3. But that is not necessarily what Pilate would hear. From Pilate's perspective, his authority was granted by the emperor; it is not inherent to Pilate's own self. This second meaning, therefore, might explain why Pilate seeks to release Jesus after this point—he could have interpreted Jesus as acknowledging the emperor's power (19:12a). It also would have made Pilate attuned to his own dependence on the emperor. When the Jewish leaders challenge his loyalty to the emperor in 19:12b, Jesus has primed Pilate to react with violence.

Sedition Committed: No King but Caesar (19:12b-16a). The title "friend of Caesar" was eventually used to describe provincial governors and therefore recognizable to the Gospel audience. It also serves the themes of John's Gospel, which contrast the "friend of Caesar" with those who would be "friends" of Jesus and therefore of God. One cannot be both.

Pilate reacts to the challenge that he is not a "friend of Caesar" if he releases Jesus by approaching the judgement seat, or *bēma*. The location indicates the moment of a final verdict. The language, however, is ambiguous: is Jesus seated on the *bēma* or is Pilate? The ambiguity again serves Johannine themes. As in John 5, another attempts to judge Jesus, but Jesus himself has been given authority to judge by the Father. In 19:14, the hour is again brought to the center: "and it was the Day of Preparation of the Passover, it was about the sixth hour" (noon). The priests have spent half their day debating with Pilate over Jesus' fate, rather than in preparation for the Passover at the temple, sacrificing the lambs needed for the evening celebration and memorial (Brant 2011, 249). The intensity, therefore, reaches a fever pitch: "Take away! Take away! Crucify him!" (19:15). The command to "take away" or "lift up" does not have a direct object in 19:15, thus also leaving some ambiguity. The reference to the time of Passover in 19:14, and its association with the time of slaughtering lambs (Josephus, *Spec.* 2.145; Brown 1970, 883; contra Thompson 2015, 389–90), encourages the audience to recall 1:29 where John (the Baptist) declared Jesus to be "The Lamb of God, the one who takes away the sin of the world!" (cf. 1:36).

Pilate repeats his previous description of Jesus from 19:5 with a slight adjustment in 19:14; he no longer says "behold the man (*anthrōpos*)," but instead says "behold your king." Pilate's description is certainly ironic—Jesus has twice before been identified as the King of Israel (1:49; 12:13), and the crowd in Galilee attempted to crown him in 6:15—but it is also condescending. Pilate's display of a beaten Jesus as "King of the Judeans" makes a mockery of any Judean who might think they could ever free themselves from Roman rule; it is a display of Roman power. Rather than focusing on this insult, however, the priests continue to be preoccupied with Jesus himself, and the threat they perceive him to be. When Pilate asks if he "should crucify your king?" the Jewish leaders respond, "We have no king except Caesar!" (19:15). This confession at once satisfies Pilate, who is now willing to execute Jesus because it is a complete submission to Roman rule (19:16a). Carter writes, "With these words, the Jerusalem leaders repudiate their centuries-old covenant with God as Israel's king (1 Sam 8:7; Ps 47:2; 93:1)" (2008, 309). Whether the leaders actually made this confession is not the focus here. What it reveals is how the Johannine community understood the events surrounding Jesus' execution; for them, the Jerusalem religious establishment forsook their God for another, namely Rome. Made all the more poignant on the Day of Preparation, the Gospel presents the rescued Israelites bending to another Pharaoh rather than relying on the God of their deliverance. *This* is the actual sedition of the encounter; Rome seeks to overthrow and occupy the throne that belongs to God alone.

C. John 19:16b-42: Jesus' Death and Burial

The rest of chapter 19 records Jesus' crucifixion, death, and burial. Continuing with the theme of control, Jesus' knowledge and intentionality repeatedly surfaces in the chapter, contrasting the ignorance of those around him. The section roughly divides into two portions, 19:16b-30 and 19:31-42. Each section contains interactions between the Jerusalem religious elite and Pilate; scenes of Roman soldiers unwittingly fulfilling Scripture with acts of violence; and the new household established by Jesus. This household is created when Jesus appoints his mother to the Beloved Disciple's household. Joseph and Nicodemus also participate as members of this household by caring for Jesus' body after death. The result is a twofold step pattern illustrated below:

> 19:16b-30, Jesus' Crucifixion
>   A. vv. 16b-22, Religious Leaders and Pilate: Debating the *Titulus*
>   B. vv. 23-24, The Soldiers' Fulfill Scripture: Dividing Garments
>   C. vv. 25-30, Jesus' Mother and Beloved Disciple
> 19:31-42 Jesus' Burial
>   A'. v. 31, Religious Leaders and Pilate: Removing the Bodies
>   B'. vv. 32-37, The Soldiers' Fulfill Scripture: Piercing the Side
>   C'. vv. 38-42, Joseph and Nicodemus Bury Jesus

Jesus' Crucifixion (vv. 16b-30). The first section records Jesus' crucifixion with several significant differences from the Synoptic accounts. First, Jesus carries the cross himself to the place of his crucifixion. This, again, shows Jesus' deliberate decision to fulfill his Father's will (10:17-18). Second, the naming of the location "Place of the Skull," alongside its Hebrew name "Golgotha" in 19:17, creates a parallelism with 19:13, where the "Stone Pavement" or "Gabbatha" was also named and translated. The pause on the names of these locations focuses the audience's attention and creates greater gravity for the scenes that take place there (cf. 5:1; comp. 1:38, 40; 20:16). Moreover, calling the site of Jesus' crucifixion the "place" or *topos* again calls to mind how this word has been used to describe the temple, or the place of God's presence, elsewhere in the Gospel (4:20; 5:13; 11:48; 14:2-3).

Language is also significant to the debate over the *titulus*, or title placard, placed above Jesus on the cross where he was crucified. Stationed between two additional (and anonymous) victims, Jesus' cross is the center of attention, and all eyes are drawn to the placard, which reads, "Jesus of Nazareth, King of the Jews" (19:19). The title is a continuation of Pilate's derision of any nationalistic hopes among the Jews, and he makes sure word gets out by translating the title into three languages: Hebrew, Latin (lit. "Roman"), and Greek. As Brant suggests, "Pilate has created a scene" and the priests are not happy (2011, 251). But Roman executions were meant to be a spectacle to humiliate those found to have defied Roman sovereignty and to teach those who might consider such defiance that they would face a similar fate (Marcus 2006).

With his execution of Jesus, Pilate not only kills a potential revolutionary but also triumphs over any claims of Judean sovereignty among the Jews in and around Jerusalem for the Passover. When the priests ask Pilate to change the *titulus*, Pilate refuses. The priests already gave away any right to make such a request in 19:14 when they made themselves subjects of Rome alone; they have chosen their king, and his representative has written his "scripture" for them: "Jesus of Nazareth, King of the Jews." Indeed, as Keener notes, this is the only time the word for writing ("what I have written, I have written") is used in John to describe anything other than the Scriptures of Israel (2003, 1138). When Pilate writes this new scripture, he does so as part of his larger humiliation of the Jews and priests in particular, who perhaps thought they had won the day by securing Jesus' execution (cf. Brant 2011, 251). In this reading, Jesus is just a means for Pilate to assert Roman authority over the Jerusalem religious elite; his punishment has nothing to do with any crimes he committed since Pilate never found anything with which to charge him. Jesus *is* a proxy victim, just as Caiaphas said he would be, but not in the way the high priest anticipated. According to the Gospel, Jesus is displaying the "sin of the world," which is idolatry (cf. 1 John 5:21). The fear of all those around Jesus clouds their vision, and they submit to Rome rather than the One True God and the one whom God sent (17:1-26).

In 19:23-30 the field of vision shifts from the placard to the scene beneath the cross, where soldiers gather to gamble for Jesus' clothes and Jesus' loved ones watch. The soldiers' division of Jesus' clothing reflects Roman practice of the time period; executioners were privy to the personal belongings of those whom they killed, and crucifixion victims were hung naked so as to cause the most humiliation possible. Rather than dividing Jesus' tunic (*chitōn*), however, they gamble for it because "it was seamless, woven from above (*anōthen*) in one piece" (19:23). Even though the soldiers believe they are in control of the scene—they are the ones who have crucified Jesus, stripped him, and taken possession of his belongings—they are ignorant of God's plan being wrought through them. Their actions fulfill the words that were written by the psalmist (another association with David) in Ps 22:18 (21:19 LXX): "They divided my garments for themselves and over my clothing they cast lots." Regardless of the possible symbolic possibilities of the "seamless tunic" (cf. Brown 1970, 920–22), therefore, at least one implication of this double action is clear: the soldiers ignorantly but completely reenact this Scripture. Jesus also fulfills Scripture, but with full knowledge (cf. 13:18-19; 19:25-30).

The texts turns from the soldiers, emblems of Roman power already shown to be false, to the women associated with Jesus, either three or four (the Greek is unclear), and his Beloved Disciple. The presence of Jesus' mother is significant because it closes the inclusio begun in John 2:1-12 with her first appearance. At the wedding, Jesus' mother was rebuffed before Jesus eventually responded to her implied request concerning a lack of wine, because "it was not yet" his "hour" (2:3-4). As the audience knows, *this* is now Jesus' "hour" and there will indeed be wine. This wine, though, is not "the best wine" (*to kalon oinon*, 2:10) meant for a wedding celebration but "sour" or "vinegar" wine (*oxos*). Jesus' statement, "I thirst" (*dipsō*), ties the scene specifically to Ps 69:21 (68:22 LXX), which reads, "And they gave me gall in my food, and for my thirst (*dipsan*) they gave me vinegar wine (*oxos*)." As in John 2, the wine is drunk late in the scene, after the formation of a new household. "Woman," he says, "Behold, your son" (19:26; cf. 2:4). Beverly Gaventa rightly notes that the referent "son" is ambiguous; Jesus' words could call his mother to look upon himself, the Beloved Disciple, or both (1999, 93). The language for the Beloved Disciple is clearer although the idea that Jesus is referring to himself as mother is also tantalizing (cf. John 3; Fehribach). "Behold your mother," Jesus says. This is the only verse where Jesus refers to his own mother as a mother, but it is as a mother to a different son. The creation of this household begins to fulfill the promise of 1:12-13 that those who believed in Jesus' name would become God's children, birthed through God's will rather than blood, flesh, or human desire.

Jesus' death comes in 19:30, but it is a moment of his own choosing. Once again, the Gospel emphasizes that Jesus is not a victim, despite all appearances to the contrary (7:24). Beginning in 19:28, immediately after securing a new household for his mother, Jesus "knew that already everything has been completed," and for that reason, "so that the Scripture might be completed, he said, 'I thirst.'" Whether or not Jesus was thirsty is beside the point. What is important is that Jesus, a man hanging on a cross, beaten, naked, and slowly suffocating, is completely aware of his surroundings. He chooses to speak these words; they are not forced upon him in some haphazard manner. His knowledge that "everything has been completed" recalls 13:1, where Jesus "knew that his hour had come" and that he "loved his own in the world to completion" (*eis telos*). When he speaks his final word, *tetelestai* (it has been completed), he declares this reality into the world by speaking the finality of God's will as the Word should do.

What exactly is meant by "everything" (*panta*) that has been completed in 19:30 is debatable since Jesus has not yet been resurrected, returned to the Father, or given the Holy Spirit. It seems best to see "everything" as closely related to "the work," which appears with the closely related verb *teleioō* in 4:34; 5:36; and 17:4. This "work" is the "love" Jesus shows for "his own . . . to completion" (*eis telos*) in 13:1. In John 17 he says, "I completed (*teleiōsas*) the work" from the Father, leading up to the prayer that all his disciples "might be completely one (*teteleiōmenoi*), so that the world might know that you sent me and that you loved them just as you loved me" in v. 23. Thus, Jesus' "completion" in 19:30 is his death, the ultimate act of love for his own (*ta idia*)—the world (1:11; 10:3-4; cf. 19:28)—in obedience to God's will (3:14-18; 15:12-14). With this work completed, *he* hands over his spirit; it is not forced from him (10:17-18).

Jesus' Burial (vv. 31-42). After Jesus' death, the stairstep pattern outlined above repeats, first with the Jerusalem leaders approaching Pilate for another favor. This time, they want Pilate to ensure that the victims are dead and their bodies removed, so that they will not "remain" (*meinē*) on the crosses during Passover (19:31; cf. 19:14). As in 18:28, Pilate agrees to their terms, acting once again as the ally of the Jerusalem elite by having consideration for their religious practices. Next, the soldiers again appear on the scene, and, as in 19:23-24, they unwittingly fulfill Scripture even as they attempt to humiliate and desecrate Jesus' body further. The two victims on either side of Jesus are again mentioned first (19:18), with the soldiers breaking their legs so as to hasten their suffocation (19:32). When the soldiers come to Jesus, who hangs in the middle, they find him already dead. They do not refrain from breaking his legs out of respect, but rather they choose instead to pierce him with a spear, further penetrating and scarring his body. Their actions show how, unlike in the Synoptic accounts, they are unmoved by Jesus' death (Mark 15:39; Matt 27:54; Luke 23:47).

Someone, however, is moved and keeps careful record of these events for the sake of the believing community, the new household formed by Jesus. In 19:35-37, the narrator pauses to focus the audience's attention on the scene before them. The portrait of Jesus' dead body, his unbroken bones, and the sudden flow of blood and water out of Jesus' pierced side is an example of vivid description, or *ekphrasis*, that is meant to bring "what is being shown before the eyes" (Pseudo-Hermogenes, *Prog.* 22 [Kennedy]). The flow of water is often connected to 7:38-39 and Jesus' promise of living water flowing "from the belly" or "womb" (*koilia*). Adele Fehribach traces the maternal imagery associated with this description as well, since blood and water are the two fluids that flow from the womb in childbirth (cf. 16:20-22). A number of Christian interpreters have portrayed this scene, rather than Acts 2, as the "birth" of the church.

The scene is extended with three witnesses who testify to the veracity of the image of Jesus' body: a truthful eyewitness and two Scripture passages, which offer divinely inspired testimony (Aristotle, *Rhet.* 1.15; Cicero, *Top.* 19–20; Quintilian, *Inst.* 5). These witnesses certify not only that Jesus died but also the manner in which he died and the state of his body after death. Once again, the soldiers' actions fulfill Scripture, showing God's involvement and Jesus' obedience. As the Passover lamb, Jesus' body remains unbroken (Exod 12:46; Num 9:12; Ps 34:19-20); and like the pierced Lord mourned over from Zech 12:10, Jesus' death fulfills his promise from John 12:32 that when "lifted up" he will "draw all people to himself." Whether in disgust, ignorance, or belief, the characters and the audience are collectively forced to look upon Jesus, at last "lifted up" on the cross (3:14).

Focusing on 19:35, we read, "The one having seen has testified, and his testimony is true, and *that one* knows that he speaks truly, so that you also might believe." The italicized words in my translation have unclear antecedents in the Greek. The narrator could be saying that the eyewitness knows these things about himself, but, as Jesus said, testimony on one's own behalf is not persuasive (5:31). The demonstrative pronoun "that one" could also be a gesture toward Jesus' body, or the Father himself, who endorses the disciple's witness just as he verified that of Jesus (8:13-14). The purpose of the testimony is "so that you might believe," which will be repeated in 20:31

as well. In 21:24 the audience hears the third version of this refrain: "This is the disciple, the one testifying concerning these things, and who wrote these things, and we know that his testimony is true." It is this final description that leads many to suggest the Beloved Disciple is also the eyewitness of 19:35 (e.g., Keener 2003, 1154).

Rather than interpreting these asides as awkward pauses, or false stops, the three asides in 19:35-37; 20:30-31; and 21:24-25 should be read together. They are connected by themes and vocabulary, and they begin to fulfill Jesus' prayer from John 17. In 17:20 Jesus prayed for the disciples who were with him, as well as for "the ones believing in me because of their words." With Jesus' death, his departure is underway; therefore, it is up to the disciples to begin spreading his word. These three direct appeals to the audience are made only *after* Jesus' death (19:35) and twice after his resurrection and giving of the Holy Spirit (20:30-31; 21:24-25), and all three are explicitly tied to belief. In this way, the Gospel portrays itself in the "words" of the disciples who transmit Jesus' revelation to those who did not "see" him directly. It is through their words that the audience now stops and looks upon Jesus' pierced body, drawn into the story at 19:37 as part of the collective "they" who gaze upward "at the one whom they pierced" and join in the mourning for their Lord as described in Zech 12:10 (John 16:20-22).

Action resumes in 19:38 (just as it will in 21:1). Having stepped through the first two levels of the stairstep pattern noted above, the narrative turns to the reactions among Jesus' followers. Interestingly, the witness of 19:35 is nowhere mentioned in Jesus' burial. Once again a request is made to Pilate (19:31), but this time it is from Joseph of Arimathea, who is only mentioned here in this Gospel. Joseph is called a "disciple of Jesus, but a secret one (*kekrymmenos*), because of the fear of the Jews" (19:38), perhaps a fear of being put out of the synagogue (9:22; 16:2). The genitive construction "fear of the Jews" is ambiguous in that it could be (1) an objective genitive (as it is usually taken), meaning Joseph is fearing the Jews, or (2) a subjective genitive, meaning the fear the Jews themselves have. In the context of the Gospel, that fear is of the Romans whose military might could crush Jerusalem (11:50; Josephus, *J.W.* 6.8.5). Either way, Joseph remains a covert disciple, showing the truth of the narrator's testimony from 12:42-43.

Joseph is joined by another ambiguous figure, Nicodemus, whose own secretive meeting with Jesus at night is recalled in 19:39. Brant (2011, 255) notes that the Jews permitted crucified criminals to be buried before sunset as is prescribed by the biblical law (Deut 21:22-23; Ezek 39:14-16; Josephus, *J.W.* 4.314–17). Nicodemus and Joseph may have connections to the Jerusalem elite, who might have approved of their taking Jesus' body, but they certainly would not have anticipated the type of burial he receives. Nicodemus not only comes during the daylight to take Jesus' body but also brings with him a large amount of aromatics. The amount is extravagant; Brown argues for seventy-five pounds worth (1970, 941), while Keener suggests seventy fluid ounces (2003, 1163). The combination of spices and linen cloths indicate that Joseph and Nicodemus seek to give Jesus an honorable entombment, but it is not without some lingering ambiguities. Jesus said his body was already anointed for burial in 12:1-8 when Mary poured pure nard over his feet and wiped them with her hair. Moreover, because of the time, Nicodemus and Joseph are forced to bury Jesus hastily, putting him in a nearby tomb out of convenience. How could they have expected to complete this work before sunset? Brant also highlights the "poignant but absurd picture" of these verses, concluding that "the audience . . . knows that such efforts are not necessary because Jesus's death is not humiliating and that the normal concerns of long-term internment of his body are misguided" (2011, 256). Jesus will take his life back again.

. . . And Takes It Up Again (20:1–21:25)
John 20–21 records several stories of Jesus' resurrection appearances. They are often divided at 20:30-31, which many scholars argue is the original ending of the Gospel. In this reading, John 21 was added later to explain the continued role of the church as well as its relationship to other believing communities, perhaps especially Petrine churches, and the unexpected death of the Beloved Disciple (Brown 1970, 1077–82). Even if John 21 was added later (a fact that remains unprovable for lack of manuscript evidence), it was not added haphazardly, but continues a number of themes from the Gospel, particularly the shepherding motif surrounding Jesus' death and resurrection (cf. Hasitschka). Furthermore, the pause at 20:30-31 is not unprecedented in the Gospel, as we saw earlier in the Farewell Discourse (13:31–16:33) as well as at 19:35-37 where the narrator lingered to focus on Jesus' body on the cross. Read in connection with 19:35-37, in particular, 20:30-31 and 21:24-25 form a threefold pattern that presents the Gospel as the words of the disciples through whom later believers will come to faith, thus fulfilling Jesus' prayer from 17:20 (see comments above). In what follows, I will treat John 20–21 as a unit. This section of text contains four resurrection appearances, but only three of them (20:19-23, 24-31; 21:1-25) come after Jesus' return, or ascension, to the Father.

198 Reading John and 1, 2, 3 John

A. John 20:1-18: Jesus' Resurrection Revealed

John 20:1-18 contains two parallel scenes that center on Mary's reactions to sights around and in Jesus' tomb. In vv. 1-10, Mary arrives while it is still dark and, seeing the stone removed from the tomb, concludes that Jesus' body has been stolen. She runs to Simon Peter and the anonymous Beloved Disciple, but neither offers Mary any comfort after they look into the tomb; they never explicitly tell Mary what they saw but simply abandon her, still weeping, beside the empty tomb in v. 10. In vv. 11-18, Mary herself looks into the tomb and sees something different from what the previous two disciples had seen. For the first time, we hear someone speak to Mary: the two angels seated in the tomb and, then, Jesus himself. It is Mary, therefore, who first sees the resurrected Jesus. He comforts her and gives her the first commission to tell the good news. Having been comforted, she is sent out to comfort the disciples who left the empty tomb in silence.

Where Is My Lord? (vv. 1-10). John 20:1 begins on the first day of the week, early in the morning, before sunrise. The time and day recall Jesus' early-morning arrival into the praetorium in 18:28, just after Peter's night-time denials in 18:25-27. When Mary goes to Simon Peter in 20:2, it is his first appearance in the Gospel since that fateful night. Mary's choice to go to Peter raises the question of whether or not anyone yet knows Peter's shameful behavior; unlike Mark's account, Mary seems to assume Peter is still counted among Jesus' disciples. The time and day also resonate with the opening of the Gospel by again alluding to Genesis. Although it is still dark, and elements of chaos seem to reign—the early-morning time that evokes moments of betrayal and impending death—there are glimmers of hope, hints that we are also on the cusp of a new creation.

At the beginning, however, it is too dark for Mary to see these hopes. She sees the stone rolled away from the tomb and, without looking inside, assumes the worst: someone has stolen, and therefore desecrated, the body of her Lord. She runs and gives her first report, self-conceived, of Jesus' location: "They removed my Lord from the tomb and we do not know where they placed him" (v. 2). A number of interpreters have wrestled with Mary's use of "we" here; after all, she is the only one who visited the tomb in v. 1. Brant (2011, 266) suggests that Mary includes the disciples in her report, forcing them to agree with her conclusion even before they see for themselves. Rather than responding to Mary, however, both disciples take off running back to the tomb (v. 3). The Beloved Disciple famously wins this footrace, but he pauses outside while Peter walks into the tomb. Peter sees the burial cloths, "fine linen wrappings" and the "face cloth" folded to one side, perhaps belying a rushed tomb robbery but nevertheless confirming the absence of a body. The Beloved Disciple then enters and sees the same scene, at which point "he believed" (v. 8).

The content of the Beloved Disciple's belief is often assumed: he must have believed in Jesus' resurrection. Yet, if that is what the narrator intended, it is far from clear. Instead, the sequence of events before and after this announcement of belief makes it seem more likely that he now "believed" Mary's first report: "They have removed my Lord from the tomb and we do not know where they have placed him." The Beloved Disciple is now counted among the "we." The reasons for preferring this interpretation are that the Beloved Disciple never *speaks* to anyone after coming to his belief— as though there was no need to explain anything. He and Peter have now provided witness for Mary's testimony and she is believed. Verse 9 is linked to v. 8 with a confirming causative *gar*, meaning "for" or "since": "he entered and saw and believed *since they* did not yet know the Scripture that it was necessary for him to be raised from death." If the Beloved Disciple believed in the resurrection, his silence is confounding and does not make sense with v. 9: how could he now be clumped together with Mary and Peter as joined "they" if his belief is different from their belief? When he and Peter "returned home" (lit., "went again to their own"), they leave Mary weeping outside the tomb. The scattering of these three disciples fulfills Jesus' words from 16:32, but it sets the stage for the joy he promised as well.

Mary, the First Apostle (vv. 11-18). Left alone outside the tomb, Mary continues weeping. The connections to the Lazarus episode should now be clear: a Mary (perhaps the same Mary, see Schrader) mourns the loss of a loved one. While the Jews just thought Mary was going to the tomb in 11:31, Mary *has gone* to the tomb in John 20 and she is weeping, just as she did in 11:33. Standing there instead of running away, she now looks into the tomb for herself and sees a vision different from Peter's or the Beloved Disciple's: two angels, one at the head and one at the feet of where Jesus' body had laid (20:11-12). Sandra Schneiders suggests that this portrait is evocative of the ark of the covenant, or the mercy seat, which was flanked by two cherubim (2008, 165). While the disciples remained silent before Mary, never verbally acknowledging her words or emotion, the two angels immediately speak to her, asking, "Woman, why are you weeping?" The address, "woman," reminds readers of Jesus' conversations with his mother (2:4; 19:26) and the Samaritan disciple from John 4. After she repeats her woe, she hears these words once again: "Woman, why are you weeping?" (20:14). She turns to look and sees Jesus, but she does not know that it is him just yet (20:9).

Mary's interaction with Jesus is a classic "recognition" scene (*anagnorisis*), which was common in ancient literature. In this kind of scene, two characters (either individuals or groups) reunite after a period apart, but there is a delay in recognition of the one who has returned (Larsen 2008). The delay is often due to the fact that the one returning was thought to be dead. Thus, in Aeschylus's *Libation Bearers*, Electra is not convinced of her brother, Orestes's, identity until he shows her a lock of hair (*Cho.* 212–45). Odysseus, too, must prove his identity to his wife, Penelope, as well as his son, besting the suitors who have come to claim his household thinking he was deceased. His childhood nurse, Eurycleia, who suckled him and reared him, recognizes Odysseus first. Being commanded by Penelope to wash the feet of the stranger in their midst, Eurycleia has already noticed how much this man resembles Odysseus "in stature, voice, and feet" (*Od.* 19.381) before his identity is confirmed when she recognizes a scar on his leg (19.390).

The means of recognition are often "tokens," some sort of sign that proves or unmasks a person's true identity. Larsen argues that there are three recognition scenes in John 20 (vv. 11-18, 19-23, 24-29) but also that the entire Gospel is an extended "recognition" story. Jesus comes as God's Word enfleshed, but the world is unable to recognize the tokens (signs) he gives as proof of his identity. This tragic misrecognition leads to the world's disbelief and Jesus' crucifixion; but even in this moment, God uses the world's mistake to provide means for others to recognize Jesus after his resurrection: there are now scars on his hands and his side that prove who he is anew.

Mary does not recognize Jesus based on visual signs, but on an aural one. When Jesus first calls to Mary saying, "Woman, why are you weeping? Whom are you seeking?" (vv. 13-14), he repeats the same question from 18:6, when the mob came to arrest him. Now, rather than a moment of violence, Jesus uses this same question to create an intimate reunion between himself and a single disciple. Mary, however, has not received the token yet; she cannot recognize Jesus. John 20:9 means she, too, does not know the Scripture that would have enabled her to anticipate Jesus' resurrection. Still focused on her grief, Mary requests, "Sir, if you took him, *tell me* where you placed him, and I will take him" (20:15). Jesus breaks through her sorrow with one word: "Mariam." This is the first time Jesus has called a woman by her name in the entire Gospel, and it is also the first name he says after his resurrection. He will not call another disciple by name until 21:15 when he speaks to Peter, calling him "Simon son of John." The calling of Mary's name fulfills Jesus' promise from 10:3 that the shepherd "calls his own by name and leads them out." Mary shows herself to be one of Jesus' sheep when she recognizes Jesus as he speaks her name. Immediately she cries, "Rabbouni!" *My* teacher (20:16). Mary not only recognizes Jesus; she also recognizes that she belongs to him.

Rather than lingering in this moment, the Gospel breaks with the common recognition scene typology as Jesus pushes Mary away. He says, "Stop clinging to me, for not yet have I ascended to the Father. But go to my brothers and *tell them*, 'I am ascending to my Father and your Father, even my God and your God'" (20:17). Interpreters have long debated these words from Jesus (Attridge 2003): is he rebuking Mary? Is there an inappropriateness to her grasping of him, perhaps because she is a woman? Is she touching him or clinging to him? Lost in all this focus on Jesus' first command to Mary ("stop clinging to me") is the rest of what Jesus says. Jesus' comment is not rebuking Mary for touching him but rather for clinging to him before he has finished his ascent to the Father. Mary, it seems, has encountered Jesus *right after his resurrection* and before his ascension! In John's Gospel, Jesus' death and resurrection are just parts of his return to the Father (14:28-31). He has not yet completed his return, and, therefore, he needs to complete his return before he can fulfill his promises to his disciples from the Farewell Discourse, including the giving of the Holy Spirit. In this way, Jesus shortcuts Mary's request for him to tell her something and gives her two commands: (1) "go to my brothers" and (2) "tell them, 'I am ascending to my Father and your Father, even my God and your God.'" Mary is to replay her role as a witness from 20:2, but this time she is to give good news from Jesus rather than bad from herself. Jesus' body is not missing; he is not the victim of yet another crime and humiliation; instead, he is resurrected and he is now ascending to the Father, just as he said he would.

Mary reports to the disciples a victorious "I have seen the Lord!" in v. 18, but in spite of the buildup, we never hear the response. In contrast to the footrace in 20:3-4, there is nothing but silence. The Gospel does not even tell us everything that Mary reported, but ends the scene with "and the things he said to her." After this, Mary disappears from the story, but she does not disappear from the tradition. Although 20:18 could mean that Mary only told the others of Jesus' ascension, some early Christians thought Mary was privileged with more teaching from the Risen Jesus, teaching that she now passed on to skeptical disciples. Karen King suggests that the second century (ca. 120–180 CE) *Gospel of Mary* expands on the belief that Jesus taught Mary more before she left to report to the disciples (2003, 129–34). Thus, in the *Gospel of Mary* Peter says to Mary, "Sister, we know that the Savior loved you more than all other women. Tell us the words of the Savior that you remember, the things which you know that we don't because we haven't heard them." Mary answers, "I will teach you about what is hidden from you" and then begins teaching about a vision she received.

Mary's unique role in seeing the Risen Jesus was a point of some debate among early Christians. No doubt part of this reflects the distrust of women witnesses in the Greco-Roman world generally as a part of the larger suspicion of all things female and feminine (Myers 2017a, 18–24). While some see Jesus' trust of a woman as a "proof" of his resurrection, others see this as a weakness. The transformation of Mary Magdalene in the tradition, from first witness and apostle sent by the Lord, to a redeemed and ever-weeping harlot just grateful to be in the room, is evidence of this persistent debate. Indeed, the non-canonical *Gospel of Mary* is often tied to groups that would later be considered "heretical" by the church catholic, partly because Mary, a woman, was a leading figure (Attridge 2003, 161; Schaberg). Even in the *Gospel of Mary* itself the male disciples debate whether or not they should believe Mary's words because she is a woman. King notes that a similar debate between Mary and Peter appears in the *Gospel of Thomas* (114), *Pistis Sophia*, and the *Gospel of the Egyptians*. Peter, representative of the dominant church, consistently distrusts Mary's word because of her gender. In these non-canonical writings, at least, he is consistently rebuked for it (King 1988, 525–26). These later debates among Christians, however, should not diminish Mary's special place in the canonical Gospel traditions, including outside the Gospel of John. Mary Magdalene is consistently among the first to see the Risen Lord and the first to share this news; in John, she is the first apostle commissioned by Jesus after his resurrection. As Levi says to Peter in the *Gospel of Mary*, "For if the Savior made her worthy, who are you then for your part to reject her?" Even though this *Gospel* is outside the tradition, Jesus' trust in Mary's ability is not.

B. John 20:19-31: Revelations behind Locked Doors

A new episode begins in 20:19: Mary is suddenly absent and the remaining disciples are alone, once again in darkness. John 20:19-31 in many ways repeats 20:1-18; this time, Thomas plays the part of Mary by experiencing a dramatic moment of recognition and revelation from Jesus. The two scenes bracket "the same day" (20:19), 20:1-18 starting in the darkness of early morning and 20:19-31 shrouded in the approaching darkness of evening. In contrast to the open tomb, which Peter, the Beloved Disciple, and Mary freely entered in the morning, the disciples are clustered fearfully behind locked doors meant to bar anyone's entrance. Importantly, 20:19-31 occurs *after* Jesus' ascension to the Father, enabling the giving of the Holy Spirit and the invitation for Thomas to touch Jesus in vv. 24-29. The remaining disbelief and fear of these disciples, even after they have seen the resurrected Jesus and been commissioned by him in vv. 19-23, contrasts Mary's response and also forms a bridge back to the Gospel audience who has not experienced such visions. Visions, it seems, are no guarantee of faithfulness; blessedness, Jesus says, comes from belief that is not dependent on sight.

A Renewed Creation (vv. 19-23). Jesus first appears to his disciples when they are locked behind doors "because of the fear of the Jews" (20:19). Repeated from 7:13 and 19:38, this fear has prompted secretive behavior in the past: the silencing of a crowd's burgeoning belief (7:13) and keeping Joseph a "secret" disciple, at least until his lavish burial of Jesus (19:38-42). Again, the "fear of the Jews" is an ambiguous phrase. Although most interpreters read it as the disciples being afraid of the Jews, perhaps still fearing for their lives after Jesus' crucifixion, we should remember that it was the Jews' own fears that initiated the plot against Jesus in John 11. The Jewish leadership fears the response of Rome, and these disciples fear the violence they might endure if the Jews' fear spreads. All in all, the disciples seem to think, it is just better for them to lay low.

The image of the disciples together in a confined space not only contrasts the open tomb from 20:1-18 but also brings to mind the Lazarus episode from 11:40-44. Even though the disciples are not dead, they have buried themselves, trapped behind locked doors and bound by fear. They, too, need to be resurrected. Jesus' sudden appearance "in the middle" recalls the location of his crucifixion "in the middle" of two other victims (19:18). How Jesus could manifest in a locked room has sparked some debate among scholars, and it is part of a much larger argument about the nature of Jesus' resurrected body (Frey, 221–36; Moss). Yet Jesus has made inexplicable appearances before in John's Gospel, perhaps most clearly while walking across the stormy Sea of Galilee and immediately taking himself and his disciples to the other side (6:21). He was also able to evade capture in John 7–8 and 10, even while in the middle of a crowd intent on stoning him! Jesus' ability to appear here, then, is not entirely out of character. Just as in the other scenes, John does not bother explaining *how* Jesus could do this, but simply says that he does.

Jesus offers his disciples two tokens of his identity. First, he says, "Peace to you." This conforms to Jesus' teaching in the Farewell Discourse that he is "leaving" his peace with the disciples even though they are in the world (14:27; 16:33). With these words, Jesus acknowledges that it is the world around them that has caused the disciples to fear and to remain inside. He also reminds them of his promise; Jesus has not abandoned these disciples but has worked to give them "peace." Second, Jesus shows the disciples his hands and his side as the visual tokens that correspond to the trusted disciple's witness from 19:35. Only then do the disciples "rejoice because *they saw* the Lord" (20:20). Having recognized him, Jesus repeats his words, "Peace to you," and adds his commission, "Just as the Father has sent me, I am also sending you" (20:21). Jesus' words bring to fruition his prayer from 17:18. Just like Jesus, then, they are anointed with the Holy Spirit. Rather than saving the Spirit's arrival for Pentecost as Acts does, in John's Jesus "breathed" the Spirit on the disciples the evening of his resurrection. Having ascended to the Father and requested the Spirit on their behalf, Jesus returns to his disciples, immediately fulfilling his promises not only that they would see him again but also that he would give them another Paraclete, the Spirit of Truth.

This scene is not just one of joyful recognition, however, but also of re-creation and rebirth. As in Gen 2:7, Jesus breathes life into his disciples by giving them spirit. Jesus once again acts as God's Word by issuing forth the life that God desires and on which all humanity depends. Equipped with the Spirit, Jesus commissions his disciples, saying, "Should you release the sins of anyone, they have been released; if you should grasp of anyone, they have been grasped" (John 20:23). The translation alone should indicate how difficult this verse is to interpret. It has often been connected to Matt 18:18 and Jesus' giving "the keys of the kingdom" to Peter, or to those who rightly confess Jesus' identity as the Christ. Nevertheless, the verbs are not the same in Matthew, nor does Matthew mention sins (cf. Beutler, 245–46). Moreover, John's Gospel rarely uses the plural "sins," nor does it mention "release" from sins or "grasping" (or "retaining") them anywhere but here. The closest parallel appears in John 8:21-58 as Jesus engages in an escalating dialogue with other Jews gathered to celebrate Tabernacles when Jesus warns that those listening will "die" in their "sins" unless they believe in his identity as "I am."

Sandra Schneiders suggests that rather than "grasping" sins as the implied direct object of the second portion of 20:23, the whole phrase ought to be translated as an objective genitive. This means that the second portion of the verse is not describing "sins," but the forgiven people. Schneiders translates 20:23 as "Anyone whose sins you forgive, they are forgiven to them and those [the forgiven] whom you hold fast [in the communion of the Church] are held fast" (2006, 354). According to Schneiders, the commission of the disciples is not to judge and cut off people but rather to demonstrate God's revelation of love, enabling them to let go of their unbelief. Since the disciples have now received the Holy Spirit, they are able to discern truth from falsehood in the world, in line with the promise of 16:8-9, but that does not mean they condemn the world. Like Jesus, they are to love.

Believing with and without Sight (vv. 24-31). Having seen Jesus for themselves, the disciples from 20:19-23 now believe in Jesus' resurrection. In this way, John 20:1-23 reenacts the story of John 4: a woman has a unique encounter with Jesus and then travels to share the news. Later, those she witnessed to find their own faith because of their own sight and their own experience with Jesus (4:39-42). John 20:24-31, however, immediately brings to the fore the problem with the paradigm: what about those who have not seen, let alone touched, Jesus? What about Thomas?

Thomas is sometimes maligned in Christian tradition, but more recently scholars have emphasized his sympathetic role. Thomas's disbelief is logical and understandable, but he also undergoes transformation (Popp, 523–24). When Thomas hears the other disciples now repeat Mary's words, "We have seen the Lord!" he is incredulous, perhaps even offended. "Unless I should see in his hands the impression of the nails, and cast my finger into the impression of the nails, and throw my hand into his side, I will *by no means* believe!" (20:25). Thomas's statement of disbelief is emphatic. He wants not only to see what the other disciples have seen—Jesus' hand and side—but also to touch them. Mary touched Jesus in the garden, but no mention was made there of his hands and side; Mary only needed to hear Jesus' voice to believe. According to Candida Moss, as the preeminent token for recognition, the presentation of scars and markings is a more climactic and more powerful proof (58). Thomas will not settle for anything less. He is, as Brant suggests, a killjoy (2011, 272), or, as Moss puts it, a skeptic and therefore an ideal witness to be convinced (59).

A week passes with no proof. Thomas, however, continues to gather with the other disciples and shelter inside (20:24). The other disciples may believe that Jesus is resurrected, but they are still behind locked doors (v. 25). Repeating the scene from vv. 19-23, Jesus again appears in the middle of the group and says, "Peace to you" (v. 26). Jesus, then, makes it clear that he has shown up to prove Thomas wrong and also to show evidence of his continued presence among the disciples through the Holy Spirit. In 20:27, Jesus repeats Thomas's challenge almost verbatim even though he was not present in v. 25: "Put your finger here and see my hands, and put your hand and cast it into my side, now stop being faithless and be faithful!" Jesus may not have been there, but the Spirit is already in the community. This encounter is not only the evidence of Jesus' real resurrection but also verification of the presence of the Spirit and therefore what it means to abide with God.

Moss argues that Thomas's request is to see not the open wounds of Jesus but rather his scarred body. The distinction is significant for Moss because dead bodies, even reanimated ones, do not heal; only living bodies do (63–65). Looking for the impressions, or scars, from nails that pierced skin over a week prior means that Thomas wants proof that Jesus is *alive* and not some a ghost or resuscitated flesh. Such a reading supports Jörg Frey's arguments that the Gospel of John pushes against docetic interpretations of Jesus' death and resurrection. This reading also coheres with the belief that bodies retain their distinguishing marks even after death; Jesus is resurrected not with a "perfect" body without blemish but with one that shows the literal marks of his obedience. For Moss, such an image is especially powerful for our understandings of disability. Instead of seeing disability as something to overcome, Jesus' resurrected body incorporates these attributes as a part of his person (51).

It is also significant that the Gospel of John transforms what should have been bodily marks of shame—marks from crucifixion and an open wound on his side given after his death—and transforms them into symbols of honor. Thomas's request, to touch Jesus' scars and to "cast" his hand in Jesus' side, are surprising and transgressive. As Moss notes, scars are a climactic and powerful sign for recognition, but scars are predominantly only seen, as in 20:19-23, not touched or probed as Thomas demands. Moreover, such touch and invasion of the body would have been dishonorable and emasculating in the ancient Roman context (Myers 2015, 211). Jesus' commands for Thomas to perform this corporal exploration, however, again challenge Roman ideals. The world may think that such a display and intimate touch is shameful, but Jesus shows it to be honorable and revelatory; it is a visual, aural, and tactile display of his and God's love. Indeed, Jesus' vulnerability in 20:27 elicits the most exalted confession in the Gospel. Thomas exclaims, "My Lord and my God!" (20:28), and thus transforms from the quintessential skeptic to the most profound witness.

Thomas's confession, however, is not met with unambiguous praise from Jesus. Instead, Jesus turns the focus from Thomas to the audience listening to the story, bringing them into the scene just as he did while praying to the Father before his death. "Because you have seen me, you have believed," Jesus says. "Blessed are the ones who have not seen me and who have believed" (20:29). The first portion of Jesus' statement is sometimes translated as a question ("Do you believe because you have seen me?"), but it does not need to be interpreted this way. Jesus' comment to Thomas seems also to implicate the rest of the disciples who were said to rejoice "having seen the Lord" in 20:20 only after Jesus showed them his hands and side. All these disciples, not just Thomas, needed at least visual proof of Jesus' resurrection in order to believe. The words of other disciples were not enough for any of them (vv. 18-19, 24-25). The Gospel of John, however, presents Jesus as especially aware of those believers who will come to and continue in faith by means of such words. It is for these disciples he prays in 17:20 and to whom he speaks in 20:29. In this way, the Gospel elevates the audience listening. Even though they may think themselves "lesser" disciples for not having seen (or touched) the Lord, Jesus himself calls them blessed and, in doing so, encourages them to continue in their faith. He has not left them orphans either (14:18).

John 20:30-31 continues this address to the audience. It also repeats the purpose statement from 19:35 as the second of the three interrelated narrator asides in these final chapters. The table below highlights their connections in words and themes.

John 19:35	John 20:30-31	John 21:24-25
And the one who has seen has testified, and his testimony in true, and that one knows that he speaks truly, <u>so that you yourselves might believe.</u>	*Many other signs, therefore, Jesus did before his disciples, which have not been written in this book.* But these have been written <u>so that you might believe that Jesus is the Christ the Son of God, and so that believing you might have life in his name.</u>	**This one is the disciple who testified concerning these things and who wrote these things and we know that his testimony is true.** *And there are also many other things which Jesus did, such that if they were written I suppose the world itself could not hold the books written.*

John 20:31 reaches back to 19:35 by emphasizing belief. In both of these verses there are text-critical issues showing a debate between a predominantly evangelistic purpose ("that you might come to believe") and one that emphasizes encouraging those who already believe ("that you might continue believing"). The second of these options is preferred on the basis of manuscript evidence and themes in the Gospel that call for perseverance (Talbert 2005, 267–68). Nevertheless, the Gospel also has evangelistic elements and provides testimony for anyone who might hear it regardless if they are believers or not.

Two other issues are worth noting in 20:30-31: first, 20:30 repeats a common summary technique found in ancient biographies from the Greco-Roman world, insisting that more could be written than was included in this work. Such a statement at once highlights the compositional work of the author in selecting and framing the writing in a way they considered the most persuasive, while also exalting the subject by indicating that even more could have been included. John is saying he chose the best evidence to make his points, even though he is perfectly aware that other stories are out there. This sentiment is repeated in 21:24-25. Second, 20:31 once again ties together recognition and life, a theme that runs throughout the Gospel. The grammar of this verse is imprecise and could also be translated, "But these things have been written so that you might believe that *the Christ the Son of God is Jesus*, and so that believing you might have life in his name" (Talbert 2005, 267). This translation underscores that recognizing *Jesus* is the Christ the Son of God is key to having life (1:12-13; 3:18; cf. 17:11-12). Since he is the incarnation of God's Word, one must recognize, or be in line with him, in order to experience life since, as the prologue informs, "all things came into being through [the Word] and without [the Word] not one thing became which has become" (1:3). Recognizing Jesus means recognizing God's love and will for life. Such recognition leads toward an abiding communion that is not just earthly life, but "eternal life" and "life abundant" (10:10).

C. Futures Revealed and Concealed (21:1-25)

The final chapter of John's Gospel contains Jesus' fourth and final appearance to his disciples after his resurrection (21:14). The chapter's connection to the rest of the Gospel is debated, although more recent scholars note its similarity in content to the rest of John, suggesting that even if it is a later addition, it is carefully interwoven into the narrative. Making one of the earlier arguments for reading John 21 as an integral part of the Gospel, Paul Minear argues that the chapter provides a conclusion to the stories of both the Beloved Disciple and Peter, two disciples whose lives occupy the Gospel repeatedly (91). Rather than reading John 20:30-31 as an ending, therefore, Minear and others suggest that John 21 provides a more complete ending to the Gospel, even a super-abundant ending, one that overflows just like the net of fish (Gaventa 1996).

Breakfast on the Beach (vv. 1-14). John 21 can be divided into two episodes, vv. 1-14, a third recognition scene and Jesus' breakfast with his disciples on the beach, and vv. 15-25, Peter's conversation with Jesus and competition with the Beloved Disciple. Throughout the chapter, Peter plays a prominent role, one that is perhaps surprising given that the last time he was mentioned in the Gospel he returned to his own home after a disappointing trip to Jesus' tomb. Minear suggests that Peter and the Beloved Disciple traveled back to Galilee, leaving Jerusalem, after finding the empty tomb. As a result, Minear says that Peter and the Beloved Disciple may *not* have been present for either of Jesus' two other appearances in 20:19-31; if they were there, no specific attention is paid to them. The Gospel at least leaves open the possibility of their absence. John 21 rectifies this problem. This, for Minear, is a key reason why one should not ignore John 21 when reading the Gospel of John (91–93).

The chapter opens in a new location, away from Jerusalem and back in Galilee near the "Sea of Tiberias" (6:1, 23). Peter gathers with six other disciples: Thomas (11:16; 14:5; 20:24-28), Nathanael (1:45-49), "the sons of Zebedee" who make their first explicit appearance in the story, and "two others" (21:2). Whether or not the Beloved Disciple is one of these "sons of Zebedee" is not clarified in the text. Peter, true to his role in the Gospel, continues his leadership position when he leaves to fish and is followed by the other six. After a night of catching no fish, the disciples see a stranger walking along the beach. In this final recognition scene, Jesus does not show his hands or his side but rather gives instructions: "Cast the net to the right side, and you will find [some]" (21:6). When the net is suddenly impossible to move because of the "multitude of fish" (5:3; 6:9, 11), the Beloved Disciple exclaims, "It is the Lord!" In contrast to his silence in 20:9, here he shouts aloud his recognition and prompts Peter to jump into the sea in order to beat them all to the shore.

Although the Beloved Disciple recognizes Jesus first, Peter remains the focus of the story. Jesus' "charcoal fire" to which he invites the disciples contrasts the last "charcoal fire" around which Peter warmed himself the night he betrayed his Lord (18:18). When Jesus instructs the disciples to bring the fish they caught, it is Peter who "went up and dragged the net onto the land full of fish, large ones, a hundred and fifty three of them" (21:11). Peter's ability to haul this net full of huge fish when the other six could not while in the boat again reinforces his eagerness: the same trait that has led him to profound confession (6:68-69) and failure (13:36-38; 18:10, 15-27), as well as prompting him to "throw himself" into the sea in 21:7!

The number of fish, 153, has sparked interpretations often highlighting abundance, either as a symbol of the messianic age ushered in by Jesus or of the disciples' commission to evangelize (Thompson 2015, 438–39). In spite of the great number of large fish, the net "was not divided" (*eschisthē*). The verb used here is the same verb from 19:24 when the soldiers cast lots for Jesus' seamless tunic rather than tearing, or dividing, it between them. The image of a unified tunic and net resonates with the Gospel's emphasis on oneness between the Father, Jesus, and his disciples of all generations. Indeed, the disciples in John 21 experience a brief moment of unity as they eat together. Sharing a meal reminiscent of John 6, full of bread and fish (6:9, 11; 21:9-13), they do not "scrutinize" (*exetazō*) Jesus because "they knew it was the Lord" (21:12; cf. 16:23).

Following the Shepherd (vv. 15-25). In spite of all appearances, however, Jesus knows the unity is not complete at this beach gathering. One sheep needs to be reintegrated into the flock on his way to becoming a shepherd:

Peter. In what follows Jesus engages Peter in a conversation about his present and his future rather than castigating him for his past. These final verses of the Gospel can be divided into three sections: (1) vv. 15-17; (2) vv. 18-22; and (3) vv. 23-25. These sections are connected by key words and themes: love, following, and death. They also form a transition from a focus on Peter to the Beloved Disciple, who recognized the Lord in 21:7, and finally to the Gospel community. This is the "we" who includes those responsible for finalizing and preserving the Gospel story, as well as the audience who listens and believes its testimony (21:24-25).

In 21:15-17 Jesus questions Peter concerning his love and therefore his loyalty. Most debate over these verses has focused on the shifting between the verbs used for "love"—either *agapaō* in Jesus' first two questions or *phileō* used by Jesus in his third iteration and used by Peter throughout. John A. L. Lee argues that in the first century, the verb *agapaō* had a more informal tone, while *phileō* was more respectful (29). Most other scholars, however, note that the Gospel regularly switches between *agapaō* and *phileō* in the course of the narrative, just as it does with other words (e.g., *logos* and *rhēma*) and with other elements in 21:15-17: Peter is commanded to feed (*boske*) as well as shepherd (*poimaine*) the sheep; the sheep are called *probata* and *arnia*; and Peter adds the verb *ginōskō* to his final declaration in v. 17. Noting these facts, Alan Culpepper writes, "Repeating a request three times signaled earnestness (Ps 55:17; *b. Yoma* 87a). In such repetitions, stylistic variations are the norm and do not typically convey different nuances in the variation of terms" (2010, 174). What is important in this exchange, then, is that Jesus asked Peter *three times* if he loved him, matching the three denials Peter uttered in 18:15-25. He does not simply take Peter's word for it, however, Jesus commands action: where Peter's actions have shown his lack of love in the past, Jesus commands him to show his love by loving his Lord's beloved.

Having commissioned this new shepherd, Jesus tells him where this love will lead. Like Jesus, Peter will lay down his life. While Peter thought he was prepared for such a sacrifice in 13:36–38, his behavior in John 18 revealed otherwise. With Jesus' example now complete, however, Peter can follow through with his love. Jesus says, this will happen. Just as Jesus was bound and led away, so will Peter be: "Truly, truly I am saying to you, when you were younger, you girded yourself and walked where you wanted. But when you are old, you will stretch forth your hands and others will gird you and bear you where you do not want." The verb for "girding" or "dressing" is *zōnnyō*, which is related to the compound verb *diazōnnymi* used in 13:4-5 for Jesus' girding a towel around himself before washing the disciples' feet, and for Peter's own dressing in 21:7 before he plunged into the water. As a young man, Peter chose to gird himself in 21:7, just as Jesus chose to dress himself with a servant's towel. Also like Jesus, Peter's choices will lead to a sacrifice of laying down his life. In 21:19 the narrator makes this clear by repeating a refrain used to foretell Jesus' own death from 12:33 and 18:32: "He said this signifying (*sēmainōn*) by what type of death he would glorify God." Poignantly, Jesus ends the exchange with the command, "Follow me."

Peter's gaze, however, turns to look backward, rather like the disciples from 6:66. He questions Jesus about the disciple who was following them. Continuing with an explicit reference to chapter 13, the narrator makes sure the audience knows who this disciple is: "the disciple whom Jesus loved, . . . who also reclined at the dinner upon his breast and said, 'Lord, who is the one betraying you?'" (21:20; cf. 13:23-25). Peter's question, "Lord, what about this one?" is more than just a passing comment. As in John 13, Peter wants to know, but this time he asks for himself while the Beloved Disciple is silent. Peter may have been "reinstated," but this exchange shows us that his character remains fundamentally unchanged: he still seems to speak before he thinks. As Brant suggests, he keeps trying to follow Jesus, but he repeatedly missteps. Jesus, however, does not let even this troublesome sheep wander from his flock but answers, "If I should want him to remain until I come, what is that to you? You follow me" (21:22). Peter, in spite of his tendency toward recklessness, is not only counted among Jesus' sheep but is also able to become a shepherd because of Jesus' example: this one will also glorify God.

In 21:23-25 the Gospel suddenly leaves Jesus and Peter behind, turning its own attention squarely to the Beloved Disciple. Often considered an addendum to explain this disciple's death to the community, v. 23 clarifies Jesus' prophetic word: "Therefore, this word went out to the brothers that this disciple would not die. But Jesus did not say to him that he would not die, but that 'if I should will him to remain until I come.'" In other words, the emphasis should be on Jesus' will and not on the disciple's fate. Jesus' word, and not the false "word" of the brothers, is the one that should be trusted. Verses 24-25 continue this motif of trust as well as the focus on the Gospel audience. Having encouraged the audience to trust Jesus' words, the Gospel now reinforces its own witness: "This is the disciple who is testifying concerning these things and who wrote these things, and *we know* that his testimony is true. And there are many other things which Jesus did, such that if they were written I suppose the world itself could not hold the books written." As explored above, this conclusion brings together the summaries from 19:35-37 and 20:30-31 as a capstone to the entire Gospel. It also causes the audience to become a de-facto witness, incorporated into the "we" statement just as they were in 1:14: "And the Word became flesh and dwelled among us, and we saw its glory, glory as one uniquely begotten from a father."

Sherri Brown argues that John 21 continues the transition begun in 20:29-31 from the disciples who saw the Risen Jesus to the Gospel audience who had no such access. By continuing to exalt the audience, John 21 "brings the Gospel story beyond its conclusion into the time of the community of its early audiences and clarifies the form and mission of the community it engenders" (2015b, 30; cf. Minear, 95–98). This transition, however, began much sooner than just John 20 and even precedes 19:35-37; instead, the Gospel has always been reaching toward its audience by privileging their perspective from the outset with its prologue. Even though the Gospel audience may not have "seen" Jesus' body before their eyes, they have "seen" him through this Gospel and through the words the disciples have passed down, including especially the witness of the Beloved Disciple.

As the conclusion to the Gospel, therefore, John 21 completes the narrative transition from past to present and on toward the future. Jesus is the primary point of revelation from whom disciples received God's words (1:18), but it is other disciples who now carry these words inspired and vetted by the Holy Spirit. Passing Jesus' teaching on to the later generations of believers, the Gospel itself is the means of their seeing, hearing, and even touching. Rather than bereaved, these disciples are blessed (20:29). Even beyond the death of the trustworthy Beloved Disciple, therefore, the Gospel encourages its audiences to accept this witness and, in turn, to become witnesses themselves that Jesus is the Christ, the Son of God.

Theological Threads

Crucifixion and Atonement

In the Gospel of John, as in all the canonical Gospels, Jesus' crucifixion is in accordance with God's plan for Jesus and the world. For this reason, although the event appears tragic to those who view it from the outside, it is a moment of victory and glorification for Jesus. The deep irony of this twist plays on various levels in John's Roman context. First, those living in the Roman Empire would have been familiar with crucifixion as one of the most humiliating forms of execution possible. Reserved for non-citizens (and former citizens whose actions deemed them outside the protection of the law; cf. Suetonius, *Galba* 9.1), crucifixion was torturous ridicule for the perceived crimes of the victims: it was an ironic exaltation. Often a punishment for revolutionaries, rebels, and all others convicted of sedition, crucifixion humiliated victims by raising them up, but not in order to receive honor. Rather they were put on display, naked and beaten, for scorn. Joel Marcus calls crucifixion a "parodic exaltation," where the punishment fits the crime by reminding not only the convicted of Rome's superiority, but also all those who viewed their displayed bodies (2006, 78–80).

When the Gospels present Jesus hailed as "king," dressed in purple and given a crown, the image conforms to Roman parody plays acted out in executions (82). Since Jesus was convicted of sedition, a desire to overthrow Caesar and claim himself to be king, he is now "crowned" and "exalted" to survey his kingdom from the vantage point of the cross. The association between kingship and exaltation, as Marcus notes, is in part what made crucifixion such a perfect punishment for sedition in Roman eyes (83–84). Jesus' exaltation silences him, and anyone else who might claim him to be king or have monarchical aspirations of their own (John 19:16-22). Of course, from the perspective of the canonical Gospels, the true irony is that in this moment, Jesus *is* exalted and shown to be king. As Marcus writes, "The danger of parody, however, is that it may turn into reality" (86). With this "reversal of a reversal," early Christians claimed that Jesus' kingship was shown real through the manner in which he willingly suffered on the cross in obedience to God's will. Indeed, this is the emphasis in the Gospel of John as Jesus issues orders even from the cross and controls when he dies (19:23-28). In this way, Jesus' crucifixion begins his glorification; it is a revelation of his glory to the world, as well as a revelation of the world's sin.

In John, Jesus' crucifixion is the climactic display of love. It is a display of both his love for God, his Father, to whom he has been obedient throughout life and now also in his death, and his love for the world, his own, whom he loved "to completion" (13:1). Jesus shows his love by dying "on behalf" of his friends and his sheep, not in a substitutionary sense—he is not thwarting God's judgment—but in order to save them from thieves and wolves who seek their destruction (Koester 2008, 115). Jesus' death as the Passover Lamb is not about atonement for sins, but, as Craig Koester argues, it is deliverance from sin: the mistake of misrecognition that led to the world's disbelief of Jesus and their rejection of him (113–14; cf. John 1:29). Blood and water flow from Jesus, the Passover Lamb, and mark those who look upon his crucified form, rescuing them from disbelief just as looking at the snake saved the stricken Israelites in Num 21 (cf. John 3:14; 12:32; 19:35-37). In this way, Jesus' crucifixion is revealing, loving, and glorifying. It unmasks the cruelty of the ruler of this world and lifts up the mistake of those who have been taken in by this false god, either out of fear or out of misplaced pursuits of honor (5:40-44; 11:45-53; 19:6-16).

Even though Jesus' death does not prompt a confession of belief from a centurion as it does in Mark 15:39, John's Gospel still calls us to look upon his crucified body in John 19:35-37. The way in which Jesus suffers—according to God's will, willingly, knowingly, for the benefit of others, with long-lasting and superior results—means he dies a good death (Myers 2012, 163–71). In this way, Jesus' body is no longer a sight of humiliation, but of true glory. As Marcus explains, when a prisoner died "with unaccountable dignity," audiences "might then be tempted to conclude that the crucified victim actually did possess a certain noble or regal quality" (2006, 87). In John's Gospel, therefore, the cross becomes Jesus' throne and a place of real glory, because it is the ultimate revelation of divine love.

Resurrection and Eternal Life

Jesus' resurrection, and implied ascension to the Father, should not be separated from his crucifixion in the Gospel of John. Instead, these are all parts of Jesus' return to the Father that he explains to his disciples in the Farewell Discourse (14:28-29; 20:17). In 10:17-18 Jesus also ties these events together, explaining, "For this reason the Father loves me, because I am laying down my life so that I should take it again. No one removes it from me, but I myself am laying it down from myself. I have authority to lay it down, and I have authority to take it again. This is the commandment I received from my Father." Jesus' crucifixion is the revelation of divine love, but his resurrection is equally important. Jesus does not simply love the world to be killed by it. He certainly dies, but he does not remain dead. Rather, as the Word through which all life comes and is, Jesus cannot be permanently destroyed by creation. Jesus, therefore, reveals his love by dying and confirms his identity by rising again. The resurrection is not just vindication, but victory; this is the moment that Jesus' proclamation from 16:33 is made complete: "I have spoken these things to you so that in me you should have peace. In the world you have affliction, but be courageous; I have conquered the world!"

Through his resurrection, Jesus shows the eternal life that he provides for those who believe, love, and, therefore, follow him. Even though the world will pursue and perhaps even kill Jesus' followers, they will live. Jesus' resurrection and return to the Father are what enables the believers to be courageous. Because they abide in a living God by means of a living Jesus, they too are already experiencing eternal life. It is not simply a future event; this is a present reality. This present participation in life is reinforced with Jesus' giving of the Holy Spirit in 20:19-23. The presence of the Spirit among Jesus' disciples means that they are not alone but experience communion even in Jesus' physical absence.

In this way, the resurrection is a crucial part of the Gospel story, both for the disciples in the story who receive the Spirit from Jesus himself and for the later disciples who have never seen their Lord with physical eyes. Remaining in the community and in connection to the Holy Spirit, these later disciples also participate in the oneness for which Jesus prayed in 17:22-23. And it is this connection to God's glory that results in their authentic living—that is, in living lives that imitate Jesus' type of love, no matter the cost (12:25-26; 15:12-14).

III. The Letters of John

A Brief Overview of the Letters of John

Of the three Johannine Letters, 1 John has received the most attention in Christian history and biblical scholarship. This is not altogether surprising given its length in comparison to 2 and 3 John as well as its traditional connection to the Gospel of John (see General Introduction). Second John is often seen as an "echo" of 1 John, repeating several of its themes and phrases, albeit in a much more concise form (Lieu 1986, 149). Third John, however, is something of an enigma. It is at once specific by naming its recipient (Gaius), an ally who was most likely also the letter's carrier (Demetrius), and an opponent (Diotrephes). But it is also befuddling, with a lack of details concerning the theological nature of the feud. Judith Lieu suggests that rather than theologically or doctrinally developed, the Elder's attitude toward Diotrephes in 3 John is more in response to personal insult than clearly articulated theological differences (159). If the Elder disagrees with Diotrephes's specific theology, he does not give many details in the letter itself (3 John 9-10).

These three letters, much like the rest of the Johannine corpus, should be read together and also separately. Verbal, thematic, and traditional connections demonstrate their origins from the same community, but their differences should not be ignored either. First John is more of a homily than a letter, while 2 and 3 John are similar to other ancient letters (Parsenios 2014, 26–28; Loader, xii). Altogether, these three writings provide a more sustained glimpse into the Johannine community, with 1 John offering the most robust theological reflection of the three while 2 and 3 John offer what Lieu describes as "clear contact with known issues and controversies in the early church" (166): namely, issues surrounding power, authority, itinerary, hospitality, tradition, and connections between various early Christian communities.

Historical Background

Composition Order and Dates

Most of the debates concerning the Letters of John focus on their relation-ship to the Gospel, especially between the Gospel and 1 John (see General Introduction; Culpepper and Anderson 2014). Conclusions concerning the composition of the Gospel, and its relationship to these Letters, necessarily affect suggested dates of composition. Alan Culpepper (2014) offers an over-view of five major positions in current scholarship including the following:

(1) The Gospel was written first and the Letters convey a later, internal Johannine schism usually composed in order 1, 2, 3 John (Brown 1982; Parsenios 2014; Rusam).

(2) The Letters were written before the Gospel to address a developing gnostic or docetic strand of teaching (Strecker; Schnelle). Udo Schnelle argues that 2–3 John were written first because they are so brief and opaque, acting as stop-gap measures before the more theologically robust answers of 1 John and the Gospel were constructed (see also Strecker; Talbert 2005).

(3) Lieu (1986, 2008) suggests that the Letters are not literarily depen-dent on the Gospel, although they all come from the same Johannine tradition (see also Jones 2009, 2014).

(4) Similarly, another group argues that the order of composition cannot be determined because of the complexity of written traditions. For these scholars, creating a linear progression of writing is too speculative and/or unnecessary for interpretation (Schnackenburg, 39; Reis, 51).

(5) Finally, a growing group of interpreters believe that 1 John was written in the later stages of the Gospel's composition, with 2 and 3 John being written shortly thereafter. This contingent suggests that the Johan-nine community collected and composed the Gospel over a period of time, adjusting traditions to fit their current contexts, whether facing pressures from non-Messianic Jews or from Christological debates among other believers (Culpepper 2014; Scholtissek; von Wahlde 2010, 2014; Anderson 2011, 2014).

One more option, however, can be added to Culpepper's list: namely, the theory that 2 and 3 John may have functioned as two different, or even sequential, "cover letters" for 1 John. According to this theory, 2 and 3 John were letters of introduction and recommendation, demonstrating a speaker's connection to the Elder who wrote them. The Elder presents himself as an authoritative figure in 2 and 3 John and, therefore, over those addressed in them. In this reading, 2 and 3 John would have been sent by the Elder through an approved teacher who delivered the sermon that is 1 John on the Elder's behalf. In 2 John, the audience is more general ("to the Elect Lady"), and no specific disciple is recommended by the Elder, perhaps suggesting this letter could have been taken to a number of assemblies by various speakers. In 3 John, however, we have both a more specific addressee, Gaius, and a recommended traveler, Demetrius. In 3 John, Gaius is encouraged to welcome Demetrius, who most likely carried 3 John to him and could have been sent to speak the sermon of 1 John to the assembly of which Gaius was a part. If 2 and 3 John are sequential, however, 2 John could have been sent first as the initial cover letter for 1 John. Having been prohibited from sharing the sermon with the community of the "Elect Lady and [her] children" by Diotrephes, Demetrius brings 3 John, a letter that addresses Gaius directly. Gaius's influence over the assembly seems to have rivaled that of Diotrephes. If this is the case, the composition order would be 2 and 1 John, followed by 3 John. Regardless, all three of these writings would have been composed around the same time to address the same conflicts.

Of course, this theory too is speculative, but it does have some attractive elements. It would explain (1) why 1 John begins without any sort of epistolary introduction and ends without any greeting. Both of these elements are in 2 and 3 John. It would also (2) clarify why 2 and 3 John were preserved and why they remained connected to 1 John as part of the Johannine corpus. Additionally, it would address (3) why 1 John was so readily accepted into the canon as the most theologically robust writing of the three, while 2 and 3 John, as "extras," took time to gain authority. In our canon, organized by length, 2 and 3 John were "moved" to follow 1 John rather than precede it, but that does not necessitate their later composition. And, finally, this theory would explain (4) why specific "theological" conflicts or issues are not outlined in 3 John; either these issues were already introduced in 2 and 1 John, or they were about to be with the reading of 1 John by Demetrius.

Whichever theory an interpreter follows will affect their conclusions regarding the date of final composition for each writing. Since the Gospel itself is usually dated to somewhere between 90–110 CE, the Letters fall somewhere in this same range. This twenty-year time frame spans the imperial rule of Domitian (r. 81–96 CE), Nerva (r. 96–98 CE), and Trajan (r. 98–117 CE). Domitian was an unpopular emperor, ultimately assassinated and replaced by an elderly and more docile Nerva whom the Senate hoped to control. Shortly after he was adopted by Nerva, Trajan succeeded him and brought greater stability to the empire.

In spite of this stability, Trajan's relationship with Jews and Christians was fraught. His father had served as a tribune during the First Jewish War and was eventually appointed governor of Syria by Vespasian. This status allowed Trajan to establish himself as a tribune in Syria before he was appointed to several offices in Spain and Germany. He himself quelled a rebellion that was started by Jews in the eastern portions of the empire and that eventually spread to Alexandria, Egypt, a city with a large number of Jewish inhabitants at the time. In his rule, Trajan reflected the values of the Roman ruling class: namely, that loyalty to Rome should outweigh all other commitments in a subject's life.

In a surviving correspondence between Trajan and one of his governors, Pliny the Younger, they discuss how to handle the growing number of Christians in the province of Pontus-Bithynia (northern Asia Minor). Rather than instituting a state-wide hunt for Christians, Rome was focused on ensuring loyalty from its subjects, and Pliny only executed Christians who were (1) brought to him and accused by others and (2) refused to renounce Christ and offer a sacrifice of incense to the emperor, even after Pliny demanded this three times (*Ep. Tra.*, ca. 112 CE). Although the fact that Pliny executed Christians is disturbing, it should be noted that their Christian faith was not considered the main charge. Trajan approved of these executions because disobeying Pliny, and therefore Rome, was the real crime. Warren Carter cautions against reading Pliny's policies into the Johannine situation too closely (2008, 72), but the general idea of the community wrestling with allegiances certainly comes to bear in the Johannine Letters as the author competes with named and unnamed opponents who challenge his authority.

Lieu argues that rather than seeking to be overly specific, we should see in 1–3 John the general conflicts that existed among early Christian communities who had itinerant teachers. These teachers, whenever they engaged with diverse communities, would have encountered and offered differing stories and interpretations. Without existing institutionalized structures or episcopacies, these communities and their leaders had to decipher which interpretations were "faithful" and which were false (rather like Israel in Deut 13 and 18). Itinerant Christian teachers, therefore, competed with one another, passionately defending their own authority and interpretations against others (125–35). Lieu insists, the conflict over leadership displayed in 2–3 John *is* the problem, not just for modern-day readers of these Letters but also for their first recipients; they were trying to sort out whom to follow and why (157–60). Since the Elder won out in this debate, his Letters were preserved and are reminders of the debates that propelled the process of

self-definition that the Johannine community underwent and shared with
the larger Christian movement (164; 2008, 25–28).

Authorship

Theories on the authorship of the Johannine Letters are intimately tied to
conclusions drawn from the previous section on the date and composition
of these writings, as well as their relationship to the Gospel. As noted in the
General Introduction, 1 John was associated with the Gospel early on, and
both writings stood on the authority of John of Zebedee. This apostolic background encouraged its acceptance into the canon. Like the Gospel, however,
1 John is anonymous. First John is even more anonymous than the Gospel,
which at least associates itself with the Beloved Disciple in 21:24-25. Second
and 3 John also provide some hint at authorship with the attribution of "the
Elder" (*ho presbyteros*, 2 John 1, 3 John 1), but as with the Beloved Disciple,
this Elder is never explicitly named. For this reason, Lieu suggests an "inten-
tional" anonymity in these writings that ought to be respected rather than
decoded (2008, 9).

George Parsenios urges readers to explore the theological importance
of anonymity. Like Raymond Brown (1979, 1982) and D. Moody Smith
(1991, 17–18) before him, Parsenios is confident that all four writings come
from the same "mind," whether that be the mind of an individual disciple
or the collective mind of the Johannine community, over a period of time
(2014, 26; see also Culpepper 1998, 2014; Anderson 2014). For these
scholars, the verbal, syntactical, and thematic links between these writings
make their similar origins clear. Influenced by Lieu, Parsenios also believes
that the anonymity of the Letters, and the Gospel, is significant. "[S]uch
anonymity," he writes, is "an important statement on the nature of discipleship in the Johannine tradition" (2014, 31). Specifically, it is a reflection of
the importance of "abiding" or "remaining" (*menō*) in the unity of Father,
Son, and Spirit-infused community (John 17:23; 1 John 3:24; 4:12-16;
2 John 9; 3 John 8). The Gospel and Letters of John have authoritative
speakers and teachers behind them, but their main source of authority is
unity with Christ, who himself is united to the Father. As Parsenios explains,
to read and hear these writings does not lead one to focus on the identity
of the author, but rather "to see him [the author] is to look through him to
Christ and, more specifically, to the Christ of the Gospel" (48).

The Gospel and Letters of John blend voices together, connecting
narrator, speakers, and Jesus. In John 3:11-21 and 12:27-50, Jesus' voice is
entwined with the narrator's so that determining who is "speaking" is a challenge. Even when their voices do not merge, they are always in agreement

and the narrator even knows what Jesus is thinking at 13:1-5. This same blended voice comes through in the Letters as well. As Brown concludes, "The Johannine Jesus *speaks* as the author of the Johannine epistles writes" (1982, 24, emphasis original; cf. Parsenios 2014, 48). David Reis suggests that this resonance is especially profound in 1 John, which he interprets as an imitation of Jesus' speech in John 13–17, with a special emphasis on John 15 (2003; cf. Loader, xx). Reis argues that the speaker of 1 John is the "mimetic voice of Jesus" (50) and, in this way, shows his unity with the Son, Father, and Spirit.

In terms of ancient rhetoric, 1 John portrays the authorial *ethos* (character) of Jesus, using the technique of *prosōpopoiia* (speech-in-character or impersonation). This technique was common, used whenever writing dialogue for a character, but could also be useful in teaching or persuasive speeches. Cicero, for example, uses *prosōpopoiia* to shift attention away from his client, accused of a number of charges including murder, to the character of a woman who was a witness in his trial. Rather than focusing on his client, Cicero impersonates first the witness's famous ancestor and then her brother in order to degrade her character and, therefore, the value of her testimony (*Cael.* 14–15). Unlike Cicero's speech, 1 John is not explicit in its use of *prosōpopoiia*, but subtle; Jesus' voice is woven throughout the entire work. Nevertheless, as it does for Cicero, this technique contributes to 1 John's persuasiveness; this is the voice of one who *knows* what he's talking about. Moreover, *prosōpopoiia* added emotion and vividness to speeches, perhaps enabling the author of 1 John to articulate stronger polemic and praise than otherwise would have been possible (see also Watson 1989, esp. 120). As John of Sardis writes, impersonation "makes the language alive and moves the hearer to share in the emotion of the speaker by presenting his character" (*Prog.* 194 [Kenney]; cf. Nicolaus the Sophist, *Prog.* 67). By presenting himself as Jesus' contemporary mouthpiece, and his audience as united in the same Spirit, the author of 1 John seeks to persuade his audience to continue their allegiance with him and, therefore, with the Father and the Son (1:3).

Second and 3 John, however, differ. As mentioned above, the writer of these epistles identifies himself as "the Elder," which Parsenios suggests indicates that he was in charge of several house churches in the region, presumably Asia Minor (2014, 131–32). This Elder may be another John, whom Papias identifies as "the Elder" living in Ephesus and who was confused with the "Apostle" (John son of Zebedee), but we cannot be sure (Eusebius, *Hist. eccl.* 3.39:3–4). The Elder of 2–3 John faces challenges to his authority, thus prompting him to write several of his assemblies and, perhaps, to facilitate the reading of 1 John to them.

Audience and Purpose

As with the Gospel, the audiences of the Johannine Letters are usually located in Ephesus or surrounding areas in Asia Minor. Because of the geographical location of Ephesus and its importance as the provincial capital, it was an ideal location for missionary work as Paul's presence there demonstrates (Acts 19–20; cf. Jones 2014). The Ephesian locale also means the early Johannine Christians would have been surrounded by and participating in various cultural contexts, whether Jewish, Roman, Greek, or otherwise. The importance of religious cults should not be overlooked in the city, which Carter notes had regular festivals and parades honoring the pantheon and Roman leadership that celebrated "the city's sacred identity rooted in Artemis" (2011, 1). Morna Hooker argues that Ephesus was "regarded as responsible for guarding the goddess' honour," meaning that any threat, from Christians or anyone else, could meet an intense response (42–44).

Although the Letters do not mention "the Jews/Judeans" as the Gospel does, there was a notable Jewish population in Ephesus as well. If the Johannine Christians were separated from their previous connections in synagogues, they would no longer experience the protection Jews had from participating in some aspects of Roman religious life. Paul Anderson suggests, therefore, that "disagreements between community members of Jewish and Gentile origins over assimilative issues were most likely the backdrop for controversies" in 1 John (2014, 88). In other words, the Johannine Christians were facing pressure from a number of different angles, all competing for their loyalty (Parsenios 2014, 15). Daniel Streett argues that some believers must have been tempted to return to a version of faith closer to their Jewish roots, thus denying Jesus' divinity (112–18; cf. Olsson). Dominant Greco-Roman philosophies also regularly separated human (flesh, mortality, desire, etc.) from divine. Believers persuaded by these philosophies might focus on the Christ's divinity in contrast to Jesus' flesh. Even though these pressures could have come from outside the group—from nonbelieving Jews or Gentiles—it is the conflict *within* the group that occupies the attention of these Letters. The author seeks to maintain a relationship with his audience in spite of divisions caused by the teachings and behaviors of *other* believers, whom he says are allied with "the world" (1 John 2:15-27; 2 John 7–11; 3 John 9–10).

The precise nature of this debate, as indicated above, is still a mystery. Brown's reconstruction continues to be the most prevalent theory. He argues that there was a group of believers who separated themselves from the tradition associated with the Elder. These believers had clear doctrinal differences in four areas:

(1) *Christology:* they denied the significance (or occurrence) of the incarnation (1 John 2:22; 4:2-3; 2 John 7);

(2) *Ethics and ecclesiology:* they understood themselves to be "sinless" even though they treated others poorly (1 John 1:10; 2:9-11; 5:2; 2 John 6; 3 John 11);

(3) *Eschatology:* as sinless ones, they were experiencing a realized eschatology rather than looking for a return of Christ (1 John 3:2); and

(4) *Pneumatology:* they emphasized revelation received through the Holy Spirit rather than the traditions passed down by the Elder or other disciples (1 John 3:23–4:13).

Interpreters who follow Brown's reconstruction, even if they modify it, often call this group the "secessionists" because, as 2 John 9 explains, they have "gone beyond" (*proagōn*) the teaching of Christ rather than abiding in it (cf. Smith 1991; Culpepper 1998; von Wahlde 2010; Anderson 2011, 2014). According to Brown's reading, the Johannine Letters are predominately polemical in intent and in their presentation of opponents.

Lieu (1991, 11–16; 2008, 9–14) and David Rensberger (21–25), however, have noted that while there is polemical language in the Letters, they are not specific about the content of the conflict. Pheme Perkins agrees, suggesting that the Letters are more focused on building up the community through pastoral encouragement than they are on outlining the specific flaws of various opponents (xxi–xxii; cf. Streett, 112–18). According to Lieu, the focus of the Letters is to create and affirm the "fellowship" (*koinōnia*) that currently exists between the author and recipients (1 John 1:3). Indeed, she argues, the rhetorical effect of 1 John's switching between "we," "you," and "I" language brings the audience together to be a part of the united "we" of the author, so that "the audience loses any separate identity or possibility within the encompassing 'we'" (2014, 136). Second and 3 John differ from 1 John with greater specificity. In Lieu's reading, 2 John justifies the exclusion of believers who no longer confess the importance of Jesus' flesh, while 3 John continues discussing issues of hospitality. On its own, 3 John does not offer insight into the theological positions that created the division between Diotrophes and the Elder. Scholars who read the three letters together, however, suggest that the same Christological concerns must be at the core of 1 and 2 John.

Parsenios, for example, seeks to find a middle ground between these two positions. He suggests that while Brown's outline of disagreements might be too confident and precise, the diminishment of the dispute by Perkins and others risks downplaying the crisis in the community (2014, 17–19).

Focusing on 1 and 2 John, Parsenios argues that the opponents have a "deficient Christology" that denies Jesus' humanity in favor of his divinity: "in their certainty that he [Jesus] is God, they have come to deny that he was a human" (22). Given the language of 1 and 2 John, that emphasizes unity between the identities of Jesus and the Christ (2:22; 4:2; 5:1, 5, 13, 20; 2 John 3, 7-10), however, it might be better to suggest that the opponents divided the divine "Christ" from the human "Jesus" (Thatcher 2001, 242). Having received the Spirit, these opponents no longer see any significance to Jesus' flesh. He served his purpose when he died and gave the disciples the Spirit. In contrast, the Elder emphasizes that Jesus' flesh still matters, not only because of his death but also because of his current intercessory work before the Father and his coming return (1 John 1:7–2:2; 2:28-29; 4:9-10, 17-18; 5:6-8).

Literary Features

Even though 1–3 John are all called "letters" or "epistles," only 2 and 3 John reflect that ancient genre. Both 2 and 3 John begin with identifying the sender, followed by the addressee, before offering a short greeting. The Letters are also short, a common feature of private correspondence in the ancient Mediterranean world, and they include a desire from the sender to see the recipients before concluding with final greetings. Although 2 and 3 John stand out in the NT canon due to their brevity and some of their contents, such as the health wish in 3 John 2, they are more like other ancient letters from the Roman world than any other letters in our NT (Lieu 2008, 4–6; cf. Stowers). Third John is a letter of introduction, or a recommendation letter, seeking hospitality for Demetrius (Parsenios 2014, 26–28). Second John is a paraenetic letter, offering advice and encouragement for the believers facing division. The advice 2 John gives is explicit: whenever they encounter a believer who denies "Jesus Christ coming in the flesh" they are to discontinue hospitality with them (v. 7).

First John, however, is different. Rather than a "letter," this writing is often described as a homily or sermon, similar to Hebrews (Heb 13:22-25; Lieu 2008, 5). It lacks an epistolary opening of sender, recipient, or greeting and ends with an abrupt command to "keep yourselves from idols!" (1 John 5:21). Parsenios writes that it is "broadly and loosely speaking, an example of paraenetic literature" like 2 John, but it lacks the specificity of response that 2 John has (24). Instead, 1 John uses insider language of maxims (or *sententiae*) that encourage the audience to agree with the author out of a shared set of understandings. "*Sententiae*," he writes, "have a social function, drawing boundaries and establishing a social connection between author and audience" (18; cf. Aristotle, *Rhet.* 2.21). The boundaries the author draws with these maxims is between "believ[ing] and behave[ing] rightly" or "wrongly" (19). The need to choose is reinforced with dualistic language that Parsenios identifies as paradoxes, antitheses, and double-meaning (*paronomasia*), which is also evident in the Gospel (John 3:5-6; 12:25; 1 John 3:6-8).

Duane Watson focuses on repetition in 1 John, arguing that 1 John employs almost every technique of amplification outlined in ancient *progymnasmata* and rhetorical handbooks to encourage the audience to remain in fellowship with the author. Instead of making a theological argument full of proofs meant to convince an audience of outsiders, the author uses familiar language and agreed-upon definitions to reinforce their allegiance (1993, 117–18; cf. 1989). "Far from being boringly *redundant*," he writes, "the rhetor is carefully *emphatic*" in order to strengthen the loyalty and connection he already has with the audience (1993, 123). For Watson, the author does not doubt the basic connection, but only its strength, especially in the face of other, perhaps rhetorically capable, opponents.

First John's incorporation of Johannine traditions reflected in John 13–17 also supports the conclusion that 1 John is epideictic. Jo-Ann Brant argues John 13–17 forms the most epideictic section of the Gospel, since this speech encourages the disciples to "remain" in the community in spite of the hostility they face from the world around them (2011, 210). Like 1 John, the Farewell Discourse contains a number of repetitions, also making it a challenge for interpreting and outlining (see commentary). Taking on the voice of Jesus, therefore, the speaker of 1 John repeats Jesus' epideictic style from the FD in order to encourage his own audience living in a time long after Jesus' return to the Father.

Outlines

The outlines below will guide the commentary that follows. While outlining 2 and 3 John is straightforward, given their adherence to the letter genre, 1 John is a challenge. The repetition described by Watson adds to the rhetorical effectiveness of the work, but it also prevents an easy outline. Brown argues that 1 John mirrors the Gospel of John in its progression, but this seems driven by Brown's argument about their interrelationship rather than necessitated by the text itself (1982, 123–29). Brown supposes that the Gospel was written before 1 John and that 1 John is offering a corrective to misinterpretations of it. Even Culpepper's emphasis on the similarities between 1 John 5:13 and John 21:24-25 does not require that 1 John as a whole reflect the Gospel's format (2014, 100–101). Indeed, 1 John is missing a number of elements found within the Gospel, focusing instead on themes found in John 5–6, 8, and 13–17 rather than rehearsing the entire narrative (see also Smith 1991, 24).

First John's focus on these Gospel scenes also coheres with the observation that 1 John is imitating Jesus' voice since these chapters each contain significant portions of Jesus' discourses. Instead of tying 1 John so tightly to a Gospel outline, then, this commentary will focus on the arguments of 1 John as its own work, even though it is doubtless indebted to Johannine tradition. In what follows, I divide 1 John into three chapters focusing on 1:1–2:17; 2:18–4:6; and 4:7–5:21 in order to devote sufficient space to its theological perspectives. First John as a whole, however, has a chiastic structure that is outlined below. The chiasm shows the sermon's emphasis on behavior as revealing one's loyalties and, therefore, one's identity. Second and 3 John follow the standard pattern of ancient epistles and will be analyzed in separate chapters. These two letters will be treated as potential cover letters and therefore related in content to 1 John, reflecting the same conflicts.

First John
A Sermonic Prologue (1:1–4)
Body of the Letter: Exhortations to Remain in Fellowship (1:5–5:21)
    A. 1:5–2:2, Sin's Solution Is Jesus Christ, Righteous One
        B. 2:3-17, The Commandments: Love One Another, Not the World
            C. 2:18–4:6, Behavior Reveals Identity
                i. Antichrists: Going Out vs. Remaining In (2:18-27)
                ii. Revealing Identities (2:28–3:24)
                i'. Antichrist Identified: Testing Spirits (4:1-6)
        B'. 4:7–5:4, Let Us Love because God Is Love
    A'. 5:5-21 Jesus Christ, Son, True God, Eternal Life

Second John
Opening Greeting (vv. 1-3)
Body of Letter (vv. 4-11)
Praise and First Command (vv. 4-6)
    Rationale: Deceivers and Antichrist (v. 7)
    Warnings and More Commands (vv. 8-11)
Closing Greeting (vv. 12-13)

Third John
Opening Greetings (vv. 1-4)
Body of the Letter (vv. 5-12)
    Praise for Gaius (vv. 5-8)

Blame for Diotrephes (vv. 9-10)
Recommending Demetrius (vv. 11-12)
Closing Greetings (vv. 13-15)

Remain in Fellowship

1 John 1:1–2:17

Throughout 1 John, the author encourages the audience to remain in fellowship. Speaking to believers rather than non-Christians, 1 John acknowledges the pressures of living in a world that is full of factions demanding loyalty, especially "the desire of the flesh and the desire of the eyes and the arrogance of livelihood" that comes from loving the "world" (*kosmos*, 2:15-16). For 1 John, this sort of misguided love is nothing less than idolatry because it prioritizes created things rather than the Creator (5:21). In contrast, one is connected to real love (that is, to God) by means of the example and teachings of Jesus, who is God's One-of-a-kind Son and revelation of divine love (3:16; 4:7-11). The author's urgent encouragement, therefore, is for the audience to *continue* abiding in the love revealed to them, in spite of the alluring arguments or lifestyles of those who have "gone out" from them (2:18).

Emphasizing Jesus' authority, the speaker of 1 John takes on Jesus' voice, reflecting many traditions also found in John 13–17 (the Farewell Discourse) and elsewhere in the Gospel (esp., John 5–6; 8). Just as Jesus encouraged his disciples to remain in him, loving him by following his commandment to love one another, so too does 1 John (e.g., John 13:34-35; 14:15, 21-24; 15:14; 1 John 2:3-5; 3:22-24; 5:3, 18). Rather than consoling the disciples in light of Jesus' approaching departure, 1 John encourages an audience who already lives without the physical presence of Jesus. This physical absence is part of the challenge that 1 John faces as various believers claim inspiration by the Holy Spirit and offer competing interpretations about Jesus or divine truth (4:1-6). By speaking like Jesus, the author shows continuity with him; the person delivering 1 John would literally offer the breath (*pneuma*, spirit) of Jesus because 1 John quotes and paraphrases Jesus traditions so frequently. This speech-in-character (*prosōpopoiia*) creates a compelling authorial persona (*ethos*) to convince the audience to remain allied to him and the tradition he represents, while also making space for subtle additions and tweaks as he interprets Jesus' teachings in light of the community's current situation.

In this chapter, I will focus on 1 John 1:1–2:17, which includes the
so-called "prologue" (1:1-4) followed by a section meant to encourage
and admonish the believers to continue confessing their sins because of
the work of Jesus Christ, Righteous One, who is even now their Advocate
(*paraklētos*) before the Father (1:5–2:2). In 2:3-17, the sermon shifts to a
discussion of commandments by (1) rephrasing Jesus' "love command" from
John 13:34-35 and 15:12-14, which is called the "old command" in 1 John
2:3-11; (2) praising the audience of 1 John with a digression at 2:12-14; and
(3) issuing the speaker's "new command" in 2:15-17: namely, not to love the
world.

Commentary

A Sermonic Prologue (1:1-4)
The opening lines of 1 John lead a number of scholars to conclude that it
is not a letter, at least not in the classic sense. Instead, it opens much more
like Hebrews, which describes itself as a "word of exhortation" (13:22). First
John provides no such explicit self-designation, but the author does describe
the writing as a means of proclamation in 1:1-4; it is written proclamation
to be sure, but proclamation nonetheless. For this reason, interpreters have
suggested reading 1 John more as a homily or sermon and not as a letter
(Parsenios 2014, 36–37). This is a helpful starting point because 1 John
proceeds not with linear argumentation but rather with looping repetition,
chain-links, inclusios, and chiasms that reward the one who is listening
closely. The author is not trying to convince the audience to become Christians, but rather to remain in fellowship with the believing tradition that
the speaker represents: the "we" who have heard, seen, touched, and are
proclaiming the message to them.

The exalted and enigmatic language of 1 John 1:1-4 encourages some
interpreters to read it as a "prologue" similar in purpose, and also themes,
as the "prologue" to the Gospel (by which they mean John 1:1-18; see
commentary). Raymond Brown (1982, 176–80) might offer the most robust
interpretation in this vein by suggesting that 1:1-4 was intentionally shaped
to reflect John 1:1-18. This is part of Brown's larger structural argument that
all of 1 John mirrors the Gospel. Even if unconvinced by Brown's specificity,
other scholars note connections between the passages, such as mention of
the "beginning" (*archē*), a "word" (*logos*), "life" (*zōē*), "testimony" (*martyria*),
that which was seen by and revealed to an "us" (*hēmin*), and the identification of Jesus that occurs near the end of the passage rather than at its outset
(John 1:17; 1 John 1:3; see Parsenios 2014, 37–38; Smith 1991, 38–39).
These connections are not precise enough, however, to necessitate a literary

relationship between 1 John 1:1-4 and John 1:1-18; they could be explained by shared language in the Johannine community (Lieu 2008, 45–46). As George Parsenios writes, the passages are similar, but it is "similarity-in-difference" (2014, 38). First John has its own agenda and purpose that, while resonant with parts of the Gospel, are nonetheless distinct and should be appreciated on their own terms even as we acknowledge the sermon's roots in Johannine traditions.

First John begins in mid-thought with a series of relative clauses. Although this is not "good Greek," it is gripping for an audience (Brown 1982, 152). The opening verses sweep them into the world of the sermon, pulling the hearers along to discover just what the author is proclaiming. Below is my translation:

[1]That which was from the beginning (*ap archēs*),
　　which we have heard,
　　　　which we have seen with our eyes,
　　　　　　which we beheld and our hands touched
　concerning the word of life—
[2]indeed, the life was revealed
　　and we have seen
　　　and are testifying
　　　　and are proclaiming to you
　the eternal life which was before the Father and was revealed to us—
[3]that which we have seen and have heard,
　　we are proclaiming also to you,
　　　so that you yourselves also might continue having fellowship
　　　with us.
And indeed our own fellowship is with the Father and with his Son, Jesus
　Christ.
[4]Indeed, we ourselves are writing these things to you,
　so that our joy might be fulfilled.

These verses are repetitious, using multiple relative and subordinate clauses to describe the proclamation while also delaying a clear articulation of purpose. The result is a circling prologue that slowly moves forward only to digress before resuming its main thought again.

In v. 1, the author focuses on the credibility of the witness provided, highlighting physical interactions with "that which was from the beginning." In v. 2, the author pauses to describe "the life" and brackets another triplet of descriptions that emphasize the authority of the "we" who received God's revelation. Verse 3 returns to the thought of v. 1, repeating the opening verse but also building to a climax by switching the order of verbs ("we have seen and have heard") and adding "we are proclaiming to you," a repetition from v. 2. Verses 3-4, therefore, are a crescendo, containing two purpose clauses that disclose the intentions of the homily: (1) that the audience "might continue having fellowship with us" and, therefore, with the Father and Son, and (2) that "our joy might be fulfilled."

This second purpose in 1:4 is somewhat surprising, given the focus that has so far been on what the "we" is bringing to the "you" (plural) of the audience. Why would the "we" be proclaiming something that was just for their own benefit—"so that *our* joy might be fulfilled"? Early scribes also struggled with this inconsistency, and a number of manuscripts contain *"your"*(*hymōn*) rather than "our" (*hēmōn*) in this verse. The more original reading is probably "our joy," however, for two reasons: (1) the change to "your" makes the text easier to understand, and scribes generally clarify passages rather than make them more confusing; and (2) this verse is close to Jesus' promises in the Farewell Discourse that his departure, and the disciples' continual "abiding" in him (and the Father), was for their joy. In John 15:11, for example, after telling the disciples the parable of the vine and branches, Jesus says, "I have said these things to you so that my joy might be in you and *your joy might be fulfilled* (*hē chara hymōn plērōthē*)." Again in 16:24, he says, "Until now you asked nothing in my name. Ask and you will receive so that *your joy might be fulfilled*." A scribe, therefore, could have recalled Jesus' promise in the Gospel of John and made 1 John 1:4 match (cf. 2 John 12).

Rather than seeing the meaning of this verse as a contradiction to 1:1-3, however, there is another possibility for interpreting 1:4, particularly in light of the emphasis on fellowship that this verse also has. In the first three verses the author provides information that underscores the authority of the "we" testifying to the audience. These descriptions parallel traditions from the Gospel, particularly John 3:11, where another unknown "we" creeps into the text. During Jesus' conversation with Nicodemus, he suddenly switches from first singular verbs to first plural, proclaiming, "Truly, truly I am saying to you, *that which we know we are saying and that which we have seen we are testifying*, and you are not receiving *our* testimony." Similar phrases appear in John 3:32 as well as in 19:35, 20:30-31, and 21:25; the latter three are references to testimony about the manner of Jesus' death, the reality of Jesus' resurrection, and the validity of the Gospel's message.

While these parallels could imply that the author was one of these witnesses, if not the Beloved Disciple himself, the author could also simply be tapping into the collective tradition of testimony of the Johannine community, just as the Johannine Jesus does in John 3:11 (cf. Brown 1982,

163). Without concluding whether this author did or did not see the risen Christ with certainty, the authorial "we" of 1 John unites the speaker with the Johannine tradition and, more important, with Jesus himself, the initiator of that tradition. Moreover, the switch to "our" in 1 John 1:4 merges the authorial "we" and the audience "you" into one: the "our" whose joy is being fulfilled. Since the hope is that they will all share in fellowship, the joy they experience is a unified joy.

Exhortations to Remain in Fellowship (1:5–2:17)

First John 1:5–5:12 comprises the main body of the homily. The chiastic structure highlights the sermon's emphasis on behavior (i.e., love for one another) as the key to revealing one's identity and, therefore, showing the fellowship to which one belongs. For the author of 1 John, love is the key marker of God's children. Only those who mimic the true example of love displayed and continually expressed in the ongoing work of Jesus, God's Son and Christ, are able to show such love because they live in relationship with the Father and Son and are empowered by God's Spirit. First John 1:5–2:17 begins the body of 1 John explaining how believers maintain their place in this unity in spite of sins (1:5–2:2), and expanding Jesus' command to love with a new command: not to love the world (2:3-17).

A. 1 John 1:5–2:2: Sin's Solution Is Jesus Christ, Righteous One

First John 1:5–2:2 can be divided into three parts: (1) 1:5; (2) 1:6-10; (3) 2:1-2. First John 1:5 resumes the themes of 1:1-3 with the verbs *akēkoamen* ("we have heard") and *anangellomen* ("we are reporting back"). This is the third and final use of *akēkoamen* in 1 John, and it once again follows a relative pronoun ("which"). This time, however, there is a noun that grounds this pronoun; it is no longer an unknown thing "which we have heard" but is now "the message" (*hē angelia*). Having emphasized their connection to the revelation in 1:1-3 as well as its source from the Father, 1:5 moves on to offer the content: "And *this* is the message which we have heard from him and we are reporting back to you: God is light and darkness is not in him, not at all." The contrast of light and darkness resonates with the larger Johannine tradition, especially the opening verses of the Gospel of John where the Word is identified as "the light" and "the true light" that the "darkness" did not "overcome" (1:4-9; cf. 3:19-21). The image appears elsewhere in the Gospel when Jesus calls himself "the light of the world" (8:12; 9:5; 11:9-10; 12:46) and encourages those around him to "walk in the light" while they can (12:35-36).

As 1 John continues, the author also describes fellowship with God as "walking in the light" (1:6-7) with the first in a series of contrasting conditional statements in 1:6-10. This section rotates between a negative description (A) followed by a positive one (B). The negative descriptions outnumber the positive and thus bracket the entire section. Yet this is only one aspect of the pervasive parallelisms in this passage as seen below:

A. [6]<u>If we should say</u>, "We have fellowship with him" and in darkness we are walking,
> we are lying and not doing the truth.
B. [7]*If in the light we are walking*, as he is in the light,
> we continue having fellowship with one another,
> > and the blood of Jesus his Son continues cleansing us from all sin.
A'. [8]<u>If we should say</u>, "We are no longer having sin,"
> we are deceiving ourselves and the truth is not in us.
B'. [9]*If we continue confessing our sins*,
> he is faithful and righteous,
> > that he should release sins for us and cleanse us from all unrighteousness.
A". [10]<u>If we should say</u>, "We have not sinned,"
> we are making him a liar and his word is not in us.

In each negative conditional statement (A), the comment "we should say" is contrasted with the behavior, or the reality experienced, by the "we." The "we" of these verses is denying having sinned and, therefore, the need to be cleansed from sin. Such a posture, however, serves only to reveal one's distance from God. The sin that threatens fellowship with God, and with others, continues to cause alienation. According to 1 John, such denial is itself a sin: it is lying and not doing the truth (v. 6), self-deception (v. 8), and making God a liar (v. 10). These three descriptions build on one another, rotating between "lying/liar" (*pseudometha/pseudēn*) and "deception" (*planōmen*), and moving from "not doing the truth" to a statement about what is "not in us"—either "the truth" (*alētheia*) or "his word" (*logos*). These descriptions recur in the sermon but begin the transition from language of "fellowship" (*koinōnian*, 1:3, 6, 7) toward "abiding" or "remaining in" (*menō en*) that dominates the remainder of the homily (2:6–4:16).

The positive conditional statements (B) contrast the (A) clauses not only by excluding a "if we should say" claim but also by shifting the focus from the "we" to a description of Jesus (vv. 7, 9). Rather than saying they are "walking in the light," the "we" is encouraged simply to do it and, as a result, continue experiencing fellowship with one another and with the Father and his Son, Jesus (cf. 1:3-4). As v. 9 indicates, walking in the light does not mean that one never makes a mistake, or misses the mark, which is to sin (*hamartia*); instead, walking in the light means continually confessing the sins that one commits. This confession means telling the truth to others, to oneself, and to God, thereby trusting in God's provision for cleansing rather than relying on oneself or living in denial. Learning about Jesus in these verses means the author is explaining why the audience can trust God in spite of their own sinfulness: namely, because of Jesus his Son. As in the Gospel, walking toward and in the light means moving toward life rather than hiding in the shadows of fear and wrath (John 3:19-21; 9:40-41).

The final section of the passage is 2:1-2. It is a sudden direct address to the audience, breaking the flow of the argument with an emotional appeal of comfort. Like 1:5, 2:1 resumes the theme of telling the audience why the author is writing them, this time using the first person singular *graphō* rather than the first person plural. The author encourages the audience by expanding on the reasons that they can hope and should continue confessing. Their hope is manifest in the person and *continuing* work of Jesus Christ. The author explains:

> [1]Little children (*teknia*), I am writing to you so that you might not sin.
> But if someone should sin,
>> we continue having an Advocate (*paraklēton*) before the Father,
>> Jesus Christ, Righteous One.
> [2]And he himself is expiation (*hilasmos*) for our sins,
>> and not only for ours, but also for the whole world.

According to 1 John, Jesus continues being an Advocate and Comforter (*paraklētos*) for the believers, even though he is no longer physically present with them. Such a reality is related to the continuing work he administers by means of his blood from 1:7 and 9. Jesus' advocacy is before the Father, it is effective for cleansing believers, and it is more than sufficient. Calling him "Righteous One" (*dikaion*) reflects 1:9 as well, where he was called "faithful and righteous" (*pistos estin kai dikaios*) and demonstrated these qualities by releasing believers from sins and purifying them "from all unrighteousness." As "expiation" (*hilasmos*), Jesus intercedes for believers and continues helping them, long after his return to the Father. This, explains 1 John, is why believers *must* continue relying on him (see Theological Threads).

B. 1 John 2:3-17: New Commandment: Love One Another, Not the World
The next section of 1 John continues with the contrast of light and dark but shifts gradually from first person plural language to third singular ("he" or "she") in its hypothetical constructions. This is part of the gradual turn from discussing the "we" of the community, who is aligned with the author in fellowship with God through the continuing confession of Jesus and in loving one another, to identifying the "antichrists" who reject Jesus and mimic the world's behavior (2:18–4:6). This passage also turns from the topic of "sin" (*hamartia*) to keeping the commandments or word of God as given by Jesus: loving one another. This section incorporates traditions from John 13–17, especially John 15, as well as John 8. This latter passage is a difficult text with a disturbing history of interpretation, but the traditions it conveys will occupy a major portion of the upcoming argument in 1 John 3 as the author identifies who is "from God" (*ek tou theou*) and who is "from the devil" (*ek tou diablou*).

First John 2:3-17 has four parts: vv. 3-5, 6-11, 12-14, and 15-17. The overriding theme of the section is that keeping the commandments is the evidence of one's fellowship or "abiding" with God. This means that one continuously loves the siblings in the faith *and*, therefore, does not love the things world values.

1 John 2:3-5: Knowing through Keeping. The literary artistry demonstrated above through the extensive use of repetitions, contrasts, and various parallelisms continues in 1 John 2:3-17. First John 2:3-5 is another inclusio that brackets two contrasting couplets to create an A/B/B'/A' pattern. Verse 3 sets the topic: how we recognize that we are knowing (and therefore having fellowship with) God. Verses 4-5 digress with two contrasting couplets, a negative example followed by a positive one. The negative language repeats themes from 1:6, 8, and 10 as the hypocrite is again called a "liar" (*pseustē*), and "the truth" (*hē alētheia*) is not in him. The positive example continues building on 1 John's definition of "the word" (*ho logos*) by making it parallel to "commandments" from v. 4. So far, the "word" of 1 John has been linked to "life" (*zōē*, 1:1), "truth" (1:8, 10), and now "commandments." As 2:5 continues, it is also made parallel to "the love of God." "The love of God" will continue to be an important topic in 1 John, especially in 4:7-21, which runs parallel to 2:3-17 in my outline of the sermon. The completion or perfection of "the love of God" is demonstrated when believers show Jesus' kind of love to one another. As 1 John 3:16 will explain, this means loving even if it means laying down one's life (*psychē*; cf. John 10:17-18; 13:2; 19:28). First John 2:6 returns to the main topic by summarizing the teaching and emphasizing that this behavior is how "we are knowing that we are in him" (*ginōskomen en autō esmen*).

1 John 2:6-11: Remaining in the Light. First John 2:6-11 contains two shorter sections (vv. 6-8, 9-11), both of which have the following pattern:

(A) a statement about "the one saying." Verse 6 offers a positive example, while v. 9 returns to the negative.
(B) a two-verse section that expands or clarifies the example with two contrasting parallel clauses (vv. 7-8a, 10-11a).
(C) an ending with a causal statement about "the darkness" (*hoti hē skotia*, vv. 8b, 11b).

The construction of v. 6 is difficult to render into English but is particularly poignant in Greek. Below is my translation alongside a transliteration with portions emphasized to highlight assonance.

The one saying he remains in him ought,   *ho legōn en autō menein opheilei,*
just as <u>that one</u> *walked,*   **kathōs** <u>ekeinos</u> *periepatēsen,*
<u>he himself</u> also **thusly** *to walk.*   *kai* <u>autos</u> **houtōs** *peripatein.*

Even though this is a stuttering translation that shifts subjects in the middle of the verse, it illustrates the claim of "remaining in him" with which the verse begins. Just as "the one" should remain in him, "that one" (Jesus) is also *in him.* This cohabitation is demonstrated by Jesus' sudden presence in the middle of the verse describing the faithful believer. The believer cannot "remain in him" if Jesus does not also remain in the believer, showing the believer how to walk (and to live).

Following the positive example in v. 6, 2:7-8 is a digression in the form of a direct address, mirroring 2:1-2 (on *digressio* see Guzmán and Martin, 297–99). This time, however, the audience is called "beloved" (*agapētoi*). This title repeats in the rest of the sermon (3:2, 21; 4:1, 7, 11) and serves not only to unite the author with the audience but also to identify the author as one who loves and, as such, one who obeys God's commands. This digression introduces the theme of "commandments" (*entolē*) that continues throughout the sermon. The author is not writing an entirely new commandment in the homily because he paraphrases Jesus' commandment from John 13:34-35 in the digression that follows in 1 John 2:10-11 and again in 3:11 (cf. 3:14, 23; 4:7, 12, 19; 5:2). He *is*, however, writing a new commandment as well, which he introduces in 2:8 but will not offer explicitly until 2:15-17.

The pattern repeats in 2:9-11 and builds on a negative example. As in v. 6, it begins with a form of indirect speech but does not exhibit the abiding principle of that verse. It reads, "The one saying he is in the light, but continues hating (*misōn*) his brother, is in the darkness even now." The hypocrite's claim repeats from 1:6: "If we should say, 'We are having fellowship with him,' but are walking *in the darkness*, we are lying and are not doing the truth," thereby bringing the descriptions of these opening portions full circle (1:5–2:11). Indeed, this parallelism is one reason why Parsenios (2014, 55–72) treats all of 1:5–2:11 together as a single section. As we will see, however, the section extends to 2:17 because of the resumption of the commandment theme in 2:15-17.

The expansion that follows in 2:10-11 does not directly address the audience but again returns to the motif of love while also introducing hatred (*miseō*). These verses also unite the ideas of loving, remaining, and walking in the light that have rotated throughout the opening portions of the sermon. In contrast to these positive attributes is hating and darkness. First John 2:10-11 reads:

> [10] The one loving his brother remains (*menei*) in the light,
>   and there is no scandal (*skandalon*) in him (*en autō*)
> [11] But the one hating his brother is in the darkness,
>   and he walks in the darkness and does not know where he is going,
>   because the darkness blinded his eyes.

The imagery of these verses coheres well with the story of the man born blind in John 9. Although the man has stumbled in darkness from his physical condition, he hears Jesus' word, and because of his obedient trust, he is cured. This sudden sight results in insight as well as physical sight when the man first testifies about Jesus and then worships him in 9:35-38. In contrast, the religious leaders in John 9 have physical sight, but they exhibit blindness by stumbling in their questioning and prosecution of the cured man, as well as in their judgment concerning him and Jesus. Their stumbling ultimately results in their expulsion of the cured man, an act of hatred that cuts him off from his family and kinship networks. Jesus' words to them are also cutting: "If you were blind, then you would have no sin. But now, because you say, 'We see,' your sin remains (*menei*)" (John 9:40-41). As in 1 John 1:6-10, the sin here is self-sufficiency, pride, and fear that keeps one from admitting shortcomings (cf. John 3:19-21).

1 John 2:12–14: Digression Praising the Audience. First John 2:12-14 is another digression that shifts from the main thought of the passage. Like the two previous digressions in 2:1-2 and 2:7-8, this digression also includes direct address and reasons for why the author is writing ("I am writing to you," *graphō hymin*, 2:1, 7, 12, 13). In this way, the lengthier and more rhetorically embellished digression in 2:12-14 culminates the beginning series of arguments in the sermon and prepares for the transition that will follow.

Duane Watson (1989) argues that the author combines the rhetorical techniques of *distributio, conduplicatio,* and *expolitio* in these verses (cf. *Rhet. Her.* 4.28.38; 4.35.47; 4.42.54; Cicero, *De or.* 40.138; Quintilian, *Inst.* 9.3.28–29; 10.5.7–9). Awareness of these techniques clarifies the passage, showing that the author first addresses the group as a whole, first as *teknia* and then as *paidia* (both mean "little children"), before distributing more specific praise for two distinct groups within the larger collection (*distributio*): the "elders" (lit. "fathers," *pateres*) and the "young ones" (*neaniskoi*). Watson argues that the titles for "little children" refer to the entire community because the author uses them throughout the sermon when addressing the group as a whole (*teknia* in 2:1, 12, 28; 3:18; 4:4; 5:21; *paidia* in 2:14, 18; 3:7).

In addition to *distributio*, the author also uses *conduplicatio* (or repetition), the most obvious of which are the three-fold uses of "I am writing" (*graphō*) in vv. 12-13 followed by "I wrote" (*egrapsa*) in v. 14. These two sets of three also reflect what Watson (99) calls John's "penchant for groupings of three" that we have seen elsewhere—for example, the uses of *akēkoamen* in 1:1-5; "If we should say" in 1:6-10; "The one saying" in 2:4-9; and the three descriptions of the "young ones" in 2:14 to end the digression. Other repetitions include the praise of the elders "because you have known the one from the beginning," as well as of the youth who "have conquered the evil one." These repetitions, Watson argues, make the entire digression an *expolitio*, which uses parallel statements to expand on main ideas without changing themes (103).

In other words, the author creates definitions through parallel phrases, just as he has in the previous sections of 1 John, but 2:12-14 is a single concentrated passage of focused repetition. In 2:12-14, the release of sins is described as knowing the Father, and conquering the evil one means being strong, that is, having the word of God remaining in you. Both *conduplicatio* and *expolitio* are forms of amplification, often used to create an emotional appeal. This use of *pathos* is common in digressions, which Quintilian explains "amplify or abridge a topic" and "add charm and elegance to oratory" (*Inst.* 4.3.15). In 2:12-14, the author amplifies the message by praising the audience, seeking to win their allegiance before he transitions to harder subjects: a new command (2:15-17) and a description of the "anti-christs" who threaten their fellowship (2:18–4:6).

1 John 2:15-17: The New Commandment. After the digression in 2:12-14, the author returns to the topic of commandments from 2:3-11. In 2:7, the author explains, "I am not writing to you a new commandment," but in v. 8 he follows with, "on the other hand, I am writing to you a new commandment." The "old commandment" is the loving of one's siblings (*adelphos*) implied by 2:9-11. This is 1 John's first paraphrase and invention on the tradition reflected in John 13:34-35 when Jesus commands his disciples to "love one another" (*agapate allēlous*). The "new commandment," then, comes in 2:15a with the first imperative used thus far in the sermon. In contrast to Jesus' positive command, 1 John gives the negative command that results from it, writing, "Do not keep loving the world or the things in the world (*mē agapate ton kosmon mēde ta en tō kosmō*)." For 1 John, to love one another means showing the love of God: both the love for God and loving the way God does. While this does include loving the world in the Gospel of John (cf. 3:16), the way that God loves is in sending his Son, Jesus Christ. First John will repeat this description of God's self-revelatory love in 4:7-11. First John 2:15, however, is a command not to keep on loving the world (present tense) or the things of the world, meaning that loving God should come before loving all else. Loving God means one cannot love the world in the way the world expects.

First John 2:15b-17 explains:

> [15b]If someone should keep loving the world, the love of the Father is not in him.
>   [16]Because everything in the world,
>   the desire of the flesh,
>   and the desire of the eyes,
>   and the arrogance of livelihood,
>   is not from the Father, but from the world.
> [17]And the world is passing away, also its desire.
> But the one doing the will of God remains into eternity.

The explanation in these verses returns to a third-class conditional clause, which was used throughout 1 John 1–2, but particularly repeats 2:1, where the author writes, "If someone should sin" or "if someone should keep on sinning (*ean tis hamartē*, present tense)." While 2:1 followed this protasis with a hopeful apodosis ("we continue having an Advocate before the Father"), 2:15b moves in a decidedly negative direction: "the love of the Father is not in him." According to our speaker, there is no room for dual allegiances. If one loves the world, and the things of the world, one is not loving the Father. As 2:16-17 goes on to describe, loving the world means setting the created in the place only the Creator can rightfully occupy.

In 2:16-17, 1 John continues with its patterns of three, further defining "everything in the world" as "desires" or "seductions" (*epithymia*), and "arrogance" (*alazoneia*). That "the world" (*ho kosmos*) is the main topic of these verses is emphasized by the use of *traductio* or *polytoton*, which is the repetition of the same word in different cases in rapid succession (*Rhet. Her.* 4.14.20–21; Quintilian, *Inst.* 9.3.41–42). The word *kosmos* appears six times in four different cases. The first four appearances create an A/B/A'/B' pattern by rotating between the accusative (direct object) and dative (indirect object) cases in vv. 15-16a; it then shifts to the genitive (v. 16b) and, finally, the nominative (subject) case in v. 17. This is also an example of *epistrophē* or *conversio* because *kosmos* appears as the last word three times in vv. 15-16a (*Rhet. Her.* 4.13.19). For the audience listening in Greek, therefore, the focus on "the world" is unmistakable.

The word *epithymia* is also a significant word in 2:15-17. It occurs three times, always in the nominative case. This means *epithymia* is always a subject, which fits the word's meaning: unchecked desires have a way of ruling people. *Epithymia* can mean simple yearning, but it often implies excessive passion or lust (Rev 18:14). In the Pastoral Epistles, *epithymia* are temptations that draw people into ruin, particularly those who wish for riches (1 Tim 6:9; 2 Tim 2:22) and the so-called "little women" (*gynaikaria*) who are controlled by their desires, making them easy to fool (2 Tim 3:6). William Loader argues that these desires include sexual desires, suggesting that the three negative attributes (desires of the flesh, eyes, and greed) correspond to general criticisms of the "depraved excesses of the rich at their often pretentious banquets" (2014, 231). In the Gospel of John, this word appears in 8:44 when Jesus rebukes his opponents, saying,

> For you yourselves are from the devil (*ek tou diabolou*) and you want to do your father's desires (*epithymias*). That one was a murderer (*anthrōpktonos*) from the beginning (*ap archēs*) and he has not stood in the truth because the truth is not in him. Whenever the liar should speak, he speaks from himself, because he is a liar and the father of it.

Several of these terms resonate with portions of 1 John, including "from the beginning" (1:1; 2:7, 13, 14; cf. 2:24; 3:8, 11), liar and lying (1:6, 10; cf. 2:21, 27) in contrast to truth (1:6, 8; 2:4; cf. 2:21; 3:18, 19; 4:6), a focus on one's father (1:2, 3; 2:1, 13-16; cf. 2:22-24; 3:1), as well as what is or "is not" in someone (1:5, 8, 10; 2:4, 10, 15-16; cf. 2:22, 27; 3:5, 10; 4:3, 6). The connections with John 8 here prepare the audience for more extensive use of these traditions in the rest of 1 John 2:18–4:6. They also introduce the important idea of determining where one is "from" (*ek*) that will be a main topic in 1 John 3.

According to the author of 1 John, "the world" is aligned with the devil; it is fooled by its own desires rather than loving its Creator. As a result, loving the way the world does means being "arrogant" of what one can acquire in life (*bios*, 2:16; 3:17) rather than looking toward the eternal (*aiōna*, 2:17). Like "the darkness" (*hē skotia*), "the world" is "passing away" (*paragetai*, 2:8, 17) because it is a created thing and not the eternal Creator. It cannot overcome its Maker any more than darkness can overcome Light (2:8; John 1:1-5). Having been caught up in pursuits, the world, and those who love the way it loves, seek after idols that cannot provide eternal life. United to these false gods, they are passing away in contrast to those who continue "doing the will of God" and who "are remaining forever."

Theological Threads

Sin, Atonement, and Jesus' Continuing Ministry

The portrait of atonement in 1 John is often regarded as being different from the Gospel, at least in its explicitness (Lieu 2008, 55–57). In the Gospel, there is mention of Jesus' being the "Lamb of God" (1:29, 36), but there is not much emphasis on his dying a sacrificially atoning death. Instead, his death is a display of complete love (13:2; 19:28) and deliverance as the Passover Lamb (19:14, 34-37). In 1 John 1:7 and 9, however, the author describes Jesus' "blood" as "continuing to cleanse" (present tense) believers from sins. This purifying action in v. 7 is expanded in v. 9, which describes Jesus "releasing" sins along with "cleansing us from all unrighteousness." Most scholars regard these verses as descriptions of Jesus' death, sometimes tying the mention of "blood" in 1:7 with the dripping blood and water from Jesus' side in John 19:34 (cf. 1 John 5:6). For these scholars, the emphasis is placed on the continuing importance of Jesus' *death* in 1 John 1:7-9 and is evidence that the author is facing opponents who devalue its salvific value (e.g., Brown 1982, 53–54; Schnelle, 47–73; de Boer 1996, 86–93; cf. Streett, 19–89).

Without disregarding the image of Jesus' death in these verses, however, I suggest that this is too narrow a reading for 1 John because it is also too narrow a reading of sacrificial atonement and purity from the Old Testament and ancient Judaism (Klawans 2000, 2006; Meshel). Certainly the author's mention of Jesus' blood recalls his death, but it also points toward his incarnation *and* his resurrection and return to the Father. Jesus' blood, according to the author, is continuing to cleanse believers from sins and all unrighteousness. Death on its own, however, does not render one pure according to Leviticus. Purity comes only when an entire ritual of atonement is completed, especially when the blood is manipulated—sprinkled and flicked around or upon the altars (Lev 16; cf. Douglas; Moffitt). In other words, a priest is needed not only to kill the chosen victim but also to present the blood before the Lord. The blood, Leviticus tells us, is able to atone not because it represents the victim's *death* but rather because it is their *life* (Lev 17:10-16). For Jesus' blood to atone and cleanse, therefore, it needed to be presented to God. This, it seems, is what 1 John implies Jesus is doing even now. First John assumes the reality and importance not only of Jesus' death but *also* of his resurrection and return to the Father. It is there that Jesus continues working on behalf of the believers.

This interpretation is reinforced by 2:1-2. In 2:1, the author abruptly switches tone by addressing the audience directly: "Little children!" (*teknia*). This is the same word Jesus uses to address his disciples in John 13:33 just before he gives them the love command that will also surface in 1 John 2:3-17. The declaration of this identity once again unites the audience to the author, showing the author's confidence in them. Even though the author is aware that the "little children" could still sin, that is no reason to lose hope or to lose fellowship with God. Instead, the author says "we continue to have an Advocate before the Father: Jesus Christ, Righteous One" (2:1). Unlike the Gospel, which seems to indicate that the role of Advocate (*paraklētos*) has shifted to the Spirit once Jesus is physically absent from the disciples (14:16, 26; 15:26; 16:7), 1 John insists that Jesus does not cease in his own advocacy for believers. Instead, he continues as an Advocate before the Father while the Spirit, as we will see, operates among the believers in the world (1 John 3:24; 4:1-6, 13).

Jesus' advocacy before the Father is the way that his blood is continuing to cleanse believers. Having returned to the Father, Jesus now acts as a sort of high priest presenting his blood before the Father. Noticing the overlap in language, Christopher Holmes offers a similar reading of 1 John, arguing that there are "priestly gestures" in this sermon. As the "Righteous One," Jesus is the ideal high priest who not only offers "expiation" (*hilasmos*, on translation, see Parsenios 2014, 66–67) but also *is* expiation because it is his blood and, therefore, his life that brings about purity and restored fellowship. Indeed, Jesus' offering is so effective that it is sufficient not only for the sins of the believers past, present, and future but also for the "whole world." Jesus' act of love and display of God's love is much greater than all the hatred and denial mustered by "the world" that opposes him. Although such expiation certainly does not occur without Jesus' death, it also requires his resurrection and ascension. Like the Gospel, 1 John too collapses Jesus' death with his resurrection as part of his glorification and return to the Father (cf. John 14:28-29; 17:1-5). First John, therefore, should be read as emphasizing Jesus' continuing work before the Father as resurrected and ascended Son, and not only the continued value of his death.

Ethics in 1 John

Unlike with the Gospel of John, scholars have long recognized the importance of ethics in 1 John. Nevertheless, the ethics of 1 John can be confusing because although it is a homily about the love of God, it also contains harsh polemic against its opponents and "the world" (van der Watt 2014, 197). Does this mean the Johannine community did not care about nonbelievers? First John's ethics can also be confusing because of its language about "sin" (*hamartia*). The sermon not only switches between singular and plural nouns (sin and sins) but also describes believers both as needing to continue confessing their sins in 1:5–2:2 and as being unable to sin "because the seed of God is in them" (3:9; cf. 5:18). As we will see in the next chapter, part of the confusion from 3:9 is resolved by noticing the present tense of the verb "doing." According to our author, it is not that believers *never* sin but rather that they do not "continue doing sin" because they confess and reaffirm their fellowship and love of God (2:1-2; 3:6-9; 5:16). But where does the ability to confess, stop sinning, and love come from?

Ethics are much more explicit in 1 John than in the Gospel, at least partly because of its genre: this is a sermon rather than a narrative. In addition, the inward focus on the Johannine community makes sense for this sermon: it is directed toward believers who are facing some sort of division in their community, a division that the author sees as a threat to the fellowship they have with God and with one another. In his study, Jan van der Watt emphasizes the familial language of 1 John; the threat is to the family of God and, therefore, deeply personal (2014, 208). The author is not concerned with how believers ought to love nonbelievers, but with how they should treat one another in contrast to the ways of those he perceives as the "antichrists" who have abandoned the family.

Furthermore, 1 John reminds its audience that God's love comes before all other acts of love. This means God has loved long before there was a division of those "in him" and "in the world." If the believers are loving the way that God loves, they too should love the world and be sent into the world. By abiding in God's love, the believers keep their priorities in line: it is God's identity and desire that motivate them. They love because God loved, and no other love can supersede this divine prerogative.

First John's ethical emphasis should not be read as a claim of self-sufficiency or "works" salvation. Rather, as argued above, self-sufficiency is a sinful posture because it alienates one from the love and life that God gives through the work and mediation of Jesus. Instead, the author is consistent that the motivation and ability for an ethical life, or, in Johannine terms, a life lived in fellowship with the God who is love, only come from abiding in God. On their own, believers lose sight of authentic love and become driven by desires that may appear "good" to the eyes and to the flesh but that are ultimately selfish and lifeless (2:15-17). According to 1 John, at their worst, these desires lead to murder because people place their own wants, and fears, above all else. Like Cain, rather than laying our lives down, we take the lives of others (3:11-19a).

Freedom and life come when believers participate in fellowship with the Father, Son, Spirit, and a community of faith. When believers abide in this family, freedom and life come not only for the believer but also for the entire fellowship and even the world. The love expressed by believers comes not from within but from outside, from God and from the love of God that they receive from others. When believers continue experiencing the love of God, they are transformed (or reborn), enabled to live out that love and, therefore, to participate in God's continuing revelation of love to the world.

Behavior Reveals Identity

1 John 2:18–4:6

First John 2:18–4:6 comprises the middle portion of the sermon. Having laid the foundational calls for the audience to remain in fellowship, the author now moves to explain the threats to that fellowship. In 1:5–2:17 those threats were sins of self-deception, hypocrisy, and, ultimately, idolatry since through such delusions people come to seek life from sources other than God. These are not accidental mistakes or even necessarily sin done knowingly; rather, this is a disposition firmly held. As long as believers continue confessing their sins, they continue relying on and participating in the fellowship that includes the Father, Son, and community as a product of the intercessory and expiatory work that Jesus does before the Father (2:1-2). It is only when believers decide they do not need such assistance that they cut themselves off from this fellowship and therefore from life.

In 2:18–4:6, the author delves more deeply into the characteristics of those who have "gone out" from the community in contrast to those remaining in it. The departure of people from a community, especially if they are charismatic or well liked, is difficult for those who remain behind; anyone who has experienced an end to friendships, estranged family relationships, or church division can attest to this fact. The author of 1 John encourages these who remain by affirming their identity as children of God, reminding them of the promise of eternal life that they received, and reinforcing their continuous connection to God through his Son. In contrast, those who "went out" (*exēlthan*) are depicted in starkly polemical terms. They are "antichrists" (*antichristoi*, 2:18; 4:3), ones who are "denying" (*ho arnoumenos*, 2:22-23), liars (2:21, 22, 27), ones who have neither the Father nor the Son (2:23), and children of the devil, just like Cain (3:10-12). The harsh language against these deserters amplifies the positive descriptions of the believers who remain. It also reinforces God's control and stability even though the community itself seems to be in disarray. Rather than a mistake, the departure of these "antichrists" only helps the *true* children of God by

(1) showing them "it is the last hour" (2:18) and (2) revealing to them that they are the "children of God" in contrast to the "children of the devil" (3:10). The result, then, should be boldness rather than shame (2:28; 3:21-22).

Commentary

Antichrists Left, but You Abide (2:18-27)

Coming right after the author's new commandment to "stop loving the world" in 2:15-17, 1 John 2:18 turns to a new but related subject: the division in the community. George Parsenios (2014, 83) considers 2:18 an announcement:

> A. Little children! It is now the last hour,
> B. and just as you heard that an antichrist is coming,
> B'. even now many antichrists have become!
> A'. Thus, we know that it is the last hour.

This verse is a chiasm that pivots on the word "antichrist/s" (*antichristos*), which is bracketed by repetitions of "it is the last hour" (*eschatē hora estin*). The effect is an emphasis on these two ideas, cementing their relationship to one another. First John's interest in the antichrist has not only been a challenging aspect of this writing (e.g., how does such harsh polemic fit in a sermon devoted to "love"?) but has also fostered reflections on who or what is the "antichrist" throughout Christian tradition.

In his study of the term, Craig Koester (2014a, 189) notes that our recent fascination with identifying what or who is the "antichrist" is not a new trend. Rather, he explains, "two of the principal architects of the antichrist tradition were Irenaeus and Hippolytus" from the late second and into the early third centuries CE (see further discussion below). The term "antichrist," however, is unique to 1 and 2 John and is only used a total of five times (1 John 2:18, 22; 4:3; 2 John 7). It is important, therefore, to focus on 1 and 2 John to get an idea of how this community understood the term based on its place in the Letters.

As Koester notes, the word itself means "one opposed to Christ" an *anti-Christ*. First John 2:18 does not provide much detail on how to identify this figure, but it *does* say that there are "many antichrists" rather than just one. As the passage continues, the audience learns that anyone who "is denying [by saying], 'Jesus is not the Christ'" is the antichrist (v. 22). The antichrist, thus, is not limited to a single individual but is revealed by anyone who denies that Jesus is God's Christ and Son. Moreover, as 2:19 emphasizes, these deniers are ones who used to be part of the community, or family, of God:

From us (*ex hēmōn*) they went out, but they were not *from us*,
For if they were *from us*, they would have remained <u>with us</u>,
But, so that they might be revealed [they went out], because all of them
are not *from us*.

The repetition of "from us" (*ex hēmōn*) continues the author's emphasis on one's origins, which will become an even more important theme in what follows (2:28–3:24). This repetition also highlights that these antichrists are not nonbelievers, but they are former members of the community who have now "left" by denying Jesus' identity. This is what makes them liars. Moreover, this description connects these antichrists to all the previous negative examples given in 1 John 1–2 who were also called "liars" and ones who "deceive" (1:6, 8, 10; 2:21-22, 27). The author is emphatic in renouncing these former members: by denying Jesus is the Christ, these opponents have forsaken not only their fellowship with the community but also their connection to the Father himself (2:23).

As harsh as 1 John is against the opponents, however, the author is equally complimentary of the audience. They are "little children" (*paidia*) and have "an anointing from the Holy One" that "teaches" them so that they "know all things" (2:20, 27). The language of "anointing" surrounds the descriptions of the antichrists, disrupting the polemic with direct addresses to the audience that affirm their status with God and praise their knowledge. Having introduced the antichrists, the author confirms the audience's security before diving into 2:22-25, which contains a contrast between the antichrists and the audience and also shifts the topic back to a command for the believers themselves. The passage can be divided as follows:

A. 2:18-19, Antichrists Revealed
    B. 2:20-21, Your Anointing Means You Know the Truth
        C. 2:22-25, Pivot Contrast: The Antichrist/s vs. You/Us
            1. 2:22-23a, The Antichrist Has Neither the Son nor the Father
            2. 2:23b-24, You Remain in the Son and the Father
            3. 2:25, We Have the Promise of Eternal Life
    B'. 2:24-27, Your Anointing Teaches You: Remain in It/Him

Affirming his audience, the author uses epideictic rhetoric to encourage them to *continue* living as they have lived, rather than joining those called "antichrists." If they, too, leave they will not only reveal themselves to be antichrists but will also have forsaken God's anointing as well as his promise of eternal life.

Finally, this passage contains several allusions to traditions also reflected in John 6:60-71. I agree with Jan Heilmann that John 6 is about the selection of the Twelve: a test initiated by Jesus in John 6:4 that comes to a climax in 6:60-71 when "many" (*polloi*) disciples are "scandalized" (*skandalizei*) by Jesus' teaching and turn back and stop "walking" (*peripatoun*, 6:66) with him. Peter, at Jesus' instigation, then communicates the confession of the remainder: "Lord, to whom should we go? You have the words of eternal life. We ourselves have believed and have known that you, yourself, are the Holy One of God (*ho hagios tou theou*)" (6:69). The connection to "Holy One" (*tou hagiou*) in 1 John 2:20 is the clearest allusion in our passage, but there is also the mention of "many" in 2:18 as well as the previous discussion about where one "walks" in 2:3-11, and the author's statement that the one "remaining in the light" has "no scandal in him" (*skandalon*, 2:10).

These allusions to the story of disciples' abandoning Jesus in John 6, therefore, create a comparison between that past event from Jesus' lifetime and the situation of the Johannine community. Just like Jesus, the believers in 1 John are facing a split that is happening not because they have made a mistake but rather because they are teaching and living in accordance with God's will. Even though "many" have left, they can be encouraged because Jesus faced a similar situation. Moreover, those who remain in John 6 have been "chosen" (*exelexamēn*, 6:70) by Jesus and "drawn" (*elkysē*, 6:44) by the Father to him, to receive his teaching and life. Jesus is the "Holy One" whose anointing is his teaching. When one remains in that teaching, which includes the scandal of Jesus' flesh as bread and his blood as drink, one remains in life (6:53-58). Nevertheless, the connections to John 6 also caution the audience of 1 John that they are not above possibilities for desertion. Indeed, Jesus knew there was a "devil" in the mix in 6:70-71, and even Peter himself betrays Jesus before the story ends. Even so, when Peter returns to Jesus, he receives forgiveness and is restored to fellowship. He is an example of the promise and hope of 1 John 1:5–2:2.

Recognizing the Children by Their Behavior (2:28–3:24)

The largest chunk of this middle section is 2:28–3:24. I will analyze it in three parts: (1) 2:28–3:6; (2) 3:7-18; and (3) 3:19-24. Overall, this passage focuses on the identity of the "children of God" in contrast to the "children of the devil" (3:9-10). Throughout 2:28–3:24, the author confirms the audience's identity as God's children even while describing the means for examining oneself and members of the community. This comparison and contrast continues ideas from earlier in the sermon about the "antichrists" and those who are not *really* part of the family from 2:18-27, as well as the emphasis on behavior and especially love versus hate from 2:3-17. This central part of the sermon focuses on the theme that behavior reveals identity: where one abides (or remains) will demonstrate one's origins and will manifest itself in daily living, either as ones who love or ones who hate. This does not mean that the children of God never sin; instead, the prior instructions from 1:5–2:2 should be allowed to carry weight in 2:28–3:24. It is not that the children of God will not make mistakes but rather that they will not abide in a sinful lifestyle that continuously places one's own desires or fears over those of others. The children of God show themselves not in perfection but in love and faithfulness: they rely on God's agent and Son, Jesus, for forgiveness and continually return to the practice of loving based on the revelation of that same Son (3:16).

A. We Are God's Children (2:28–3:6)

First John 2:28–3:6 begins with a hinge or transitional passage in 2:28-29. The verses continue the command and themes from 2:18-27 by once again admonishing the audience to "remain in it" or "him." The location of one's remaining is ambiguous in Greek because the pronoun could either be masculine (him) or neuter (it). In 2:25-27, the audience was commanded to "let it [i.e., that which you heard from the beginning (*ho ap archēs ēkousate*)] remain in you" as well as the "anointing (*chrisma*) which you received from him is remaining in you"; as a result, they were also promised that they would "remain in the Son and in the Father." When the "little children" (*teknia*) are again told to "remain in it/him" in 2:28, this could be a repetition of 2:25 and 27 that they are to remain in what they heard and their anointing, but it is not separate from their abiding in the Father and the Son from 2:26.

After 2:28 recapitulates the previous command, it shifts forward by pointing to the revelation of Jesus at his second coming. This "revelation" certainly resonates with the previous discussion of ones being revealed, but this time the revelation is of Jesus rather than the antichrists. The emphasis for our author is that remaining in the teaching and anointing given, as well as in the Son and Father, means that one has nothing to be ashamed of when Jesus comes again. First John 4:17-18 will return to this theme, clarifying that Jesus' return is a time of judgment. As David Rensberger writes, the boldness or confidence (*parrēsia*) experienced by the believers results from their abiding fellowship with God and one another: "*they are already . . .* on the other side of judgment" (2014, 250; emphasis original). Looking back at the Gospel, we recall that Jesus repeatedly speaks with *parrēsia* in the world but is rejected as a result. Nevertheless, he is also bold before and heard by his Father because he lives as God desires (John 7:13; 11:38-44; 16:24-33;

18:20). Believers live in a similar situation: they are rejected, and even hated, by the world (3:13), but they are beloved of God and heard by him (3:21-22; 4:4-6). Indeed, according to 1 John, these believers "have been born" (*gegennētai*) from God and now experience a new identity in him (2:29).

The author exemplifies such *parrēsia* in 3:1-2 with a declaration about the audience (repeated words and phrases are highlighted):

> A. [1]Look at what kind of <u>love</u> the Father has given to us,
>   that we should be called **children of God** (*tekna theou*)! And *we are*!
> B. On account of this, <u>the world does not know us</u>, because <u>it did not know him</u>.
> A'. [2]<u>Beloved</u>, *we are now* **children of God** (*tekna theou*)!
>   And what *we will be* <u>was not revealed</u> yet.
> B'. <u>We know</u> that when <u>he should be revealed</u> (cf. 2:28),
>   *we will be* like him because we will see him just as he is.

The structure in these verses creates a contrast between the children of God and the world. As God's children, the audience knows they "will be like him" when "he should be revealed." The referent in these verses is ambiguous: will they be like Jesus or like God? This ambiguity reflects the consistent conflation of the Father and Son throughout 1 John, similar to Jesus' comment in John 14:9: "The one who has seen me has seen the Father." To be like Jesus is to be like God because Jesus so completely enacts God's will. In contrast to the children, the world is ignorant: it does not know "us" and did not know "him." While the world will face "shame" at Jesus' coming, the children are able to be bold because they already share in the will and love of God.

The announcement of the children's identity reinforces the author's calling them "little children" and "children" throughout the sermon (2:1, 12, 14, 18, 28; 3:7, 18; 4:4; 5:21). It also reflects the promise also recorded in John 1:12-13 that, "to the ones who received him, he gave authority to them to become children of God (*tekna theou*); to the ones who are believing in his name, they were not from bloods or from the will of flesh or from the will of a man, but from God born (*ek theou egennēthēsan*)!" These are the only places in the Gospel and 1 John that the shortened *tekna theou* is used instead of *tekna tou theou*, perhaps indicating a closer connection between these two passages than we might otherwise conclude (cf. John 11:52; 1 John 3:10; 5:2). Just as John 1:12-13 helps set the stage for the revelation of Jesus' identity in the Gospel, so too does 1 John 2:28–3:2. Having been recognized as children of God, the audience is made to participate in God's mission, continuing Jesus' work from the Gospel narrative. Just like Jesus, their mission is to "love one another" and, in so doing, to destroy the "works of the devil" that lead to death (3:7-18).

Indeed, 3:3-6 develops further what it means to be a child of God before pivoting with another direct address and command in v. 7. The author creates two contrasts that hinge on a description of Jesus in 3:5 as follows:

A. Positive: Each one having hope purifies, just as *that one* is pure (3:3)
   B. Negative: Each one still doing sin is doing lawlessness (3:4)
      C. You know why *that one* was revealed: to take away sin (3:5)
A'. Positive: Each one abiding in him does not continue sinning (3:6a)
   B'. Negative: Each one still sinning has not seen or known him (3:6b)

In v. 3, having "this hope on the basis of" Jesus enables believers to purify themselves continually in imitation of him. But how? The answer lies in the connections between this passage and 1:5–2:2. The verb translated "purify" is *hagnizei* and has cultic overtones, just as *katharizei* and *homologōmen* in 1:7 and 9, where Jesus is also said to "take away sin" because of his righteousness and continual intercession (2:1-2; cf. John 11:55). Believers are not purifying themselves on their own, therefore, but only by means of Jesus' continued work on their behalf.

Indeed, the related verb *hagiazō* is also used twice by Jesus in John 17:19 when he describes his coming death and return to the Father, saying:

And on behalf of them, I myself am sanctifying (*hagiazō*) myself,
so that they themselves might be ones having been sanctified (*hēgiasmenoi*)
in truth.

According to Jesus, his death and return to the Father are actions that sanctify himself *on behalf* of others. Jesus does not need purifying in order to approach the Father, but his followers *do*. His demonstration of complete love in laying down his life shows his followers how to love as well. That this is also the intention of 1 John 3:3 is made clear when the author explicitly appeals to Jesus' laying down of his life "on behalf" of the believers in 3:16-18. In contrast, the ones who keep on sinning have not seen or known Jesus because they fail to imitate his example (cf. John 19:36-37).

B. The Children of God vs. Children of the Devil (3:7-18)

Having made the proclamation of the audience's identity as "children of God" in the present time, as well as into the future, the author shifts in 3:7-18 to give three prohibitions to these children: do not be deceived

(v. 7), do not be amazed (v. 13), and do not love in word only, but with action (v. 18). The passage both begins and ends with the direct address, "little children," using *paidia* in v. 7 and *teknia* in v. 18, thus creating an inclusio that mirrors the rotation between these two titles elsewhere in the sermon and reinforces the audience's identity as God's children. This section, however, also contains some of the most piercing polemic of the sermon as the author narrows in on ways to identify the "children of the devil" (*tekna tou diabolou*, v. 10) who contrast God's children by hating their siblings (*adelphoi*) rather than loving them. In this section, Cain is set apart as the paradigmatic sinner who hates, and therefore "slaughters" his brother; in contrast, the Son of God is the paradigmatic example of love for all God's children to imitate by laying down his own life on their behalf (v. 16).

The first section of this passage is 3:7-12, which focuses on the command, "Little children, let no one deceive you." The reference to deception ties back to the description of the antichrists and ones who deny Jesus is the Christ in 2:18-27. First John 3:7-12 can be broken down further into vv. 7-9 and 10-12. In vv. 7-9, two positive descriptions of the children of God as "the one continuing to do righteousness" and "having been born from God" surround v. 8, which offers negative contrasts and frames Jesus' work in cosmic terms. Jesus' example of love not only enables believers to be cleansed from sin, but he "was revealed so that he might destroy the works of the devil." This introduction of the devil, who "continues sinning since the beginning," paves the way for the introduction of Cain in 3:10-12, to which I will turn shortly.

Verse 9 rounds out the opening section with a particularly difficult phrase about "each one having been born" from God. The ambiguity of the Greek makes translation tricky: the third person verbs "is not able" (*dynatai*) and "has been begotten" (*gegennētai*) do not have explicit subjects, but they must be determined from the surrounding context. Moreover, the verb *gennaō* can mean either "born" or "beget," also depending on context. Most translations render the verse as follows: "Those who have been born of God do not sin, because God's seed abides in them; they cannot sin, because they have been born of God" (NRSV). As many interpreters note, however, the idea that believers are unable to sin contradicts the previous remarks in 1:5–2:2 that believers need to continue confessing their sins in order to receive cleansing (Lieu 2008, 136–41; Parsenios 2014, 93). Part of the solution comes by recognizing the present tense of the verbs in this verse: 1 John says that each one born from God will not *continue doing sin*, meaning they will turn from it through confession. Even with this recognition, however, the final clause remains problematic: how can anyone "not be able to sin"? The Greek, however, leaves open that the subject of "be able," and perhaps even "has been born/begotten," could be the "seed" (*sperma*) rather than the "each one" from the beginning of the sentence. This results in the following translation: "Each one having been born from God does not continue doing sin because God's seed remains in him, and it is not able to sin because it has been begotten from him." According to this interpretation, it is God's seed that cannot sin because it has its origins entirely in God himself, whom the audience already knows has no darkness in him at all (1:5). The seed that God provides, like other procreative seed in ancient embryological theories, continues as part of the child long after birth. This reasoning is why ancients believed that children imitated their parents, particularly their fathers (Myers 2017a, 43–57).

The importance of fathers remains the focus in 3:10-12, where Cain comes firmly into view. As Judith Lieu notes, these verses should be read together even though a number of scholars follow Raymond Brown's classic breakdown of 1 John at 3:11 (e.g., Parsenios 2014, 99). Lieu suggests that 3:10 is a topic sentence that is then expounded by the example of Cain in vv. 11-12 (2008, 141). Verse 10 also forms a pivot turning from the positive description of "each one" in v. 9 to the negative "each one" in vv. 10b-12. A number of ancient interpreters understood Cain's killing of Abel in Gen 4 as the beginning of sin in the world instead of the garden scene of Gen 3 (cf. *Tg. Ps.-J.*; Snyman; Scarlata). Even those who anchored sin's beginning in Gen 3 bound Gen 4 closely to those earlier events, often mitigating Adam's role and reinforcing Eve's treachery.

Rather than noting Adam's presence with Eve when the serpent came, various Hellenistic interpreters suggest that Eve was seduced by the serpent and her "conversation" resulted in her conception of Cain (*GLAE*; Philo, *Post.* 172–74; Josephus, *Ant.* 1.52–29; cf. Lieu 2008, 139). According to these traditions, Cain was literally a child of the devil rather than a child of Adam. This wicked origin, therefore, explained Cain's unacceptable offering before God as well as his move to "slaughter" Abel either as revenge or, in some texts, as a substitute offering to make up for his original, rejected one (*Jub.* 4.1-6; Gen. Rab. 22.8; Ephrem the Syrian, *Comm. Gen.* 3.4.3). As John Byron (532–33) notes, the word *sphazō* ("slaughter") in 1 John 3:12 is a common verb for sacrificial killing in the Greco-Roman world and LXX. Tom Thatcher argues that the Johannine community highlighted Cain's diabolical origins here in 1 John 3 and in John 8 in order to explain the divisions this community experienced (2012, 365–73). If the believers were at a loss at how former members of their community could "deceive" or "hate" them (as the author of 1 John implies), these believers needed only look to Gen 3–4.

The passage shifts in 1 John 3:13-18 with another prohibition: "Do not be amazed, brothers, if the world continues hating you." Retaining the imagery of "brothers," the sermon continues its use of Cain but now identifies the one hating as "the world" (*ho kosmos*). Like Jesus in his Farewell Discourse, the speaker of 1 John classifies the world as hating the community. This hatred, moreover, results in the world "remaining in death" because hatred leads to "murder," just as it did between Cain and Abel. In addition, with the continuation of the Cain theme and resonance with Jesus' teaching from John 15:18-25, 1 John 3:13-18 also incorporates traditions similar to John 5. In John 5, Jesus likewise commands his audience, "do not be amazed" (5:28), and tells them, "Truly, truly I am saying to you, 'The one who is hearing my word and continues believing in the one who sent me has eternal life and he does not come into judgment, but *he has passed from death into life*'" (5:24; cf. 1 John 3:14). First John interprets this tradition by explaining what Jesus' word is: it is loving the brothers, or "loving one another," the very commandment emphasized throughout 1 John (2:7-11; 3:11, 24; 4:21; 5:2).

First John 3:16 now offers the positive paradigm to contrast the example of Cain from 3:10-12. Rather than the hatred of Cain, the believers are to imitate the superior love of Jesus, who, although unnamed, is clearly the referent in 3:16 that reflects his words from John 10:17-18.

> [16]By this we have known love:
> For that one, on behalf of *us*, laid down his life,
> and we ourselves ought, on behalf of our *brothers*, to lay down our lives.

As in John 10:17-18, the word for "life" in this verse is *psychē* not *zōē*. The giving of one's *psychē* should not be read as incorporeal, however, as though Jesus only laid down his "soul" or "mind." Instead, Lev 17:10 LXX states that it is blood that contains the *psychē* of all living beings (cf. Douglas). Jesus' laying down of his *psychē* "on behalf of us" is the complete model of love for others to follow. In an argument from greater to lesser, the speaker urges the audience not to "slaughter" their brothers but rather to be slaughtered for their sakes if necessary. If brothers (and sisters) should be willing to lay down their *psychai* for one another, they should certainly be willing to give of their *bios*—that is, their worldly livelihood. Returning to themes from 2:15-17, the sermon outlines practical demonstrations of God's love. If the "love of God" is remaining in believers, their lives should reflect it. Closing out this section, the speaker concludes, "Little children, let us not love in word nor in speech, but in work and in truth" (3:18).

C. Reassurance that God Is Greater (3:19-24)

Parsenios considers 3:19-24 a digression directed toward the audience (2014, 104). This digression is full of complicated translation and text critical issues, but its focus is clear: to encourage and reassure the audience that they are indeed God's children. Although some scholars argue that 3:7-18 points toward clearly identified opponents who have left the community (cf. Brown; von Wahlde 2010; Thatcher 2012), Koester's reading of the antichrist language of 1 John better explains this encouraging turn in 3:19-24. Koester argues that although it can be easy to single out "others" as antichrists, 1 John also makes it clear that antichrists (and the spirit of the antichrist) can exist within the community as well. Therefore, he explains, the language of 1 John also invites the community members to examine themselves: are they exhibiting characteristics of the devil's children or of God's Son?

Such examination is unsettling when it is rooted in ourselves and not in the assurance of God's faithfulness. In 3:19-20, the sermon encourages its audience not to be too myopic: while our hearts may condemn us, God is greater than our hearts. Parsenios's translation of these verses is helpful for making this point clear:

> [19]And in this we shall know that we are of the truth, and in his presence we will reassure our heart [20][that] even if our heart condemns us, that God is greater than our heart and he knows all things.

In this context, God's knowledge reinforces the believers' knowledge. First John has highlighted what they "know" (*ginōskō*) and "have known" (*egnōka*) throughout the sermon (2:5, 13-14, 18, 29; 3:16, 24). Their knowledge is rooted in what God has revealed through his Son, which is love that leads to abiding with one another and with the divine. The God who knows everything is greater, and that greatness is an assurance of mercy rather than judgment (2:28-29; 4:17-18).

Released from their condemnation, therefore, 1 John 3:21 says "we have boldness before God" (*parrēsian exomen pros ton theon*). Focusing in again on *parrēsia*, Lieu clarifies that among the Greeks this word "denoted the freedom of speech, which was the democratic privilege of the free citizen who had the right to be heard and who could expect a response" (2008, 156). Although 1 John is not evoking a specifically political context, the parallel is helpful, especially when we remember that politics and religion were never isolated from each other in the ancient world. In the Gospel of John, Jesus promises his disciples that they will receive whatever they ask from God in Jesus' name (14:13-14; 15:7, 16; 16:23-24). The closest parallel to 1 John 3:22

comes in John 16:24 when Jesus says, "Ask and receive, so that your joy might be made complete." Jesus' command is for boldness on the part of his disciples; he continues, "In that day you will ask in my name, indeed I am not saying that I will ask the Father for you" (John 16:26). According to 1 John, the time of asking God directly is *now*. Enabled by the example of Jesus' love, they are released and can approach God because "we are keeping his commandment and are doing the things that are pleasing before him" (3:22; cf. 5:13-15). Just as Jesus was bold before the world, he was also bold before his Father, asking and knowing that he was heard (cf. John 9:30-33; 11:22, 41-42; 12:27-28). Indeed, in John 17 he models a bold prayer for his disciples after instructing them to ask the Father in his name. According to 1 John, believers should imitate not only Jesus' love but also his boldness because they too can be confident of God's response to them, even if God responds in unexpected ways.

First John 3 ends with a synopsis of the commandments that disciples are to continue keeping, along with the abiding that results:

> [23]And this is his commandment:
>   that we should believe in the name of his Son, Jesus Christ
>   and that we should love one another,
> just as he gave the command to us.

The twofold commandment of 1 John 3:23 combines the love command from John 13:34-35 (15:12-14; 1 John 5:1-5, 13) with a command to believe in the name of Jesus as God's Son and Christ. This latter command connects to the emphasis on asking in Jesus' name from John 16, but it also reflects a broader focus on Jesus' name in the Johannine tradition. Recognizing Jesus' name is a shorthand for deciphering his identity throughout the Gospel of John. In John 1:12-13, this belief is the foundation for believers to become God's children; in 3:14-18, the one who believes in "the name of the Unique Son of God does not come into judgment but has eternal life"; and 20:31 culminates with a hope that the Gospel audience will keep "believing that Jesus is the Christ the Son of God, and that by believing [they] should have life in his name" (cf. Myers 2018a). First John, too, emphasizes Jesus' identity as God's Son over and against those who deny that he is the Christ (2:22). First John underscores that belief is not simply cognitive: true belief shows itself in love. Love and belief keep the community connected to the Father and to the Son because it is in confessing belief and in living out love that God's Spirit enables (3:24).

Examining the Spirits (4:1-6)

First John 4:1-6 contains a number of overlaps with 3:19-24. As in 3:19-24, 4:1 begins with a statement that "in this we are knowing" and addresses the audience as "beloved" (3:19, 21). The themes in 3:19-24 progress from boldness to commandments to abiding and, finally, to the Spirit that occupies 4:1-6. First John 4:1 also mirrors what comes before by issuing another prohibition just as in 3:7, 13, and 18. As in 3:18, the negative command is followed by a positive one; in 4:1 the believers are told, "Do not continue believing every spirit but examine (*dokiamazete*) the spirits if they are from God because many lying prophets have gone out into the world." This description of "lying prophets" (*pseudoprophētai*) returns to the motif of liars and antichrists from 2:18-22 (cf. 1:6-10; 2:4; 4:20; 5:10). Rather than focusing on the people, however, the sermon now turns to discuss the spirits that possess them. According to 1 John, the spirits that possess a person are "examined" by the confessions, and, therefore, the breath (*pneuma*) issued forth.

First John 4:3 recapitulates 2:18-22 explicitly, explaining, "And each spirit which is not confessing Jesus is not from God, but this is the one of the antichrists which you have heard is coming and now is already in the world." Koester suggests that this language continues the cosmic battle 1 John depicts between Christ and his followers against the devil, who possesses and motivates the antichrist in the world. For Koester, 1 John presents "the cosmic battle between Christ and antichrist . . . being fought and won in the present" with "claim and counterclaim" over Jesus' identity as Christ and Son (2014a, 192–93). Instead of an event completed in the past, Jesus' defeat over the devil and his works is ongoing. The believers, too, participate in this battle *and* in the victory by continuing to confess Jesus' identity, loving one another, and sharing words of life in a world that shows them hatred (2:13-14; 4:4; 5:4-5).

In 4:4-6 the sermon concludes the discussion of antichrists for the moment, building to the dramatic admonitions of love in 4:7-21. First John 4:4-6 works through second person, third person, and finally first-person language to unite the audience again with the speaker.

[4]You yourselves are from God, little children (*teknia*),
   and you have conquered them,
     because the one who is in you is greater than the one that is in the
      world.
[5]They themselves are from the world,

on account of this they are speaking from the world and the world
listens to them.
[6]We ourselves are from God.
The one knowing God listens to us.
The one who is not from God does not listen to us.
From this we are knowing the spirit of truth and the spirit of deception.

The progression both culminates the proclamation of the audience's identity as children of God from 3:1-2 and reinforces the author's identity and
authority. The audience is reminded again of God's greatness (3:19-22) in
spite of their rejection by the world (3:13). Furthermore, as long as the audience continues listening to these teachings, they will remain God's children
and avoid being deceived (3:7). In 4:7-21, the subject returns to the importance of loving one another in community. Inspired by God's Spirit, given
through Jesus Christ, these believers are enabled to show completed love for
one another: unity that is only made possible by abiding in and with the
divine.

Theological Threads

Antichrists in 1 John and the Christian Imagination

As mentioned above, even though the idea of an "antichrist" has a developed
history in Christian tradition, the term itself is only found in 1 and 2 John.
This fact may come as a surprise to many modern-day readers of the Bible
who often assume that this figure is an individual described in Revelation.
Craig Koester (2014a) helpfully discusses some of the reception history of
the notion of the antichrist, acknowledging its long and ancient construction
in Christian circles. Indeed, 1 John indicates that its audience already knew
about "the antichrist," explaining that "the one of whom you have heard,
'he is coming,' even now he is already in the world" (4:3). In referencing
the antichrist, therefore, 1 John is participating in a larger Christian tradition that figured the antichrist as the primary, human opponent of God,
possessed by Satan and carrying out his eschatological battle with God and
against believers on earth (187).

Koester notes that early Christians built this image by combining the
language of "antichrist" with the "man of lawlessness" described in 2 Thess
2:8 and the beast of Rev 13; nevertheless, these same assumptions of a political leader persecuting Christians is nowhere to be seen in 1 and 2 John, the
two writings that supply the name "antichrist." Instead, 1 and 2 John describe
being "antichrist" as denying that Jesus is the Christ or that Jesus Christ has

come in the flesh (1 John 2:22; 4:2; 2 John 7). Moreover, these deniers are not nonbelievers but rather had their origins in the Christian community and then "went out" by denying Jesus' identity. Rather than looking outside for the antichrist, or the spirit of the antichrist, the author of 1 John directs the Johannine community to examine itself. The eschatological battle with these antichrist elements is not coming at some point in the future but rather is happening now, and the believers in the Johannine community are already combatants. Indeed, 1 John 4:3 reports, "the antichrist . . . is *already* in the world" (4:3). In this way, 1 John makes the conflict immediate and gives the audience a responsibility: they cannot just sit safely on the sidelines; they, too, are participants in the battle even as they already experience victory alongside Jesus (4:4).

Tom Thatcher notes how such polemic seems to undercut the love language for which 1 John, in particular, is known. "Was John simply hypocritical?" he asks (2012, 350). For Thatcher, the solution comes from recognizing the impact of deep memories of conflict and rejection experienced by the Johannine community. Like other minority groups, the Johannine community understands its suffering as reinforcing its elect status against a world opposed to and oppressing them (cf. Mark 4:1-20). Yet it should also be noted that 1 John does not encourage its audience to "hate" anyone, including the world that hates them. Instead, the believers are characterized by love and are to imitate the love that Jesus himself showed, not only on behalf of those who would eventually come to believe in him but also on behalf of the world. As 2:1-2 reads, "My little children, I am writing these things to you so that you might not sin. But if anyone should sin, we have a Paraclete before the Father: Jesus Christ, Righteous One. And he himself is expiation concerning our sins, and not only concerning ours, but also concerning the whole world." Regardless of "the world's" wickedness, its fear, and its continual allegiance with the devil and his prophets, Jesus' self-sacrifice and continual intercession are greater. In this way, 1 John maintains that love is greater than hate.

Spirits in 1 John

The role of the Spirit in 1 John (and the rest of the Letters) is often highlighted as a key difference between these writings and the Gospel. As we saw in the previous chapter, it is Jesus who continues to exist as the *Paraclete* in 1 John rather than the Spirit, who is never called by this title (contra John 14–16). This difference is part of what has led a number of scholars to see the debate behind 1–3 John as primarily Christological (e.g., Brown; Schnelle). If the opponents are stressing the importance of the Spirit now over and against any need for Jesus (especially if he is no longer considered the Son or the Christ), then the Letters' insistence on Jesus' identity and continued importance makes sense. Nevertheless, while there is a difference of emphasis between the Gospel and 1 John with regard to the Spirit, these are differences of degree rather than kind. Indeed, 1 John's references to Spirit not only resonate with understandings of spirit possession and indwelling in the ancient Mediterranean world but also connect back to the well-known Johannine metaphor of new birth.

In her study of spirit possession and Christology in the Gospel and Letters of John, Pamela Kinlaw argues that the key conflict behind all of the Johannine writings is an early form of docetism that separated the human being, Jesus, from the divine and preexistent Son and Christ. The tradition represented by the writings combats this separation by insisting "on the permanent union between the divine and human and what belief in that union entails for the community" (99). For Kinlaw, this union means that Jesus was not temporarily "possessed" by God's Spirit but rather that God's Spirit is a part of him, permanently "indwelling" in his being so that he can also offer that same divine indwelling Spirit to those who believe in his name. This spiritual indwelling connects the believers not only to the Father and the Son but also to one another, effectively creating the community unity for which various Jewish traditions had longed (64–67; cf. Isa 11:2; 42:1; 59:21; Joel 2:28-29; *Ps. Sol.* 17; *1 En.* 49.1-4; *T. Levi* 18). It is for this reason, suggests Kinlaw (99–100), that 1 John is emphatic that "Jesus is the Christ" (2:22; 5:1) and "the Son of God" (4:15; 5:5) by regularly combining titles as a part of his name: he is God's "Son Jesus Christ" (1:3; 5:20); "Jesus his Son" (1:7); and "Jesus Christ" (2:1; 3:23; 4:2; 5:6, 20; cf. 2 John 3, 7).

While I do not have the same certitude as Kinlaw of the conflict behind the Johannine writings, her understanding of the Spirit in 1 John is helpful and makes sense of the present passage. Only the Spirit, or breath (*pneuma*), that comes from God—as delivered by his Son, Jesus Christ—can make the *true* confession: "Jesus Christ has come in the flesh" (4:2). Moreover, such an image builds on the previous emphasis on being "born from" or begotten by God in 3:1-24. Along with "seed" (*sperma*, 3:9), spirit was also understood to play an important role in conception and generation for a child, as well as being one of the nutrients taken in by the body to continue living. For the Hippocratics, it was the woman who provided this nourishment during pregnancy by taking in "cold breath" (*pneuma psychron*) and passing it along to the fetus (*Nat. puer.* 1.486). For Aristotle, however, it was the male seed that provided hot and therefore animating *pneuma* to the fetus, thus giving it life (*Gen. an.* 735b33–35, 737a20–22). Jewish texts again differ, emphasizing that it is God alone who gives the *pneuma* that brings about life (*b. Nid.* 31). The metaphorical conception, generation, and birth language of 1 John (and the rest of the Johannine writings), therefore, also maps onto its turn to the Spirit in 3:24–4:6 (cf. 5:1-12). Having been begotten by God and born again as God's children through their connection to Jesus Christ, believers are shaped by God's seed and continue to live as his children by means of his Spirit. It is *this* Spirit that continues to provide their life and breath; and it is this Spirit that will continue confessing Jesus' identity: he "has come in the flesh" and he *is* God's Christ and Son. Just as actions reveal identity, so too do spoken words.

Love, Faith, and Life

1 John 4:7–5:21

The final section of 1 John stretches from 4:7–5:21. Overall the progression of this section moves from the polemic of 2:18–4:6 to a digression of encouragement in 4:7-18 (cf. 2:13-14) before returning again to a series of contrasts in 4:19–5:21 (cf. 1:5–2:12). In 1 John 4:7-10, the author declares again Jesus' command from John 13 and 15: "Let us love one another" (*agapōmen allēlous*) but grounds it not as much in Jesus' actions (1 John 3:16) as in God's prior motivation and very identity as "the Love" (4:8, 16). It is God who "loved first" (4:10, 19) and enables believers likewise to love. First John 4 calls on the believers to imitate Jesus by bringing God's love to completion, or maturity, in continuing to love one another (4:10-18). First John then contrasts those who offer genuine confessions of belief, shown by their love for one another, with the hypocrites who hate their "siblings" (*adelphōn*) in spite of their claims to love God (4:19–5:5). These contrasts continue throughout the rest of the sermon, reinforcing once again the author's aim to keep these believers in fellowship as well as the traditions 1 John represents, which the author sees as the only means of unification with the Father and Son.

In what follows, I will analyze 1 John 4:7–5:21 in two subunits: (1) 4:7–5:5, which contains a chiastic structure pivoting on the proclamation that completed love is casting out fear in 4:16-18; and (2) 5:5-21, which focuses on Jesus' identity as the Christ, the Son of God. When read as a whole, 5:5-21 summarizes the sermon by highlighting the main points of belief, using language similar to John 20:30-31. In these verses, Jesus' identity as the Son of God and the Christ is emphasized, as well as the life that "the ones believing in his name" have (1 John 5:5, 13). Rather than upsetting the unity of the *Shema*, that God is One, 1 John joins the Gospel's claims that Jesus is united with the Father, so that they are One (cf. John 10:30). Indeed, 1 John 5:6-8 also argues that "the Spirit and the water and the blood . . . are in the One," and in 5:20 God's "Son Jesus Christ" is "the True God and Eternal Life." In this way, 1 John ends with a similar point of emphasis as it began: stressing the continued need for Jesus' flesh in spite of any claims that believers can move on and learn to love without the Risen and Advocating Son (4:10; 1:5–2:2).

Commentary

Let Us Love because God Is Love (4:7–5:5)

First John 4:7–5:4, like the rest of the sermon, can be divided in a variety of ways. Raymond Brown reviews several possible divisions in his 1982 commentary (542–44). He ultimately divides the passage into five parts: 4:7-10, 11-16b, 16c-19, and 4:20–5:4a. Georg Strecker offers a similar division (1996, 162) while Karen Jobes ends the section at 5:3. Judith Lieu and George Parsenios, however, argue that there is a "shift in thought" with 5:1, which offers the positive counterpoint to 2:22 and 4:7 (Parsenios 2014, 121; Lieu 2008, 200). Nevertheless, as Brown and others have noted, even if there is a "shift" at 5:1, these verses are not entirely separate from what comes before either. Indeed, the section continues (and perhaps culminates) the discussion of "love" (*agapē*) from 4:7 onward.

Rather than seeing a clear break at 5:1, therefore, I suggest it is better to view 5:1-5 as a transitional section that reaches both backward and forward. It reaches forward to 5:5-21 by highlighting Jesus' identity as the Christ, the Son of God. It reaches backward by finishing a chiastic section that begins in 4:7 and focuses on the overall theme of love. This chiasm is outlined below and centers on statements surrounding "completed love" (*teteleiōtai hē agapē*) in 4:16-18.

> A. 4:7-10, Let Us Love as Ones Born from God
>   B. 4:11-15, If We Love One Another, God Remains in Us
>   C. 4:16-18, Completed Love Casts Out Fear
>   B'. 4:19-21, The One Not Loving Is a Liar
> A'. 5:1-5, The One Believing Is Born from God

Sections A through B' all begin with a first-person plural ("we") statement or verb. First John 5:1 repeats again the idea from 4:7 that those loving "have been born from God" (4:7; 5:1) before resuming first person plural address in 5:2. Sections B and B' mention confessions as well as sight (*theamai, horaō*), with B focusing on positive descriptions and B' on negative ones; and, finally, section C lies in the center as a pivotal statement about God's love reaching its goal in believers, resulting in their freedom from fear.

First John 4:7-10 again addresses the audience as "Beloved" (3:21; 4:1) and then shifts to rhythmic lines similar to the digression of 2:13-14. As Lieu notes, "The short balanced paragraphs [of 4:7-10] have led some to describe this as a hymn to love, and in some editions of the New Testament it is set out in poetic form, although it is not technically verse" (2008, 175). The effect of this poetry-like unit is an amplification of the themes found in these verses, drawing them together from what has come before and setting up their exposition in what follows. Their importance, therefore, merits a translation here (highlighted portions show repetition):

> [7] *Beloved, let us continue loving* one another because the *love is from God.*
> Indeed, each one *continuing to love has been born from God* and is knowing God.
> [8] The one *not continuing to love* does not know God, because *God is love.*
> [9] In this the *love of God* has been revealed in us (*en hēmin*):
> Because his Son, the Unique-One, God sent into the world
> so that we might live through him (*di autou*).
> [10] In this is *the love:*
> *Not that we have loved* God,
> But that *he himself loved* us (*ēgapēsen*) and sent his Son,
> an expiation concerning our sins.

By calling his audience "beloved," the speaker again stresses God's initiative and endurance in loving. Indeed, in 4:8 the speaker claims that God is "the Love," meaning this is the epitome of his will and identity. This definition is expanded in vv. 9-10 with two parallel clauses beginning "in this" (*en toutō*). Both of these verses emphasize that the "love of God," that is, the way of God's loving (subjective genitive), is his sending his Unique (*monogenēs*) Son for the life of those in the world, an "expiation" (*hilasmos*) for sins.

These verses once again highlight the importance of the Son's flesh, that is, his unified identity as "Jesus Christ." Indeed, 4:9 could also be translated "in this the love of God has been *made visible* among us." In this way, 4:9 resonates with the claim of John 1:14 that "the Word became flesh and dwelt *among us* (*en hēmin*), and we have seen (*eseasametha*) his glory, glory as *a unique one from a father* (*monogenous para patros*), full of grace and truth." It is through physical interaction with Jesus that the world, and the first believers, beheld and interacted with God's love made visible in a person and his life. First John 4:9-10 also resonates with John 3:16-17, another passage that employs the descriptor *monogenēs* for Jesus:

[16]For thusly (*houtōs*) did God love (*ēgapēsen*) the world, that his Son, the Unique-One, he gave, so that each one believing in him might not perish but have eternal life. [17]For God did not send (*apesteilen*) the Son into the world that he should judge the world, but so that the world might be saved through him (*di autou*).

Like the Gospel, 1 John 4 presents God as the one who loves *first* and indicates that his love is most clearly shown in the sending of his Unique Son into the world.

For all these similarities, the metaphor in 1 John of how life is received from God's sending of his Son is different from that in the Gospel. As in 1 John 1:5–2:2, the image in 4:7-10 is cultic: the Son of God was sent so that we might live through him, which is accomplished because of his "expiation concerning our sins." Although the language of "expiation" is usually tied to Jesus' death by interpreters of 1 John, we should remember the present tense of the verbs in 1:5–2:2, where the first use of *hilasmos* is. As in 2:1-2, Jesus' identity as *hilasmos* is permanent; his identity as expiation has not somehow ended now that he has suffered and returned to the Father. Just as Jesus' identity as "Son" does not end, neither does his identity as *hilasmos*; indeed, in 4:10 *hilasmos* is in apposition to *huios* ("Son") as a further explanation of what that identity is as well as how believers "live through him" (4:9). Just as in 1:5–2:2, therefore, 1 John reminds the audience of the crucial role of Jesus' flesh for believers—in the present as well as in the past and future; the Son is still *hilasmos*.

In 4:11-15 and 16-18, 1 John moves to talk about God's love in a different way: namely, its "completion" among believers. In his analysis of this passage, David Rensberger (2014, 238–43) notes the confusion over translating the verb *teleioō* (perfection, completion) in English Bibles and commentaries. When translated as "perfection," this verb implies a blamelessness that again contradicts the emphasis on continual confession and the need for Jesus as *hilasmos* in 1 John. As such, it can set up an ideal of discipleship that is impossible for believers to follow. Focusing on 4:18, for example, one could walk away thinking that believers should never be afraid. Rensberger argues convincingly that we should translate *teleioō* as "to bring to completion" because this is closer to the meaning of the Greek term. A *telos* is a goal or an end, a point of maturity; the related verb *teleioō*, therefore, also communicates the idea of reaching completion or reaching a goal (243–49). The resulting interpretation clarifies not only the difficult statement of 4:18 but also the surrounding context.

In 4:12, 1 John shifts seemingly abruptly to saying that "no one has seen God before" (cf. John 1:18). It promises, however, that "if we should continue loving one another, God remains in us (*en hēmin*) and his love reaches its goal in us (*en hēmin*)." For Rensberger, the promise of 1 John is that, even though believers have not yet seen God face to face—and, indeed, did not even see Jesus himself—they can "see" God when they continue loving one another (250). In other words, when the believers imitate Jesus' type of love—the love that he showed through his willing obedience to the Father in both laying down his life *and* taking it back up again—the believers, too, gain a glimpse of the divine. Even though this love brought Jesus to a "goal" of crucifixion (John 13:2; 19:28), it also resulted in his resurrection and return to the Father (14:28-29; 17:1-5; 20:17-18). Believers, therefore, can anticipate their own continued living regardless of where loving might lead them.

Indeed, 1 John 4:17 promises, "just as that one [Jesus] is, also we ourselves are in this world" (cf. 1 John 3:1-2). This is the reason, then, that believers have no fear when they experience the type of love that was God's goal in sending Jesus. They "have known and have believed the love which God has" for them because they have known and believed Jesus Christ the Son (1 John 4:16; cf. John 6:69). By imitating him in their present lives, believers know God hears their prayers (1 John 3:21-22; 5:14-17) and watches over them in the present and in the future to come (5:18-21). For this reason, the believers can be "bold" (*parrēsia*) instead of fearful or ashamed (2:28; 4:17-18). Rather than a condemnation for those who are afraid, therefore, 4:11-18 is an encouragement for believers to remember the type of love revealed to them, as well as the type of love they are to show and to experience from one another.

First John 4:19-21 once again reminds the audience that love has its source in God, before offering a negative contrast to vv. 11-15. In this section, there is also a transition from discussing "the love of God" as a subjective genitive (God's way of loving) to an objective sense: how people are loving God. This change is made explicit in 4:20 when the speaker returns to negative and hypocritical confessions of the hypothetical "someone" (*tis*), similar to the liars and self-deceivers in 2:3-11 and 1:6-10. As in those previous sections, 4:20 compares this one's confession to their actions: "If someone should say, 'I am loving God' and is hating his brother, he is a liar" (cf. 2:9, 11; 3:15). According to 1 John, since people cannot see God, believers cannot love him with actions directly. Instead, genuine disciples love God and show God's type of love by loving others, particularly those in the community of faith who face similar ostracism from "the world" as they do (3:13). In this way, believers "see" God in one another by loving and by experiencing this love.

This, 1 John 4:21 concludes, is God's commandment: "The one loving God is also loving his brother." One side of the equation does not exist without the other. As mentioned above, 5:1-5 is a transitional section; it both rounds out the chiastic structure begun at 4:7 and looks forward with its naming of the Son, whose being sent is the manifestation of God's love from 4:7-21. Repeating motifs of being born from God, the love of God, commandments, and belief from 4:7-21, 5:1-4 also mixes subjective and objective understandings of "the love of God," finishing the blending that began in 4:19-21. It also picks up on the verb "to believe" or "trust" (*piseteuō*) from 4:16. In 4:7-15, the speaker paired loving with knowing (*ginōskō*), which is a common verb throughout the sermon. In 4:16, however, the notion of "believing" also enters the equation. In 5:1-2, these three ideas combine: the one believing loves and knows. The focus then shifts squarely to belief (*pistis*) in v. 4, specifically, belief "that Jesus is the Christ the Son of God" (5:1). This belief is "conquering the world," recalling Jesus' statement of victory from John 16:33. First John 5:5 continues the statement on conquest, thus working with 5:4 to create a hinge. In the rest of 1 John, the focus turns to the importance of recognizing Jesus' identity as God's Christ and Son. Jesus persists in being the crucial point of connection between the Father and all his children, long after his life, death, resurrection, and return to the Father (cf. 1 John 1:5–2:2; John 17:1-5).

Jesus Is Christ, the Son of God, the True God, and Eternal Life (5:4-21)
The final section of 1 John details the identity of Jesus, the Christ, the Son of God (5:5, 12-13). As Brown (1982, 631) notes, this final chapter resembles John 20 with its connection between believing in the name of Jesus and receiving eternal life (John 20:30-31; cf. 1:12-13). Moreover, as with Thomas's final exchange with Jesus in John 20, 1 John has a more elevated statement about Jesus than any other part of the sermon by ending with a clearly divine confession: "This one is the True God and Eternal Life" (5:20). The sermon then ends with the enigmatic command, "Little children, guard yourselves from idols" (5:21). This command has often confused readers of 1 John, but it is usually understood to be in some sort of relationship with the nebulous opponents whose teaching prompted the sermon (Painter, 328–30; Griffith; Streett, 233). Parsenios concludes that while these theories can be compellingly argued, we need to remain cautious, writing, "But as with any attempt to define too carefully what the beliefs of the opponents are in 1 John, the evidence does not allow us to arrive at any amount of certainty" (2014, 125–26).

Although I agree with Parsenios, the final section of 5:5-21 does provide some interesting possibilities for understanding the background of 1 John. Indeed, rather than (or perhaps in addition to) the Platonic, Stoic, gnostic, and docetic depictions of the opponents usually offered, Daniel Streett's analysis may be more accurate. According to Streett (90–111), the problem that 1 John tackles is the departure of Johannine Christians *back* to synagogues and, therefore, away from the confession of Jesus' continued significance as Christ and Son. Streett finds evidence for this conclusion throughout 1 John, and especially 5:6-8, which I will mention in more detail below. First John 5:5-21 shows more clearly than any part of the sermon that at least one concern the author is combatting is that Jesus' divinity disrupts God's unique oneness as articulated in the *Shema* (Deut 6:4-5). Lori Baron argues that this is also a key problem Jesus faced in the narrative of the Gospel, prompting disputes with the Jews (John 5:18, 40-47; 10:30). First John 5:5-21 likewise emphasizes that rather than a threat to God's oneness, Jesus is the revelation of God's identity on earth and continues his ministry before the Father in the present. Thus, believers need to continue trusting in him and his name so that they can experience him: that is, Eternal Life (1:1-4; 5:20).

In what follows, I will analyze this section in two subunits: 5:4-13 and 5:14-21. Verses 4-13 focus on the witness of God concerning his Son, while vv. 14-21 remind the audience again what they know and the boldness they have before the Father.

A. 1 John 5:4-13: God Is the Witness

First John 5:4-13 focuses on the theme of witness or testimony (*martyria, martyreō*). In contrast to previous portions of 1 John, however, the emphasis is on the believers' willingness to accept, or receive, certain testimony over others; specifically, human or divine. As outlined in the commentary section on John 5, human and divine testimony were categories of proofs (*pisteis*) in the ancient Mediterranean world. Although human testimony could be good, particularly if it was from virtuous and well-known individuals, divine testimony was always superior because, as Cicero explains, "the surpassing virtue of the gods is the result of their nature, but the virtue of men is the result of hard work" (*Top.* 20.76–77 [Hubbell, LCL]; cf. Quintilian, *Inst.* 5.11.37–42; McConnell, 47–52). In other words, gods are simply more trustworthy. The Gospel of John operates with this same outlook. Jesus repeatedly distrusts (*ouk episteuen*) the "testimony of people" because "he himself knew what was in humanity" (John 2:23-25; 5:31-34). In contrast, Jesus repeatedly affirms and delivers the testimony of God made visible in his works, words, and relationship with Scripture (5:36-47; 8:13-20). Indeed, one of the key arguments in John's Gospel is that Jesus' crucifixion came about because neither he nor the divine testimony from him and about him was received by the world (3:11, 31-36). Just as the Gospel admonishes its audience to accept God's testimony that Jesus is his Son, sent on his behalf to show his love to the world (3:16-18), so too does 1 John. Rather than trusting human testimony, the believers are encouraged to rely on God's.

As mentioned above, 5:4-5 is a hinge, moving from the discussion of love to the identity of Jesus. The rhetorical question of 5:5-6b is the positive counterpart to the description of the antichrist in 2:22. In 2:22, the author asks, "Who is the liar if not the one denying [saying], 'Jesus is not the Christ'? This one is the antichrist, the one denying the Father and the Son." First John 5:5-6b asks, "And who is the one conquering the world if not the one believing, 'Jesus is the Son of God'? This one is the one who came through water and blood, Jesus Christ, not in the water only, but in the water and in the blood." In addition to the parallel between the rhetorical questions (*tis estin . . . ei mē*), both questions follow with a statement of identity: *This one is* (*houtos estin*). In 2:22, the "one" identified is the antichrist; in 5:6 the one is "Jesus Christ." The parallel, therefore, is established not between the antichrist and the believer who conquers but rather between the antichrist (and perhaps "the spirit of deception" from 4:1-6) and Jesus Christ himself. Such a contrast is more in keeping with later interpretations of "antichrist" by Hippolytus and Irenaeus (Koester 2014a, 189).

Significantly, these parallels help us understand several confusing elements in 5:4-8 and support the conclusion that the speaker's emphasis on water, blood, and Spirit is somehow in response to the false teachings he perceives in his community. Verses 6-8 read,

> [6]This one is the one who came through water and blood, Jesus Christ—not in the water only, but in the water and in the blood—and the Spirit is the witness: for the Spirit is the truth. [7]For three are the witnesses: [8]the Spirit and the water and the blood, and the three are in the One.

Many scholars debate what precisely 1 John means by water and blood (see Streett, 256–337). Several suggest that this is a reference to Jesus' death from John 19:34-35, where blood and water come from Jesus' pierced side. Supporting this view, Parsenios highlights the presence of the Spirit in 19:30 and the idea of conquest from 16:33 (2014, 122). For Parsenios, then, 1 John 5:6-8 is emphatic that Jesus, the Christ, did die, in contrast to opponents who argued against this view (cf. Brown 1982, 595–98; Thatcher 2001, 247–48; Lieu 2008, 214–15; von Wahlde 2010, 3:188). Others, however, suggest that "the water" is a description of Jesus' baptism while blood is his death. In this way, 5:6-8 covers the entirety of his ministry (Smith, 122–25; Heil, 106; Streett, 326–27). Still others argue that the combination refers to Jesus' birth, with water and blood being an allusion to amniotic fluid. Annette Weissen-rieder supports this view, noting the role that spirit (*pneuma*) had in ancient understandings of birth since fetuses took in *pneuma* both while in the womb and after birth as life-giving nourishment (2014, 79–81). Significantly, Weis-senrieder notes that *pneuma* is *physical* nourishment taken in by the body; indeed, it is the crucial nourishment that enables life. Although these arguments differ in their particulars, they agree that the overall emphasis is on Jesus' incarnation, thereby reaffirming the confession from God's Spirit in 4:2: "Jesus Christ has come (*elēlytha*) in flesh."

There are strengths and weaknesses to each of the suggestions given for 5:6-8 above. One key problem is their temporal focus: namely, they all highlight the former realities of Jesus' flesh, either as one who really died, as one who had a ministry from baptism to his death, or as one who was really born. Certainly, as 4:2 makes clear, 1 John agrees with each of these elements; however, I suggest, the flesh of Jesus is also an ongoing, salvific reality for 1 John, which is made clear in 1:5–2:2. For 1 John, it is not just that Jesus Christ *was* in the flesh for a time, but rather than he is still flesh and that it is as a flesh-and-blood Advocate that he is still ministering before the Father on behalf of confessing believers. Indeed, this is what the perfect tense from 4:2 means: not just that Jesus Christ came in the flesh but that he *has come and remains* in the flesh, even though he has returned to the Father. As 1:5–2:2 explains, Jesus' blood is still "cleansing" believers when they confess and rely on him. Understood this way, 1 John 5:6-8 takes on a different tone: Jesus Christ came in water and in the blood, and, regardless of the specific events associated with them, these elements continue testifying to his identity along with the Spirit. They continue testifying because they remain part of him, not as superfluous or separate and temporary locations but as part of his, and therefore God's, divine unity.

Such a reading makes sense of the Greek in 5:7-8 that, translated literally, reads, "For three are the witnesses: the Spirit and the water and the blood, and the three are in the One." Although interpreters regularly translate 5:8 as "the three are in agreement," the actual phrase is "the three are in the One (*eis to hen eisin*)." This is the same language that Jesus uses in John 10:30 when he says, "I and the Father are One (*hen esmen*)." Moreover, it is also similar to Jesus' prayer for his followers in 17:23 that "they might become completed into One (*hōsin teteleiōmenoi eis hen*)." Baron has argued that Jesus' words are a reference to the *Shema*, and his perceived threat to that divine unity is what sparks the violent reaction against him in 10:31. If 1 John 5:8 is also a reference to the *Shema*, rather than an idiomatic statement about agreement, it communicates a similar claim as Jesus in 10:30: namely, that he, even as a physical being, is "in the One." As a result, these *physical* elements—Spirit, water, and blood—are also a part of the One, the divine unity that is God. This is the audacity of the Johannine confession: Jesus' physicality is not a threat to God's unity, but part of it. Moreover, this physicality provides the hope for believers also to share in the divine abiding (cf. Kinlaw, 167–71).

This interpretation also explains why, in 5:9-13, this same testimony is said to be from God "concerning his Son" (vv. 9-10). First John 5:9 explains, "If we are receiving testimony from people, the testimony of God is greater, for this is the testimony of God which he has testified concerning his Son." Rather than concluding, as most interpreters do, that readers must wait until 5:11 to know what "this testimony" is, I suggest that v. 9 is a summative statement about 5:6-8. The testimony of the water, blood, and Spirit is God's testimony because they are "in the One." First John 5:11-12, therefore, explains God's testimony in a different way: namely that "God gave eternal life to us, and this life is in his Son. The one having the Son has the life. The one not having the Son of God does not have the life" (cf. 2:22-23). Having the Son of God, v. 13 clarifies, means "believing" or "trusting in the name of the Son of God": Jesus Christ (cf. John 1:12, 17; 3:18; 20:30-31; 1 John 2:12; 3:23).

B. 1 John 5:14-21: Boldness from What We Know

First John ends with final words of encouragement in 5:14-21. Summarizing what the audience "knows," these verses remind them to continue relying on God rather than acquiescing to the pressures of "the whole world," and "the Evil One," around them. The passage can be broken down into three smaller portions: 5:14-15, 16-17, 18-20.

First John 5:14-15 introduces the main topic of knowledge, continuing from the author's purpose statement from v. 13: "I wrote these things to you so that you might know (*eidēte*) that you have eternal life." The possession of eternal life from believing that the Son of God is Jesus Christ leads the audience to have "boldness before him," that is, before God. This is the fourth and final reference to "boldness" (*parrēsia*) in 1 John. In 2:28 and 4:17, such "boldness" is the confidence believers will have on the day of judgment when Jesus returns. Rather than fearing this day, believers can look forward to it because they are living in fellowship with him. In 3:21 and 5:14, *parrēsia* is rooted in the present time so that believers can ask God for assistance with the confidence that he hears and will answer them, just as he answered Jesus in the Gospel of John (11:41-44). In both 1 John 3:21 and 5:14, believers have confidence "before God" or "before him" and ask God directly. Such an image resonates with Jesus' promise from John 16:25-26 when he says, "I have spoken these things to you in parables. The hour is coming when I will no longer speak in parables to you, but with *parrēsia* I will proclaim to you concerning the Father. In that day, you will ask in my name, and I am not saying that I will ask the Father on your behalf." For 1 John, "that day" is not only in the future (2:28; 4:17) but also in the present, post-resurrection life of the community.

On the one hand, 1 John 5:16-17 is a brief digression that interrupts the series of "knowing" statements in 5:14-15, 18-20. On the other, it is an example of what believers can be confident of asking God.

> [16]If someone should see his brother sinning a sin not toward (*pros*) death, he will ask and he [God] will give to him life, to the one sinning not toward (*pros*) death. There is a sin toward (*pros*) death, not concerning that one am I saying that he should ask. [17]All unrighteousness is sin, but there is a sin not toward (*pros*) death.

Lieu contends that these verses articulate a felt concern within the community (2008, 225–26). Having argued vehemently in 1 John 3 against the continuation of sin among the children of God, the author of 1 John now poses the question, what should believers do if they see their siblings struggling with sins? The answer, 1 John responds, is to ask God on their behalf. Such a response is similar to the role of Jesus, who continues his advocacy for believers by cleansing them from sins and unrighteousness when they confess and trust him to do so (1:5–2:2).

What is more difficult to answer, however, is the definition of "a sin not toward death" versus "a sin toward death." Lieu notes that distinction of types of sins is present in the larger biblical tradition, corresponding to different forms of punishment or ritual offerings (Lev 7:19-20; Mark 3:28-30; Matt 12:31-32; Luke 12:10). Streett adds to this list the commands against false prophets from Deut 13, which condemns to death those who deceive Israel to worship idols and draws them away from worshiping God alone (cf. Deut 18:20). As Streett (232–33) observes, Deut 13 is stringent in its condemnation; even loved ones are not immune from capital punishment (vv. 6-9). He suggests, therefore, that God will not give life to the false teachers that are luring the believers of 1 John away from their recognition of Jesus and God's Son because these ones are like the false prophets of Deut 13. In practical terms, 1 John 5:16-17 could comfort believers when their siblings do not return to the fold, or stop sinning, even after they pray for them. It is not that God did not listen to them but rather that their siblings are unwilling to stop sinning to receive life. As 1 John 1:7-10 explains, those who do not continue confessing their sins, or who think that they have never sinned, deceive themselves and, as a result, cut themselves off from the cleansing ministry of Jesus.

Recognizing the allusion to Deut 13 and 18 in 1 John 5:16-17 resonates not only with the reading of 5:6-8 offered above but also with 5:18-21. Both of these passages emphasize God's unity as *the* One, just as the *Shema* does (cf. Deut 13:3-4). In 5:18-21, 1 John returns to the list of what the audience knows: that each one having been born of God does not continue sinning but instead, "keeps himself" (*tērei heauton*) so that the Evil One cannot "touch him." At the same time, however, believers also know that "the whole world is lying with the Evil One," which explains the hatred the world has for believers. The reference to "the whole world" in 5:19 brings to mind this same description from 2:2, where 1 John emphasizes that the expiation available through Jesus is more than sufficient for "the whole world." The separation, therefore, is not because God is not able to save but rather because the world has chosen darkness over light (cf. John 3:19-21).

Finally, 1 John 5:20 concludes with a list of what believers know because of the Son of God: "he has come and has given us understanding so that we might know the truth, and we are in the truth, in his Son Jesus Christ. *This One* is the True God and Eternal Life." The use of *houtos estin*, "this One is," in 5:20 connects this verse back to 5:5-6 and, therefore, back to 2:22-23, the only three verses in 1 John to use this phrase. All three of these verses focus on recognizing Jesus' identity as Christ and Son, and this recognition, this "having the Son," means also having eternal life. Rather than a sudden shift in subjects, then, 5:20 and 21 continue the emphasis on unity: the confession of Jesus Christ as God's Son does not disrupt the oneness of God but rather is an acknowledgment of *how* this One God has chosen to reveal himself, and his love, to the world. Instead of being deceived by false prophets who are urging believers away from this confession and therefore to the worship of false gods who cannot give life (cf. Ps 115:4; 135:15; Isa 41:28; 48:5-12; Jer 9:13; 14:22), 1 John admonishes believers to *remain* in the confession and life they already experience.

According to 1 John, believers "keep" themselves by "keeping" God's commandments: loving one another and not loving the world (see "keep," *tēreō*, in 2:3-5; 3:22-24; 5:3). They can only do so, however, when they remain in the fellowship made possible by Jesus' past, present, and future ministry. Jesus' blood continues cleansing believers from sins when they stray but then confess and return. God's Spirit enables them to confess the truth of Jesus' identity, that he "has come in the flesh" and is God's Son. And Jesus' example of love upon the cross enables believers to imitate his selfless obedience to the Father (3:16). This "keeping" (*tēreō*) is expanded in 5:21 with the related verb *phylassō* ("guard"), which the Gospel interchanges with *tēreō* in John 12:47 and connects with Jesus' care for his disciples in 17:12. Rather than a throwaway statement, therefore, "Little children, guard yourselves from idols" in 1 John 5:21 is the culmination of the entire sermon. Having been told that they "have eternal life" already, the believers are encouraged to remain in life rather than forfeiting it by following the deceivers who have gone out from among them. For 1 John, the choice is clear: continue in fellowship with us and, therefore, with the Father and the Son (1:3).

Theological Threads

Three in One: Trinity in 1 John?

Like the Gospel of John, 1 John has been a source of debate over the possible presence of Trinity or Trinitarian-like theology within it (cf. Köstenberger and Swain). Such thoughts are understandable given the language of Father, Son, and Spirit throughout the Johannine writings. As Adesola Akala notes, the Son-Father metaphor is pervasive throughout the Gospel, and Marianne Meye Thompson (2001) has demonstrated the importance of Fatherhood language for understanding the theology of the Gospel as well. A number of additional studies can be highlighted that focus on the Spirit in these same writings: Gary Burge, Cornelis Bennema (2007), Dorothy Lee (2012, 85–108), Gitte Buch-Hansen, and Troels Engberg-Pedersen (2015, 2017) to name just a few. Nevertheless, even as Father, Son, and Spirit *do* play significant roles in the Johannine writings, there is not *explicit* Trinitarian language in any of them. Moreover, rather than "equality" between the Persons of the Trinity that later theologians would emphasize, Jesus the Son always subordinates himself to the Father in the Gospel, and the role of the Spirit seems even more difficult: is the Spirit given by the Father (John 14:26) or the Son (15:26; 16:7; 20:20-21)? Rather than looking within these writings for a *clear and complete* communication of Trinitarian theology, it is better to see how important the Gospel and writings of John were for the later articulation of Trinity.

This view is especially important when we come to 1 John 5:7-8, or the so-called "Johannine comma." If you have a King James Version (KJV) of the Bible, you will notice a significant portion of text is missing from the commentary above; this section is called the "Johannine comma" (*comma* is Latin for "clause" or "phrase" rather than a punctuation mark). This clause is a Trinitarian explanation for the confusing statement from 5:7-8: "Because three are the witnesses: the Spirit and the water and the blood, and the three are in the One." I have given an interpretation of these verses above, but for earlier scribes and interpreters, this verse was an invitation for Trinitarian readings. Later Latin, Greek, Coptic, Ethiopic, and Arabic versions of 1 John 5:7-8 read as follows (based on Greek ms.):

> Because there are three who testify in heaven: Father, Word, and Holy Spirit, and these three are one. And three are testifying on the earth: Spirit, water, and blood, and these three are in the One.

This longer reading eventually found its way into the KJV because of Erasmus, who published the first Greek New Testament in 1516, the base text used for the KJV translation published in 1611.

According to Lieu, even though these verses are clearly later additions to 1 John, "once the doctrine of the Trinity began to develop, the presence of the spirit and the final phrase of verse 8, understood as 'and the three are a unity,' were bound to evoke the unity of the three persons of the Godhead" (2008, 215). For this reason, it was also difficult to remove this addition once it found its way into the text. As Parsenios concludes, "The comma tells us much more about the history of Christian thought than it does about the history of the text of the NT or the theology of 1 John" (2014, 123). Rather than being a point of contention, or even concern, therefore, the "Johannine comma" is a demonstration of how present context impacts theological interpretations of Scripture. Although 1 John is not "Trinitarian" in a full sense, one can see how the Johannine writings were later interpreted in Trinitarian ways, even to the extent that later scribes added to the text to make such readings explicit.

God Is Love, Jesus Is Life

The final portions of 1 John offer several explicit divine titles that contribute significantly to the overall theological perspective of the sermon. First, God is called "the Love" (*hē agapē*) in 4:8, but this love is not abstract; rather, it is specifically revealed in God's sending of his "Son" the "Unique One into the world, so that we might live through him" (4:9). This "living" is expanded again when the Son is called "expiation concerning our sins" (4:10). Having been forgiven and cleansed, believers are now able to *live*, that is, to have fellowship with God. Moreover, believers express this type of life—eternal life—when they imitate God's love modeled through the sending of his Son: self-sacrificing love that benefits others (3:16). It is when believers live this way that their Spirit-infused confessions of Jesus' identity cohere with their manner of life. *This*, 1 John says, is what it means to have the type of love God wants; this is "completed love."

Not only is God's identity as "Love" not abstract; neither is the Son's identity who manifests, or reveals, God's love to the world (4:9-10). Turning to the second set of titles, we find the Son identified in the following ways: in addition to being God's Son and expiation, he is also called "Savior of the world" in 4:14, and he is explicitly named "Jesus" in 4:15 and 5:5, the "Christ" in 5:1, and "Jesus Christ" in 5:6. All of these titles build to the climax of 5:20 that Jesus is "True God and Eternal Life." Like the Gospel, 1 John understands God's Son to be a perfect reflection of God's will: namely, love for the world that results in life (John 1:1-16). Just as in John 1:17-18, the Son's name is "Jesus Christ" and "he shows the way" to the Father in ways no one has been able to before (1 John 4:12). Knowing Jesus, therefore, means also knowing God as Father: Jesus' work as his Son reveals who the Father is by showing what he desires for the world (cf. Thompson 2001, 57–100).

The unity that exists between the Father and Son is complete, according to 1 John (and the Gospel of John). It may appear divided because of Jesus' incarnation and physical manifestation, but such is only appearance rather than reality. Instead, Jesus' physicality makes God visible: it is a revelation of God's identity rather than a division of it. Without Jesus' being sent, 1 John argues, the world would have no firsthand experience with Light (1:5). Moreover, Jesus' incarnation is *still* relevant to believers and needs to be confessed because believers *still* rely on his blood and his advocacy before the Father whenever they sin (1:7–2:2). Such confession and reliance reunites them with the divine and enables them again to confess truthfully of Jesus' identity because they can live out the love he exemplifies (4:19-20). Thus, according to 1 John, the Spirit, the water, and the blood are in the One, not in competition with the One. Jesus Christ is True God and Eternal Life, flesh and all. To deny this reality is to divide God and therefore to seek life from a mere idol (5:21).

Abide in the Teaching of Christ

2 John

Second John shares many of the same themes and language with 1 John. Like 1 John, 2 John calls its addressees "children" (2 John 1, 4, 13); mentions the command to love one another (2 John 5; 1 John 3:11, 23; 4:7, 12) as that which was given to the believers "from the beginning" and in opposition to novel teaching (2 John 6, 9-10; 1 John 2:7, 27; 3:11); focuses on truth; and warns of deceivers and an antichrist who has "gone out into the world" and does not confess "Jesus Christ coming in the flesh" (2 John 7; 1 John 2:18-22; 4:2). Second John also repeats admonitions to "abide" or "remain" (*menō*, 2 John 9; 1 John 2:24-29; 3:21-24) and to "walk" or "live" in truth by following the commandments (*peripateō*, 2 John 4-6; 1 John 2:6-11), has language of "fellowshipping" (2 John 11; 1 John 1:3-4), describes "having" the Father and the Son (2 John 9; 1 John 2:23; 5:10-12), and notes the fulfillment of joy (2 John 12; 1 John 1:4). The similarities are so extensive that Parsenios asks, if 2 John "merely duplicates 1 John . . . [w]hy was 2 John written at all?" (2014, 130). Moreover, why was it preserved and eventually canonized?

I have offered a variety of answers to these questions in the introductions preceding this section, but I will include my own perspective here as well. I agree with the majority of scholars that while it is not possible to define the precise composition order of the Johannine writings, it does seem that the Letters were written around the same time (ca. 90–110 CE). One reasonable suggestion is to see 2 and 3 John as different cover letters for 1 John. Second and 3 John could have been composed for two or more different communities (2 John being more general and 3 John more specific), or they may be sequential: having sent 2 John with 1 John, the Elder's representative was rejected by Diotrephes. This would have prompted the Elder to resend 1 John along with 3 John as the cover letter to Gaius, probably in the hands of Demetrius whom the Elder recommends (3 John 12). While no single sequence is provable beyond a doubt, these situations could explain why

2 and 3 John were preserved *and* associated with 1 John, particularly if they were all kept by a single community who remained persuaded by the Elder's instructions.

If read together in this way, 1–3 John can be understood to deal with the same, primarily Christological, controversy described in 1 John: namely, that some in the community had left the fellowship because they either no longer considered Jesus to be relevant to their salvation, and/or they no longer considered Jesus to be "the Christ" (2:18-19; 4:2). First John, therefore, argues extensively that Jesus *remains* the Christ and God's Son in the flesh long after his death, resurrection, and return to the Father. He is the Advocate (*paraklētos*) on behalf of believers before the Father, cleansing them by means of his blood (1:7–2:2; 2:18-29; 4:1-10; 5:6-21). Jesus' physicality, therefore, does not disappear after his death but remains a part of his identity and a part of the divine unity—just as Jesus proclaims in John 10:30 (cf. 20:1-29). As I argued in the commentary on 1 John 5:6-8, it is Jesus' continued physicality that gives believers hope that they too can become one with God even in the present, thereby fulfilling Jesus' prayer in John 17:23.

As a cover letter or preface to 1 John, 2 John is not a mere duplicate but a synopsis that introduces the main ideas of 1 John prior to its performance before the community. It prepares the assembly and offers the following advice: (1) continue walking in the truth by loving one another and keeping the traditional teaching "of Christ" (vv. 4-7); and (2) be careful to disassociate from those who reject Jesus Christ "coming in the flesh" to avoid being swept up in the false teaching or "evil works" (vv. 8-11). These positive and negative exhortations lead Parsenios to conclude that 2 John is a "typical paraenetic," or advice, letter (2014, 130–31). The letter coheres to the expected form and length of most private, ancient letters but has a more general addressee, similar to Paul's letters. Indeed, Judith Lieu (2008, 247) suggests that 2 John has been influenced by "a distinctive developing 'Christian' letter style" with its greetings that include "grace" and "peace" (v. 3). The structure of 2 John pivots on v. 7, which is the focal point of the dispute in the Johannine Letters. The outline of 2 John below guides the commentary that follows:

A. Opening Greetings (vv. 1-3)
   B. Praise and First Commands (vv. 4-6)
      C. Rationale: There Are Deceivers and Antichrist (v. 7)
   B'. Warnings and More Commands (vv. 8-11)
A'. Closing Greetings (vv. 12-13)

Commentary

Opening Greetings: The Elect Lady and Her Children (vv. 1-3)

Although there has been some debate over the identity of the "Elect Lady" and her "children" in 2 John 1, the majority of interpreters agree that this is an assembly or *ekklēsia* ("church"). While one could translate *eklektē kyria* as "Lady Electa," it is more probable that this is a description of a house-church community for several reasons: first, it was not uncommon to address groups (cities, nations, or the earth) with feminine markers such as "daughter," "Lady," "sister," or "wife." As Birger Olsson (61) notes, this is a common feature in a number of OT prophetic texts, but it was also a standard trope in Greco-Roman cultures more generally (cf. Lieu 2008, 244–45). Second, and more telling for 2 John in particular, in his closing greeting the Elder writes, "The children of your elect sister (*tēs adelphēs tēs elektēs*) greet you" (v. 13). Rather than a literal "sister," the closing greeting of 2 John indicates that members of another community are greeting the gathered "lady and children" addressed in 2 John. The use of such language fosters the fictive kinship, or family, of the Johannine communities. They are all sister-communities, filled with children who trace their paternity to God as Father. Jesus alone is called a "Son," thereby establishing his superiority over the children. The Elder occupies an authoritative place in this familial hierarchy, but he is clear that his status does not impinge on the Son's. Instead, he is most likely a leader of the community, likely also literally older in age, and therefore regarded as a keeper of the traditions passed down to him (Brown 1982, 647–51).

In vv. 1b-2, the Elder immediately turns to include several key concepts: love, truth, knowledge, abiding, and eternity. His confessed continual love for the Lady and her children identifies him as an ally, one who is seeking the best for his family of faith. He is no flatterer or deceiver but rather a true friend who will speak frankly with the intention of helping his beloved. It is for this reason, then, that the Elder is also an ally of truth. In his letter to Antiochus Philopappus titled *How to Tell a Flatterer from a Friend*, Plutarch explores the overlap of love and truth, explaining that "Truth is a thing divine" while the "flatterer is in all likelihood an enemy to the gods" (*Adul. amic.* 2). The flatterer deceives by playing on a person's inflated self-love rather than offering true advice, legitimate requests, and even warranted criticism. In contrast, a friend speaks openly, with *parrēsia*, the same virtue with which Jesus speaks to the people in the Gospel and that 1 John says believers can do before God (John 7:13; 11:14; 16:25, 29; 18:20; 1 John 2:28; 3:21; 4:17; 5:14). Even though 2 John does not use the language of either "flatterer" or "friend," it operates with many of the same ideas as Plutarch's letter: the Elder presents himself not just as a friend but also as a family member who is seeking the good of the entire family of God by speaking openly to his sister and her children. This open speech commends the Lady and her children when they are due praise, but it also criticizes and warns them so that they will not fall into the traps of deceivers (v. 7). The deceivers, then, are the flatterers who seek to beguile the Lady and her children, drawing them away from what is truly good and into a way that only seems good.

Verse 3 rounds out the greeting by promising, "With us will be grace, mercy, peace from God the Father and from Jesus Christ the Son of the Father, in truth and in love." The "us" assumes unity between the Elder and his addressees as well as the wider family of "all those knowing the truth because the abiding truth (*tēn alētheian tēn menousan*) will be in us and with us forever" (v. 2). The "truth" of which the Elder writes is not fleeting, but eternal. This introduction paves the way for his later censure of those who "lead beyond (*proagōn*) and do not abide (*mē menōn*) in the teaching of Christ" (v. 9). Moreover, v. 3 also emphasizes the divine unity of God as including the Father as well as the Son, whose name is Jesus Christ. This, too, corresponds to the admonition in v. 9 that one cannot "have God" if they do not have "the Father and the Son."

Keep on Living in Truth and Loving One Another (vv. 4-6)
After the opening greetings, the letter shifts into a section of praise for the audience in v. 4. The Elder says that he "was greatly overjoyed" to have found some of the Lady's children "living in truth, just as we received command from the Father" (cf. 1 John 1:6, 7; 2:6, 11). The word for "living" can also be translated "walking around" (*peripateō*), indicating the way in which someone is living or their behavior (BDAG, 803). The way in which one walks is the way in which they live. For the Gospel and 1 John, this is either in light and truth or in darkness and lies (John 8:12; 11:9-10; 12:35; 1 John 1:6-7; 2:6-11). The continued use of the first person plural in 2 John 4 ("we received," *elabomen*) again links the Lady, her obedient children, and the Elder, but he also implies that there is room for improvement: only *some* of her children are walking in this way (*ek tōn teknōn sou*). The implication that *some* of the children, therefore, are *not* walking in truth justifies the Elder's command in v. 5. The Elder uses second person singular pronouns in v. 5 but switches to the second plural in v. 6.

In his command, the Elder again reminds his audience of the source of the truth of which he writes that it is a commandment (*entolē*) from the Father and, the Elder explains, a restatement of what the believers already know. Parsenios's connection of this rhetoric to classic paraenesis is helpful. He notes, "writers and speakers who compose paraenetic texts and speeches not only acknowledge but often freely admit that the advice they encourage people to follow is *not* new or novel but something that the recipient of the instruction *already knows*" (2014, 131; emphasis added). This same argumentation is used repeatedly in 1 John; even though 1 John 2:15-17 includes a "new" commandment, the emphasis is on continuity with what the audience knows "from the beginning" (1 John 1:1; 2:7, 13-14, 24; 3:11; 2 John 5, 6). The Elder's attention to paraenetic argumentation is especially significant because he contends that his opponents *are* giving "new" and, therefore, false teachings—teachings that have their origins not "from the Father" but from themselves or, worse, from the Evil One ("evil works," *ergois . . . tois ponērois*, 2 John 11; "evil" and Evil One, *ponēros*, John 3:19; 7:7; 17:15; 1 John 2:1-14; 3:12; 5:18-19; 3 John 10).

Second John 5-6 also demonstrates the Johannine proclivity for threefold repetition, reading:

A. [5]And now I am asking you (*se*), dear Lady,
    not as though I am writing a new commandment to you (*soi*),
    B. but one which we have had from the beginning:
        C. (*hina*) that we should love one another.
A'. [6]And this is the love:
        C'. (*hina*) that we should live according to his commandments.
A". And this is the commandment,
    B'. just as you heard (*ēkousate*) from the beginning:
        C". (*hina*) that you should live in it.

The repetition of these verses results in the following meaning: the commandment, heard from the beginning, is to live loving one another. Whole phrases from these verses also appear in 1 John (cf. 3:11; 5:3) as does the theme of keeping the commandments given. These commandments are expressed by means of love, and they also show one's love of God, the Father, and the Son, Jesus Christ (2:3-4; 3:22-24; 5:2-3; cf. John 14:15, 21; 15:10). Parsenios notes that the logic of 2 John 5-6 is tautological, or circular. Moreover, the gender of the pronoun at the end of v. 6a ("it") makes it impossible to pin down: is the "it" the commandment or love? "The impression one gets," Parsenios concludes, "is that the mere repetition of phrases is precisely the point" (2014, 136). This is an argument not based on logic but made through emphasis.

In his own analysis, Duane Watson (1993) suggests that 1 John uses as many types of repetition as possible to amplify the argument. Amplification, when used effectively, is "a forcible method of arguing" that underscores the main points of an argument (Cicero, *Part. or.* 8.27; Watson 1993, 101). According to Parsenios (2014, 136) 2 John 5-6 is similar, using *expolitio*, or the repetition of a single idea in a different form (*Rhet. Her.* 4.42.54). These verses also include "accumulation," which involve "accumulations of definitions" (Cicero, *Part. or.* 16.55). Second John 5-6a has a sequence of three definitions that close the circle of vv. 4-6, tying together the themes of walking/living, commandments, loving one another, and the equation of "from the beginning" with "from the Father." The result of this repetition is amplification of the Elder's thesis: obedience is inseparable from love lived out.

Rationale: There are Deceivers and Antichrist (v. 7)

Up to v. 7, 2 John has been largely positive, hinting at censure in v. 4 but otherwise encouraging the audience to continue their loving behavior. Having earned the trust of his audience, the Elder changes his tone in v. 7. All of 2 John pivots on v. 7, which is both connected to what comes before by the causal conjunction *hoti* ("because") and introduces the theme of false teachers that dominates vv. 8-11. In contrast to the eternal and abiding truth that the Elder *repeats* to his audience in vv. 4-6, the false teachers offer new teachings that are outside, or "beyond," the teachings of Christ (v. 9). Read alongside v. 6, v. 7 gives justification for continuing to keep God's commandment of loving one another. The Elder writes

> [6]And this is the commandment, just as you heard from the beginning, that you should live in it [7]because many deceivers went out into the world, the ones not confessing Jesus Christ coming in the flesh. This one is the deceiver and the antichrist.

In other words, continuing to walk according to the Father's command of love ensures maintaining one's connection to God, thereby providing protection from "the deceiver and the antichrist" (cf. 1 John 5:18-21).

Second John 7 is regularly highlighted as communicating the core of the disagreement between the Elder and those who have left the community. As in 1 John 2:18-19 and 4:2, the ones who "went out" are denying Jesus Christ's flesh. Second John 7 repeats much of 1 John 2:18-19, including the description of "many" (*polloi*), "went out" (*exēlthon*; cf. 1 John 4:1, *exelēlythasin eis ton kosmon*), "just as you heard" (*kathōs ēkousate*), and *antichristos*.

First John also uses the terms "deceiver" and "deceive" (*planos, planaō*) as synonyms for liar and lying, which also appear in 2:22 and 4:1-2. Finally, 1 John 2:22 also uses the emphatic demonstrative pronoun to underscore the identity of the antichrist: "*This one* is (*houtos estin*) the antichrist, the one denying the Father and the Son." Indeed, so similar are these sections of 1 and 2 John that Lieu writes, "2 John 7 presupposes and has been formulated in the light of the longer letter. It is much less probable that the author here introduced an unfamiliar idea, which he subsequently had to explain in 1 John" (2008, 252). For Lieu, this is an argument in favor of canonical order as compositional order, but even 1 John uses antichrist language with the understanding that his audience has heard of "antichrist" before (2:18). While the idea might be unfamiliar to modern-day readers, it seems that it was not novel for the Johannine community.

Even though 1 John can help us understand 2 John 7, it does not clarify one significant aspect of this verse: namely, the present tense participle *erchomenon* (coming). Readers familiar with 1 John 4:2 expect here another perfect participle, "has come" (*elēlythota*), and, as Lieu notes, a number of English translations accommodate such an expectation (NRSV "has come," CEB and NLT "came"; cf. von Wahlde 2010, 3:230). Nevertheless, the use of the present participle in 2 John indicates that the Elder has in mind a broad category of Jesus' enfleshed identity. The present tense is ongoing or continuous in meaning, indicating not only that Jesus has been in the flesh but also that he continues being in the flesh even in the present and into the future (cf. Brown 1982, 669–70; Kinlaw, 94). This use is similar to the use of the perfect tense in 1 John 4:2, just not in the way most scholars interpret it (see commentary). Second John 7, therefore, highlights the continued, and enduring, existence of Jesus' flesh. This interpretation is consistent with arguments from 1 John, including 4:2 (1:5–2:2; 5:6-8). What the deceivers are guilty of is separating the Christ from the flesh-and-blood Jesus (Kinlaw, 95). For the Elder, this teaching is anti-Christ.

Watch Out and Exclude False Teachers (vv. 8-11)

The warning tone of v. 7 continues in vv. 8-11. "Watch yourselves," the Elder writes, "so that you should not lose the things for which we have worked but receive a full reward." This warning is a bit awkward in English, but the Greek contains assonance and rhyming that highlight its main components: do not destroy (*mē apolesēte*) but receive back in full (*plērē apolabēte*). These two subjunctive verbs sit at the beginning and end of the purpose clause (*hina*, "so that"), also adding emphasis. Like 1 John 5:18-21, the Elder indicates God's protection for the ones who continue abiding in love and, therefore, remain connected to the Father and the Son. This does not, however, remove responsibility for believers. They still need to "watch themselves" just as they need to "guard themselves from idols" (1 John 5:21). The implication is that abiding, or remaining, in the truth is not a static reality; rather, it is one that requires action as well as reflection.

In 2 John 9 the Elder returns to his concern for preserving the community's traditional teaching about Christ (v. 7). Using substantival participles in a style also characteristic of 1 John, he creates a contrast, moving from negative example to positive.

> A. Each one who is going beyond (*proagōn*)
>> B. and does not continue remaining (*menōn*) in the teaching of Christ
>> C. does not have God.
> B'. The one who continues remaining in the teaching,
> C'. *this one* has both the Father and the Son.

Just as 2 John 7 mirrors 1 John 2:18-19, 2 John 9 resembles 1 John 2:23 by explaining that one cannot have the Father without also having the Son. As in 1 John, the concern is not simply the content of the deceivers' message but also that it is potentially persuasive; indeed, "persuade" is another definition for *proagō* (LSJ; cf. 1 John 3:7). Implied is that teachers may come offering instructions on how to "have God," but for the Elder, such "possession" is impossible if one does not have both the Father and the Son. These teachers might indeed be possessed, but it is not by God's Spirit (cf. 1 John 4:1-6).

For this reason, the Elder commands his audience to discontinue fellowship with anyone who does not "offer" the "teaching of Christ." The "teaching of Christ" is best understood as an objective genitive, meaning the teaching about Christ, but it could also have a subjective flavor since Jesus taught that he was the Christ and of his unity with the Father (John 4:26; 5:19-23; 8:26; 10:30). Second John 10-11 prohibits the believers from "receiving" false teachers into a "household" (*oikia*). The use of the feminine form of "household" (*oikia* instead of *oikios*) corresponds to the addressee, the Elect Lady (*kyria*), fitting for believers gathering in a house-church (Parsenios 2014, 141; Lieu 2008, 259–60). The household language also continues the family metaphor of the Lady, Elect Sister, and children of the letter (vv. 1, 4-5, 13).

The Elder continues the initial prohibition with another in v. 11, repeating his warning with an "augmentation" that builds on the first command with an even more restrictive one (Cicero, *Part. or.* 15.52–54; Quintilian, *Inst.* 8.4.3–9; cf. Watson 1993, 102). Not only are the believers forbidden to welcome such a teacher into the household, but they also cannot even "speak greetings" to him. Pushing the command yet further, the Elder provides his rationale: "for the one speaking greetings to him shares in his evil works" (v. 11). The verb for "sharing" is *koinōnei*, the verbal form of the noun *koinōnia*, "fellowship," used in 1 John 1:3-4. According to the Elder, hosting or even speaking in a welcoming way to a suspicious teacher is enough to transition one away from fellowship with "the Father and with his Son Jesus Christ" (1 John 1:3; cf. 2 John 3)! How such a statement coheres with the Elder's simultaneous command to love is discussed in the theological section below.

Closing Greetings from Your Elect Sister's Children (vv. 12-13)

The letter closes abruptly with an implied promise of an upcoming visit from the Elder, as well as "greetings" from "the children of [the] Elect Sister." The Elder explains that this short letter is only the beginning of what he has to say to the community, yet he would rather speak face to face rather than rely on "papyrus and ink." As Lieu (2008, 262) notes, this is a "conventional" way to end a letter, but it is also indicative of the preference for oral communication in the ancient Greco-Roman world. Philosophers, for example, complained of possible miscommunication that could happen through written mediums, worried that reliance on written words would diminish memorization, and criticized the elite who would collect writings but never bother trying to understand them (Plato, *Ph.*; *Symp.*; cf. Cambron-Goulet)! Letters were often necessary correspondence, but they only filled in for one's absence until one was able to reunite with their addressee. The Elder's conclusion, therefore, resembles that of many other letters, including several in the NT (Phlm 22-25; Rom 15:31-32; 1 Cor 16:5-7). As in Paul's letter to Philemon, the Elder's desire to come is both a promise and a bit of a threat: he will see for himself if they are remaining in the teaching as he instructed.

The final greetings in v. 13 are also typical, but their context as part of 2 John makes them significant. In vv. 10-11 the Elder warned the community against welcoming, or "speaking greetings (*chairein*)" to, those who are not "remaining in the teaching of Christ." His incorporation of greetings (*aspazetai*) from another community to the "Elect Lady and her children" means that he still considers them to be within the Johannine fold. He might be concerned that they could be led astray, but his letter communicates confidence that they have not departed yet.

Theological Threads

Although 2 John is substantially less theologically developed than 1 John, it nevertheless operates on several theological assumptions. First, it emphasizes the enduring nature of Jesus' incarnation and unification with the Father. For the Elder, there is no "going beyond" this fundamental "teaching of Christ" in order to "have God" in some more profound way. Instead, leaving this teaching means leaving the divine fellowship. Second, 2 John assumes a future eschatology with its warnings about destroying the "rewards" or "wages" for which the believers have worked (v. 8). The warning "watch yourselves" is reminiscent of Jesus' apocalyptic counsel in Mark 13; the believers need to stay on guard because their salvation is not yet entirely realized. There is still the need to abide and love, *and* there are threats in the form of deceivers and the antichrist.

Finally, because 2 John is concerned with preserving a community relationship, it offers a dualistic ecclesiology: either one is in, or one is out. There is no fence-straddling in 2 John. In some sense, the harsh polemic of 2 John contrasts with, and perhaps even contradicts, its focus on the command to love in vv. 4-6. In interpreting this Letter, therefore, it is important to keep context in mind. The Elder is addressing not nonbelievers but rather a community that has experienced (and is still in the midst of) some sort of division. Moreover, he is writing at a time when itinerant teachers of all sorts of traditions and philosophies were common.

Lucian of Samosata (ca. 125–90 CE) was a traveling speaker, but he also regularly mocked the hypocritical traveling philosopher who wears the costume of a lover of wisdom but whose life proves him hollow. In his *Life of Peregrinus*, Lucian includes in his criticism false Christians who easily dupe church communities into providing them lavish hospitality in exchange for their empty teachings. Christians also acknowledged this problem in their own writings. The *Didache* (ca. 96 CE), for example, includes specific prohibitions for traveling teachers as well as guidance for determining if itinerants were genuine or not. In the NT, Paul frequently describes travelling teachers with whom he competes for loyalty (e.g., 2 Cor; Gal; Rom), while the Pastorals and Catholic Letters use the trope of false teachers as a sign of the approaching eschaton (2 Tim 3:1-9; 2 Pet 3; Jude). The Elder's warnings, therefore, fit his context and emphasize the severity of his concern for his audience. He sees in his competition a real threat.

Whether or not the Elder's response is appropriate in our own time is another question altogether. Western Christians do not understand, need, or practice hospitality in the same ways that ancient Christians did. Moreover, they do not live in a context where their faith puts them in direct odds with the political establishment in the same way it did in the Roman world. Rather than using 2 John to cast blame on others, then, perhaps believers can learn from the struggle by acknowledging the difficulty of "remaining in" a teaching that continues to astound: we are to love one another, just like Jesus did, regardless of the cost.

Coworkers in Truth

3 John

Third John, like 2 John, receives significantly less attention than the other Johannine writings. Third John is often considered the most "un-Johannine" of the Johannine corpus with its unique vocabulary (e.g., Gentiles, coworkers, church/assembly, imitate) and its unusual specificity (Olsson, 30; cf. Brown 1982, 727; Lieu 2008, 264; Parsenios 2014, 146; Jobes, 281). While the Elder remains something of a mystery, 3 John names its addressee (Gaius), an opponent (Diotrephes), and an emissary (Demetrius). Moreover, 3 John contains a number of elements common among ancient letters including brevity and an apology for being so brief; a named recipient; a prayer for health and thanksgiving; specific requests; and closing greetings. As a result, Judith Lieu concludes, "More than any other NT writing, 3 John displays many of the features of ordinary letters surviving from the ancient world" (2008, 265). And yet, even with all its specificity and comparability, much about 3 John remains unknown. Despite the Elder's fervency in the letter, no clear reference to the figures it names or to the controversy it describes remains recorded in Christian tradition. Third John, therefore, at once offers readers the most transparent description of a conflict in the Johannine community while also remaining remarkably opaque.

Although 3 John is different from the other Johannine writings, it is still a Johannine writing (Schnackenburg, 290; Strecker, 253). This is affirmed not only by tradition but also by the vocabulary and themes in the writing. As Karen Jobes (282) argues, the differences between 3 John and the rest of the writings is a feature of its genre: this is a genuine, personal letter, in contrast to a sermon (1 John), a general letter to a community (2 John), or a biography (Gospel). The opening and closings of 3 John mirror closely those of 2 John, as do the concerns over walking and being "in truth" (3 John 1, 3, 4; 2 John 1, 3, 4; John 17:19), joy for children (*chara*, 3 John 4; 2 John 12; 1 John 1:4; cf. John 15:11; 16:20-24; 17:13), and the "evil" (*ponēros*) works and words of false teachers (3 John 10; 2 John 11; cf. 1 John 2:13-14; 3:12;

5:18-19; John 3:19; 7:7; 17:15). Third John also has a number of additional
links to 1 John and the Gospel such as its concern with truthful testimony
(3 John 3, 6, 12; 1 John 1:2; 4:14; 5:6-10; John 5:31; 8:14-17; 19:35;
21:24); an emphasis on "the name" (*to onoma*, 3 John 7, 15; 1 John 2:12;
3:23; 5:13; John 1:12; 3:18; 17:6-26; 20:30-31); separation among communities by "casting out" (*ek ekballō*) perceived bad influences (3 John 10; John
9:34-35); and an overall concern for recognition and hospitality. All the
Johannine writings ask if people can recognize that *Jesus* is the Christ and,
therefore, if they receive (*lambanō*, 3 John 7; 2 John 4, 10; John 1:12, 16)
him, his teachings, and his "friends" (*philoi*, 3 John 15; John 15:13-15). In
3 John, the Elder is calling on Gaius to remain a friend of Jesus, and therefore of the community, by welcoming the Elder and his allies while rejecting
Diotrephes.

Third John describes itself as part of a series of letters. Having sent a
previous letter to the church, the Elder found that his teaching and emissaries ("brothers") were rejected by Diotrephes (v. 9). This situation is what
prompted the Elder to write to Gaius, and he promises that he will also visit
soon in person (v. 14). Third John may have been a single missive sent to
Gaius prior to the Elder's arrival and subsequent teaching, or it could have
functioned as a cover letter affixed to teaching sent before the Elder's arrival.
Unfortunately, we cannot know the answer to this question for certain, but
its connection to 1 John could suggest that 3 John was an introduction to
that sermon, perhaps resent after the initial rejection by Diotrephes. Third
John proceeds as follows:

A. Opening Greetings: Gaius, the Beloved (vv. 1-4)
   B. Beloved: Praise for Gaius (vv. 5-8)
      C. Blame for Diotrephes (vv. 9-10)
   B'. Beloved: Recommending Demetrius (vv. 11-12)
A'. Closing Greetings (vv. 13-15)

Commentary

Opening Greetings: The Beloved Gaius (vv. 1–4)
The opening words of 3 John repeat much of 2 John 1: the Elder addresses
his audience and describes his love for them "in truth." The new character
of 3 John is Gaius, the only personal recipient named in the Gospel and
Letters of John. Although it is tempting to identify this Gaius in more detail,
"Gaius" was a popular name in Roman antiquity. It was the given name for
Julius Caesar, his successor Augustus, and later emperors Nero and Caligula,
as well as a number of notable Roman generals (Coriolanus), historians

(Tacitus), and politicians (Gracchus, etc.). There are three other men named Gaius mentioned in the NT alone: Gaius from Macedonia who traveled with Paul (Acts 19:29); a Gaius of Derbe (Acts 20:4); and a Gaius from Corinth who was baptized by Paul and who also hosted him (1 Cor 1:4; Rom 16:23). The Gaius of 3 John is not to be confused with any of these other figures, but he was apparently influential enough to receive this letter from the Elder and may have been a member of the same community as Diotrephes. Gaius was also a householder of enough means to welcome and host travelling teachers, an activity the Elder wishes Gaius to continue by welcoming himself as well as those he sends (Demetrius) in contrast to Diotrephes's rejection (3 John 5-8, 12).

The Elder's writing to Gaius has the implicit goal of reinforcing, or at least gauging, his relationship with him. Although the Elder will ask for practical help—welcoming the brothers and Demetrius, sending them on their way "worthily," and preparing for the Elder's immediate visit—all of these actions are based on Gaius's loyalty to the Elder. The Elder, therefore, begins his Letter with emphatic declarations of his own love for Gaius: "To Gaius, the Beloved, whom I myself am loving in truth" (v. 1). Recalling Lori Baron's (2010, 53) note that love in the ancient world is not just a feeling but also loyalty, this opening statement is not a gushing emotional moment but a stark statement of fidelity: the Elder is writing Gaius out of his love for him, his loyalty to him; he is only writing because he desires the best for Gaius. In other words, the Elder is treating Gaius as a true friend ought to do (v. 15). That the Elder also places himself in an authoritative, and even paternal, position by calling Gaius one of his children (*ta ema tekna*, v. 4) does not diminish the notion of friendship, since ancients did not assume that friendships existed only between people of the same status. Indeed, Aristotle describes family relationships as types of friendships, including between fathers and sons (Eth. nic. 8.7-14).

The Elder's wish for Gaius's health in v. 2 is typical of letters in the ancient Mediterranean world, but it also has specifically Johannine elements. Such wishes were common in personal letters, letters that assume a close relationship between sender and recipient, thus continuing to build on the Elder's appeal to intimacy with Gaius (see examples in Lieu 2008, 264; Parsenios 2014, 148). Nevertheless, the precise wording of this health wish stands out from the preserved letter fragments from Egypt. The Elder writes, "I am praying for you about all things, for you to prosper and be in good health, just as your life (*psychē*) prospers" (v. 2). As Raymond Brown (1982, 704) argues, this use of *psychē* corresponds to its use elsewhere in the Johannine writings, where it means not "soul" in contrast to a physical body but rather a holistic sense of "life." In the Johannine writings, Brown explains, a *psychē* is "a life that one can lay down, as differentiated from a *zoē*, 'eternal life'" (e.g., John 10:17-28; 12:25; 1 John 3:16). It is the "life" that one should be willing to give on behalf of the siblings in imitation of Jesus' own actions of love that reveal his loyalty to the world.

In v. 2 the Elder's wish is not for prosperity in the sense of wealth or health that puts Gaius's needs over those of others. Rather, his prayer is for "prosperity" in the sense of continued actions that Gaius has shown on behalf of the Elder and brothers in the past (3 John 3, 5-8, 11-12). The Elder wishes for Gaius to continue loving by living out his loyalty "in truth." Indeed, the Elder's requests for hospitality are a chance for Gaius to demonstrate this continued "prosperity" by imitating "the Good" (v. 11). The Elder's message should not be confused with a health and wealth gospel.

Praise for Gaius: Faithful Hospitality Makes Us Coworkers in Truth (vv. 5-8)

The Elder moves into the body of the Letter in v. 5, continuing his praise for Gaius. Gaius has welcomed the brethren in the past, even though they were strangers (*xenous*) before they came to him. The care for "strangers" is an important tenant in the OT and the ancient world generally since there were not public inns or hotels for people to use, particularly in smaller towns or wilderness regions. Hospitality was not merely caring for friends and relatives but also opening one's house and sharing goods with strangers who were traveling away from their homeland. It was a virtue for which ancient figures were praised when they exhibited it in extraordinary levels (e.g., Abraham in Gen 18; Philo, *Abr.* 22; *T. Ab.*; cf. Arterbury 2010, 69–76) and censured when they failed to offer it or when they broke the trust enacted by hospitality codes (*Il.*; Ovid, *Metam.* 1.212–44; 8.626–724). Offering hospitality was an act of trust and was often the beginning of sustained relationships, such as covenants, marriages, and treaties of peace (Gen 24:10-61; 29:1-20; Exod 2:15-21; 2 Sam 9:11-13; *Jos. As.*; Tobit). Early Christian missionaries relied on this ancient custom, which also made it useful as a litmus test for teachers and communities depending on whom they welcomed, in what ways, and for how long (e.g., *Did.* 11–12; Lucian, *Peregr.*; Mark 6:7-11 and parallels; Acts; Gal 4:14; 1 Tim 1:3-7; 4:9-10; 2 Tim 3:1-9; 2 Pet 2).

Using epideictic rhetoric of praise and blame, the Elder seeks to convince Gaius to "imitate not the wicked but the Good" (v. 11), specifically by continuing his acts of hospitality. George Parsenios notes the close similarity between 3 John and letters of recommendation, introduction, and commendation from the ancient world (2014, 148–49; cf. Libanius, *Epis. Styles* 8, 55;

Demetrius, *Eloc.* 2). Third John is "proof of support for a person abroad, a passport of sorts, identifying that the person should be treated and given a certain kind of privilege. Given this background," Parsenios concludes, "we should assume that 3 John is being carried by Demetrius as he travels to Gaius" (149). Even though Demetrius is also a stranger (*xenos*) to Gaius, the Elder is hopeful that their shared love/loyalty will result in Gaius's acceptance (and defense) of him despite Diotrephes and the opposition he represents (v. 10).

The Elder uses language that resonates with larger Johannine themes of appropriate recognition (see below). The Elder describes Gaius as "doing faithfulness (*poieis piston*) whenever [he] should work for the brothers" (v. 5). Moreover, the Elder says Gaius does "well" (*kalōs*) when he sends these brothers out "in a manner worthy of God" (v. 6). The translation of *kalōs* with the simple word "well" does not capture the nuance this word carries in Johannine tradition (cf. John 4:17; 8:48; 13:13; 18:23). While it can simply mean "well," as in a "good job," this adverb is related to the adjective that Jesus uses to describe himself as the "good" or "noble shepherd" (*kalos*, 10:11, 14), his works (10:32-33), and the type of wine he provides at Cana (2:10). Jane Heath suggests that in the Gospel of John, the language of *kalos*, along with *agathos*, is part of the "discussion of *unity*" between the Father and Son (530, emphasis original). Picking up on the use of these terms to describe God's singular goodness in Second Temple Jewish writings, Heath argues that John's calling Jesus "good" or "noble" is his interpretation of the *Shema* through his Christology: Jesus *is* good, just as God is good, because he is part of the divine unity. When Gaius does "well" or "nobly," therefore, he acts in ways that are also consistent with this unity.

Brown does show, however, that the statement "to do well" (*poien kalōs*) is a standard formula for requests in ancient letters (1982, 792). Nevertheless, the Elder's Johannine perspective influences how he uses such language, just as it did in his previous statement that Gaius is "doing faithfulness." Even though the Elder imitates his literary context by issuing a request with the same words (you do well), what he means by "good" is shaped by the underlying Jesus story: the Elder is asking Gaius to continue imitating Jesus' goodness by welcoming the visitor who comes in truth (this time Demetrius) on the basis of testimony, that is, on the basis of faith rather than sight (20:29; 21:24-25).

Indeed, asking Gaius to continue doing "faithfulness" (*piston*) resonates with Jesus' command for Thomas in John 20:27 to "become faithful" (*ginou . . . pistos*). Thomas responds with the most elevated confession of Jesus' identity in the Gospel, calling him "My Lord and my God" (20:28). In return, however, Jesus does not bless Thomas but instead blesses all those who believe (or trust) in spite of not seeing Jesus in person (20:29). Gaius, like the general audience of the Gospel, must rely on testimony (*martyria*) rather than on his own sight. Thus, in 3 John "testimony" is an important motif and test: if Gaius trusts, believes, and loves the Elder, he will accept not only his teaching but also his representative, Demetrius (comp. 3 John 12; John 19:35; 21:24). This acceptance, as in the Gospel, is not without risk. Bringing Demetrius into his home means Gaius could be expelled from his faith community (v. 10), just like the man born blind (John 9:34-35).

Blame for Diotrephes: Wickedness from the Love of Being First (vv. 9-10)
Moving to the center of the letter, the Elder describes his opponent. Unlike the other Johannine writings, 3 John provides a name: Diotrephes. This name means "nurtured by God," and while not nearly as common as Gaius, it was common enough that it is also impossible to pinpoint his identity outside of this reference in 3 John (Brown 1982, 716). Diotrephes's description contrasts sharply with that of Gaius, the Elder, and those allied with him.

Introducing Diotrephes in v. 9, the Elder writes, "I wrote something to the assembly, but the one seeking to be first among them (*ho philoprōteuōn autōn*), Diotrephes, does not welcome us." The Elder's explanation for writing resembles other language in the Johannine writings, where the authors give different purpose statements (1 John 2:1, 7-8, 12-14, 21, 26; 5:13; 2 John 5, 12; John 20:30-31; 21:24-25). The description of Diotrephes, however, as "the one seeking to be first among them," is a unique feature; this is the only time the verb *philoprōteuō* (or the related words *philoprōton, philoprōteia*) is used in the NT.

To "desire" or "seek to be first" is a vice, a desire wrought from too much self-love. Plutarch argues that "tranquility of mind" is disturbed when people "do not manage their impulses" (*Tranq. an.* 12.471d–e). "And self-love (*philautia*) is chiefly to blame, which makes men *eager to be first* and to be victorious in everything and insatiably desirous of engaging in everything" (Helmbold, LCL). Elsewhere, Plutarch quotes Sophocles as saying,

> he was glad to have escaped, now that he was old, from sexual love, as from a cruel and raging tyrant; but in public life one must escape, not from one tyrant, the love of boys and women, but from many loves which are more insane than that: love of contention, love of fame, *the desire to be first and greatest*, which is a disease most prolific of envy, jealousy, and discord. (*An seni* 8 [Helmbold, LCL])

Plutarch ascribes this vice to contentious leaders of the past, including Alcibiades, the famous Athenian general turned traitor during the Peloponnesian War (*Alc.* 2.1), and the Athenian tyrant, Peisistratus (*Sol.* 29.1–3). Both Peisistratus and Alcibiades were chameleons, able to charm crowds with apparent magnanimity, but all the time simply wanting prestige for themselves alone. Both men were willing to go to any extreme in order to win: Alcibiades cheats, betrays, and conspires to lead the Athenians into unwise battles while Peisistratus inflicts fake battle wounds to provoke the Athenians to war. Rather than leading their followers to peace, these men sow dissention and violence (see also Cassius Dio, *Hist.* 9.40).

To call Diotrephes "the one seeking to be first among them" is, therefore, the same as calling him a tyrant. Like Peisistratus, he rules over the assembly with force and falseness: not only does he not welcome the brothers sent by the Elder; he also spreads "evil words" by "talking nonsense" or "playing the fool" (*phlyareō*; LSJ). From his position of power, he even "casts out from the assembly" (*ek tēs ekklēsias ekballei*, v. 10) anyone who challenges him. Diotrephes puts on a show to deceive, and he takes out his wrath on those who dare usurp him. The implication is, therefore, that Diotrephes's treachery will out him just as it did Alcibiades and Peisistratus, but at the cost of much suffering by those under his rule. The Elder, like Solon and Nicias long before him (Plutarch, *Nic.* 9.1–2; *Alc* 18.1–2; *Sol.* 29.3), sees through the act and seeks to "liberate" the assembly from the tyrant Diotrephes. The Elder himself will arrive soon, but in the meantime, he is sending Demetrius as his emissary in order to gauge if Gaius is his ally.

The Elder also uses emphatic pronouns (a feature common to all the Johannine writings) to draw connections and divisions in vv. 3, 8, 10, and 12. In v. 3, he underscores Gaius's positive behavior: "just as you yourself (*sy*) continue walking in truth." In vv. 8 and 12, the emphasis is on "we": "We ourselves (*hēmeis*), therefore, ought to continue receiving (*hypolambanein*) ones such as these so that we might become co-workers (*synergoi*) in truth" (v. 10); "And we ourselves (*hēmeis*) are continuing to testify, and you know that our testimony is true" (v. 12). In v. 8, the "we" includes Gaius (cf. 1 John 1:6–2:3), while in v. 12 it is an authoritative "we" whom Gaius is to trust, similar to the language of 1 John 1:1-5. Diotrephes is described with an emphatic pronoun in v. 10: "And not satisfied with this, he himself (*autos*) does not welcome the brothers and forbids the ones wishing [to welcome them] and throws them out of the assembly." Because he does not receive (*hypolambanein*, v. 4) the brethren with the Elder, the Elder promises to "remember" (*hypomnēsō*) Diotrephes's works "which he does with evil words by bringing unjust charges against us (*hēmas*)" (v. 10; cf. 2 John

11). The battle in 3 John is in large part one of words and the actions they inspire: positive words are given in commendation of Gaius, the brothers, and Demetrius versus Diotrephes's "evil words" and "nonsense." The Elder praises Gaius but also challenges him: his actions of welcoming or rejecting Demetrius will reveal whom he believes—and whom he loves.

Recommending Demetrius: An Opportunity to Imitate the Good (vv. 11-12)

In v. 11, the Elder addresses Gaius directly again with the title "Beloved" (*agapēte*, v. 5). Instead of another request for Gaius to continue offering hospitality, in v. 11 the Elder issues a clear command: "Do not imitate the Wicked (*to kakon*), but the Good (*to agathon*). The one doing good is from God; the one doing evil has not seen God." The Elder uses the present tense in his prohibition *mē mimou*, which could be translated "stop imitating," thus indicating that Gaius may be influenced, or at least intimidated, by Diotrephes's prohibitions despite the praise for him in vv. 3-8.

The contrast of these specific terms for "wicked" (*kakos*) and "good" (*agathos*) is not found elsewhere in the Johannine writings, but both of these words do appear in the Gospel and Letters of John. "Wicked," *kakos*, and its comparative *cheirōn* are used three times in the Gospel (5:14; 18:23, 30), once as a contrast to *kalōs* (John 18:23; 3 John 6). In John 18, Jesus is accused of doing *kakos*, but there is no one to testify to that fact. As Ruth Sheridan (2015) and Jane Heath (525–28) note in their analyses of John 7–8, the Jews (and especially the religious leaders) perceive Jesus as a threat to their monotheistic faith—meaning he is a false prophet and, thus, deserving of death, specifically by stoning (Deut 13:10). The irony of John is that Jesus is *agathos* and *kalos* (1:46; 2:10; 7:12; 10:11, 14, 32-33) in the same way that God alone is. Those who reject him as God's messenger who speaks truth (*alētheia*, 8:31, 32, 40, 44, 45, 46) are doing *kakos*.

Just as the traditions embedded in the Tabernacles section of the Gospel of John (7–10) figure prominently in 1 John, they also seem to lurk in the background of 3 John. Indeed, the use of *agathos* in 3 John 11 may provide a clue to the theological debate behind the scenes. Returning to Heath, she argues that the crowd's "grumbling" division in John 7:12 is much more than just a query of Jesus' general "goodness"; instead it is a statement comparing Jesus to the Good that is God alone. In John 7:12, the crowd debates, saying, "He is Good (*agathos estin*)," and others, "No! but he is deceiving (*plana*) the crowd" (cf. *planaō* in Deut 13; John 7:47; 1 John 1:8; 2:26; 3:7; *planos*, 2 John 7). Whether or not Jesus is "the Good"—that is, the embodiment and realization of God's goodness on earth in accordance with the messianic expectation associated with Tabernacles—or a deceiver is crucial to determining the crowd's reaction to him (Deut 18:15-20). Like the Israelites gathered around Mt. Horeb, the crowd must determine "the good and the wicked (*to agathon kai to kakon*)" (Deut 30:15). The crowd in John, unfortunately, misjudges Jesus' identity and chooses wrong (*kakos*, John 7:24; 8:59; 10:31; 18:20).

In 3 John Gaius has a chance to get things right. Will he imitate "the Good" shown to him in the life and works of Jesus, or will he imitate "the Wicked" of the world who rejected him? In this narrative setup, Demetrius stands in Jesus' stead, and his acceptance or rejection is paralleled to Jesus' divine visitation into the world. Third John 12 reinforces this reading by confirming the Elder's testimony on Demetrius's behalf with the phrase "and you know that our testimony is true." This is the same slogan that accompanies the Gospel's description of the Beloved Disciple's witness about Jesus in John 19:35 and 21:24-25. Demetrius is proven not only by this testimony but also by the witness of "the truth itself" (*autēs tēs alētheias*), a description used for Jesus and the Spirit in the Gospel and 1 John (John 14:6, 17; 15:26; 16:13; 1 John 5:6). The implication is, therefore, that in rejecting the Elder's emissaries, Diotrephes also rejects Jesus as "the Good" and "the Truth" (John 7:12; cf. 1:46). Gaius should choose differently; he should do well (*kalōs* v. 6; *agathos* v. 11).

It is impossible to determine with exact precision whether or not Diotrephes's rejection is connected to the larger debates of the Gospel and 1–2 John. Nevertheless, since Johannine interpretations of the *Shema*, and Jesus' place in the divine unity, run in the background of its use of *agathos*, it is possible. Indeed, the Elder continues that "the one doing good is from God (*ek theou*)," the same language that 1 John uses to describe the children of God and those who acknowledge Jesus' identity as the Christ, Son of God, True God, and Eternal Life (5:18-21). In contrast, "the one doing wickedness has not seen God" (3 John 11). This description mirrors several passages in the Gospel and 1 John. In the Gospel, Jesus rectifies the fact that "no one has seen God before" by manifesting God's glory, truth, and grace in the world (John 1:18; 3:32; 6:46; 14:9). First John 4:20 repeats this understanding, and 3:6 emphasizes that it is by seeing Jesus, the one sent to destroy the works of the devil, that believers are able to stop sinning. In the Gospel and 1 John, therefore, no one can "see" God without seeing—that is, recognizing—Jesus as his Son and Christ. Second John 9 concurs: "Each one who leads astray (*proagōn*) and does not remain in the teaching of Christ does not have God; the one who remains in the teaching, this one has both the Father and the Son."

Closing Greetings from the Friends (vv. 13-15)

Third John ends with greetings that are strikingly similar to those of 2 John, but more urgent: "I have many things to write to you, but I do not wish to write to you by ink and reed. Rather I hope immediately to see you, and we will speak face to face. Peace to you. The friends (*philoi*) greet you. Greet the friends (*philoi*) by name" (3 John 13-15). The Elder expresses his need to share more with Gaius, but promises that he will come "immediately" (*eutheōs*) so they can continue the conversation face to face (lit. *stoma pros stoma*) rather than through writing (or through Demetrius). The Elder's decision to visit also ensures that he will personally see whether or not Gaius has obeyed his commands and that his promise "to remember" Diotrephes's wickedness will be enacted (v. 10).

The Elder's words, "peace to you (*eirēnē soi*)," imitate those of Jesus, which he gives to his disciples after his resurrection and return to the Father in John 20:19, 21, and 26. In the Gospel of John, only Jesus can give peace: "Peace I leave for you, my peace I give to you. Not just as the world gives do I give to you. Do not let your heart be troubled or be fearful" (14:27; cf. 16:33). The Elder also greets with "peace" in 2 John 3 but uses the future tense to describe what "will be" for the believers. The issuance of "peace" in 3 John, therefore, resonates with Jesus' promise to the Johannine community, and the Elder's ability to speak it for Gaius once again associates him with his Lord (cf. the use of *prosōpopoiia* in 1 John). The Elder is in continuity with Jesus by speaking in accordance with him; he can offer "peace" because he is connected to the peace that comes from God alone.

Finally, as in 2 John, the Elder closes with "greetings." Rather than an Elect Sister and children, however, this time the greetings are shared between "friends" (*philoi*). The term "friends" also reflects traditions from the Gospel of John and continues the Elder's distinction of those who are allied with him and those who oppose him. In the Gospel, John (the Baptist) characterizes himself as Jesus' "friend" in 3:29 because he prepares the way for Jesus to take center stage. In 11:11, Lazarus is called a "friend" of Jesus before Jesus travels to raise him from the dead. In John 15:13-15, Jesus defines what it means to be his "friend," saying (1) friends show their "love" (*agapē*) by laying down their lives (*psychē*) for each other; (2) the disciples are his friends "if they should do the things I am commanding (*entellomai*) you" (15:14); and (3) friends know each other's plans just as Jesus has revealed the Father's will to them (15:15). Not only are the disciples "friends" with Jesus; but Jesus says they are also friends of God who "loves (*philei*) you because you have loved (*pephilēkēte*) me and have believed that I came from God" (16:27).

To use the language of "friends" in 3 John, therefore, the Elder closes with a final reminder of the stakes in this battle of words: to ally with the Elder is to remain a friend not just to him but also to the community and God whom he represents, the Good. In contrast, to ally (or submit) to Diotrephes is to ally with the Wicked and with a tyrant, who does not display the selfless love demonstrated by the true friendship of Jesus (John 15:12-15) but who will always desire to be first himself. This is the false peace of the world. The Elder seeks, instead, to keep Gaius in true peace. This does not mean being free of pain or suffering to have "prosperity" in the world's sense, but it is to live a life mimicking the Good made visible in the true testimony of Jesus the Christ. Certainly this can lead to suffering, but it also leads to the peace that comes from authentic friendships, grounded in God's type of love.

Theological Threads

Third John, the shortest letter of the NT, is too short to have a developed theological perspective on its own. As a part of the Johannine corpus, however, we see that it resonates with the theology of the other writings explored in this commentary. In particular, 3 John participates in the larger Johannine theme of recognition: can one recognize the ones God has sent as messengers of the truth, or do they mistake these messengers for deceivers? As Kasper Bro Larsen (2008) notes, the entire Gospel of John is full of recognition type scenes that emphasize this motif. Jesus is the messenger sent by God, but he is mistaken as a false prophet, one who leads the people astray by "making himself equal to God" and "God's Son," thereby threatening Jewish monotheism (John 5:18; 10:33; 19:7). According to Deuteronomy, therefore, Jesus is deserving of capital punishment, specifically by stoning (Deut 13:10; 17:6; 18:20). The tragedy of the Gospel, therefore, is one of blindness: the world does not recognize its Creator come down in flesh. Instead, the world accepts false gods, such as Rome (John 19:12), seeks glory from mortals (5:40-47; 7:18; 12:42), and fearfully submits to diabolical tyranny (11:45-54; 12:31; 14:30; 16:11).

Third John does not repeat the Gospel narrative, but it does resonate with these general themes. Instead of accepting or rejecting Jesus, Gaius is now faced with the decision of trusting the Elder and his emissary, Demetrius. Does he believe that Demetrius carries "the truth" as the Elder and the brethren testify in v. 12? Or will he submit to Diotrephes's tyrannical desire to be first, regardless of the cost to the community around him? The notion of hospitality in 3 John, just as in the Gospel, is a theological issue because it exposes what one believes and who one loves or fears. The Elder knows that there is risk in this choice, but he and Diotrephes (and perhaps

Gaius) see the risk differently. For the Elder, being cast out of the assembly by Diotrephes is difficult, but ultimately it is a cost one should be willing to pay (cf. John 9:34-35; 12:42-43; 16:2). Departure from Diotrephes means that one is a friend of God: one who shares in "doing good," seeing God, and experiencing love in truth and in true community. After all, separation from Diotrephes's assembly does not mean Gaius will be alone but rather that he will have a new family of siblings, brothers and sisters, and true friends, including the Elder, Demetrius, and the Father and his Son, Jesus Christ.

Works Cited

Akala, Adesola Joan. *The Son-Father Relationship and Christological Symbolism in the Gospel of John.* LNTS 505. London: Bloomsbury T&T Clark, 2014.

Aland, Kurt and Barbara. *The Text of the New Testament: An Introduction to the Critical Editions and to the Theory and Practice of Modern Textual Criticism.* Revised. Grand Rapids: Eerdmans, 1995.

Alter, Robert. *The Art of Biblical Narrative.* New York: Basic Books, 1981.

Anderson, Paul N. "The Community that Raymond Brown Left Behind: Reflections on the Johannine Dialectical Situation." Pages 47–93 in *Communities in Dispute: Current Scholarship on the Johannine Epistles.* Edited by R. Alan Culpepper and Paul N. Anderson. ECL 13. Atlanta: SBL Press, 2014.

———. *The Fourth Gospel and the Quest for Jesus: Modern Foundations Reconsidered.* T&T Clark Biblical Studies. London: T&T Clark, 2006.

———. *The Riddles of the Fourth Gospel: An Introduction to John.* Minneapolis: Fortress, 2011.

Arterbury, Andrew E. "Breaking the Betrothal Bonds: Hospitality in John 4." *CBQ* 72 (2010): 63–83.

———. *Entertaining Angels: Early Christian Hospitality in its Mediterranean Setting.* NTM 8. Sheffield: Sheffield Phoenix, 2005.

Ashton, John. "Really a Prologue?" Pages 27–44 in *The Prologue of the Gospel of John: Its Literary, Theological, and Philosophical Contexts. Papers read at the Colloquium Ioanneaum 2013.* Edited by Jan G. van der Watt, R. Alan Culpepper, Udo Schnelle. WUNT 359. Tübingen: Mohr Siebeck, 2016.

Attridge, Harold W. "Argumentation in John 5." Pages 188–99 in *Rhetorical Argumentation in Biblical Texts: Essays from the Lund 2000 Conference*. Edited by Anders Eriksson, Thomas H. Olbricht, and Walter Übelacker. ESEC 8. Harrisburg: Trinity Press International, 2002a.

———. "'Don't Be Touching Me': Recent Feminist Scholarship on Mary Magdalene." Pages 140–66 in *A Feminist Companion to John. Vol II*. Edited by Amy-Jill Levine with Marianne Blickenstaff. Cleveland: Pilgrim Press, 2003.

———. "Genre Bending in the Fourth Gospel." *JBL* 121 (2002b): 3–21.

———. "How Priestly Is the 'High Priestly Prayer' of John 17." *CBQ* 75 (2013): 1–14.

Barker, James W. *John's Use of Matthew*. Minneapolis: Fortress, 2015.

Baron, Lori. "Interpreting the *Shema*: Liturgy and Identity in the Fourth Gospel." *Annali di storia dell'esegesi* 27 (2010): 53–60.

———. "The Shema in John's Gospel and Jewish Restoration Eschatology." Pages 165–73 in *John and Judaism: A Contested Relationship in Context*. Edited by R. Alan Culpepper and Paul N. Anderson. SBLRBS 87. Atlanta: SBL Press, 2017.

Bauckham, Richard. *The Testimony of the Beloved Disciple: Narrative, History, and Theology in the Gospel of John*. Grand Rapids: Baker, 2007.

Beavis, Mary Ann. "Reconsidering Mary of Bethany." *CBQ* 74 (2012): 281–97.

Bennema, Cornelis. *Encountering Jesus: Character Studies in the Gospel of John*. 2d ed. Minneapolis: Fortress Press, 2014.

———. *The Power of Saving Wisdom: An Investigation of Spirit and Wisdom in Relations to the Soteriology of the Fourth Gospel*. Reprint. Eugene: Wipf & Stock, 2007.

Bernier, Jonathan. Aposynagōgos *and the Historical Jesus in John: Rethinking the Historicity of the Johannine Expulsion Passages*. BIS 122. Leiden: Brill, 2013.

Beutler, Johannes. "Resurrection and the Forgiveness of Sins. John 20:23 against Its Traditional Background." Pages 237–51 in *The Resurrection of Jesus in the Gospel of John*. Edited by Craig R. Koester and Reimund Bieringer. WUNT 222. Tübingen: Mohr Siebeck, 2008.

de Boer, Esther A. *The Gospel of Mary: Beyond a Gnostic and a Biblical Mary Magdalene*. LNTS 260. London: T&T Clark, 2004.

de Boer, Martinus C. "The Depiction of 'the Jews' in John's Gospel: Matters of Behavior and Identity." Pages 141–57 in *Anti-Judaism and the Fourth Gospel*. Edited by Reimund Bieringer, Didier Pollefeyt, and Frederique Vandecasteele-Vanneuville. Louisville: Westminster John Knox, 2001.

———. "Jesus' Departure to the Father in John: Death or Resurrection?" Pages 1–19 in *Theology and Christology in the Fourth Gospel: Essays by the Members of the SNTS Johannine Writings Seminar*. Edited by G. van Belle, J. G. van der Watt, and P. Martiz. BETL 184. Leuven: Leuven University Press, 2005.

———. *Johannine Perspectives on the Death of Jesus*. CBET 17. Kampen: Pharos, 1996.

Borgen, Peder. *Bread from Heaven: An Exegetical Study of the Concept of Manna in the Gospel of John and the Writings of Philo*. NovTSup 10. Leiden: Brill, 1965.

Boyarin, Daniel. "The Gospel of the *Memra*: Jewish Binitarianism and the Prologue to John." *HTR* 94 (2001): 243–84.

Brant, Jo-Ann A. *Dialogue and Drama: Elements of Greek Tragedy in the Fourth Gospel*. Peabody: Hendrickson, 2004.

———. *John*. PCNT. Grand Rapids: Baker Academic, 2011.

Brown, Raymond E. *The Community of the Beloved Disciple*. New York: Paulist Press, 1979.

———. *The Epistles of John*. AB 30. Garden City: Doubleday, 1982.

———. *The Gospel according to St. John*. AB 29-29A. Garden City: Doubleday, 1966–70.

Brown, Raymond E., and Francis J. Moloney. *An Introduction to the Gospel of John*. ABRL. Garden City: Doubleday, 2003.

Brown, Sherri. "Believing in the Gospel of John: The Ethical Imperative to Becoming Children of God." Pages 3–24 in *Johannine Ethics: The Moral World of the Gospel and Epistles of John.* Edited by Sherri Brown and Christopher W. Skinner. Minneapolis: Fortress, 2017.

———. "Water Imagery and the Power of Presence in the Gospel of John." *Theology Today* 72 (2015a): 289–98.

———. "What's in an Ending? John 21 and the Performative Force of an Epilogue." *PRSt* 42 (2015b): 29–42.

Brown, Sherri, and Christopher W. Skinner, eds. *Johannine Ethics: The Moral World of the Gospels and Epistles of John.* Minneapolis: Fortress, 2017.

Brunson, Andrew C. *Psalm 118 in the Gospel of John: An Intertextual Study on the New Exodus Pattern in the Theology of John.* WUNT 2/158. Tübingen: Mohr Siebeck, 2003.

Buch-Hansen, Gitte. *"It Is the Spirit that Gives Life": A Stoic Understanding of Pneuma in John's Gospel.* BZNT 173. Berlin: de Gruyter, 2010.

Bultmann, Rudolf. "New Testament and Mythology: The Problem of Demythologizing the New Testament Proclamation (1941)." Pages 1–45 in *New Testament and Mythology and Other Basic Writings.* Edited and translated by Schubert M. Ogden. Minneapolis: Fortress, 1989.

———. *Theology of the New Testament.* Orig. 1951–55. Translated by Kendrick Grobel. Waco: Baylor University Press, 2007.

Burge, Gary M. *The Anointed Community: The Holy Spirit in the Johannine Tradition.* Grand Rapids: Eerdmans, 1987.

Burridge, Richard. *What are the Gospels? A Comparison with Graeco-Roman Biography.* 2d ed. Grand Rapids: Eerdmans, 2004.

Bynum, William Randolph. "Quotations of Zechariah in the Fourth Gospel." Pages 47–74 in *Abiding Words: Perspectives on the Use of Scripture in the Gospel of John.* Edited by Alicia D. Myers and Bruce G. Schuchard. SBLRBS 81. Atlanta: SBL Press, 2015.

Byron, John. "Slaughter, Fratricide and Sacrilege: Cain and Abel Traditions in 1 John 3." *Bib* 88 (2007): 526–34.

Cambron-Goulet, Mathilde. "The Criticism—and Practice—of Literacy in the Ancient Philosophical Tradition." Pages 201–26 in *Orality, Literacy and Performance in the Ancient World*. Edited by Elizabeth Minchin. Leiden: Brill, 2012.

Carter, Warren. "Festivals, Cultural Intertextuality, and the Gospel of John's Rhetoric of Distance." *HTS* 67/1 (2011): Art. #802, 7 pages. DOI:10.4102/hts.v67i1.802.

———. *John and Empire: Initial Explorations*. New York: T&T Clark, 2008.

Clark-Soles, Jaime. "John, First–Third John, and Revelation." Pages 333–78 in *The Bible and Disability: A Commentary*. Edited by Sarah J. Melcher, Mikeal C. Parsons, and Amos Yong. Waco: Baylor University Press, 2017.

———. *The Scripture Cannot Be Broken: The Social Function of the Use of Scripture in the Fourth Gospel*. Leiden: Brill, 2003.

Cohen, Shaye J. D. *The Beginnings of Jewishness: Boundaries, Varieties, Uncertainties*. Hellenistic Culture and Society. Berkeley: University of California Press, 2001.

Coloe, Mary L. "Gentiles in the Gospel of John: Narrative Possibilities— John 12:12–43." Pages 209–23 in *Attitudes to Gentiles in Ancient Judaism and Early Christianity*. LNTS 499. Edited by David C. Sim and James S. McLaren. London: Bloomsbury/T&T Clark, 2013a.

———. *God Dwells with Us: Temple Symbolism in the Fourth Gospel*. Collegeville MN: Liturgical Press, 2001.

———. "The Johannine Pentecost: John 1.19–2.12." *ABR* 55 (2007): 41–56.

———. "Like Father, Like Son: The Role of Abraham in Tabernacles— John 8:31–59." *Pacifica* 12 (1999): 1–11.

———. "The Structure of the Johannine Prologue and Genesis 1." *ABR* 45 (1997): 40–55.

———. "The Woman of Samaria: Her Characterization, Narrative, and Theological Significance." Pages 182–96 in *Characters and Characterization in the Gospel of John*. Edited by Christopher W. Skinner. LNTS 461. London: Bloomsbury T&T Clark, 2013b.

Conway, Colleen. *Behold the Man: Jesus and Greco-Roman Masculinity.*
Oxford: Oxford University Press, 2008.

———. "Speaking through Ambiguity: Minor Characters in the Fourth
Gospel." *BibInt* 10 (2002): 324–41.

Corbeill, Anthony. *Nature Embodied: Gesture in Ancient Rome.* Princeton:
Princeton University Press, 2003.

Croy, N. Clayton. "The Messianic Whippersnapper: Did Jesus Use a Whip
on People in the Temple (John 2:15)?" *JBL* 128 (2009): 555–68.

Culpepper, R. Alan. *Anatomy of the Fourth Gospel: A Study in Literary
Design.* Philadelphia: Fortress Press, 1983.

———. *The Gospel and Letters of John.* Interpreting Biblical Texts. Nashville: Abingdon, 1998.

———. "The Johannine *Hypodeigma*: A Reading of John 13." *Sem* 53
(1991): 133–52.

———. *The Johannine School: An Evaluation of the Johannine-school
Hypothesis Based on an Investigation of the Nature of Ancient Schools.*
SBLDS 26. Missoula: Scholars, 1975.

———. "Peter as Exemplary Disciple in John 21:15–19." *PRSt* 37 (2010):
165–78.

———. "The Pivot of John's Prologue." *NTS* 27 (1981): 1–31.

———. "The Prologue as Theological Prolegomenon to the Gospel of
John." Pages 3–26 in *The Prologue of the Gospel of John: Its Literary,
Theological, and Philosophical Contexts. Papers read at the Collo-
quium Ioanneaum 2013.* Edited by Jan G. van der Watt, R. Alan
Culpepper, and Udo Schnelle. WUNT 359. Tübingen: Mohr
Siebeck, 2016.

———. "The Relationship between the Gospel of John and 1 John."
Pages 93–119 in *Communities in Dispute: Current Scholarship on
the Johannine Epistles.* Edited by R. Alan Culpepper and Paul N.
Anderson. ECL 13. Atlanta: SBL Press, 2014.

Culpepper, R. Alan and Paul N. Anderson, eds. *John and Judaism: A
Contested Relationship in Context.* SBLRBS 87. Atlanta: SBL Press,
2017.

Culy, Martin M. *Echoes of Friendship in the Gospel of John.* NTM 30. Sheffield: Sheffield Phoenix, 2010.

Daly-Denton, Margaret. *David in the Fourth Gospel: The Johannine Reception of the Psalms.* AGJU 47. Leiden: Brill, 2000.

Daise, Michael A. *Feasts in John: Jewish Festivals and Jesus' 'Hour' in the Fourth Gospel.* WUNT 2/229. Tübingen: Mohr Siebeck, 2007.

Dixon, Suzanne. *The Roman Mother.* Norman: University of Oklahoma Press, 1987.

Dodd, C. H. *Historical Tradition in the Fourth Gospel.* Cambridge: Cambridge University Press, 1963.

Douglas, Mary. "Sacred Contagion." Pages 86–106 in *Reading Leviticus: A Conversation with Mary Douglas.* Edited by John F. A. Sawyer. JSOT 227. Sheffield: Sheffield Academic, 1996.

Engberg-Pedersen, Troels. *Friendship, Flattery, and Frankness of Speech: Studies on Friendship in the New Testament World.* NovTSup 82. Leiden: Brill, 2014.

———. *John and Philosophy: A New Reading of the Fourth Gospel.* Oxford: Oxford University Press, 2017.

———. "A Question of Genre: John 13–17 as *Paraklēsis.*" Pages 283–302 in *The Gospel of John as Genre Mosaic.* Edited by Kasper Bro Larsen. SANT 3. Göttingen: Vandenhoeck & Ruprecht, 2015.

Evans, Craig A. *To See and Not Perceive: Isaiah 6.9–10 in Early Jewish and Christian Interpretation.* JSOT Sup 64. Sheffield: Sheffield Academic, 1989.

Fehribach, Adele. "The 'Birthing' Bridegroom: The Portrayal of Jesus in the Fourth Gospel." Pages 104–29 in *A Feminist Companion to the Gospel of John. Vol. 2.* Edited by Amy-Jill Levine with Marianne Blickenstaff. Cleveland: Pilgrim Press, 2003.

Flemming, Rebecca. *Medicine and the Making of Roman Women: Gender, Nature, and Authority from Celsus to Galen.* Oxford: Oxford University Press, 2000.

Frey, Jörg. *The Glory of the Crucified One: Christology and Theology in the Gospel of John.* Waco: Baylor University Press, 2018.

Gaventa, Beverly Roberts. "The Archive of Excess: John 21 and the Problem of Narrative Closure." Pages 220–39 in *Exploring the Gospel of John*. Edited by R. Alan Culpepper and C. Clifton Black. Louisville: Westminster John Knox, 1996.

———. *Mary: Glimpses of the Mother of Jesus*. Minneapolis: Fortress, 1999.

Glancy, Jennifer. *Slavery in Early Christianity*. 2nd ed. Minneapolis: Fortress, 2006.

———. "Torture: Flesh, Truth, and the Fourth Gospel." *BibInt* 13 (2005): 107–36.

Gleason, Maud W. *Making Men: Sophists and Self-Presentation in Ancient Rome*. Princeton: Princeton University Press, 1995.

Gregory, Andrew. "The Third Gospel? The Relationship of John and Luke Reconsidered." Pages 109–34 in *Challenging Perspectives on the Gospel of John*. Edited by John Lierman. WUNT 2/219. Tübingen: Mohr Siebeck, 2006.

Griffith, Terry. *Keep Yourselves from Idols: A New Look at 1 John*. JSNT 233. Sheffield: Sheffield Academic, 2002.

Gruen, Erich S. *Diaspora: Jews amidst Greeks and Romans*. Cambridge: Harvard University Press, 2004.

Harstine, Stan. *Moses as a Character in the Fourth Gospel: A Study of Ancient Reading Techniques*. JSNTSup 229. Sheffield: Sheffield Academic, 2002.

Hartsock, Chad. *Sight and Blindness in Luke-Acts: The Use of Physical Features in Characterization*. Leiden: Brill, 2008.

Hasitschka, Martin. "The Significance of the Resurrection Appearance in John 21." Pages 311–28 in *The Resurrection of Jesus in the Gospel of John*. Edited by Craig R. Koester and Reimund Bieringer. WUNT 222. Tübingen: Mohr Siebeck, 2008.

Hays, Richard B. *Echoes of Scripture in the Gospels*. Waco TX: Baylor University Press, 2016.

Heath, Jane. "Some were saying, 'He is Good' (John 7.12b): 'Good' Christology in John's Gospel." *NTS* 56 (2010): 513–35.

Heil, John Paul. *Blood and Water: The Death and Resurrection of Jesus John 18–21*. CBQMS 27. Washington DC: CBA, 1995.

Heilmann, Jan. "A Meal in the Background of John 6:51–58?" *JBL* 137 (2018): 481–500.

Hill, Charles. E. *The Johannine Corpus in the Early Church.* Oxford: Oxford University Press, 2004.

Holmes, Christopher T. "Gestures to the Priesthood: Exploring Jesus' Priestly Function in 1 John," *RevExp* 114 (2017): 564–73.

Hooker, Morna D. "Artemis of Ephesus." *JTS* 64 (2013): 37–46.

Huizenga, Leroy A. *The New Isaac: Tradition and Intertextuality in the Gospel of Matthew.* NovTSup 131. Leiden: Brill, 2009.

Hylen, Susan E. *Imperfect Believers: Ambiguous Characters in the Gospel of John.* Louisville: Westminster John Knox, 2009.

Ilan, Tal. *Jewish Women in Greco-Roman Palestine.* Peabody: Hendrickson, 1996.

Jones, Peter Rhea. *1, 2, and 3 John.* SHBC 29B. Macon: Smyth & Helwys, 2009.

———. "The Missional Role of ὁ ΠΡΕΣΒΥΤΕΡΟΣ." Pages 141–54 in *Communities in Dispute: Current Scholarship on the Johannine Epistles.* Edited by R. Alan Culpepper and Paul N. Anderson. ECL 13. Atlanta: SBL Press, 2014.

Keener, Craig S. *The Gospel of John.* 2 vols. Peabody: Hendrickson, 2003.

Keith, Chris. "Jesus the Galilean in the Gospel of John: The Significance of Earthly Origins in the Fourth Gospel." Pages 45–60 in *Portraits of Jesus in the Gospel of John: A Christological Spectrum.* Edited by Craig R. Koester. LNTS 589. London: T&T Clark/Bloomsbury, 2018.

———. *The* Pericope Adulterae, *the Gospel of John, and the Literacy of Jesus.* New Testament Tools, Studies and Documents 38. Leiden: Brill, 2009.

Kennedy, George A., ed. and trans. *Progymnasmata: Greek Textbooks of Prose Composition.* Atlanta: SBL, 2003.

Kessler, Gwynn. *Conceiving Israel: The Fetus in Rabbinic Narratives.* Divinations. Philadelphia: University of Pennsylvania Press, 2009.

King, Helen. *Hippocrates' Woman: Reading the Female Body in Ancient Greece.* London: Routledge, 1998.

King, Karen L. "The Gospel of Mary (BG 8502,1)." Pages 523–27 in *The Nag Hammadi Library in English*. Edited by James M. Robinson. San Francisco: Harper & Row, 1988.

——. *The Gospel of Mary: Jesus and the First Woman Apostle*. Santa Rosa: Polebridge, 2003.

Kinlaw, Pamela E. *The Christ Is Jesus: Metamorphosis, Possession, and Johannine Christology*. AB 18. Atlanta: SBL, 2005.

Klawans, Jonathan. *Impurity and Sin in Ancient Judaism*. Oxford: Oxford University Press, 2000.

——. *Purity, Sacrifice, and the Temple: Symbolism and Supersessionism in the Study of Ancient Judaism*. Oxford: Oxford University Press, 2006.

Klink, Edward W, III. *The Sheep of the Fold: The Audience and Origin of the Gospel of John*. SNTSMS 141. Cambridge: Cambridge University Press, 2007.

Koester, Craig R. "The Antichrist Theme in the Johannine Epistles and its Role in Christian Tradition." Pages 187–96 in *Communities in Dispute: Current Scholarship on the Johannine Epistles*. Edited by R. Alan Culpepper and Paul N. Anderson. ECL 13. Atlanta: SBL Press, 2014a.

——. "The Gospel of John as a Source for First-Century Judaism." Pages 59–76 in *John and Judaism: A Contested Relationship in Context*. Edited by R. Alan Culpepper and Paul N. Anderson. SBLRBS 87. Atlanta: SBL Press, 2017.

——. *Revelation: A New Translation with Introduction and Commentary*. AYB 38. New Haven: Yale University Press, 2014b.

——. "'The Savior of the World' (John 4:42)." *JBL* 109 (1990): 665–80.

——. "'Spirit' (*Pneuma*) in Greco-Roman Philosophy and the Gospel of John." Pages 235–50 in *The Prologue of the Gospel of John*. Edited by Jan G. van der Watt, R. Alan Culpepper, and Udo Schnelle. WUNT 359. Tübingen: Mohr Siebeck, 2016.

——. *Symbolism in the Fourth Gospel: Meaning, Mystery, Community*. 2nd ed. Minneapolis: Fortress, 2003.

——. *The Word of Life: A Theology of John's Gospel*. Grand Rapids: Eerdmans, 2008.

Koester, Helmut. "Ephesos in Early Christian Literature." Pages 119–40 in *Ephesos Metropolis of Asia: An Interdisciplinary Approach to its Archaeology, Religion, and Culture.* Edited by Helmut Koester. HTS 41. Valley Forge: Trinity Press International, 1995.

Köstenberger, Andreas J., and Scott R. Swain. *Father, Son, and Spirit: The Trinity and John's Gospel.* NSBT 24. Downers Grove: InterVarsity, 2008.

Kurek-Chomycz, Dominika A. "The Fragrance of Her Perfume: The Significance of Sense Imagery in John's Account of the Anointing in Bethany." *NovT* 52 (2010): 334–54.

Kysar, Robert. *Voyages with John: Charting the Fourth Gospel.* Waco: Baylor University Press, 2006.

Lamb, David A. *Text, Context and the Johannine Community: A Sociolinguistic Analysis of the Johannine Writings.* LNTS 477. London: Bloomsbury/T&T Clark, 2014.

Lappenga, Benjamin J. "Whose Zeal is it Anyway? The Citation of Psalm 69:9 in John 2:17 as a Double Entendre." Pages 141–60 in *Abiding Words: The Use of Scripture in the Gospel of John.* Edited by Alicia D. Myers and Bruce G. Schuchard. SBLRBS 81. Atlanta: SBL Press, 2015.

Larson, Kasper Bro. *Recognizing the Stranger: Recognition Scenes in the Gospel of John.* BibInt 93. Leiden: Brill, 2008.

Lee, Dorothy A. *Hallowed in Truth and Love: Spirituality in the Johannine Literature.* Eugene: Wipf and Stock, 2012.

———. "Martha and Mary: Levels of Characterization in Luke and John." Pages 197–220 in *Characters and Characterization in the Gospel of John.* Edited by Christopher W. Skinner. LNTS 461. Bloomsbury/T&T Clark, 2013.

Lee, John A. L. "The Puzzle of John 21:15–17: A Formality Solution." *NovT* 59 (2017): 27–30.

Lieu, Judith M. *I, II, & III John: A Commentary.* NTL. Louisville KY: Westminster John Knox, 2008.

———. "The Audience of the Johannine Epistles." Pages 123–40 in *Communities in Dispute: Current Scholarship on the Johannine Epistles.* Edited by R. Alan Culpepper and Paul N. Anderson. ECL 13. Atlanta: SBL Press, 2014.

————. "Blindness in the Johannine Tradition." *NTS* 34 (1988): 83–95.

————. *The Second and Third Epistles of John: History and Background.* Edited by John Riches. Edinburgh: T & T Clark, 1986.

————. *The Theology of the Johannine Epistles.* NTT. Cambridge: Cambridge University Press, 1991.

Lincoln, Andrew T. *Truth on Trial: The Lawsuit Motif in the Fourth Gospel.* Peabody: Hendrickson, 2000.

Lipsett, B. Diane. *Desiring Conversion: Hermas, Thecla, Aseneth.* Oxford: Oxford University Press, 2010.

Loader, William R. G. *The Johannine Epistles.* Epworth Commentaries. London: Epworth, 1992.

————. "The Significance of 2:15–17 for Understanding the Ethics of 1 John." Pages 223–35 in *Communities in Dispute: Current Scholarship on the Johannine Epistles.* Edited by R. Alan Culpepper and Paul N. Anderson. ECL 13. Atlanta: SBL Press, 2014.

Longenecker, Bruce W. *Rhetoric at the Boundaries: The Art and Theology of the New Testament Chain-Link Transitions.* Waco: Baylor University Press, 2005.

Manning, Gary T., Jr. *Echoes of a Prophet: The Use of Ezekiel in the Gospel of John and in Literature of the Second Temple Period.* LNTS 270. London: T&T Clark, 2004.

Matera, Frank J. *New Testament Theology: Exploring Diversity and Unity.* Louisville: Westminster John Knox, 2007.

Marcus, Joel. "Crucifixion as Parodic Exaltation." *JBL* 125 (2006): 73–87.

————. *Mark 1–8.* AB 27. New York: Doubleday, 2000.

Martin, Troy W. "Paul's Argument from Nature for the Veil in 1 Corinthians 11:13–15: A Testicle instead of a Head Covering." *JBL* 123 (2004): 75–84.

Martyn, J. Louis. *History & Theology in the Fourth Gospel.* Rev. ed. Nashville: Abingdon, 1979.

Matson, Mark A. *In Dialogue with another Gospel? The Influence of the Fourth Gospel on the Passion Narrative of the Gospel of Luke.* SBLDS 178. Atlanta: SBL, 2001.

McConnell, James R., Jr. *The* Topos *of Divine Testimony in Luke-Acts.* Eugene: Pickwick, 2014.

Mead, A. H. "The βασιλικός in John 4.46–53." *JSNT* 23 (1985): 69–72.

Meeks, Wayne A. "The Man from Heaven in Johannine Sectarianism." *JBL* 91 (1972): 44–72.

———. *The Prophet-King: Moses Traditions and the Johannine Christology.* NovTSup 14. Leiden: Brill, 1967.

Menken, Maarten J. J. *Old Testament Quotations in the Fourth Gospel: Studies in Textual Form.* CBET 15. Kampen: Pharos, 1996.

Meshel, Naphtali. *The 'Grammar' of Sacrifice with a 'Grammar' of Σ: A Generativist Study of the Israelite Sacrificial System in the Priestly Writings.* Oxford: Oxford University Press, 2014.

Minear, Paul S. "The Original Functions of John 21." *JBL* 102 (1983): 85–98.

Moffitt, David M. *Atonement and the Logic of Resurrection in the Epistle to the Hebrews.* NovT Sup 141. Leiden: Brill, 2011.

Moloney, Francis J. *Belief in the Word: Reading the Fourth Gospel: John 1–4.* Minneapolis MN: Fortress Press, 1993.

———. "'In the Bosom of' or 'Turned towards' the Father?" *ABR* 31 (1983): 63–71.

Moss, Candida R. "The Marks of the Nails: Scars, Wounds and the Resurrection of Jesus in John." *EC* 8 (2017): 48–68.

Moss, Candida R., and Joel S. Baden. *Reconceiving Infertility: Biblical Perspectives on Procreation and Childlessness.* Princeton: Princeton University Press, 2015.

Myers, Alicia D. *Blessed Among Women? Mothers and Motherhood in the New Testament.* Oxford: Oxford University Press, 2017a.

———. *Characterizing Jesus: A Rhetorical Analysis on the Fourth Gospel's Use of Scripture in Its Presentation of Jesus.* LNTS 458. London: T&T Clark, 2012.

———. "Gender, Rhetoric, and Recognition: Characterizing Jesus and (Re)defining Masculinity in the Gospel of John." *JSNT* 38 (2015): 191–218.

———. "'Jesus Said to Them . . .' : The Adaptation of Juridical Rhetoric in John 5:19–47." *JBL* 132 (2013): 415–30.

———. "Jesus the Son of God in John's Gospel: The Life-Making *Logos*." Pages 141–55 in *Portraits of Jesus in the Gospel of John: A Christological Spectrum.* Edited by Craig R. Koester. LNTS 589. London: T&T Clark/Bloomsbury, 2018a.

———. "Just Opponents? The Jews and Ethic Formation in the Gospel of John." Pages 159–76 in *Johannine Ethics: The Moral World of the Gospel and Epistles of John.* Edited by Sherri Brown and Christopher W. Skinner. Minneapolis: Fortress, 2017b.

———. "*Prosopopoetics* and Conflict: Speech and Expectations in John 8." *Bib* 92 (2011): 580–96.

———. "Remember the Greatest: Remaining in Love and Casting Out Fear in 1 John." *RevExp* 115 (2018b): 50–61.

———. "Rhetoric." Pages 187–203 in *How John Works: Storytelling in the Fourth Gospel.* Edited by Douglas Estes and Ruth Sheridan. SBLRBS 86. Atlanta: SBL Press, 2016.

———. "A Voice in the Wilderness: Classical Rhetoric and the Testimony of John (the Baptist) in John 1:19–34." Pages 119–39 in *Abiding Words: Perspectives on the Use of Scripture in the Gospel of John.* Edited by Myers and Schuchard. SBLRBS 81. Atlanta: SBL Press, 2015.

Myers, Alicia D., and Bruce G. Schuchard (eds.). *Abiding Words: Perspectives on the Use of Scripture in the Gospel of John.* SBLRBS 81. Atlanta GA: SBL Press, 2015.

Nässelqvist, Dan. "Stylistic Levels in Hebrews 1.1–4 and John 1.1–18." *JSNT* 35 (2012): 31–53.

Neirynck, Frans. "The Question of John and the Synoptics: D. Moody Smith 1992–1999." *ETL* 76 (2000): 122–32.

Neyrey, Jerome H. *The Gospel of John in Cultural and Rhetorical Perspective.* Grand Rapids: Eerdmans, 2009.

———. "'Without Beginning or Days or End of Life' (Hebrews 7:3): Topos for a True Deity." *CBQ* 53 (1991): 439–55.

Nongbri, Brent. "The Use and Abuse of P^{52}: Papyrological Pitfalls in the Dating of the Fourth Gospel." *HTR* 98 (2005): 23–48.

O'Day, Gail R. "'I Have Overcome the World' (John 16:33): Narrative Time in John 13–17." *Sem* 53 (1991): 153–66.

———. "Martha: Seeing the Glory of God." Pages 487–503 in *Character Studies in the Fourth Gospel: Narrative Approaches to Seventy Figures in John*. Edited by Steven A. Hunt, D. Francois Tolmie, and Ruben Zimmermann. WUNT 314. Tübingen: Mohr Siebeck, 2013.

Olsson, Birger. *A Commentary on the Letters of John: An Intra-Jewish Approach*. Translated by Richard J. Erickson. Eugene: Pickwick, 2013.

Painter, John. *1, 2, and 3 John*. Sacra Pagina. Collegeville: Liturgical Press, 2002.

Parsenios, George L. "Confounding Foes and Counseling Friends: *Parrēsia* in the Fourth Gospel and Greco-Roman Philosophy." Pages 251–72 in *The Prologue of the Gospel of John*. Edited by Jan G. van der Watt, R. Alan Culpepper, and Udo Schnelle. WUNT 359. Tübingen: Mohr Siebeck, 2016.

———. *Departure and Consolation: The Johannine Farewell Discourses in Light of Greco-Roman Literature*. NovTSup 117. Leiden: Brill, 2005.

———. *First, Second, and Third John*. PCNT. Grand Rapids: Baker Academic, 2014.

———. *Rhetoric and Drama in the Johannine Lawsuit Motif*. WUNT 258. Tübingen: Mohr Siebeck, 2010.

Parsons, Mikeal C. *Body and Character in Luke and Acts: The Subversion of Physiognomy in Early Christianity*. Rev. Waco: Baylor University Press, 2011.

Perkins, Pheme. *The Johannine Epistles*. New Testament Message 21. Wilmington: Glazier, 1979.

Popp, Thomas. "Thomas: Question Marks and Exclamation Marks." Pages 504–29 in *Character Studies in the Gospel of John*. Edited by Steven A. Hunt, D. Francois Tolmie, and Ruben Zimmermann. WUNT 314. Tübingen: Mohr Siebeck, 2013.

Quek, Tze-Ming. "A Text-Critical Study of John 1.34." *NTS* 55 (2009): 22–34.

Reeder, Caryn A. *Gendering War and Peace in the Gospel of Luke*. Cambridge: Cambridge University Press, 2018.

Reinhartz, Adele. "'And the Word Was Begotten': Divine Epigenesis in the Gospel of John." *Sem* 85 (1999): 83–103.

———. *Befriending the Beloved Disciple: A Jewish Reading of the Gospel of John*. London: Continuum, 2001.

———. "Building Skyscrapers on Toothpicks: The Literary-Critical Challenge to Historical Criticism." Pages 55–76 in *Anatomies of the Fourth Gospel: The Past, Present, and Futures of the Fourth Gospel as Literature*. SBLRBS 55. Atlanta: SBL, 2008.

———. "Caiaphas and Annas: The Villains of the Piece?" Pages 530–36 in *Character Studies in the Fourth Gospel: Narrative Approaches to Seventy Figures in John*. Edited by Steven A. Hunt, D. Francois Tolmie, and Ruben Zimmermann. WUNT 314. Tübingen: Mohr Siebeck, 2013.

———. "Incarnation and Covenant: The Fourth Gospel through the Lens of Trauma Theory." *Int* 69 (2015): 35–48.

———. "Story and History: John, Judaism, and the Historical Imagination." Pages 113–26 in *John and Judaism: A Contested Relationship in Context*. Edited by R. Alan Culpepper and Paul N. Anderson. SBLRBS 87. Atlanta: SBL Press, 2017.

———. *The Word in the World: The Cosmological Tale in the Fourth Gospel*. SBLMS 45. Atlanta: Scholars Press, 1992.

Reis, David M. "Jesus' Farewell Discourse, 'Otherness,' and the Construction of a Johannine Identity." *SR* 32 (2003): 39–58.

Regev, Eyal. "The Temple Cult, Romanization, and the Rebels." *Journal of Ancient Judaism* 5 (2014): 40–60.

Rensberger, David. "Completed Love: 1 John 4:11–18 and the Mission of the New Testament Church." Pages 237–71 in *Communities in the Dispute: Current Scholarship on the Johannine Epistles*. Edited by R. Alan Culpepper and Paul N. Anderson. ECL 13. Atlanta: SBL Press, 2014.

———. *Johannine Faith and Liberating Community*. Philadelphia: Westminster Press, 1988.

Ringe, Sharon H. *Wisdom's Friends: Community and Christology in the Fourth Gospel*. Louisville: Westminster John Knox, 1999.

Robertson, Jesse E. *The Death of Judas: The Characterization of Judas Iscariot in Three Early Christian Accounts of His Death*. Sheffield: Sheffield Phoenix, 2012.

Rusam, Dietrich. *Der erste, zweite und dritte Johannesbrief*. BNT. Göttingen: Vandenhoeck & Ruprecht, 2017.

Scarlata, Mark William. *Outside of Eden: Cain in the Ancient Versions of Genesis 4:1–16*. LBS. London: T&T Clark/Bloomsbury, 2012.

Schaberg, Jane. *The Resurrection of Mary Magdalene: Legends, Apocrypha, and the Christian Testament*. New York: Continuum, 2002.

Schnackenberg, Rudolf. *The Johannine Epistles: Introduction and Commentary*. Translated by Reginald and Ilse Fuller. New York: Crossroad, 1992.

Schneiders, Sandra M. "The Raising of the New Temple: John 20.19–23 and Johannine Ecclesiology." *NTS* 52 (2006): 337–55.

———. "Touching the Risen Jesus: Mary Magdalen and Thomas the Twin in John 20." Pages 153–76 in *The Resurrection of Jesus in the Gospel of John*. Edited by Craig R. Koester and Reimund Bieringer. WUNT 222. Tübingen: Mohr Siebeck, 2008.

Schnelle, Udo. *Antidocetic Christology in the Gospel of John: An Investigation of the Place of the Fourth Gospel in the Johannine School*. Translated by Linda M. Maloney. Minneapolis: Fortress, 1992.

Scholtissek, Klaus. "Relecture und réécriture: Neue Paradigmen zu Methode und Inhalt der Johannesauslegung aufgewiesen am Prolog 1,1–18 und der ersten Abschiedsrede 13,31–14,31." *ThPh* 75 (2000): 1–29.

Schrader, Elizabeth. "Was Martha of Bethany Added to the Fourth Gospel in the Second Century?" *HTR* 110 (2017): 360–92.

Schüssler-Fiorenza, Elisabeth. *Jesus: Miriam's Child, Sophia's Prophet: Critical Issues in Feminist Christology.* New York: Continuum, 1994.

Segovia, Fernando F. "John 15:18–16:4a: A First Addition to the Original Farewell Discourse?" *CBQ* 45 (1983): 210–30.

Seim, Turid Karlsen. "Descent and Divine Paternity in the Gospel of John: Does the Mother Matter?" *NTS* 51 (2005): 361–75.

Sharon, Nadav. *Judea under Roman Domination: The First Generation of Statelessness and Its Legacy.* EJL 46. Atlanta: SBL Press, 2017.

Sheridan, Ruth. *The Figure of Abraham in John 8: Text and Intertext.* LNTS. London: T&T Clark/Bloomsbury, 2019.

———. "Identity, Alerity, and the Gospel of John." *BibInt* 22 (2014): 188–209.

———. *Retelling Scripture: 'The Jews' and the Scriptural Citations in John 1:19–12:15.* BIS Series 110. Leiden: Brill, 2012.

———. "Seed of Abraham, Slavery, and Sin: Reproducing Johannine Anti-Judaism in the Modern Commentaries on John 8:30–34." Pages 313–32 in in *John and Judaism: A Contested Relationship in Context.* Edited by R. Alan Culpepper and Paul N. Anderson. SBLRBS 87. Atlanta: SBL Press, 2017.

———. "She Forgets Her Suffering in Her Joy: The Parable of the Laboring Woman (John 16:20–22)." Pages 45–64 in *Making Sense of Motherhood: Biblical and Theological Perspectives.* Edited by Beth M. Stovell. Eugene: Wipf & Stock, 2016.

———. "The Testimony of Two Witnesses: John 8:17." Pages 161–84 in *Abiding Words: Perspectives on the Use of Scripture in the Gospel of John.* Edited by Myers and Schuchard. SBLRBS 81. Atlanta: SBL Press, 2015.

Skinner, Christopher W. "(How) Can We Talk About Johannine Ethics? Looking Back and Moving Forward." Pages xvii–xxxvi in *Johannine Ethics: The Moral World of the Gospel and Epistles of John.* Edited by Sherri Brown and Christopher W. Skinner. Minneapolis: Fortress, 2017.

———. *John and Thomas—Gospels in Conflict? Johannine Characterization and the Thomas Question.* Princeton Theological Monograph Series 115. Eugene: Pickwick, 2009.

———. "'Son of God' or 'God's Chosen One' (John 1:34)? A Narrative-Critical Solution to a Text-Critical Problem." *BBR* 25 (2015): 341–57.

Smith, D. Moody. *First, Second, and Third John.* IBC. Louisville: John Knox Press, 1991.

———. *John.* ANTC. Nashville: Abingdon, 1999.

———. *John among the Gospels.* Columbia: South Carolina University Press, 2001.

Smith, Julien C. H. *Christ the Ideal King: Cultural Context, Rhetorical Strategy, and the Power of Divine Monarchy in Ephesians.* WUNT 2/313. Tübingen: Mohr Siebeck, 2011.

Snyman, Gerrie F. "Cain and Vulnerability: The Reception of Cain in *Genesis Rabbah* 22 and *Targum Onkelos, Targum Neofiti*, and *Targum Pseudo-Jonathan.*" *OTE* 29/3 (2016): 601–32.

Staley, Jeffrey Lloyd. *The Print's First Kiss: A Rhetorical Investigation of the Implied Reader in the Fourth Gospel.* SBLDS 82. Atlanta: SBL, 1988.

Standhartinger, Angela. "'What Women Were Accustomed to Do for the Dead Beloved by Them' (*Gospel of Peter* 12.50): Traces of Laments and Mourning Rituals in Early Easter, Passion, and Lord's Supper Traditions." *JBL* 129 (2010): 559–74.

Stibbe, Mark. *John as Storyteller: Narrative Criticism and the Fourth Gospel.* SNTSMS 73. Cambridge: Cambridge University Press, 1992.

Stowers, Stanley K. *Letter Writing in Greco-Roman Antiquity.* LEC 5. Philadelphia: Westminster Press, 1989.

Strecker, Georg. *The Johannine Letters: A Commentary on 1, 2, and 3 John.* Hermeneia. Minneapolis: Fortress, 1996.

Streett, Daniel R. *They Went Out from Us: The Identity of the Opponents in First John.* BZNT 117. Berlin: deGruyter, 2010.

Sturdevant, Jason S. "Incarnation as Psychagogy: The Purpose of the Word's Descent in John's Gospel." *NovT* 56 (2014): 24–44.

Talbert, Charles H. *Reading John: A Literary and Theological Commentary on the Fourth Gospel and the Johannine Epistles*. Rev. ed. RNT. Macon GA: Smyth & Helwys, 2005.

———. *What Is a Gospel?* Philadelphia: Fortress, 1977.

Thatcher, Tom. "Cain the Jew the AntiChrist: Collective Memory and the Johannine Ethic of Loving and Hating." Pages 350–73 in *Rethinking the Ethics of John: "Implicit" Ethics in the Johannine Writings.* CNNTE 3. Edited by Jan G. van der Watt and Ruben Zimmermann. Tübingen: Mohr Siebeck, 2012.

———. "'Water and Blood' in AntiChrist Christianity (1 John 5:6)." *SCJ* 4 (2001): 235–48.

———. *Why John Wrote a Gospel: Jesus, Memory, History.* Louisville: Westminster John Knox, 2006.

Theobald, Michael. Dav Evangelium nach Johannes: Kapitel 1–12. RNT. Regensburg: Pustet, 2009.

Thompson, Marianne Meye. *The God of the Gospel of John.* Grand Rapids: Eerdmans, 2001.

———. *John: A Commentary.* New Testament Library. Louisville: Westminster John Knox, 2015.

———. "'Light' (φῶς): The Philosophical Content of the Term and the Gospel of John." Pages 273–83 in *The Prologue of the Gospel of John.* Edited by Jan G. van der Watt, R. Alan Culpepper, and Udo Schnelle. WUNT 359. Tübingen: Mohr Siebeck, 2016.

Trozzo, Lindsey M. *Exploring Johannine Ethics: A Rhetorical Approach to Moral Efficacy in the Fourth Gospel Narrative.* WUNT 2/449. Tübingen: Mohr Siebeck, 2017.

Voorwinde, Stephen. *Jesus' Emotions in the Fourth Gospel: Human or Divine?* LNTS 284. London: T&T Clark, 2005.

Waetjen, Herman C. "Logos πρὸς τὸν θεόν and the Objectification of Truth in the Prologue of the Fourth Gospel." *CBQ* 63 (2001): 265–86.

von Wahlde, Urban C. *A Commentary on the Gospel and Letters of John.* 3 vols. Eerdmans Critical Commentary. Grand Rapids: Eerdmans, 2010.

———. "Raymond Brown's View of the Crisis of 1 John: In the Light of Some Peculiar Features of the Johannine Gospel." Pages 19–45 in *Communities in Dispute: Current Scholarship on the Johannine Epistles.* Edited by R. Alan Culpepper and Paul N. Anderson. ECL13. Atlanta: SBL Press, 2014.

van der Watt, Jan. *An Introduction to the Johannine Gospel and Letters.* T&T Clark Approaches to Biblical Studies. London: T&T Clark, 2007.

———. "Between Torah and Stoa: How Could Readers Have Understood the Johannine Logos?" Pages 189–234 in *The Prologue of the Gospel of John.* Edited by Jan G. van der Watt, R. Alan Culpepper, Udo Schnelle. WUNT 359. Tübingen: Mohr Siebeck, 2016.

———. *The Family of the King: Dynamics of Metaphor in the Gospel According to John.* Leiden: Brill, 2000.

_____. "On Ethics in 1 John." Pages 197–222 in *Communities in Dispute: Current Scholarship on the Johannine Epistles.* Edited by R. Alan Culpepper and Paul N. Anderson. ECL13. Atlant: SBL Press, 2014.

van der Watt, Jan and Ruben Zimmermann, eds. *Rethinking the Ethics of John: "Implicit Ethics" in the Johannine Writings.* WUNT 291. Tübingen: Mohr Siebeck, 2012.

Watson, Duane F. "Amplification Techniques in 1 John: The Interaction of Rhetorical Style and Invention." *JSNT* 51 (1993): 99–123.

_____. "1 John 2.12–14 as *Distributio, Conduplicatio,* and *Expolitio*: A Rhetorical Understanding." *JSNT* 35 (1989): 97–110.

Weissenrieder, Annette. "Spirit and Rebirth in the Gospel of John." *R&T* 21 (2014): 58–85.

Whitenton, Michael R. "The Dissembler of John 3: A Cognitive and Rhetorical Approach to the Characterization of Nicodemus." *JBL* 135 (2016): 141–58.

Williams, Catrin H. *I am He: The Interpretation of 'Anî Hû' in Jewish and Early Christian Literature.* WUNT 2/113. Tübingen: Mohr Siebeck, 2000.

———. "Isaiah in John's Gospel." Pages 101–16 in *Isaiah in the New Testament.* Edited by Steve Moyise and Maarten J. J. Menken. The New Testament and the Scriptures of Israel. London: T&T Clark, 2005.

Williams, P. J. "Not the Prologue." *JSNT* 33 (2011): 375–86.

Wright, William M, IV. "Greco-Roman Character Typing and the Presentation of Judas in the Fourth Gospel." *CBQ* 71 (2009): 544–59.

Zimmermann, Ruben. "Imagery in John: Opening Up Paths into the Tangled Thicket of John's Figurative World." Pages 1–43 in *Imagery in the Gospel of John: Texts, Forms, Themes, and Theology of Johannine Figurative Language.* Edited by Jörg Frey, J. G. van der Watt, Ruben Zimmermann, and Gabriele Kern. WUNT 200. Tübingen: Mohr Siebeck, 2007.

———. "Jesus' Parables and Ancient Rhetoric: The Contributions of Aristotle and Quintilian to the Form Criticism of the Parables." Pages 238–58 in *Hermeneutik der Gleichnisse Jesu: Methodische Neuansätze zum Verstehen urchristlicher Parabeltexte.* Edited by R. Zimmermann. WUNT 231. Tübingen: Mohr Siebeck, 2008.

———. *Puzzling the Parables of Jesus: Methods and Interpretation.* Minneapolis: Fortress, 2015.

CPSIA information can be obtained
at www.ICGtesting.com
Printed in the USA
LVHW012037041121
702456LV00014B/1873